TEKAHIONWAKE

broadview editions
series editor: Martin R. Boyne

E. Pauline Johnson publicity photo, 1892. Photo: Cochran, Brantford. Vancouver Public Library. VPL #9229

TEKAHIONWAKE:
E. PAULINE JOHNSON'S WRITINGS
ON NATIVE NORTH AMERICA

edited by Margery Fee and Dory Nason

broadview editions

BROADVIEW PRESS – www.broadviewpress.com
Peterborough, Ontario, Canada

Founded in 1985, Broadview Press remains a wholly independent publishing house. Broadview's focus is on academic publishing; our titles are accessible to university and college students as well as scholars and general readers. With over 600 titles in print, Broadview has become a leading international publisher in the humanities, with world-wide distribution. Broadview is committed to environmentally responsible publishing and fair business practices.

The interior of this book is printed on 100% recycled paper.

© 2016 Margery Fee and Dory Nason

Library and Archives Canada Cataloguing in Publication

Johnson, E. Pauline (Emily Pauline), 1861-1913
[Works. Selections]
    Tekahionwake : E. Pauline Johnson's writings on native North America / edited by Margery Fee and Dory Nason.

(Broadview editions)
Includes bibliographical references.
ISBN 978-1-55481-191-5 (paperback)

    I. Fee, Margery, 1948-, editor II. Nason, Dory, editor III. Title.
IV. Title: Works. Selections. V. Series: Broadview editions

PS8469.O283A6 2015   C811'.4   C2015-907187-9

Broadview Editions
The Broadview Editions series is an effort to represent the ever-evolving canon of texts in the disciplines of literary studies, history, philosophy, and political theory. A distinguishing feature of the series is the inclusion of primary source documents contemporaneous with the work.

Advisory editor for this volume: Michel Pharand

Broadview Press handles its own distribution in North America
PO Box 1243, Peterborough, Ontario K9J 7H5, Canada
555 Riverwalk Parkway, Tonawanda, NY 14150, USA
Tel: (705) 743-8990; Fax: (705) 743-8353
email: customerservice@broadviewpress.com

Distribution is handled by Eurospan Group in the UK, Europe, Central Asia, Middle East, Africa, India, Southeast Asia, Central America, South America, and the Caribbean. Distribution is handled by Footprint Books in Australia and New Zealand.

Broadview Press acknowledges the financial support of the Government of Canada through the Canada Book Fund for our publishing activities.

Typesetting by Aldo Fierro
Cover design by Lisa Brawn

PRINTED IN CANADA

Contents

List of Illustrations

Cover image: Blackfoot Indians, Fort McLeod, Alberta, 1905; photograph by Miss Campbell. Notman Photographic Archives, McCord Museum, Montreal. MP-1986.64.1

Acknowledgements

We would like to thank our research assistants Veronika Khvorostukhina, Jamie Paris, and Claire Wilson for their help with researching, annotating, and proofreading the documents; Carole Gerson, English, Simon Fraser University, for generously providing us with scans of her research materials and offering much good advice; Andrew Sly, Victoria, for transcribing and digitizing a large number of E. Pauline Johnson's uncollected prose works and putting them on the web where we could easily read them; Karen Dearlove, former curator at Chiefswood National Historical Site, for providing a tour of Chiefswood out of season and answering our questions; Wendy Nicholls at the Museum of Vancouver for allowing us to view E. Pauline Johnson's buckskin dress in storage; and the University of British Columbia Faculty of Arts for its funding support.

All royalties from this book will be donated to Chiefswood National Historic Site, Six Nations Grand River, Ohsweken, Ontario.

Introduction

E. Pauline Johnson / Tekahionwake (1861–1913) is remarkable as one of a very few early North American Indigenous poets and fiction writers. Most Indigenous writers of her time were men educated for the ministry who published religious, anthropological, autobiographical, political, and historical works, rather than poetry and fiction. More extraordinary still, she became both a canonical poet and a literary celebrity, performing on stage for fifteen years across Canada, in the United States, and in London. Because of her unusual circumstances and ability, she was afforded the self-confidence and education not only to publish literary work, but also to undertake a long performing career, albeit one that was physically demanding, socially risky, and financially unrewarding.

Johnson was born in 1861 on the Six Nations Reserve on the Grand River near Brantford, Ontario. Her father, George Henry Martin Johnson (1816–84), was a Mohawk[1] member of the Iroquois Confederacy Council, and her mother, Emily Howells Johnson (1824–98), was a cultivated Englishwoman. Pauline and her three older siblings, Allen, Evelyn, and Beverly, grew up in a large home, Chiefswood, now Chiefswood National Historic Site. Johnson was well educated by her parents, by governesses, in a reserve school, and at Brantford Collegiate Institute. When George Johnson died, a consequence of several brutal beatings by white liquor traders, the family could no longer afford to live at Chiefswood.

Johnson, her sister Evelyn, and their mother moved to Brantford, where Johnson read, wrote poetry, engaged in an active social life, participated in amateur theatricals, and published "some sixty poems in various North American serials" (Gerson and Strong-Boag xvi). Her first published poem appeared in 1883 or 1884, when she was in her early twenties (Gerson and Strong-Boag 290). She was commissioned to write poems for

---

1 Although we use "Mohawk" and "Iroquois," the terms Johnson used for herself, now the former is being replaced by "Kanien'ke-há:ka" for the people, meaning People of the Flint (Alfred xxv). "Haudenosaunee," meaning People of the Longhouse, is often used as a synonym for Six Nations.

the re-interment of Red Jacket, a famous Seneca leader, in 1884, and for the unveiling of a monument commemorating Joseph Brant, a famous Mohawk leader, in 1886. Two of her poems appeared in the major national anthology, *Songs of the Great Dominion*, published in 1889. In January 1892, she was invited to participate in a poetry reading in Toronto, where her recitation of "A Cry from an Indian Wife" was the success of the evening (Keller 58). Frank Yeigh, the organizer, launched a reading tour for her in Ontario for which she made her famous buckskin costume, now in the Museum of Vancouver. After this, she began a career that took her across Canada, to the United States, and twice to London. She travelled to perform in London first in 1894. There she undertook public recitals, made connections with influential patrons, and arranged for the publication of her first book, *The White Wampum*, which appeared in 1895 from John Lane's The Bodley Head, a well-known literary press. She continued to perform until 1909, sometimes alone, but usually with a male stage partner: first Owen Smily and then Walter McRaye (1876–1946). Then she retired to Vancouver, only to discover that she was suffering from incurable breast cancer. In her last years, friends and admirers helped her pay for her medical care by collecting the many stories she had published in magazines and newspapers into books.

On her second trip to London in 1906, she met Chief Joe Capilano (Sahp-luk), a Squamish chief. He was heading a delegation of British Columbia chiefs that met with King Edward VII to discuss land issues. On Johnson's retirement, Capilano welcomed her to Vancouver and she became friends with him and his wife Mary Agnes (Líxwelut). After his death in 1910, Johnson began to publish her versions of the stories they had told her in the *Saturday Magazine* of the Vancouver newspaper, the *Province*; most of these stories were collected in *Legends of Vancouver*. On her death, the city shut down for her funeral and mourners lined the streets to pay their respects. Chief Joe Mathias (Chief Capilano's son) and many other Indigenous people followed the cortège. Her ashes are buried in Stanley Park, where she had loved to canoe on Lost Lagoon.

Overview of the Collection and Principles of Selection

This edition groups selected poems, stories, and prose pieces into six sections. The first section reflects Johnson's connections to her birthplace, her family, and the Six Nations of Grand River;

the second section reflects her interest in the Plains Peoples and the Riel Resistance of 1885; the third section presents some of her lyric and satirical poetry; the fourth contains writings on women and children; the fifth, writings about residential schools; and the last, writing that emerged from her life on the West Coast. Carole Gerson and Veronica Strong-Boag include all of Johnson's poetry in *Collected Poems and Selected Prose* (2002). They comment of her prose, however, that "To reprint all this material would fill many thick volumes, and is therefore not possible here...." (xxviii–xxix). This collection relies on their foundational edition, as well as on the chronological list of Johnson's writing published in their biographical study, *Paddling Her Own Canoe: The Times and Texts of E. Pauline Johnson (Tekahionwake)* (2000). Although we could not include all of Johnson's prose writings either, we do include some works that do not appear in their anthology: "Heroic Indian Mothers," "A Brother Chief," "The Haunting Thaw," and "The Legend of the Ice Babies."

Despite some very real interpretative dangers, we have decided to focus this collection on the writing that bears on what was called at the time "the Indian question" or on the issue of Johnson's own identity. We do this for two reasons. First, it is as a Mohawk and as an Indigenous woman that she is now usually read, and, if Ernest Thompson Seton is to be believed, this is how she wanted to be remembered (see Appendix A8, pp. 279–80). And she was what Canadian law labels a "Status Indian," albeit an unusually privileged one. Therefore, in this collection, with only a few exceptions ("Canadian Born," the six poems in section three, and the last poem in the collection, "The Lost Lagoon"), we collect writing with explicit Indigenous themes. Johnson published only twenty poems that fit this category during her lifetime, all between 1884 and 1898—we include all but four love ballads, "The Quill Worker," "The Legend of Qu'appelle Valley," "The Ballad of Yaada," and the posthumously published "The Ballad of Lalloo," although we do include two love ballads on similar themes, "Dawendine" and "The Pilot of the Plains."[1]

To focus on Johnson's Indigenous-themed work does risk narrowing the scope of her accomplishments and identifications. The anthropologist Horatio Hale, who worked with her father and grandfather to document Mohawk traditions, writes in a review of her first poetry collection, *The White Wampum*, that

---

1 For a detailed account of the anthologization of these poems, see Fee.

"the first inclination of the reader will be to look for some Indian traits and be disappointed if these are not strikingly apparent. Her compositions will be judged as those of a 'wild Indian girl,' and not those of a well-bred and accomplished young Canadian lady with a dash of Indian blood, such as she really is" (Appendix A4, p. 267). Certainly, some critics did concern themselves with proving that "Miss Johnson's genius was wholly Indian" (Charlesworth 82), but sometimes they argued that it was not: a British newspaper reviewer wrote in 1895 that her work was "pseudo-Indian." Such struggles over the authenticity of Indigenous authors are common among critics; no matter which side they come down on, the critics are established as experts and the writers as subject to their categorization.

Like Hale, some of our contemporary critics have warned against using identity as a focus: Helen Hoy notes that writers and performers like Johnson have been restricted "to bounded cultures narrower and more visible than the culture allotted to the majority" (5). Gerson remarks that the publication of Johnson's first book, *The White Wampum* (1895), "initiated a pattern of over-determination that affected reading of her poetry for more than a century," a pattern that "excluded her ... from the mainstream of Canadian literary history as it was constructed in the middle of twentieth century" ("Postcolonialism Meets Book History" 432–33). They argue against perceiving women from racialized or "minority" groups as simply "voices of their people," a view that limits their impact and reception. Julie Rak also warns against critics producing "a kind of discourse that works to make the non-native author invisible while forcing the native 'object' of knowledge to perform in visible ways" (153). Glenn Willmott makes the case for refusing to divide "the feather from the flint" or Johnson's aestheticist "shadow writing" from her more politically engaged dramatic and narrative work (n. pag.). However, a focus on the "flint" allows us to situate Johnson in a North American context that connects her work with continental discourses of feminism, abolitionism, and Indigenous activism.

Taking Rak's comment seriously, we should make some of our own investments in Johnson visible. We both teach and write about First Nations and Indigenous literatures at the University of British Columbia. Dory Nason is an Anishinaabe enrolled in the Leech Lake Band of the Minnesota Chippewa Tribe in the United States, and Margery Fee is a white settler Canadian whose own ancestors were, like Johnson, staunchly Loyalist in their opinion (although unlike her, not their origins). As feminists whose work spans the US-Canada border, we hope this reader will be useful for courses in a range of disciplines in both countries, from Ethnic Studies, First Nations and Indigenous Studies, and Women's Studies, to Canadian and American literature courses. Further, we hope to make it possible for Johnson's work to be taught in these courses in ways that undermine stereotypes and allow her to be read in ways that are not constrained by arguments about her cultural authenticity. Reading Indigenous writers is a task that requires a willingness to take seriously the context of race, gender, and colonialism in all its complexities, and yet also to recognize that Indigenous writers create and speak from their own locations as members of specific communities, with their own knowledge systems, intellectual histories, and story traditions. Rather than trying to pin Johnson down, we will examine how and why others have read her in a variety of ways, both positive and negative, and consider how she took advantage of the options available to her to produce and refine a particular standpoint while also trying to earn a living in a society full of prejudice against independent women and those marked as racially Other. That said, Johnson shared many of the racial attitudes of her day about "lesser tribes" and other minorites.

One important reading, by Veronica Strong-Boag and Carole Gerson, connects Johnson's ideas to those of the "New Woman." They note that women who matched this description were prominent in Canada and other Western countries between 1880 and 1920, and were "[o]ften identified with feminism, although not always ... suffragist" (*Paddling Her Own Canoe* 59). These women, like Johnson, espoused more independence, better education, more opportunities for paid work, and other reforms that fostered the equality of women. Johnson found a ready audience in this group for her writing on women's issues, for example, articles on the healthful benefits of canoeing and other outdoor pastimes.

Identifications and Patriotism

Certainly, Hale saw her as a Canadian, not as a Mohawk. And she could easily have passed as white and disappeared into a bourgeois marriage (something common enough for her peers; see Barman). She received many proposals, but her only formal engagement to marry, to Charles Drayton, whose father was a law professor at Osgoode Hall in Toronto, was broken at his request. This decision was likely taken because of objections from his father about the impropriety of marrying a "half-breed" who made her living on the stage (Keller 136). Even during her engagement she showed no signs of giving up her career and consistently declared herself a Mohawk. However, unlike Hale, she clearly did not agree that someone could be a Mohawk *or* a Canadian, but not both; the last line in the Inscription to her second poetry collection, *Canadian Born*, makes this clear: "White Race and Red are one if they are but Canadian born." Further, at the time she was born, Canada did not exist as a nation; long after Confederation in 1867, Canadians were described as "British subjects" and foreign-policy decisions were left to Britain. The Six Nations under Joseph Brant had allied themselves with the British during the American War of Independence and moved to Canada in 1785 to settle on land granted them as compensation for the lands they lost in what is now New York State. Not surprisingly, then, her political attitudes were Loyalist, a strongly conservative strain of political thought that was widespread in the Anglo-Canada where she wrote "The Yankee to the south of us must south of us remain" (p. 38 below).

The Johnson family connections to the Crown descended from the Great Covenant forged first between the Dutch and then between the British Crown in North America and the Iroquois, an alliance that is represented in the famous Two-row Wampum or *Tekeni Teiohatatie Kahswentha*. Johnson's paternal great-grandfather, Jacob Tekahionwake Johnson (1758–1843) was named after his godfather Sir William Johnson (1715–74), the Crown's representative and the British Superintendent of Indian Affairs from 1756 until his death. Sir William brought the Royal Proclamation of 1763 to British North America. It was celebrated at a large gathering of around two thousand Indian leaders in order to consolidate their loyalty after the French surrender in North America. This Proclamation claims all land for the Crown, but also reserves lands for Indigenous people; it is still the basis of legal decisions about Indigenous land rights in Canada. At the outbreak of the American War of Independence, the Six Nations tried to remain neutral, but eventually most declared for the British. The Treaty of Versailles that ended the war in 1783 made no provision for the lands lost to the Americans, so in 1784 the Mohawk were granted land on the Bay of Quinte and along the Grand River as compensation, and the Johnson family moved to the Six Nations Grand River reserve. Johnson's grandfather, Jacob Johnson's son, John "Smoke" Johnson (1792–1886), was a Pine Tree chief, that is, a chief appointed on his merit, rather than by inheritance. He fought against the Americans in the War of 1812. He married Helen Martin, a high-ranking Mohawk, whose mother was a Dutch woman, Catherine Rolleston, who had been captured during the American War of Independence and adopted by a chief. As a result, Catherine and her daughter became powerful clan mothers. Helen Martin Johnson nominated Johnson's father to the Confederacy Council, a story that Johnson tells in "My Mother" (pp. 54–55 below; see also Evelyn H.C. Johnson). Johnson's father played a major role in the adoption of the third son of Queen Victoria, Prince Arthur, the Duke of Connaught and Strathearn, as a Mohawk, an event that Johnson recalls in "A Brother Chief" (pp. 94–97 below). A few months before her death, while he was Governor General of Canada, Prince Arthur visited her in Vancouver.

Her allegiance to the British Crown, Empire, and all its representatives, while quite typical of Anglo-Canada at the time, may now seem misguided, if not antithetical to Indigenous sovereignty. However, these allegiances persisted in Indigenous politics, with some First Nations refusing to negotiate with Canada. This loyalty to the Crown cleared a space for Indigenous intellectuals to criticize the government of Canada, the immediate agent of colonial rule (see, for example, Stonechild and Waiser).

Sentimentalism and Modernism

Johnson often writes in a sentimental style that is no longer easy to read with sympathy. The tropes of noble manhood and devoted motherhood that Johnson uses with such facility are now not only outmoded, they have been condemned relentlessly by modernist critics and parodied by popular writers for over a hundred years. This style was certainly commonplace, although some of her contemporaries, like Sara Jeannette Duncan (1861–1922), a high-school classmate, were moving towards realism, while others, like Isabella Valancy Crawford (1846–87), continued with the sentimental romance (see Gerson, *A Purer Taste*). Many American Indian contemporaries also used sentimental conventions, including Alice Callahan (1868–94), Sarah Winnemucca (1844–91), Mourning Dove (1888–1936), and Gertrude Bonnin / Zitkala-Ša (1876–1938). This style means extra work for present-day readers. Anishinaabe poet Armand Garnet Ruffo commented in a recent interview that "My grandmother wrote poetry and her influence was Pauline Johnson but I found the form archaic, so as a teenager I had little interest in it. It was only later when I realized what Johnson was actually saying that I revisited her work" (24).

Sentimental conventions depict and evoke strong emotions aimed at promoting ethical behaviour and the love of God, family, and country. Men were expected to marry, to lead, and to die for these values. Women were expected to support their fathers, husbands, brothers, and sons in this noble work. Johnson's story "My Mother," about her parents' lives, focuses on how her mother conformed to the expectations of the Victorian "angel in the house," while her father devoted his life to his people. However, the story also reveals that in marrying, her parents defied the wishes of both their families and challenged the attitudes of their respective communities. The children were well aware of belonging to what her brother Allen once called a "mongrel family," a sally at which even his reserved mother laughed (Evelyn H.C. Johnson 39). In many ways this knowledge underpinned both parents' high expectations that their children would behave well in all circumstances and in all company.

The Johnson children, particularly Pauline, were voracious readers and were certainly familiar with the popular sentimental literature of their childhood. In these works, abandoned, dead, disabled, and dying babies and neglected children, common enough in a world without birth control, antibiotics, or a social safety net, were transformed into famous literary figures, such as Charles Dickens's Tiny Tim in *A Christmas Carol* (1843) or Little Nell in *The Old Curiosity Shop* (1840–41). Women struggling to raise their children in difficult circumstances were also common both in reality and in literature. Louisa May Alcott (1832–88), who grew up among the Transcendentalists, a group of American intellectuals that included Henry David Thoreau (1803–82) and Ralph Waldo Emerson (1817–62), became famous for *Little Women* (1868–69) and its sequels. These books were based on her own austere childhood and adolescence with her beloved "Marmee" and sisters in Concord, Massachusetts. The novel's description of the death of one of the sisters, as well as its promotion of ideals of womanhood that include domesticity and emotional restraint, fit the sentimental model. Harriet Beecher Stowe's best-selling novel *Uncle Tom's Cabin; Or, Life among the Lowly* (1852) features an angelic child named Eva and uses sentimentalism in the service of the abolition of slavery.[1] Stowe's novel sold 300,000 copies in its first year and re-energized

---

1 Evelyn Johnson writes that her maternal grandfather, "an ardent abolitionist," had wanted her to be named after this character, but "it was decided that no little girl could be as good as 'Little Eva'" (28). Nonetheless, the family called her Eva and she took on Evelyn as her first name when she was confirmed in the family's Anglican faith.

the abolitionist movement in the North. Clearly sentimentalism could have a strong political as well as emotional impact. After Johnson retired from performing, she turned to writing stories for two mass-circulation American magazines, *Boys' World* and *Mother's Magazine*. Many of the stories collected here conform to the expectations of the editors and readers of such magazines for sentimental tropes. Nonetheless, Johnson often found a way to highlight the concerns of Indigenous people.

Marriage

Sentimental writing often depicted women and children as objects of pathos, in need of rescue by strong men. The main form of rescue for women was marriage, since single women were often unable to find respectable work that paid a living wage. Marriage, idealized as a happy ending, often led to other problems, including sexual and domestic submission, frequent and dangerous childbirth, and the loss of control over property. Marriage was often not a matter of personal choice, but intended to form alliances among those of the same religion, class, and ethnic origin. Marriages that crossed any of these lines, such as that of Johnson's parents, were both uncommon and remarked upon—when her mother died, the obituary in the local newspaper reminded readers of the general "astonishment" that had greeted the news of Emily's "unusual" marriage (Keller 137). Marriage laws in Canada both controlled and protected male property: under the law of coverture, all property that belonged to a woman became her husband's on marriage (see Chambers). Children born outside marriage were "illegitimate" and could not inherit without express provision in the father's will.

Although Johnson's stories about her parents' marriage make it clear that so-called mixed marriages could be happy, she was well aware of the social pressures that racism put on them. "A Red Girl's Reasoning" articulates how mainstream patriarchal Christian marriage laws were imposed on Indigenous people who had their own laws,[1] which usually left both men and women free to leave unhappy marriages (Carter 5). The "Red Girl" is Christy, whose husband Charlie is scandalized by the revelation that her parents were married by "Indian rites." She reasons, "Why should I recognize the rites of your nation when you do not acknowledge the rites of mine? According to your

---

1 By 1886, the courts had begun to move against the recognition of Indigenous customary law and marriage rites.

own words, my parents should have gone through your church ceremony as well as through an Indian contract; according to my words, we should go through an Indian contract as well as through a church marriage. If their union is illegal, so is ours" (p. 172 below). This stance of equality was the backbone of Six Nations alliances: the two rows in the Two-Row Wampum symbolized an equal relationship between two sovereign nations, not the subservience of one to the other. Although she is clearly from the Plains, not Six Nations, Christy's application of this principle to her marriage supported not only the equality of nations, but also the equality of men and women, a profoundly feminist idea at a time when women's submission to men was not only taken for granted, but also embodied in law (see "Heroic Indian Mothers," p. 85 below, for Iroquois divorce, and Carter for more on Plains Indian marriage customs). All women, married or not, were disadvantaged by the assumption that they were physically, morally, and intellectually weaker than men and therefore required "protection" by fathers, husbands, and sons, not to mention the state. Indigenous women's lives were further regulated by the Indian Act (1876). Those, like Christie, who married non-Status men lost their Status, nor was it passed on to their children.[1] Under these rules, which traced inheritance through the father, Johnson, her mother, and her siblings were all Status Indians; however, because the Mohawk mark inheritance through the mother, they did not have a clan, and thus, in traditionalist eyes, they were not Mohawk. Further, Status Indian women waited for the federal vote (as did Status men) until 1960, although most other women were granted this right in 1918.[2]

---

1 Before Bill C-31 (1985) was passed to remedy the unequal treatment of men and women by the Indian Act, men who married non-Status women did not lose their status, and their wives gained Status, as did their children. However, the new provisions include complex rules that mean that men or women with Status who marry partners without it may see their children or grandchildren lose Status and, thus, any claim to Aboriginal or treaty rights.

2 Racialized minorities (Chinese, Japanese, and South Asian men and women) were excluded from this bill; some pacifist religious groups, such as the Doukhobors, Mennonites, and Hutterites, had their franchise removed in 1938, although it was returned later. Incarcerated individuals could not vote until 1993. See "Voting Rights."

Johnson never married, although she received proposals from both Indigenous and non-Indigenous men (Strong-Boag and Gerson 67; Evelyn H.C. Johnson 51). And although she became a celebrity performer, she often found herself in financial difficulties that marriage to a middle-class man would have likely prevented. However, she was supported in her last illness by many friends and admirers, including members of the Canadian Women's Press Club, who helped her in many ways, including by supporting the publication and sale of *Legends of Vancouver* (Keller 256–57).

Indigenous Politics

Johnson is capable of remarkably clear dissections of the racist habits of the time, a clarity that comes out of her own standpoint as a privileged Mohawk educated in both Iroquois society and white Anglo-Canadian culture. Her deft use of analogies between Iroquois traditions of government and religion and those of the dominant culture works to show the Six Nations to be as politically responsible as, and far less sexist than, the British, the one God of the Longhouse to be more benign than the Christian God, and Iroquois traditions to be more time-tested, healthy, and virtuous than those of a corrupted urban modernity.

However, her patriotic enthusiasm for Canada and the Crown, as expressed in "Canadian Born" and elsewhere, seems at odds with her Indigenous advocacy. Rick Monture's opinion of E. Pauline Johnson's position in *We Share Our Matters: Two Centuries of Writing and Resistance at Six Nations of the Grand River* is mixed. Although he reads some poems, such as "The Corn Husker" and "The Song My Paddle Sings," as reflective of Haudenosaunee culture, he argues that "Johnson obviously served as an advocate for the benefits of Native assimilation," although he does note that she "punctuated this overarching view with the occasional harsh criticism of Canadian society's treatment of the Indigenous population" (84). He engages in close readings of several works, including "A Pagan in St. Paul's Cathedral," "The Lodge of the Law Makers," "Weh-ro's Sacrifice," and "A Royal Mohawk Chief," to make his case that her admiration for the British Crown led her to overlook the struggles of the Grand River Confederacy Council, which was abolished in 1924 by the Department of Indian Affairs.

Her political stance was certainly affected by United Empire Loyalism, then at its peak (Berger 90). In *Inventing Loyalists*, Norman Knowles summarizes the Loyalist ideology as "unfailing devotion to the Crown and Empire, a strong and pervasive anti-Americanism, suffering and sacrifice endured for the sake of principle, elite social origins and a conservative social vision" (3). The Indigenous nations who allied themselves with the British against the United States were referred to as "Feathered Loyalists." The Haudenosaunee used Loyalist discourse to claim rights in Canada. For example, Iroquois speakers featured in centenary celebrations of the arrival of the Loyalists in Canada at the end of the American War of Independence in 1784. In one celebration at Niagara, Chief A.G. Smith of Grand River asserted that the Six Nations were "anxious to be identified with the descendants of the U.E. Loyalists of Canada." He went on to argue for equality, rights, and parliamentary representation for Native people (qtd. in Knowles 86–87). As Knowles puts it, "Whereas the chiefs felt that their loyal past entitled them to justice and equality, non-Natives redefined loyalty in terms of assimilation to Anglo-Canadian ways and submission to Canadian institutions" (87). Unhappy with their reception at the celebrations in Niagara, Toronto, and Adolphustown, the Haudenosaunee held their own celebrations at the two reserves granted them in 1784: Tyendinaga and Grand River (Knowles 87–88). They were also closely involved in the raising of a monument to Joseph Brant in Brantford in 1886, where E. Pauline Johnson's "'Brant,' A Memorial Ode" was read. Rick Monture comments that the poem "merges the Haudenosaunee together with 'all British subjects'" and "ignores the relationship of military and political alliance that Brant himself had fought so hard to maintain" (82). He concludes, "Johnson's misinterpretation (or repudiation) of Six Nations nationhood could not have been lost on many of her fellow Haudenosaunee in attendance that day, and may have been one of the reasons why she received so little community support during her career" (82).

Monture's criticism of Johnson accords with that often levelled against her contemporaries in the United States, the founders of the Society for the American Indian (SAI; 1911–23), such as Charles Eastman (1858–1939), Carlos Montezuma (1866–1923), and Zitkala-Ša. These "red progressives" took a pan-Indian perspective, argued for the involvement of Indians in decisions about them, and promoted the goal of citizenship for Indians, achieved in 1924 in the US.[1] Like Johnson, they were well educated, often in white institutions, were often Christian, and frequently held professional qualifications. They all spoke and wrote to a tone-deaf general public that "knew" that Indigenous people were vanishing and that those who remained required assimilation so that they could forego their primitive ways and take up the benefits of civilization. In a 2013 special issue of *American Indian Quarterly*, Indigenous critics point out the difficulties these writers faced in mediating between home communities and mainstream society. Beth Piatote notes that the SAI is often dismissed as a "flatly 'assimilationist' organization that was willing to abandon the principles of Indigenous sovereignty" ("The Indian/Agent Aporia" 48). As Robert Warrior puts it, "Native intellectuals of the SAI generation generate anxiety exactly because of [their] overdetermined commitment to *American* belonging, and my guess is that they always will. What they said and how they said it, what they wore and why they wore it, the ways in which they displayed their patriotism—who can deny that it seems nearly constantly over the top?" (226). Johnson's costumed and performed loyalty to Canada and Crown certainly can seem over the top nowadays.

Philip J. Deloria points out in the same issue that these "strong-willed souls" lived through amazing social change and "seemed always to speak with words that doubled back on themselves" (26). Indeed, even direct speech was often misinterpreted by white audiences. One example of "double speaking" can be found in the speech that Ely S. Parker delivered at the ceremonies for

---

1 It should be noted that US citizenship granted to Indians in 1924 was a "dual citizenship" and did not supersede Indian membership in their own nations. Citizenship afforded Native Americans in the US many rights important to bringing claims against the government; therefore, arguments for citizenship were also strategically a path to land claims and other activist goals. Before 1947, Canadians were British subjects living in Canada, and Status Indians and Eskimos (Inuit) were wards of the state. The Canadian Citizenship Act (1947) was amended to include Status Indians and "Eskimos" retroactively in 1956; however, progress to citizenship has been complex and piecemeal; Bill C-31 (1985) amended the Indian Act to remove most, but not all, discrimination. Until 1960, "enfranchisement" for Status Indian men meant that they (and their wives and children) lost Status when they gained the vote.

the re-interment of Red Jacket, where Johnson and her sister were in the audience.[1] He comments that the loyalty of the Iroquois to the British caused the Americans to mistrust them, leading to the "invasion" by General Sullivan of their territories in 1779, leaving them "homeless, houseless and destitute" (Appendix C4, p. 326). He continues: "A peace was granted them, and small homes allowed in the vast domain they once claimed as absolutely and wholly theirs by the highest title known among men, viz., by the gift of God. The mercy of the American people granted them the right to occupy and cultivate certain lands until someone stronger wanted them" (p. 326 below). The irony in this speech may have been imperceptible to many in his audience, but the trope of "might makes right" on which he plays here turns up in many places in Johnson's work as well, including her poem to Brant, where she situates "Young Canada" sweeping on to power while leaving only "Indian graves" behind: "so fades the race, that unto Might and therefore right gives place" (p. 40 below). Although this image appears to validate the disappearance of the Indian, it also functions as a moral reproach. Since a reliance on might making right was the privilege of autocrats and dictators, one can see in both Parker's speech and Johnson's poem a critique of the self-justifying rhetoric of the white speakers at the two events. For example, a keynote speaker in Buffalo said: "We are here to bury the aboriginal lords of the domain in which we dwell, and which is now all our own" (Bryant 15). However, the Indian question was not so easily buried.

Johnson's Indigenous Legacy

The centennial year of Pauline Johnson's birth was 1961, and the occasion was marked by the issuing of a commemorative stamp in her honour and the pilgrimage of Six Nations leaders to her gravesite in Vancouver. As Gerson and Strong-Boag point out, this period saw the extension of the franchise to Status Indians in 1960 and an end to compulsory enfranchisement for First Nations men or bands via amendments to the Indian Act of Canada (xxxv). These changes are a fitting context for the celebration

---

1   Ely S. Parker (1828–95), like Johnson's father a hereditary Iroquois chief, was the great-uncle of Arthur C. Parker (1881–1955; see Appendix C5), a founding member of the Society of American Indians and editor of its magazine for several years. For more about Ely Parker, see Appendix C4, pp. 324–25.

of Johnson's birth, as the 1960s marked the beginning of visible and creative Indigenous rights movements in many countries. Indeed, in the years to follow, First Nations and Indigenous communities in Canada and the United States would see a resurgence of cultural traditions, political power, and sovereignty, and a surge in new literature, scholarship, and art. Johnson's commemoration would mark her importance in the context of this cultural and political shift for Native peoples.

In a special issue of *The Native Voice*, a publication of the Native Brotherhood of British Columbia, Johnson's centennial took centre stage. This special edition celebrated her legacy and connection, not to a general Canadian audience, but to First Nations peoples. While much of the issue comprises a collection of best wishes to the Six Nations delegation and excerpts of her writing, one article stands out: an interview with Chief Joe Mathias, son of Chief Joe Capilano and one of the pallbearers at Johnson's funeral in 1913. Mathias recalls Johnson's many visits to his home and the fact that she had instructed him in his early twenties on how to deliver his first public speech. Johnson's skill as a public performer, writer, and elocutionist no doubt was a great asset in mentoring a young leader. Mathias's story speaks to a history that is still being written about Johnson from a decidedly Indigenous perspective, to which we hope this volume contributes. Her work also lived on at Six Nations. Daniel David Moses, a Delaware poet and playwright, recalls memorizing Johnson's poems, including "The Song My Paddle Sings," at Six Nations School Number Four, and later singing "Lullaby of the Iroquois" in choir at Ohsweken Central School. He comments that "she was and is the one famous cultural personality from our community's history, ... the lone artist featured in the cycle of stories our Six Nations Indian Pageant then presented to the wider public.... [A]s far as we were concerned, she was always from here, she was one of our own" (127). These small anecdotes also speak to Johnson's legacy in inspiring new words from many Indigenous writers, performers, and scholars today. While her literary style may have been one that has since fallen out of favour, it is her critiques of gendered colonialism within this mode that resonate with many Indigenous women to this day.

Indeed, Johnson is now seen as a central figure in the intellectual history of Indigenous women in Canada and the United States, and as an important historical example of Indigenous feminism, alongside women such as Sarah Winnemucca and Zitkala-Ša. Like Johnson, these women are representative of countless Indigenous women in North America who were forced to leave their territories due to land dispossession, loss of Status, compulsory education in boarding schools, or simply in order to survive. However, they did not lose sight of who they were, and many spent their lives advocating for the rights and just treatment of Indigenous women and peoples to mainstream audiences in Europe, the United States, and Canada. Johnson's 1892 essay "A Strong Race Opinion: On the Indian Girl in Modern Fiction" is an important milestone in this shared history as one of the first pieces of literary criticism of mainstream literature by an Indigenous woman writer. Her insistence that the "Indian girl in cold type" was a fiction of the colonial imagination that served to dehumanize Native women everywhere still resonates.

Indeed, "A Strong Race Opinion" foresees many contemporary critiques of the princess/squaw binary in Indigenous feminist thought (see Acoose; Green). Paired with the aforementioned "A Red Girl's Reasoning," "As It Was in the Beginning," or other short stories, readers are able to assess how Johnson both engaged and rejected colonial conventions that foreclosed Indigenous women's agency, intellectual capacity, and humanity. Mohawk scholar Patricia Monture considered "A Red Girl's Reasoning" an important historical critique that expressed "not just anger but racialized analysis. Indigenous women have been naming and standing against the irony of colonialism and its impact on our lives as women for a very long time" (155). Yet Monture cautions against reading Johnson through mainstream feminist frameworks, insisting that Johnson's identity as a Mohawk woman served as the foundation for her gender politics. Contemporary Indigenous feminists argue that traditional governance systems such as those Johnson writes about in "The Lodge of the Law Makers" afforded Indigenous women power, status, and respect. Others point to her formidable women characters as representative of Indigenous women's long-standing resistance to the intrusion of colonial notions of womanhood, family, and nation. Haudenosaunee feminist Mishuana Goeman writes that "Johnson provides an avenue to examine the gendered nature of conquest" through her short stories that feature "heroines who upset the liberal rationale of settler claiming of land and bodies" (51).

In her 1994 collection of essays, *Writing as Witness*, Mohawk writer Beth Brant explains E. Pauline Johnson's legacy and importance to Indigenous women writers. She reclaims Johnson as a "spiritual grandmother to those of us who are women writers of the First Nations" (7), a woman whose work expressed the anger and frustration that Indigenous women feel in the face of racism, and more importantly, the love that Indigenous women have for themselves and their communities. As a writer and performer, Johnson, in Brant's mind, is a central figure in the literary and performance history of Indigenous women in Canada. Brant writes, "Pauline Johnson's physical body died in 1913, but her spirit still communicates to us who are Native women writers. She walked the writing path clearing the brush for us to follow" (7). Indeed, the women who have "walked the writing path" since Johnson continue to remember her in their literary efforts. For example, in 1989 Métis poet Joan Crate conjured Johnson in her book of poetry *Palé as Real Ladies: Poems for Pauline Johnson*. In 2000, Okanagan writer Jeannette Armstrong opened her novel *Whispering in Shadows* with Johnson's poem "Moonset." Two years later, Mohawk poet Janet Rogers published the play *Pauline and Emily, Two Women*, recasting Johnson as friend and interlocutor of Emily Carr, the Canadian artist who often painted Indigenous life as decayed and dying. Mohawk Shelley Niro's film *It Starts with a Whisper* (1993) includes a reading of "The Song My Paddle Sings" (Rick Monture 203). Cree poet and broadcaster Rosanna Deerchild remembers stumbling across "The Cattle Thief" in the public library: "I hand-copied that entire poem right then and there and carried it around with me, reading it over and over" (McLeod 240). Later, she wrote a poem about Johnson entitled "she writes us alive" (242). There are many other examples of Johnson's inspiration to contemporary Indigenous artists, women and men alike. It is this legacy that perhaps is the most important one.

Conclusion

On 2 June 2015, the Canada's Truth and Reconciliation Commission, charged with investigating the human costs of the Canadian residential school system (which ran from 1883 until the last school closed in 1998), declared that Canada had committed cultural genocide, defined in their report as "the destruction of those structures and practices that allow the group to continue as a group" of which residential schools, along with other assimilationist practices such as land seizure and undermining Indigenous governance and social systems, particularly women's roles, were a part. This volume, which celebrates the complicated yet important legacy of an Indigenous woman writer such as Pauline Johnson, is testament to the resiliency of Indigenous peoples, their stories, traditions, and knowledges, and to the fact that these policies, many of which Johnson criticized in her writing, did not have their desired impacts. Tekahionwake's life, writing, and performance history went against all expectations for a single, "Status-Indian" Mohawk woman at the turn of the twentieth century. Instead of reading her as the "princess" that many have positioned her to be, we hope that readers of this volume will push past such a simplistic and Euro-centric framing and see her work as a complex negotiation of identity, race, citizenship, and gender that is a contemporary reflection of Indigenous agency in the face of colonial pressures to be otherwise.

E. Pauline Johnson: A Brief Chronology

1861   Born on 10 March on the Six Nations Reserve near Brant-
        ford, Ontario, to George Henry Martin Johnson / Onwan-
        onsyshon / Teyonhehkewea and Emily Susanna Howells
        Johnson. Three siblings were born before her: Henry
        Beverly Johnson (1854), Helen Charlotte Eliza Johnson
        (1856; she was called Eva in the family and used the name
        Evelyn as an adult), and Allen Wawanosh Johnson (1858).

1862   At the death of his uncle, Henry Martin Johnson,
        George Johnson is nominated by his mother, Helen
        Martin Johnson, to a seat on the Iroquois Confederacy
        Council. Since at this time his father, John "Smoke"
        Johnson, was also on the Council and George Johnson
        was the Government Interpreter, the Council was
        reluctant to let him serve. A compromise was reached
        through the intervention of his mother, who controlled
        the seat he was to take on behalf of the Wolf Clan.

1883   Begins to publish poetry in *Gems of Poetry*.

1884   Her father dies, aged 67.
        She and Evelyn attend the ceremony in Buffalo to
        re-inter the remains of the famous Seneca orator
        Red- Jacket; her commemorative poem is published in
        the *Transactions of the Buffalo Historical Society*.
        Moves with her mother and Evelyn from Chiefswood to
        Brantford.

1886   Grandfather John "Smoke" Johnson / Sakayengwaraton
        dies on 26 August, aged 93, having spoken only two
        weeks earlier at the laying of the cornerstone for the
        Joseph Brant Memorial in Brantford.
        "'Brant,' A Memorial Ode" is read by a prominent busi-
        nessman at the unveiling of the memorial in October,
        while she stands beside him on the platform. Uses her
        great-grandfather's name "Tekahionwake" for the first
        time in a publication.

1889   "In the Shadows" and "At the Ferry" are included in
        Songs of the Great Dominion, edited by W.D. Lighthall
        and published in London.

1892   In January, performs at Frank Yeigh's Canadian Litera-
        ture evening in Toronto in a program with well-known

Canadian poets, including Duncan Campbell Scott; she is so well received that Yeigh organizes a tour of Ontario for her during which she reads in 100 villages and towns.

Begins to perform with Owen Smily as her stage partner and manager.

1894   Travels to England (April–July).

Her brother Henry dies suddenly in the United States, aged 40.

Meets the novelist and suffragist Nellie L. McClung.

1895   *The White Wampum* published in London.

Meets Charles G.D. Roberts in Fredericton.

1897   She and Owen Smily stop performing together.

1898   Her engagement to Charles R.L. Drayton announced in the Toronto *Globe and Mail* in January; in late 1899 or early 1900, he asks for her release from the engagement in order to marry another woman.

1898   Her mother dies, aged 74.

1901   After a series of illnesses and financial problems, begins touring with another performer, Walter McRaye, who also acts as their manager until she retires in 1909.

1903   *Canadian Born*, her second collection of poetry, published in Toronto.

1906   Begins to write for *Boys' World*, Chicago, Illinois.

Visits London with Walter McRaye (April–November); while there, she is introduced to Chief Joe Capilano / Sahp-luk, head of a delegation of British Columbia chiefs to King Edward VII.

1907   Begins to write for *Mother's Magazine*, Chicago, Illinois.

1909   Retires from performing and moves to Vancouver; shortly afterwards she is diagnosed with breast cancer.

1910   Chief Capilano dies; Johnson begins to publish in the Vancouver *Province* the stories that he and his wife Mary Agnes / Líxwelut had told her.

1911   *Legends of Vancouver*, a collection of some of the stories she had heard from the Capilanos, is privately printed.

1912   *Flint and Feather*, a poetry collection, published in Toronto.

1913   Dies on 7 March. Her funeral is held on what would have been her 52nd birthday; her ashes are buried in Stanley Park.

The Moccasin Maker, a collection of stories, published in Toronto.

The Shaganappi, a collection of stories, published in Toronto.

1922   A monument is erected in her honour in Stanley Park.

A Note on the Text

This collection is indebted to the work of Carole Gerson and Veronica Strong-Boag on E. Pauline Johnson's writing in *E. Pauline Johnson / Tekahionwake: Collected Poems and Selected Prose*. Their list of Johnson's complete work in *Paddling Her Own Canoe: The Times and Texts of E. Pauline Johnson (Tekahionwake)* has also been an invaluable resource. Carole Gerson kindly provided us with scans of originals where indicated below. The dates in our Table of Contents are for first publication only. The copy-texts for the works by Johnson are as follows:

From *Flint and Feather* (1912):
I.1 "Canadian Born," I.11"As Red Men Die," I.16 "The Happy Hunting Grounds," II.1 "A Cry from an Indian Wife,"II.2 "Wolverine," II.3 "Silhouette," II.4 "The Cattle Thief," II.6 "The Indian Corn Planter," III.2 "The Song My Paddle Sings," III.4 "Shadow River," III.6 "Moonset," IV.3 "Dawendine," IV.4 "Ojistoh," IV.6 "The Pilot of the Plains," IV.7 "Lullaby of the Iroquois," IV.8 "The Corn Husker," VI.7 "The Lost Lagoon"

From *Legends of Vancouver* (1911):
VI.5. "A Squamish Legend of Napoleon"

From *The Moccasin Maker* (1913):
I.5 "My Mother," I.13 "Her Majesty's Guest," I.14 "A Pagan in Saint Paul's Cathedral," IV.2 "A Red Girl's Reasoning," IV.5 "The Derelict," V.1 "As It Was in the Beginning," VI.2 "Catharine of the Crow's Nest," VI.4. "The Tenas Klootchman"

From *The Shaganappi* (1913):
I.9 "The Brotherhood," I.15 "We-hro's Sacrifice," V.3 "Little Wolf-Willow," VI.1 "The Potlatch," VI.3 "Hoolool of the Totem Poles"

From *Canadian Magazine* (May 1907), 20–22:
II.7 "The Haunting Thaw"

From Gerson and Strong-Boag, *Collected Poems and Selected Prose* (2002):

I.2 "The Re-interment of Red Jacket," Chiefswood scrapbook

I.3 "'Brant,' A Memorial Ode," *Broadside* (8 October 1886), Chiefswood scrapbook

I.4 "The Lodge of the Law-makers," *Daily Express* [London] (14 August 1902), 4

I.7. "Forty-Five Miles on the Grand," *Brantford Expositor*, Christmas Number (December 1892), 17, 20

I.10 "The Death Cry" *Saturday Night* (1 September 1888), 6

I.12 "The Avenger," *Saturday Night*, Christmas Issue (1892), 15

II.5 "A Request," *The Week* (18 November 1886), 821

III.1 "At the Ferry," *Songs of the Great Dominion*, ed. W.D. Lighthall, 1889; version amended in Chiefswood scrapbook

III.3 "His Majesty, the West Wind," *The Globe* (15 December 1894), 4

III.5 "Kicking Horse River," *The Globe* (15 December 1894), 4

IV.1 "A Strong Race Opinion: On the Indian Girl in Modern Fiction," *Toronto Sunday Globe* (22 May 1892), 1

V.2 "His Sister's Son," "Johnson-Smily Entertainment," *Fort Wayne Indiana Gazette* (25 November 1896), clipping, McMaster University.

From scans or transcriptions provided by Carole Gerson:

I.6 "Heroic Indian Mothers," *Mother's Magazine* (September 1908), 23–24

I.8 "A Brother Chief," *Weekly Detroit Free Press* (12 May 1892), 1

VI.6 "The Legend of the Ice Babies," *Mother's Magazine* (November 1911), 23–24

I. THE IROQUOIS CONFEDERACY AND LOYALISM

I. The Iroquois Confederacy and Loyalism

[The Iroquois Confederacy comprises Iroquoian-speaking nations whose traditional territories were mainly on the southern side of Lake Erie and Lake Ontario. Formed by the fifteenth century, the Confederacy consisted of five nations: the Seneca, the Mohawk, the Onondaga, the Cayuga, and the Oneida. The Tuscarora joined in 1722. Based on a system of 50 hereditary *sachems* or chiefs selected by clan mothers, the Confederacy used adoption to replace clan members lost in warfare and the epidemics that followed European arrival. The Confederacy was a powerful political force for the 200 years leading up to the American War of Independence. Those who fought as British allies lost their lands in the newly formed United States and were granted land in Canada on the Bay of Quinte and along the Grand River. Other related nations, mainly Mohawk, had long been settled in Quebec, mostly in Kahnawake near Montreal, and were major players in the fur trade. Both Iroquois and Mohawk are names imposed on these groups: Haudenosaunee is usually translated as "People of the Longhouse," and the Mohawk name for themselves, *Kanien'kehá:ka*, means "People of the Flint."]

1. "Canadian Born" (1900)

[The inscription below, which opens: Johnson's book of the same title, was not included in other reprintings of this poem, although it does have an effect on its interpretation. This poem bases the claim to citizenship on the legal principle of *jus soli*, Latin for "right of the soil."]

Inscription to *Canadian Born* (Toronto: Morang, 1903)

> Let him who is Canadian born regard these poems as written to himself—whether he be my paleface compatriot who has given to me his right hand of good fellowship, in the years I have appealed to him by pen and platform, or whether he be that dear Red brother of whatsoever tribe or Province, it matter not—White Race and Red are one if they are but Canadian born.
>
> THE AUTHOR

We first saw light in Canada, the land beloved of God;
We are the pulse of Canada, its marrow and its blood:
And we, the men of Canada, can face the world and brag
That we were born in Canada beneath the British flag.
Few of us have the blood of kings, few are of courtly birth,
But few are vagabonds or rogues of doubtful name and worth;
And all have one credential that entitles us to brag—
That we were born in Canada beneath the British flag.

We've yet to make our money, we've yet to make our fame,
But we have gold and glory in our clean colonial name;
And every man's a millionaire if only he can brag
That he was born in Canada beneath the British flag.

No title and no coronet is half so proudly worn
As that which we inherited as men Canadian born.
We count no man so noble as the one who makes the brag
That he was born in Canada beneath the British flag.

The Dutch may have their Holland, the Spaniard have his Spain,
The Yankee to the south of us must south of us remain;
For not a man dare lift a hand against the men who brag
That they were born in Canada beneath the British flag.

2. "The Re-interment of Red Jacket" (1885)

[Evelyn and Pauline Johnson attended this major ceremony, held
in Buffalo, New York, in October 1884. Many Iroquois chiefs and
dignitaries attended, including Ely S. Parker (1828–95), a Seneca
sachem, a descendant of Red Jacket (c. 1750–1830), and the first
Native American appointed as Commissioner of Indian Affairs, a
post he held from 1869 to 1871. It was the first important cross-bor-
der meeting of the Haudenosaunee Confederacy since 1784. This
poem was first published in the *Transactions of the Buffalo Historical
Society* next to one by Walt Whitman (see Appendix C3–4).]

    So still the tranquil air,
One scarcely notes the falling of a leaf;
But deeper quiet wraps the dusky Chief
Whose ashes slumber there.

Sweet Indian Summer sleeps,
Trusting a foreign and a paler race
To give her gifted son an honoured place
Where Death his vigil keeps.

Before that slumber fell,
Those ashes in their eloquence had stirred
The stubborn hearts, whose heirs to-day conferred
A Christian burial.

Through war's o'er-clouded skies
His higher flush of oratory 'woke,
And factious schemes succumbed whene'er he spoke
To bid his people rise.

The keenest flint or stone
That barbed the warrior's arrow in its flight,
Could not outreach the limit of his might
That he attained alone.

Early he learned to speak,
With thought so vast, and liberal, and strong,
He blessed the little good and passed the wrong
Embodied in the weak.

So great his mental sight,
That had his form been growing with his mind,
The fir had been within his hand a wand
With superhuman might.

The world has often seen
A master mind pulse with the waning day
That sends his waning nation to decay
Where none can intervene.

And few to-day remain;
But copper-tinted face and smoldering fire
Of wilder life, were left me by my sire
To be my proudest claim.

And so ere Indian Summer sweetly sleeps,
She beckons me where old Niagara leaps;
Superbly she extends her greeting hand,
And smiling speaks to her adopted land;

Saying, "O, rising nation of the West,
That occupies my land, so richly blest;
O, free, unfettered people that have come
To make America your rightful home,

Forgive the wrongs my children did to you,
And we, the red skins, will forgive you too;
To-day has seen your noblest action done,
The honoured re-entombment of my son."

3. "'Brant,' A Memorial Ode" (1886)

[This poem, like the previous one, was commissioned. Johnson
stood on the platform beside businessman W.F. Cockshutt as he
read the poem at the unveiling of the commemorative statue of
Joseph Brant / Thayendenega (c. 1742–1807).]

Young Canada with mighty force sweeps on
To gain in power and strength, before the dawn
That brings another era; when the sun
Shall rise again, but only shine upon
Her Indian graves, and Indian memories.
For as the carmine in the twilight skies
Will fade as night comes on, so fades the race
That unto Might and therefore Right gives place,
And as white clouds float hurriedly and high
Across the crimson of a sunset sky,
Although their depths are foamy as the snow,
Their beauty lies in their vermillion glow,
So Canada, thy plumes were hardly won
Without allegiance from thy Indian son,
Thy glories, like the cloud enhance their charm
With red reflections from the Mohawk's arm.
Then meet we as one common Brotherhood,
In peace and love, with purpose understood—
To lift a lasting tribute to the name
Of Brant—who linked his own, with Britain's fame,
Who bade his people leave their valley home,

Where nature in her fairest aspect shone,
Where rolls the Mohawk river, and the land
Is blessed with every good from Heaven's hand,
To sweep the tide of home affections back
And love the land where waves the Union Jack.
What though that home no longer ours! To-day
The Six Red Nations have their Canada,
And rest we here, no cause for us to rise
To seek protection under other skies,
Encircling us an arm both true and brave
Extends from far across the great Salt wave,
Though but a woman's hand 'tis firm and strong
Enough to guard us from all fear of wrong,
A hand on which all British subjects lean—
The loving hand of England's Noble Queen.

Fig. 1: Iroquois Chiefs from Six Nations Grand River, reading wampum, 1871. George Johnson is second from left; his father, John "Smoke" Johnson, is standing. Photo: Horatio Hale. Library and Archives Canada 319350

4. "The Lodge of the Law-makers" (1906)

Contrasts between the Parliaments of the White Man and the Red

[Here Johnson compares the government of the Iroquois Confederacy to the English parliament. She notes that while the English women have to fight for their right to participate in government, Iroquois women have had that right for more than four centuries. The article appeared at the time of female suffrage campaigns in England. "The Lodge of the Law-makers" was first published in London's *Daily Express* on 14 August 1906 with the subtitle "Contrasts between the Parliament of the White Man and the Red By Tekahionwake (The Iroquois Poetess)."]

The Paleface is a man of many moods; what he approves to-day he will disapprove to-morrow.

He is never content to let his mighty men rule for more than four or five years, after which time he wearies of their council fires, their law-giving, and their treaties with other tribes; he wants new chiefs, warriors, and braves, and he secures them by the voice and vote of the nation.

We of the ancient Iroquois race can but little understand this strange mode of government. We and our fathers, and their fathers before them, have always been pleased with our own Parliament, which has never varied through the generations—save when death leaves one seat empty, and another chief in the line of lineage steps forward to fill the vacancy.

But to more fully learn the wisdom of the white man's superior civilization, I followed the wide crowded trail that leads to his council-house. I knew I would find it on the banks of a river, for any trails, even in my own country, whether they are beaten by man, horse, or buffalo, lead always to the edge of a stream.

As I neared the place I knew it for the abode of the wise men of this nation, for the voice of power and diplomacy, and tactics and skillful intrigue, thundered out from the white man's strange time-piece set in the carven square tower that rises majestic and inviolate as the tallest pine in the undiscovered wilderness of the West; and as the mountain tornado thrashes through the topmost branches, waking them to murmuring voices that dominate all other sounds of the forest, so do the tongues of these mighty men beneath the tower proclaim their dominion over all the wilderness of mankind in these island kingdoms of the East.

The Debate

Old men and young were debating with great spirit. Their speech was not so pleasant, or so diplomatic, or so fraught with symbols, as is the speech of our Indian rulers; the law-making for the nation is not pleasant councilling; therefore, we say, use the speech that may breed dissension as one would use the stone war-club. We hide and wrap the stone in vari-colored beads and brilliantly stained moose-hair; it is then more acceptable to the eye and the touch, but the weapon and the force are there nevertheless. The white man's speech shows the grim baldness of the stone alone—no adornment, no coloring to render it less aggressive, but his tongue is arrow-headed, fleet, and direct, and where he aims is the spot he strikes.

Do the white law-makers in this great council-house on the Thames river know that there exists within my own Indian race the oldest constitutional government of America—a free Commonwealth older than any in Europe, save that of this ancient England and the land of the crags and cañons which they call Switzerland?

Hiawatha's Work

And this Commonwealth, which dominated the vast continent of North America even after the white traders set their feet on our territory, was devised and framed through the brain of the young Onondaga diplomat, Hiawatha,[1] who, conceiving an idea for a universal peace, called together the representative chiefs of all the hostile tribes. It mattered not that war and bloodshed had existed for many decades between the tribes that these envoys represented, the words of Hiawatha were as oil.

The council fires burned ceaselessly, the council pipes were filled and smoked endlessly, until the fifty chiefs in conclave all ratified the policy under discussion. And thus was framed the constitution of a government that was to live through the ages, that does exist in absolute authority to-day, where the chiefs who are the final descendants of those fifty noble families still meet, and direct the affairs of their people with no less wisdom and judgment than is displayed by these Palefaces here beneath the square tower by the Thames.

Our fifty titles are not necessarily borne by the eldest sons of the noble families, for he may be greatly lacking in the qualities that make a statesman. Is not his second, or maybe his youngest

---

1 Hiawatha founded the Iroquois Confederacy, most scholars believe, in the fifteenth century.

brother, of as noble birth as he? Why not then, put him in high places, to let him use the brain and mind that, perhaps, his elder brother lacks? This is the Iroquois policy, and we practice it; but the white man knows little of the intricate workings of our inflexible league, for we are a silent people. Will the white man who considers us a savage, unenlightened race wonder if I told him the fate of the "Senate" lies in the hands of the women of our tribes?[1]

The Daughters

I have heard that the daughters of this vast city cry out for a voice in the Parliament of this land. There is no need for an Iroquois woman to clamor for recognition in our councils; she has had it for upwards of four centuries. The highest title known to us is that of "chief matron." It is borne by the oldest woman of each of the noble families.

From her cradle-board she is taught to judge men and their intellectual qualities, their aptness for public life, and their integrity, so that when he who bears the title leaves his seat in council to join the league-makers in the happy hunting grounds she can use her wisdom and her learning in nominating his fittest successor. She must bestow the title upon one of his kinsmen, one of the blood royal so that the heritage is unbroken, so, perhaps, she passes by the inadequate eldest son and nominates the capable younger one. Thus is the council given the best of the brain and blood of the nation.

The old and powerful chiefs-in-council never attempt to question her decision; her appointment is final, and at the "condoling council," when he is installed, and his title conferred as he first takes his seat, the chief matron may, if she desires, enter the council-house and publicly make an address to the chief braves, and warriors assembled, and she is listened to not only with attention, but with respect.

There are fifty matrons possessing this right in the Iroquois Confederacy.[2] I have not yet heard of fifty white women even among those of noble birth who may speak and be listened to in the lodge of the law-makers here.

---

1 The British upper house, the House of Lords, consisted of bishops and hereditary peers at the time Johnson wrote. The upper house in Canada is called the Senate, which explains her use of this term.
2 Hereditary clan mothers still select chiefs in the modern Haudenosaunee Confederacy.

Fig. 2: Wedding portrait of Emily Howells Johnson and George Henry Martin Johnson, 1853. With permission of the Royal Ontario Museum. 922.1.103

5. "My Mother" (1909)

The Story of a Life of Unusual Experiences

[In "My Mother," E. Pauline Johnson tells the story of her mother Emily Susanna Howells (1824–98), focusing on her courtship by and marriage to Mohawk chief and interpreter George Henry

Martin Johnson (1816–84). The story was originally published in the *Mother's Magazine* in four installments—April, May, June, and July 1909.]

★ ★ ★ ★ ★

[Author's Note.—This is the story of my mother's life, every incident of which she related to me herself. I have neither exaggerated nor curtailed a single circumstance in relating this story. I have supplied nothing through imagination, nor have I heightened the coloring of her unusual experiences. Had I done so I could not possibly feel as sure of her approval as I now do, for she is as near to me to-day as she was before she left me to join her husband, my beloved father, whose feet have long since wandered to the "Happy Hunting Grounds" of my dear Red Ancestors.]

PART I

It was a very lonely little girl that stood on the deck of a huge sailing vessel while the shores of England slipped down into the horizon and the great, grey Atlantic yawned desolately westward. She was leaving so much behind her, taking so little with her, for the child was grave and old even at the age of eight, and realized that this day meant the updragging of all the tiny roots that clung to the home soil of the older land. Her father was taking his wife and family, his household goods, his fortune and his future to America, which, in the days of 1829, was indeed a venturesome step, for America was regarded as remote as the North Pole, and good-byes were, alas! very real good-byes, when travellers set sail for the New World in those times before steam and telegraph brought the two continents hand almost touching hand.

So little Lydia Bestman stood drearily watching with sorrow-filled eyes the England of her babyhood fade slowly into the distance—eyes that were fated never to see again the royal old land of her birth. Already the deepest grief that life could hold had touched her young heart. She had lost her own gentle, London-bred mother when she was but two years old. Her father had married again, and on her sixth birthday little Lydia, the youngest of a large family, had been sent away to boarding-school with an elder sister, and her home knew her no more. She was taken from school to the sailing ship; little stepbrothers and sisters had arrived and she was no longer the baby. Years afterwards she told her own little children that her one vivid recollection of England was the exquisite music of the church chimes as the ship weighed anchor in Bristol harbor—chimes that were ringing for evensong from the towers of the quaint old English churches. Thirteen weeks later that sailing vessel entered New York harbor, and life in the New World began.

Like most transplanted Englishmen, Mr. Bestman cut himself completely off from the land of his fathers; his interests and his friends henceforth were all in the country of his adoption, and he chose Ohio as a site for his new home. He was a man of vast peculiarities, prejudices and extreme ideas—a man of contradictions so glaring that even his own children never understood him. He was a very narrow religionist, of the type that say many prayers and quote much Scripture, but he beat his children—both girls and boys—so severely that outsiders were at times compelled to interfere. For years these unfortunate children carried the scars left on their backs by the thongs of cat-o'-nine-tails when he punished them for some slight misdemeanor. They were all terrified at him, all obeyed him like soldiers, but none escaped his severity. The two elder ones, a boy and a girl, had married before they left England. The next girl married in Ohio, and the boys drifted away, glad to escape from a parental tyranny that made home anything but a desirable abiding-place. Finally but two remained of the first family—Lydia and her sister Elizabeth, a most lovable girl of seventeen, whose beauty of character and self-sacrificing heart made the one bright memory that remained with these scattered fledglings throughout their entire lives.

The lady who occupied the undesirable position of step-mother to these unfortunate children was of the very cold and chilling type of Englishwoman, more frequently met with two generations ago than in this age. She simply let her husband's first family alone. She took no interest in them, neglected them absolutely, but in her neglect was far kinder and more humane than their own father. Yet she saw that all the money, all the pretty clothes, all the dainties, went to her own children.

Perhaps the reader will think these unpleasant characteristics of a harsh father and a self-centred stepmother might better be omitted from this narrative, particularly as death claimed these two many years ago; but in the light of after events, it is necessary to reveal what the home environment of these children had been, how little of companionship or kindness or spoken love had entered their baby lives. The absence of mother kisses, of father comradeship, of endeavor to understand them individually, to probe their separate and various dispositions—things so essential to the development of all that is best in a child—went far towards governing their later actions in life. It drove the unselfish, sweet-hearted Elizabeth to a loveless marriage; it flung poor, little love-hungry Lydia into alien but, fortunately, loyal and noble arms. Outsiders said, "What strange marriages!" But Lydia, at least, married where the first real kindness she had ever known called to her, and not one day of regret for that marriage ever entered into her life.

It came about so strangely, so inevitably, from such a tiny source, that it is almost incredible.

One day the stepmother, contrary to her usual custom, went into the kitchen and baked a number of little cakelets, probably what we would call cookies. For what sinister reason no one could divine, but she counted these cakes as she took them from the baking-pans and placed them in the pantry. There were forty-nine, all told. That evening she counted them again; there were forty-eight. Then she complained to her husband that one of the children had evidently stolen a cake. (In her mind the two negro servants employed in the house did not merit the suspicion.) Mr. Bestman inquired which child was fond of the cakes. Mrs. Bestman replied that she did not know, unless it was Lydia, who always liked them.

Lydia was called. Her father, frowning, asked if she had taken the cake. The child said no.

"You are not telling the truth," Mr. Bestman shouted, as the poor little downtrodden girl stood half terrified, consequently half guilty-mannered, before him.

"But I am truthful," she said. "I know nothing of the cake."

"You are not truthful. You stole it—you know you did. You shall be punished for this falsehood," he stormed, and reached for the cat-o'-nine-tails.

The child was beaten brutally and sent to her room until she could tell the truth. When she was released she still held that she had not taken the cooky. Another beating followed, then a third, when finally the stepmother interfered and said magnanimously:

"Don't whip her any more; she has been punished enough." And once during one of the beatings she protested, saying, "Don't strike the child *on the head* in that way."

But the iron had entered into Lydia's sister's soul. The injustice of it all drove gentle Elizabeth's gentleness to the winds.

"Liddy darling," she said, taking the thirteen-year-old girlchild into her strong young arms, "*I* know truth when I hear it. *You* never stole that cake."

"I didn't," sobbed the child, "I didn't."

"And you have been beaten three times for it!" And the sweet young mouth hardened into lines that were far too severe for a girl of seventeen. Then: "Liddy, do you know that Mr. Evans has asked me to marry him?"

"Mr. Evans!" exclaimed the child. "Why, you can't marry *him*, 'Liza! He's ever so old, and he lives away up in Canada, among the Indians."

"That's one of the reasons that I should like to marry him," said Elizabeth, her young eyes starry with zeal. "I want to work among the Indians, to help in Christianizing them, to—oh! just to help."

"But Mr. Evans is so *old*," reiterated Lydia.

"Only thirty," answered the sister; "and he is such a splendid missionary, dear."

Love? No one talked of love in that household except the contradictory father, who continually talked of the love of God, but forgot to reflect that love towards his own children.

Human love was considered a non-essential in that family. Beautiful-spirited Elizabeth had hardly heard the word. Even Mr. Evans had not made use of it. He had selected her as his wife more for her loveliness of character than from any personal attraction, and she in her untaught womanhood married him, more for the reason that she desired to be a laborer in Christ's vineyard than because of any wish to be the wife of this one man.

But after the marriage ceremony, this gentle girl looked boldly into her father's eyes and said:

"I am going to take Liddy with me into the wilds of Canada."

"Well, well, well!" said her father, English-fashion. "If she wants to go, she may."

Go? The child fairly clung to the fingers of this saviour-sister—the poor little, inexperienced, seventeen-year-old bride who was giving up her youth and her girlhood to lay it all upon the shrine of endeavour to bring the radiance of the Star that shone above Bethlehem to reflect its glories upon a forest-bred people of the North!

It was a long, strange journey that the bride and her little sister took. A stage coach conveyed them from their home in Ohio to Erie, Pennsylvania, where they went aboard a sailing vessel bound for Buffalo. There they crossed the Niagara River, and at Chippewa, on the Canadian side, again took a stage coach for the village of Brantford, sixty miles west.

At this place they remained over night, and the following day Mr. Evans' own conveyance arrived to fetch them to the Indian Reserve, ten miles to the south-east.

In after years little Lydia used to tell that during that entire drive she thought she was going through an English avenue leading up to some great estate, for the trees crowded up close to the roadway on either side, giant forest trees—gnarled oaks, singing firs, jaunty maples, graceful elms—all stretching their branches overhead. But the "avenue" seemed endless. "When do we come to the house?" she asked, innocently. "This lane is very long."

But it was three hours, over a rough corduroy road,[1] before the little white frame parsonage lifted its roof through the forest, its broad verandahs and green outside shutters welcoming the travellers with an atmosphere of home at last.

As the horses drew up before the porch the great front door was noiselessly opened and a lad of seventeen, lithe, clean-limbed, erect, copper-colored, ran swiftly down the steps, lifted his hat, smiled, and assisted the ladies to alight. The boy was Indian to the finger-tips, with that peculiar native polish and courtesy, that absolute ease of manner and direction of glance, possessed only by the old-fashioned type of red man of this continent. The missionary introduced him as "My young friend, the church interpreter, Mr. George Mansion, who is one of our household." (Mansion, or "Grand Mansion," is the English meaning of this young Mohawk's native name.)[2]

The entire personality of the missionary seemed to undergo a change as his eyes rested on this youth. His hitherto rather stilted manner relaxed, his eyes softened and glowed, he invited confidence rather than repelled it; truly his heart was bound up with these forest people; he fairly exhaled love for them with every breath. He was a man of marked shyness, and these silent Indians made him forget this peculiarity of which he was sorrowfully conscious. It was probably this shyness that caused him to open the door and turn to his young wife with the ill-selected remark: "Welcome home, madam."

Madam! The little bride was chilled to the heart with the austere word. She hurried within, followed by her wondering child-sister, as soon as possible sought her room, then gave way to a storm of tears.

"Don't mind me, Liddy," she sobbed. "There's nothing wrong; we'll be happy enough here, only I think I looked for a little—petting."

With a wisdom beyond her years, Lydia did not reply, but went to the window and gazed absently at the tiny patch of flowers beyond

---

1 A road over swampy or muddy terrain built of logs laid side by side at right angles to the way (*Dictionary of Canadianisms on Historical Principles Online* [DCHP-1 Online]. Web. 12 July 2014).

2 One of Johnson's father's Mohawk names, Onwanonsyshon, means "Lord of the great mansion."

the door—the two lilac trees in full blossom, the thread of glisten-ing river, and behind it all, the northern wilderness. Just below the window stood the missionary and the Indian boy talking eagerly.

"Isn't George Mansion *splendid*!" said the child.

"You must call him Mr. Mansion; be very careful about the *Mister*, Liddy dear," said her sister, rising and drying her eyes bravely. "I have always heard that the Indians treat one just as they are treated by one. Respect Mr. Mansion, treat him as you would treat a city gentleman. Be sure he will gauge his deport-ment by ours. Yes, dear, he *is* splendid. I like him already."

"Yes, 'Liza, so do I, and he *is* a gentleman. He looks it and acts it. I believe he *thinks* gentlemanly things."

Elizabeth laughed. "You dear little soul!" she said. "I know what you mean, and I agree with you."

That laugh was all that Lydia wanted to hear in this world, and presently the two sisters, with arms entwined, descended the stairway and joined in the conversation between Mr. Evans and young George Mansion.

"Mrs. Evans," said the boy, addressing her directly for the first time, "I hoped you were fond of game. Yesterday I hunted; it was partridge I got, and one fine deer. Will you offer me the compliment of having some for dinner to-night?"

His voice was low and very distinct, his accent and expres-sions very marked as a foreigner to the tongue, but his English was perfect.

"Indeed I shall, Mr. Mansion," smiled the girl-bride, "but I'm afraid that I don't know how to cook it."

"We have an excellent cook," said Mr. Evans. "She has been with George and me ever since I came here. George is a splendid shot, and keeps her busy getting us game suppers."

Meanwhile Lydia had been observing the boy. She had never seen an Indian, consequently was trying to reform her ideas regard-ing them. She had not expected to see anything like this self-poised, scrupulously-dressed, fine-featured, dark stripling. She thought all Indians wore savage-looking clothes, had fierce eyes and stern, set mouths. This boy's eyes were narrow and shrewd, but warm and kindly, his lips were like Cupid's bow, his hands were narrower, smaller, than her own, but the firmness of those slim fingers, the power in those small palms, as he had helped her from the carriage, remained with her through all the years to come.

That evening at supper she noted his table deportment; it was correct in every detail. He ate leisurely, silently, gracefully; his knife and fork never clattered, his elbows never were in evidence, he made use of the right plates, spoons, forks, knives; he bore an ease, an unconsciousness of manner that amazed her. The missionary himself was a stiff man, and his very shyness made him angular. Against such a setting young Mansion gleamed like a brown gem.

* * * * *

For seven years life rolled slowly by. At times Lydia went to visit her two other married sisters, sometimes she remained for weeks with a married brother, and at rare intervals made brief trips to her father's house; but she never received a penny from her strange parent, and knew of but one home which was worthy the name. That was in the Canadian wilderness where the Indian Mission held out its arms to her, and the beloved sister made her more welcome than words could imply. Four pretty children had come to grace this forest household, where young George Mansion, still the veriest right hand of the missionary, had grown into a magnificent type of Mohawk manhood. These years had brought him much, and he had accomplished far more than idle chance could ever throw in his way. He had saved his salary that he earned as interpreter in the church, and had purchased some desirable property, a beautiful estate of two hundred acres, upon which he some day hoped to build a home. He had mastered six Indian languages, which, with his knowledge of English and his wonderful fluency in his own tribal Mohawk, gave him command of eight tongues, an advantage which soon brought him the position of Government interpreter in the Council of the great "Six Nations," composing the Iroquois race. Added to this, through the death of an uncle he came into the younger title of his family, which boasted blood of two noble lines. His father, speaker of the Council, held the elder title, but that did not lessen the importance of young George's title of chief.

Lydia never forgot the first time she saw him robed in the full costume of his office. Hitherto she had regarded him through all her comings and goings as her playmate, friend and boon companion; he had been to her something that had never before entered her life—he had brought warmth, kindness, fellowship and a peculiar confidential humanity that had been entirely lacking in the chill English home of her childhood. But this day, as he stood beside his veteran father, ready to take his place among the chiefs of the Grand Council, she saw revealed another phase of his life and character; she saw that he was destined to be a man among men, and for the first time she realized that her boy companion had gone a little beyond her, perhaps a little above her. They were a strange pair as they stood somewhat apart, unconscious of the picture they made. She, a gentle-born, fair English girl of twenty, her simple blue muslin frock vying with her eyes in color. He, tawny skinned, lithe, straight as an arrow, the royal blood of generations of chiefs and warriors pulsing through his arteries, his clinging buckskin tunic and leggings fringed and embroidered with countless quills, and endless stitches of colored moosehair. From his small, neat moccasins to his jet black hair tipped with an eagle plume he was every inch a man, a gentleman, a warrior.

But he was approaching her with the same ease with which he wore his ordinary "white" clothes—garments, whether buckskin or broadcloth, seemed to make but slight impression on him.

"Miss Bestman," he said, "I should like you to meet my mother and father. They are here, and are old friends of your sister and Mr. Evans. My mother does not speak English, but she knows you are my friend."

And presently Lydia found herself shaking hands with the elder chief, speaker of the council, who spoke English rather well, and with a little dark woman folded within a "broadcloth" and wearing the leggings, moccasins and short dress of her people. A curious feeling of shyness overcame the girl as her hand met that of George Mansion's mother, who herself was the most retiring, most thoroughly old-fashioned woman of her tribe. But Lydia felt that she was in the presence of one whom the young chief held far and away as above himself, as above her, as the best and greatest woman of his world; his very manner revealed it, and Lydia honored him within her heart at that moment more than she had ever done before.

But Chief George Mansion's mother, small and silent through long habit and custom, had acquired a certain masterful dignity of her own, for within her slender brown fingers she held a power that no man of her nation could wrest from her. She was "Chief Matron" of her entire blood relations, and commanded the enviable position of being the one and only person, man or woman, who could appoint a chief to fill the vacancy of one of the great Mohawk law-makers whose seat in Council had been left vacant when the voice of the Great Spirit called him to the happy hunting grounds. Lydia had heard of this national honor which was the right and title of this frail little moccasined Indian woman with whom she was shaking hands, and the thought flashed rapidly through her girlish mind: "Suppose some *one* lady in England had the marvellous power of appointing who the member should be in the British House of Lords or Commons. *Wouldn't* Great Britain honor and tremble before her?"

And here was Chief George Mansion's silent, unpretentious little mother possessing all this power among her people, and she, Lydia Bestman, was shaking hands with her! It seemed very marvellous.

But that night the power of this same slender Indian mother was brought vividly before her when, unintentionally, she overheard young George say to the missionary:

"I almost lost my new title to-day, after you and the ladies had left the Council."

"Why, George boy!" exclaimed Mr. Evans. "What have you done?"

"Nothing, it seems, except to be successful. The Council objected to my holding the title of chief and having a chief's vote in the affairs of the people, and at the same time being Government interpreter. They said it would give me too much power to retain both positions. I must give up one—my title or my Government position."

"What did you do?" demanded Mr. Evans, eagerly.

"Nothing, again," smiled the young chief. "But my mother did something. She took the floor of the Council, and spoke for forty minutes. She said I must hold the positions of chief which she had made for me, as well as of interpreter which I had made for myself; that if the Council objected, she would forever annul the chief's title in her own family; she would never appoint one in my place, and that we proud, arrogant Mohawks would then have only eight representatives in Council—only be on a level with, as she expressed it, 'those dogs of Senecas.' Then she clutched her broadcloth about her, turned her back on us all, and left the Council."[1]

---

1   "His title of chief"—George Henry Martin Johnson's father, John "Smoke" Johnson / Sakayengwaraton (1792–1886), was a Pine Tree chief; he was elected to this non-hereditary post because of his oratorical skills. George Johnson inherited his position from his uncle, Henry Martin, through the nomination of his mother, Helen Martin Johnson. At this time he also received the chief's name Teyonhahkewea, or "Double Life," previously held by Henry Martin. In the Iroquois system, cousins or nephews were chosen as successors, rather than eldest sons, as in the British system. Indeed, the fact that John "Smoke" Johnson and his son would be on the Council together was almost unheard of since the Confederacy was concerned that sons would vote with their fathers. George Johnson's role as a translator complicated things further. The compromise reached was that as long as George Johnson worked as government translator, he could speak in the Council but his vote would not be required to make a decision unanimous, as was generally the case (see Evelyn H.C. Johnson 78).

"What did the Council do?" gasped Mr. Evans.

"Accepted me as chief and interpreter," replied the young man, smiling. "There was nothing else to do."

"Oh, you royal woman! You loyal, loyal mother!" cried Lydia to herself. "How I love you for it!"

Then she crept away just as Mr. Evans had sprung forward with both hands extended towards the young chief, his eyes beaming with almost fatherly delight.

Unconsciously to herself, the English girl's interest in the young chief had grown rapidly year after year. She was also unconscious of his aim at constant companionship with herself. His devotion to her sister, whose delicate health alarmed them all, more and more, as time went on, was only another royal road to Lydia's heart. Elizabeth was becoming frail, shadowy, her appetite was fitful, her eyes larger and more wistful, her fingers smaller and weaker. No one seemed to realize the insidious on-creepings of "the white man's disease," consumption,[1] that was paling Elizabeth's fine English skin, heightening her glorious English color, sapping her delicate English veins. Only young George would tell himself over and over: "Mrs. Evans is going away from us some day, and Lydia will be left with no one in the world but me—no one but me to understand—or to—care."

So he scoured the forest for dainties, wild fruits, game, flowers, to tempt the appetite and the eye of the fading wife of the man who had taught him all the English and the white man's etiquette that he had ever mastered. Night after night he would return from day-long hunting trips, his game-bag filled with delicate quail, rare woodcock, snowy-breasted partridge, and when the illusive appetite of the sick woman could be coaxed to partake of a morsel, he felt repaid for miles of tramping through forest trails, for hours of search and skill.

PART II

Perhaps it was this grey shadow stealing on the forest mission, the thought of the day when that beautiful mothering sister would leave his little friend Lydia alone with a bereft man and four small children, or perhaps it was a yet more personal note in his life that brought George Mansion to the realization of what this girl had grown to be to him.

Indian-wise, his parents had arranged a suitable marriage

---

1 Tuberculosis.

for him, selecting a girl of his own tribe, of the correct clan to mate with his own, so that the line of blood heritage would be intact, and the sons of the next generation would be of the "Blood Royal," qualified by rightful lineage to inherit the title of chief.

This Mohawk girl was attractive, young, and had a partial English education. Her parents were fairly prosperous, owners of many acres, and much forest and timber country. The arrangement was regarded as an ideal one—the young people as perfectly and diplomatically mated as it was possible to be; but when his parents approached the young chief with the proposition, he met it with instant refusal.

"My father, my mother," he begged, "I ask you to forgive me this one disobedience. I ask you to forgive that I have, amid my fight and struggle for English education, forgotten a single custom of my people. I have tried to honor all the ancient rules and usages of my forefathers, but I forgot this one thing, and I cannot, cannot do it! My wife I must choose for myself."

"You will marry—whom, then?" asked the old chief.

"I have given no thought to it—yet," he faltered.

"Yes," said his mother, urged by the knowing heart of a woman, "yes, George, you have thought of it."

"Only this hour," he answered, looking directly into his mother's eyes. "Only now that I see you want me to give my life to someone else. But my life belongs to the white girl, Mrs. Evans' sister, if she will take it. I shall offer it to her to-morrow—to-day."

His mother's face took on the shadow of age. "You would marry a *white* girl?" she exclaimed, incredulously.

"Yes," came the reply, briefly, decidedly.

"But your children, your sons and hers—they could never hold the title, never be chief," she said, rising to her feet.

He winced. "I know it. I had not thought of it before—but I know it. Still, I would marry her."

"But there would be no more chiefs of the Grand Mansion name," cut in his father. "The title would go to your aunt's sons. She is a Grand Mansion no longer; she, being married, is merely a Straight-Shot, her husband's name. The Straight-Shots never had noble blood, never wore a title. Shall our family title go to a *Straight-Shot*?" and the elder chief mouthed the name contemptuously.

Again the boy winced. The hurt of it all was sinking in—he hated the Straight-Shots, he loved his own blood and bone. With lightning rapidity he weighed it all mentally, then spoke: "Perhaps the white girl will not marry me," he said slowly, and the thought of it drove the dark red from his cheeks, drove his finger-nails into his palms.

"Then, then you will marry Dawendine, our choice?" cried his mother, hopefully.

"I shall marry no one but the white girl," he answered, with set lips. "If she will not marry me, I shall never marry, so the Straight-Shots will have our title, anyway."

The door closed behind him. It was as if it had shut forever between him and his own.

But even with this threatened calamity looming before her, the old Indian mother's hurt heart swelled with a certain pride in his wilful actions.

"What bravery!" she exclaimed. "What courage to hold to his own choice! What a *man*!"

"Yes," half bemoaned his father, "he is a red man through and through. He defies his whole nation in his fearlessness, his lawlessness. Even I bow to his bravery, his self-will, but that bravery is hurting me here, here!" and the ancient chief laid his hand above his heart.

There was no reply to be made by the proud though pained mother. She folded her "broadcloth" about her, filled her small carved pipe and sat for many hours smoking silently, silently, silently. Now and again she shook her head mournfully, but her dark eyes would flash at times with an emotion that contradicted her dejected attitude. It was an emotion born of self-exaltation, for had she not mothered a *man*?—albeit that manhood was revealing itself in scorning the traditions and customs of her ancient race.

And young George was returning from his father's house to the Mission with equally mixed emotions. He knew he had dealt an almost unforgivable blow to those beloved parents whom he had honored and obeyed from his babyhood. Once he almost turned back. Then a vision arose of a fair young English girl whose unhappy childhood he had learned of years ago, a sweet, homeless face of great beauty, lips that were made for love they had never had, eyes that had already known more of tears than they should have shed in a lifetime. Suppose some other youth should win this girl away from him? Already several of the young men from the town drove over more frequently than they had cause to. Only the week before he had found her seated at the little old melodeon playing and singing a duet with one of these gallants. He locked his teeth together and strode rapidly through the forest path, with the first full realization that she was the only woman in all the world for him.

Some inevitable force seemed to be driving him towards—

circumstances seemed to pave the way to—their ultimate union; even now chance placed her in the path, literally, for as he threaded his way uphill, across the open, and on to the little log bridge which crossed the ravine immediately behind the Mission, he saw her standing at the further side, leaning upon the unpeeled sapling which formed the bridge guard. She was looking into the tiny stream beneath. He made no sound as he approached. Generations of moccasin-shod ancestors had made his own movements swift and silent. Notwithstanding this, she turned, and, with a bright girlish smile, she said:

"I knew you were coming, Chief."

"Why? How?" he asked, accepting his new title from her with a graceful indifference almost beyond his four and twenty years.

"I can hardly say just how—but—" she ended with only a smile. For a full minute he caught and held her glance. She seemed unable to look away, but her grave, blue English eyes were neither shy nor confident. They just seemed to answer his—then,

"Miss Bestman, will you be my wife?" he asked gently. She was neither surprised nor dismayed, only stood silent, as if she had forgotten the art of speech. "You knew I should ask this some day," he continued, rather rapidly. "This is the day."

"I did not really know—I don't know how I feel—" she began, faltering.

"I did not know how I felt, either, until an hour ago," he explained. "When my father and my mother told me they had arranged my marriage with—"

"With whom?" she almost demanded.

"A girl of my own people," he said, grudgingly. "A girl I honor and respect, but—"

"But what?" she said weakly, for the mention of his possible marriage with another had flung her own feelings into her very face.

"But unless you will be my wife, I shall never marry." He folded his arms across his chest as he said it—the very action expressed finality. For a second he stood erect, dark, slender, lithe, immovable, then with sudden impulse he held out one hand to her and spoke very quietly. "I love you, Lydia. Will you come to me?"

"Yes," she answered clearly. "I will come."

He caught her hands very tightly, bending his head until his fine face rested against her hair. She knew then that she had loved him through all these years, and that come what might, she would love him through all the years to be.

That night she told her frail and fading sister, whom she found alone resting among her pillows.

"'Liza dear, you are crying," she half sobbed in alarm, as the great tears rolled slowly down the wan cheeks. "I have made you unhappy, and you are ill, too. Oh, how selfish I am! I did not think that perhaps it might distress you."

"Liddy, Liddy darling, these are the only tears of joy that I have ever shed!" cried Elizabeth. "Joy, joy, girlie! I have wished this to come before I left you, wished it for years. I love George Mansion better than I ever loved brother of mine. Of all the world I should have chosen him for your husband. Oh! I am happy, happy, child, and you will be happy with him, too."

And that night Lydia Bestman laid her down to rest, with her heart knowing the greatest human love that had ever entered into her life.

Mr. Evans was almost beside himself with joyousness when the young people rather shyly confessed their engagement to him. He was deeply attached to his wife's young sister, and George Mansion had been more to him than many a man's son ever is. Seemingly cold and undemonstrative, this reserved Scotch missionary had given all his heart and life to the Indians, and this one boy was the apple of his eye. Far-sighted and cautious, he saw endless trouble shadowing the young lovers—opposition to the marriage from both sides of the house. He could already see Lydia's family smarting under the seeming disgrace of her marriage to an Indian; he could see George's family indignant and hurt to the core at his marriage with a white girl; he could see how impossible it would be for Lydia's people to ever understand the fierce resentment of the Indian parents that the family title could never continue under the family name. He could see how little George's people would ever understand the "white" prejudice against them. But the good man kept his own counsel, determining only that when the war did break out, he would stand shoulder to shoulder with these young lovers and be their friend and helper when even their own blood and kin should cut them off.

★ ★ ★ ★ ★

It was two years before this shy and taciturn man fully realized what the young chief and the English girl really were to him, for affliction had laid a heavy hand on his heart. First, his gentle and angel-natured wife said her long, last good-night to him. Then an unrelenting scourge of scarlet fever[1] swept three of his children

---

1 An infectious disease that mainly affects children, causing fever and a red rash.

into graves. Then the eldest, just on the threshold of sweet young maidenhood, faded like a flower, until she, too, said good-night and slept beside her mother. Wifeless, childless, the stricken missionary hugged to his heart these two—George and Lydia—and they, who had labored weeks and months, night and day, nursing and tending these loved ones, who had helped fight and grapple with death five times within two years, only to be driven back heartsore and conquered by the enemy—these two put away the thought of marriage for the time. Joy would have been ill-fitting in that household. Youth was theirs, health was theirs, and duty also was theirs—duty to this man of God, whose house was their home, whose hand had brought them together. So the marriage did not take place at once, but the young chief began making preparations on the estate he had purchased to build a fitting home for this homeless girl who was giving her life into his hands. After so many dark days, it was a relief to get Mr. Evans interested in the plans of the house George was to build, to select the proper situation, to arrange for a barn, a carriage house, a stable, for young Mansion had saved money and acquired property of sufficient value to give his wife a home that would vie with anything in the large border towns. Like most Indians, he was recklessly extravagant, and many a time the thrifty Scotch blood of the missionary would urge more economy, less expenditure. But the building went on; George determined it was to be a "Grand Mansion." His very title demanded that he give his wife an abode worthy of the ancestors who appropriated the name as their own.

"When you both go from me, even if it is only across the fields to the new home, I shall be very much alone," Mr. Evans had once said. Then in an agony of fear that his solitary life would shadow their happiness, he added quickly, "But I have a very sweet and lovely niece who writes me she will come to look after this desolated home if I wish it, and perhaps her brother will come, too, if I want him. I am afraid I *shall* want him sorely, George. For though you will be but five minutes walk from me, your face will not be at my breakfast table to help me begin each day with a courage it has always inspired. So I beg that you two will not delay your marriage; give no thought to me. You are young but once, and youth has wings of wonderful swiftness. Margaret and Christopher shall come to me; but although they are my own flesh and blood, they will never become to me what you two have been, and always will be."

Within their recollection, the lovers had never heard the missionary make so long a speech. They felt the earnestness of it, the truth of it, and arranged to be married when the golden days of August came. Lydia was to go to her married sister, in the eastern part of Canada, whose husband was a clergyman, and at whose home she had spent many of her girlhood years. George was to follow. They were to be quietly married and return by sailing vessel up the lakes, then take the stage from what is now the city of Toronto, arrive at the Indian Reserve, and go direct to the handsome home the young chief had erected for his English bride. So Lydia Bestman set forth on her long journey from which she was to return as the wife of the head chief of a powerful tribe of Indians—a man revered, respected, looked up to by a vast nation, a man of sterling worth, of considerable wealth as riches were counted in those days, a man polished in the usages and etiquette of her own people, who conducted himself with faultless grace, who would have shone brilliantly in any drawing-room (and who in after years was the guest of honor at many a great reception by the governors of the land), a man young, stalwart, handsome, with an aristocratic lineage that bred him a native gentleman, with a grand old title that had come down to him through six hundred years of honor in warfare and high places of his people. That this man should be despised by her relatives and family connections because of his warm, red skin and Indian blood, never occurred to Lydia. Her angel sister had loved the youth, the old Scotch missionary little short of adored him. Why, then, this shocked amazement of her relatives, that she should wish to wed the finest gentleman she had ever met, the man whose love and kindness had made her erstwhile blackened and cruel world a paradise of sunshine and contentment? She was but little prepared for the storm of indignation that met her announcement that she was engaged to marry a Mohawk Indian chief.

Her sister, with whom she never had anything in common, who was years older, and had been married in England when Lydia was but three years of age, implored, entreated, sneered, ridiculed and stormed. Lydia sat motionless through it all, and then the outraged sister struck a vital spot with: "I don't know what Elizabeth has been thinking of all these years, to let you associate with Indians on an equality. *She* is to blame for this."

Then and only then, did Lydia blaze forth. "Don't you *dare* speak of 'Liza like that!" flung the girl. "She was the only human being in our whole family, the only one who ever took me in her arms, who ever called me 'dear,' who ever kissed me as if she meant it. I tell you, she loved George Mansion better than she loved her cold, chilly English brothers. She loved *me*, and her house was my home, which yours never was. Yes, she loved me, angel girl that she was, and she died in a halo of happiness because I was happy and because I was to marry the noblest, kingliest gentleman I ever met." The girl ceased, breathless.

"Yes," sneered her sister, "yes, marry an *Indian*!"

"Yes," defied Lydia, "an *Indian*, who can give me not only a better home than this threadbare parsonage of yours"—here she swept scornful eyes about the meagre little, shabby room—"yes, a home that any Bestman would be proud to own; but better than that," she continued ragingly, "he has given me love—*love*, that you in your chilly, inhuman home sneer at, but that I have cried out for; love that my dead mother prayed should come to me, from the moment she left me a baby, alone, in England, until the hour when this one splendid man took me into his heart."

"Poor mother!" sighed the sister. "I am grateful she is spared *this*."

"Don't think that she doesn't know it!" cried Lydia. "If 'Liza approved, mother does, and she is glad of her child's happiness."

"Her child—yes, her child," taunted the sister. "Child! child! Yes, and what of the *child* you will probably mother?"

The crimson swept painfully down the young girl's face, but she braved it out.

"Yes," she stammered, "a child, perhaps a *son*, a son of mine, who, poor boy, can never inherit his father's title."

"And why not, pray?" remarked her sister.

"Because the female line of lineage will be broken," explained the girl. "He *should* marry someone else, so that the family title could follow the family name. His father and mother have practically cast him off because of me. *Don't* you see? Can't you understand that I am only an untitled commoner to his people? I am only a white girl."

"*Only* a white girl!" repeated the sister, sarcastically. "Do you mean to tell me that you believe these wretched Indians don't want him to marry you? *You*, a *Bestman*, and an English girl? Nonsense, Lydia! You are talking utter nonsense." But the sister's voice weakened, nevertheless.

"But it's true," asserted the girl. "You don't understand the Indian nation as 'Liza did; it's perfectly true—a son of mine can claim no family title; the honor of it must leave the name of Mansion forever. Oh, his parents have completely shut him out of their lives because I am only a white girl!" and the sweet young voice trembled woefully.

"I decline to discuss this disgraceful matter with you any further," said the sister coldly. "Perhaps my good husband can bring you to your senses," and the lady left the room in a fever of indignation.

But her "good husband," the city clergyman, declined the task of "bringing Lydia to her senses." He merely sent for her to go to his study, and, as she stood timidly in the doorway, he set his small steely eyes on her and said:

"You will leave this house at once, to-night. *To-night*, do you hear? I'll have no Indian come *here* after my wife's sister. I hope you quite understand me?"[1]

"Quite, sir," replied the girl, and with a stiff bow she turned and went back to her room.

In the haste of packing up her poor and scanty wardrobe, she heard her sister's voice saying to the clergyman: "Oh! how *could* you send her away? You know she has no home, she has nowhere to go. How *could* you do it?" All Lydia caught of his reply was: "Not another night, not another meal, in this house while *I* am its master."

Presently her sister came upstairs carrying a plate of pudding. Her eyes were red with tears, and her hands trembled. "Do eat this, my dear; some tea is coming presently," she said.

But Lydia only shook her head, strapped her little box, and, putting on her bonnet, she commanded her voice sufficiently to say: "I am going now. I'll send for this box later."

"Where are you going to?" her sister's voice trembled.

"I—don't know," said the girl. "But wherever I do go, it will be a kindlier place than this. Good-bye, sister." She kissed the distressed wife softly on each cheek, then paused at the bedroom door to say, "The man I am to marry loves me, honors me too much to treat me as a mere possession. I know that *he* will never tell me he is 'master.' George Mansion may have savage blood in his veins, but he has grasped the meaning of the word 'Christianity' far more fully than your husband has."

Her sister could not reply, but stood with streaming eyes and watched the girl slip down the back stairs and out of a side door.

For a moment Lydia Bestman stood on the pavement and glanced up and down the street. The city was what was known as a garrison town in the days when the British regular troops were quartered in Canada. Far down the street two gay young officers

---

1 Emily Howells hoped that her brother-in-law, The Rev. R.V. Rogers, of St. George's Church (now Cathedral) in Kingston, Ontario, would perform the marriage. However, after he refused, the couple were married in St. Mark's Church, in nearby Barriefield.

were walking, their brilliant uniforms making a pleasant splash of color in the sunlight. They seemed to suggest to the girl's mind a more than welcome thought. She knew the major's wife well, a gracious, whole-souled English lady whose kindness had oftentimes brightened her otherwise colorless life. Instinctively the girl turned to the quarters of the married officers. She found the major's wife at home, and, burying her drawn little face in the good lady's lap, she poured forth her entire story.

"My dear," blazed out the usually placid lady, "if I were only the major for a few moments, instead of his wife, I should—I should—well, I should just *swear*! There, now I've said it, and I'd *do* it, too. Why, I never heard of such an outrage! My dear, kiss me, and tell me—when, how, do you expect your young chief to come for you?"

"Next week," said the girl, from the depths of those sheltering arms.

"Then here you stay, right here with me. The major and I shall go to the church with you, see you safely married, bring you and your Hiawatha home for a cosy little breakfast, put you aboard the boat for Toronto, and give you both our blessing and our love." And the major's wife nodded her head with such emphasis that her quaint English curls bobbed about, setting Lydia off into a fit of laughter. "That's right, my dear. You just begin to laugh now, and keep it up for all the days to come. I'll warrant you've had little of laughter in your young life," she said knowingly. "From what I've known of your father, he never ordered laughter as a daily ingredient in his children's food. Then that sweet Elizabeth leaving you alone, so terribly alone, must have chased the sunshine far from your little world. But after this," she added brightly, "it's just going to be love and laughter. And now, my dear, we must get back the rosy English color in your cheeks, or your young Hiawatha won't know his little white sweetheart. Run away to my spare room, girlie. The orderly will get a man to fetch your box. Then you can change your frock. Leave yesterday behind you forever. Have a little rest; you look as if you had not slept for a week. Then join the major and me at dinner, and we'll toast you and your redskin lover in true garrison style."

And Lydia, with the glorious recuperation of youth, ran joyously upstairs, smiling and singing like a lark, transformed with the first unadulterated happiness she had ever felt or known.

PART III

Upon George Mansion's arrival at the garrison town he had been met on the wharf by the major, who took him to the hotel, while hurriedly explaining just why he must not go near Lydia's sister and the clergyman whom George had expected would perform the marriage ceremony. "So," continued the major, "you and Lydia are not to be married at the cathedral after all, but Mrs. Harold and I have arranged that the ceremony shall take place at little St. Swithin's Church in the West End. So you'll be there at eleven o'clock, eh, boy?"

"Yes, major, I'll be there, and before eleven, I'm afraid, I'm so anxious to take her home. I shall not endeavour to thank you and Mrs. Harold for what you have done for my homeless girl. I can't even—"

"Tut, tut, tut!" growled the major. "Haven't done anything. Bless my soul, Chief, take my word for it, haven't done a thing to be thanked for. Here's your hotel. Get some coffee to brace your nerves up with, for I can assure you, boy, a wedding is a trying ordeal, even if there is but a handful of folks to see it through. Be a good boy, now—good-bye until eleven—St. Swithin's, remember, and God bless you!" and the big-hearted, blustering major was whisked away in his carriage, leaving the young Indian half overwhelmed with his kindness, but as happy as the golden day.

An hour or so later he stood at the hotel door a moment awaiting the cab that was to take him to the church. He was dressed in the height of the fashion of the early fifties—very dark wine broadcloth, the coat shaped tightly to the waist and adorned with a silk velvet collar, a pale lavender, flowered satin waistcoat, a dull white silk stock collar, a bell-shaped black silk hat. He carried his gloves, for throughout his entire life he declared he breathed through his hands, and the wearing of gloves was abhorrent to him. Suddenly a gentleman accosted him with:

"I hear an Indian chief is in town. Going to be married here this morning. Where is the ceremony to take place? Do you know anything of it?"

Like all his race, George Mansion had a subtle sense of humor. It seized upon him now.

"Certainly I know," he replied. "I happened to come down on the boat with the chief. I intend to go to the wedding myself. I understand the ceremony was arranged to be at the cathedral."

"Splendid!" said the gentleman. "And thank you, sir."

Just then the cab arrived. Young Mansion stepped hastily in, nodded good-bye to his acquaintance, and smilingly said in an undertone to the driver, "St. Swithin's Church—and quickly."

★ ★ ★ ★ ★

"With this ring I thee wed," he found himself saying to a little figure in a soft grey gown at his side, while a gentle-faced old clergyman in a snowy surplice stood before him, and a square-shouldered, soldierly person in a brilliant uniform almost hugged his elbow.

"I pronounce you man and wife." At the words she turned towards her husband like a carrier pigeon winging for home. Then somehow the solemnity all disappeared. The major, the major's wife, two handsome young officers, one girl friend, the clergyman, the clergyman's wife, were all embracing her, and she was dimpling with laughter and happiness; and George Mansion stood proudly by, his fine dark face eager, tender and very noble.

"My dear," whispered the major's wife, "he's a perfect prince—he's just as royal as he can be! I never saw such manners, such ease. Why, girlie, he's a courtier!"

"Confound the young rogue!" growled the major, in her ear. "I haven't an officer on my staff that can equal him. You're a lucky girl. Yes, confound him, I say!"

"Bless you, child," said the clergyman's wife. "I think he'll make you happy. Be very sure that you make *him* happy."

And to all these whole-hearted wishes and comments, Lydia replied with smiles and care-free words. Then came the major, watch in hand, military precision and promptitude in his very tone.

"Time's up, everybody! There's a bite to eat at the barracks, then these youngsters must be gone. The boat is due at one o'clock—time's up."

As the little party drove past the cathedral they observed a huge crowd outside, waiting for the doors to be opened. Lydia laughed like a child as George told her of his duplicity of the morning, when he had misled the inquiring stranger into thinking the Indian chief was to be married there. The little tale furnished fun for all at the pretty breakfast in the major's quarters.

"Nice way to begin your wedding morning, young man!" scowled the major, fiercely. "Starting this great day with a network of falsehoods."

"Not at all," smiled the Indian. "It was arranged for the cathedral, and I did attend the ceremony."

"No excuses, you bare-faced scoundrel! I won't listen to

them. Here you are happily married and all those poor would-be sight-seers sizzling out there in this glaring August sun. I'm ashamed of you!" But his arm was about George's shoulders, and he was wringing the dark, slender hand with a genuine good fellowship that was pleasant to see. "Bless my soul, I love you, boy!" he added, sincerely. "Love you through and through; and remember, I'm your white father from this day forth."

"And I am your white mother," said the major's wife, placing her hands on his shoulders.

For a second the bridegroom's face sobered. Before him flashed a picture of a little old Indian woman with a broadcloth folded about her shoulders, a small carven pipe between her lips, a world of sorrow in her deep eyes—sorrow that he had brought there. He bent suddenly and kissed Mrs. Harold's fingers with a grave and courtly deference. "Thank you," he said simply.

But motherlike, she knew that his heart was bleeding. Lydia had told of his parents' antagonism, of the lost Mansion title. So the good lady just gave his hand a little extra, understanding squeeze, and the good-byes began.

"Be off with you, youngsters!" growled the major. "The boat is in—post haste now, or you'll miss it. Begone, both of you!"

And presently they found themselves once more in the carriage, the horses galloping down to the wharf. And almost before they realized it they were aboard, with the hearty "God bless you's" of the splendid old major and his lovable wife still echoing in their happy young hearts.

★ ★ ★ ★ ★

It was evening, five days later, when they arrived at their new home. All about the hills, and the woods, above the winding river, and along the edge of the distant forest, brooded that purple smokiness that haunts the late days of August—the smokiness that was born of distant fires, where the Indians and pioneers were "clearing" their lands. The air was like amethyst, the setting sun a fire opal. As on the day when she first had come into his life, George helped her to alight from the carriage, and they stood a moment, hand in hand, and looked over the ample acres that composed their estate. The young Indian had worked hard to have most of the land cleared, leaving here and there vast stretches of walnut groves, and long lines of majestic elms, groups of sturdy oaks, and occasionally a single regal pine tree. Many a time in later years his utilitarian friends would say, "Chief, these trees you are preserving so jealously are eating up a great deal of your land. Why not cut away and grow wheat?" But he would always resent the suggestion, saying that his wheat lands lay back from the river. They were for his body, doubtless, but here, by the river, the trees must be—they were for his soul. And Lydia would champion him immediately with, "Yes, they were there to welcome me as a bride, those grand old trees, and they will remain there, I think, as long as we both shall live." So, that first evening at home they stood and watched the imperial trees, the long, open flats bordering the river, the nearby lawns which he had taken such pains to woo from the wilderness; stood palm to palm, and that moment seemed to govern all their after life.

Someone has said that never in the history of the world have two people been perfectly mated. However true this may be, it is an undeniable fact that between the most devoted of life-mates there will come inharmonious moments. Individuality would cease to exist were it not so.

These two lived together for upwards of thirty years, and never had one single quarrel, but oddly enough, when the rare inharmonious moments came, these groups of trees bridged the fleeting difference of opinion or any slight antagonism of will and purpose; when these unresponsive moments came, one or the other would begin to admire those forest giants, to suggest improvements, to repeat the admiration of others for their graceful outlines—to, in fact, direct thought and conversation into the common channel of love for those trees. This peculiarity was noticeable to outsiders, to their own circle, to their children. At mere mention of the trees the shadow of coming cloud would lessen, then waste, then grow invisible. Their mutual love for these voiceless yet voiceful and kingly creations was as the love of children for a flower—simple, nameless, beautiful and powerful beyond words.

That first home night, as she stepped within doors, there awaited two inexpressible surprises for her. First, on the dining-room table a silver tea service of seven pieces, imported from England—his wedding gift to her. Second, in the quaint little drawing-room stood a piano. In the "early fifties" this latter was indeed a luxury, even in city homes. She uttered a little cry of delight, and flinging herself before the instrument, ran her fingers over the keys, and broke into his favorite song, "Oft in the Stilly Night."[1] She had a beautiful voice, the possession of

---

1   A poem by Irish poet Thomas Moore (1779–1851), published in 1816 and set to music by Sir John Stevenson in 1818.

which would have made her renowned had opportunity afforded its cultivation. She had "picked up" music and read it remarkably well, and he, Indian wise, was passionately fond of melody. So they laughed and loved together over this new luxurious toy, until Milly, the ancient Mohawk maid, tapped softly at the drawing-room and bade them come to tea. With that first meal in her new home, the darkened hours and days and years smothered their haunting voices. She had "left yesterday behind her," as the major's royal wife had wished her to, and for the first time in all her checkered and neglected life she laughed with the gladness of a bird at song, flung her past behind her, and the grim unhappiness of her former life left her forever.

★ ★ ★ ★ ★

It was a golden morning in July when the doctor stood grasping George Mansion's slender hands, searching into his dusky, anxious eyes, and saying with ringing cheeriness, "Chief, I congratulate you. You've got the most beautiful son upstairs—the finest boy I ever saw. Hail to the young chief, I say!"

The doctor was white. He did not know of the broken line of lineage—that "the boy upstairs" could never wear his father's title. A swift shadow fought for a second with glorious happiness. The battlefield was George Mansion's face, his heart. His unfilled duty to his parents assailed him like a monstrous enemy, then happiness conquered, came forth a triumphant victor, and the young father dashed noiselessly, fleetly up the staircase, and, despite the protesting physician, in another moment his wife and son were in his arms. Title did not count in that moment; only Love in its tyrannical majesty reigned in that sacred room.

The boy was a being of a new world, a new nation. Before he was two weeks old he began to show the undeniable physique of the two great races from whence he came; all the better qualities of both bloods seemed to blend within his small body. He was his father's son, he was his mother's baby. His grey-blue eyes held a hint of the dreaming forest, but also a touch of old England's skies. His hair, thick and black, was straight as his father's, except just above the temples, where a suggestion of his mother's pretty English curls waved like strands of fine silk. His small mouth was thin-lipped; his nose, which even in babyhood never had the infantile "snub," but grew straight, thin as his Indian ancestors', yet displayed a half-haughty English nostril; his straight little back—all combined likenesses to his parents. But who could say which blood dominated his tiny person? Only the exquisite soft, pale brown of his satiny skin called loudly and insistently that he was of a race older than the composite English could ever boast; it was the hallmark of his ancient heritage—the birthright of his father's son.

But the odd little half-blood was extraordinarily handsome even as an infant. In after years when he grew into glorious manhood he was generally acknowledged to be the handsomest man in the Province of Ontario, but to-day—his first day in these strange, new surroundings—he was but a wee, brown, lovable bundle, whose tiny gossamer hands cuddled into his father's palm, while his little velvet cheek lay rich and russet against the pearly whiteness of his mother's arm.

"I believe he is like you, George," she murmured, with a wealth of love in her voice and eyes.

"Yes," smiled the young chief, "he certainly has Mansion blood; but your eyes, Lydia, your dear eyes."

"Which eyes must go to sleep and rest," interrupted the physician, severely. "Come, Chief, you've seen your son, you've satisfied yourself that Mrs. Mansion is doing splendidly, so away you go, or I shall scold."

And George slipped down the staircase, and out into the radiant July sunshine, where his beloved trees arose about him, grand and majestic, seeming to understand how full of joy, of exultation, had been this great new day.

★ ★ ★ ★ ★

The whims of women are proverbial, but the whims of men are things never to be accounted for. This beautiful child was but a few weeks old when Mr. Bestman wrote, announcing to his daughter his intention of visiting her for a few days.

So he came to the Indian Reserve, to the handsome country home his Indian son-in-law had built. He was amazed, surprised, delighted. His English heart revelled in the trees. "Like an Old Country gentleman's estate in the Counties," he declared. He kissed his daughter with affection, wrung his son-in-law's hand with a warmth and cordiality unmistakable in its sincerity, took the baby in his arms and said over and over, "Oh, you sweet little child! You sweet little child!" Then the darkness of all those harsh years fell away from Lydia. She could afford to be magnanimous, so with a sweet silence, a loving forgetfulness of all the dead miseries and bygone whip-lashes, she accepted her strange parent just as he presented himself, in the guise of a man whom the years had changed from harshness to tenderness, and let herself thoroughly enjoy his visit.

But when he drove away she had but one thing to say; it was, "George, I wonder when *your* father will come to us, when your *mother* will come. Oh, I want her to see the baby, for I think my own mother sees him."

"Some day, dear," he answered hopefully. "They will come some day; and when they do, be sure it will be to take you to their hearts."

She sighed and shook her head unbelievingly. But the "some day" that he prophesied, but which she doubted, came in a manner all too soon—all too unwelcome. The little son had just begun to walk about nicely, when George Mansion was laid low with a lingering fever that he had contracted among the marshes where much of his business as an employee of the Government took him. Evils had begun to creep into his forest world. The black and subtle evil of the white man's firewater had commenced to touch with its poisonous finger the lives and lodges of his beloved people. The curse began to spread, until it grew into a menace to the community. It was the same old story: the white man had come with the Bible in one hand, the bottle in the other. George Mansion had striven side by side with Mr. Evans to overcome the dread scourge. Together they fought the enemy hand to hand, but it gained ground in spite of all their efforts. The entire plan of the white liquor dealer's campaign was simply an effort to exchange a quart of bad whiskey for a cord of first-class firewood, or timber, which could be hauled off the Indian Reserve and sold in the nearby town markets for five or six dollars; thus a hundred dollars worth of bad whiskey, if judiciously traded, would net the white dealer a thousand dollars cash. And the traffic went on, to the depletion of the Indian forests and the degradation of the Indian souls.

Then the Canadian Government appointed young Mansion special forest warden, gave him a "V.R." hammer,[1] with which he was to stamp each and every stick of timber he could catch being hauled off the Reserve by white men; licensed him to carry firearms for self-protection, and told him to "go ahead." He "went ahead." Night after night he lay, concealing himself in the marshes, the forests, the trails, the concession lines, the river road, the Queen's highway, seizing all the timber he could, destroying all the whisky, turning the white liquor traders off

---

1 V.R., for Victoria Regina ("Queen Victoria"), would brand the trees as Crown property.

Indian lands, and fighting as only a young, earnest and inspired man can fight. These hours and conditions began to tell on his physique. The marshes breathed their miasma[1] into his blood— the dreaded fever had him in its claws. Lydia was a born nurse. She knew little of thermometers, of charts, of technical terms, but her ability and instincts in the sick-room were unerring; and, when her husband succumbed to a raging fever, love lent her hands an inspiration and her brain a clarity that would have shamed many a professional nurse.

For hours, days, weeks, she waited, tended, watched, administered, labored and loved beside the sick man's bed. She neither slept nor ate enough to carry her through the ordeal, but love lent her strength, and she battled and fought for his life as only an adoring woman can. Her wonderful devotion was the common talk of the country. She saw no one save Mr. Evans and the doctors. She never left the sick-room save when her baby needed her. But it all seemed so useless, so in vain, when one dark morning the doctor said, "We had better send for his father and mother."

Poor Lydia! Her heart was nearly breaking. She hurriedly told the doctor the cause that had kept them away so long, adding, "Is it so bad as that? Oh, doctor, *must I send for them?* They don't want to come." Before the good man could reply, there was a muffled knock at the door. Then Milly's old wrinkled face peered in, and Milly's voice said whisperingly, "His people—they here."

"Whose people? Who are here?" almost gasped Lydia.

"His father and his mother," answered the old woman. "They downstairs."

For a brief moment there was silence. Lydia could not trust herself to speak, but ill as he was, George's quick Indian ear had caught Milly's words. He murmured, "Mother! mother! Oh, my mother!"

"Bring her, quickly, *quickly!*" said Lydia to the doctor.

It seemed to the careworn girl that a lifetime followed before the door opened noiselessly, and there entered a slender little old Indian woman, in beaded leggings, moccasins, "short skirt," and a blue "broadcloth" folded about her shoulders. She glanced swiftly at the bed, but with the heroism of her race went first towards Lydia, laid her cheek silently beside the white girl's, then looked directly into her eyes.

"Lydia!" whispered George, "Lydia!" At the word both women moved swiftly to his side. "Lydia," he repeated, "my mother

---

1 Miasma, meaning polluted air, was thought to cause disease until replaced by the germ theory in the 1880s.

cannot speak the English, but her cheek to yours means that you are her blood relation."

The effort of speech almost cost him a swoon, but his mother's cheek was now against his own, and the sweet, dulcet Mohawk language of his boyhood returned to his tongue; he was speaking it to his mother, speaking it lovingly, rapidly. Yet, although Lydia never understood a word, she did not feel an outsider, for the old mother's hand held her own, and she knew that at last the gulf was bridged.

* * * * *

It was two days later, when the doctor pronounced George Mansion out of danger, that the sick man said to his wife: "Lydia, it is all over—the pain, the estrangement. My mother says that you are her daughter. My father says that you are his child. They heard of your love, your nursing, your sweetness. They want to know if you will call them 'father, mother.' They love you, for you are one of their own."

"At last, at last!" half sobbed the weary girl. "Oh, George, I am so happy! *You* are going to get well, and *they* have come to us at last."

"Yes, dear," he replied. Then with a half humorous yet wholly pathetic smile flitting across his wan face, he added, "And my mother has a little gift for you." He nodded then towards the quaint old figure at the further side of the bed. His mother arose, and, drawing from her bosom a tiny, russet-colored object, laid it in Lydia's hand. It was a little moccasin, just three and a quarter inches in length. "Its mate is lost," added the sick man, "but I wore it as a baby. My mother says it is yours, and should have been yours all these years."[1]

For a second the two women faced each other, then Lydia sat down abruptly on the bedside, her arms slipped about the older woman's shoulders, and her face dropped quickly, heavily—at last on a mother's breast.

George Mansion sighed in absolute happiness, then closed his eyes and slept the great, strong, vitalizing sleep of reviving forces.

PART IV

How closely the years chased one another after this! But many a happy day within each year found Lydia and her husband's mother sitting together, hour upon hour, needle in hand, sewing

---

1 This moccasin was left by Johnson to the Museum of Vancouver.

and harmonizing—the best friends in all the world. It mattered not that "mother" could not speak one word of English, or that Lydia never mastered but a half dozen words of Mohawk. These two were friends in the sweetest sense of the word, and their lives swept forward in a unison of sympathy that was dear to the heart of the man who held them as the two most precious beings in all the world.

And with the years came new duties, new responsibilities, new little babies to love and care for until a family, usually called "A King's Desire,"[1] gathered at their hearthside—four children, the eldest a boy, the second a girl, then another boy, then another girl. These children were reared on the strictest lines of both Indian and English principles. They were taught the legends, the traditions, the culture and the etiquette of both races to which they belonged; but above all, their mother instilled into them from the very cradle that they were of their father's people, not of hers. Her marriage had made her an Indian by the laws which govern Canada,[2] as well as by the sympathies and yearnings and affections of her own heart. When she married George Mansion she had repeated to him the centuries-old vow of allegiance, "Thy people shall be my people, and thy God my God." She determined that should she ever be mother to his children, those children should be reared as Indians in spirit and patriotism, and in loyalty to their father's race as well as by heritage of blood. The laws of Canada held these children as Indians. They were wards of the Government; they were born on Indian lands, on Indian Reservations. They could own and hold Indian lands, and their mother, English though she was, made it her life service to inspire, foster and elaborate within these children the pride of the race, the value of that copper-tinted skin which they all displayed. When people spoke of blood and lineage and nationality, these children would say, "We are Indians," with the air with which a young Spanish don might say, "I am a Castilian." She wanted them to grow up nationalists, and they did, every mother's son and daughter of them. Things could never have been otherwise, for George Mansion and his wife had so much in common that their offspring could scarcely evince other than inherited paren-

---

1 The desire for a male heir (or, as the British press now terms it, "an heir and a spare").
2 Any woman who married a Status Indian man was given Status, as were their children. However, Status women who married non-Status men lost their Status and any associated rights, as did their children.

tal traits. Their tastes and distastes were so synonymous; they hated hypocrisy, vulgarity, slovenliness, imitations.

After forty years spent on a Canadian Indian Reserve, Lydia Mansion still wore real lace, real tortoise shell combs, real furs. If she could not have procured these she would have worn plain linen collars, no combs, and a woven woolen scarf about her throat; but the imitation fabrics, as well as the "imitation people," had no more part in her life than they had in her husband's, who abhorred all such pinchbeck.[1] Their loves were identical. They loved nature—the trees, best of all, and the river, and the birds. They loved the Anglican Church, they loved the British flag, they loved Queen Victoria, they loved beautiful, dead Elizabeth Evans, they loved strange, reticent Mr. Evans. They loved music, pictures and dainty china, with which George Mansion filled his beautiful home. They loved books and animals, but, most of all, these two loved the Indian people, loved their legends, their habits, their customs—loved the people themselves. Small wonder, then, that their children should be born with pride of race and heritage, and should face the world with that peculiar, unconquerable courage that only a fighting ancestry can give.

As the years drifted on, many distinctions came to the little family of the "Grand Mansions." The chief's ability as an orator, his fluency of speech, his ceaseless war against the inroads of the border white men and their lawlessness among his own people—all gradually but surely brought him, inch by inch, before the notice of those who sat in the "seats of the mighty" of both church and state. His presence was frequently demanded at Ottawa, fighting for the cause of his people before the House of Commons, the Senate, and the Governor-General himself. At such times he would always wear his native buckskin costume, and his amazing rhetoric, augmented by the gorgeous trappings of his office and his inimitable courtesy of manner, won him friends and followers among the lawmakers of the land. He never fought for a cause and lost it, never returned to Lydia and his people except in a triumph of victory. Social honors came to him as well as political distinctions. Once, soon after his marriage, a special review of the British troops quartered at Toronto was called in his honor and he rode beside the general, making a brilliant picture, clad as he was in buckskins and scarlet blanket and astride his pet black pony, as he received the salutes of company

---

1 A brass alloy of zinc and copper that resembles gold. It came to mean any cheap imitation.

after company of England's picked soldiers as they wheeled past. And when King Edward of England visited Canada as Prince of Wales,[1] he fastened with his own royal hands a heavy silver medal to the buckskin covering George Mansion's breast, and the royal words were very sincere as they fell from the prince's lips: "This medal is for recognition of your loyalty in battling for your own people, even as your ancestors battled for the British Crown." Then in later years, when Prince Arthur of Connaught accepted the title of "Chief," conferred upon him with elaborate ceremony by the chiefs, braves and warriors of the great Iroquois Council,[2] it was George Mansion who was chosen as special escort to the royal visitor—George Mansion and his ancient and honored father, who, hand-in-hand with the young prince, walked to and fro, chanting the impressive ritual of bestowing the title. Even Bismarck, the "Iron Chancellor" of Germany,[3] heard of this young Indian warring for the welfare of his race, and sent a few kindly words, with his own photograph, from across seas to encourage the one who was fighting, single-handed, the menace of white man's greed and white man's firewater.

And Lydia, with her glad and still girlish heart, gloried in her husband's achievements and in the recognition accorded him by the great world beyond the Indian Reserve, beyond the wilderness, beyond the threshold of their own home. In only one thing were their lives at all separated. She took no part in his public life. She hated the glare of the fierce light that beat upon prominent lives, the unrest of fame, the disquiet of public careers.

"No," she would answer, when oftentimes he begged her to accompany him and share his success and honors, "no, I was homeless so long that 'home' is now my ambition. My babies need me here, and you need me here when you return, far more than you need me on platform or parade. Go forth and fight the enemy, storm the battlements and win the laurels, but let me keep the garrison—here at home, with our babies all about me and a welcome to our warrior husband and father when he returns from war."

---

1 The young Edward VII (as Prince of Wales) visited Canada in 1860.
2 The Iroquois Confederacy Council, composed of 50 chiefs, governed Six Nations Grand River.
3 Prussian leader Otto von Bismarck (1815–98), nicknamed "The Iron Chancellor," presided over the unification of Germany in 1871 and dominated Europe as its first chancellor from 1873 to 1890.

Then he would laugh and coax again, but always with the same result. Every day, whether he went forth to the Indian Council across the river, or when more urgent duties called him to the Capital, she always stood at the highest window waving her handkerchief until he was out of sight, and that dainty flag lent strength to his purpose and courage to his heart, for he knew the home citadel was there awaiting his return—knew that she would be at that selfsame window, their children clustered about her skirts, her welcoming hands waving a greeting instead of a good-bye, as soon as he faced the home portals once more, and in his heart of hearts George Mansion felt that his wife had chosen the wiser, greater part; that their children would some day arise and call her blessed because she refused to wing away from the home nest, even if by so doing she left him to take his flights alone.

But in all their world there was no one prouder of his laurels and successes than his home-loving, little English wife, and the mother-heart of her must be forgiven for welcoming each new honor as a so much greater heritage for their children. Each distinction won by her husband only established a higher standard for their children to live up to. She prayed and hoped and prayed again that they would all be worthy such a father, that they would never fall short of his excellence. To this end she taught, labored for, and loved them, and they, in turn, child-wise, responded to her teaching, imitating her allegiance to their father, reflecting her fealty, and duplicating her actions. So she molded these little ones with the mother-hand that they felt through all their after lives, which were but images of her own in all that concerned their father.

★ ★ ★ ★ ★

The first great shadow that fell on this united little circle was when George Mansion's mother quietly folded her "broadcloth" about her shoulders for the last time, when the little old tobacco pipe lay unfilled and unlighted, when the finely-beaded moccasins were empty of the dear feet that had wandered so gently, so silently into the Happy Hunting Grounds. George Mansion was bowed with woe. His mother had been to him the queen of all women, and her death left a desolation in his heart that even his wife could not assuage. It was a grief he really never overcame. Fortunately his mother had grown so attached to Lydia that his one disobedience—that of his marriage—never reproached him.

Had the gentle little old Indian woman died before the episode of the moccasin which brought complete reconciliation, it is doubtful if her son would ever have been quite the same again. As it was, with the silence and stoicism of his race he buried his grief in his own heart, without allowing it to cast a gloom over his immediate household.

But after that the ancient chief, his father, came more frequently to George's home, and was always an honored guest. The children loved him, Lydia had the greatest respect and affection for him, the greatest sympathy for his loneliness, and she ever made him welcome and her constant companion when he visited them. He used to talk to her much of George, and once or twice gave her grave warnings as to his recklessness and lack of caution in dealing with the ever-growing menace of the whisky traffic among the Indians. The white men who supplied and traded this liquor were desperadoes, a lawless set of ruffians who for some time had determined to rid their stamping-ground of George Mansion, as he was the chief opponent to their business, and with the way well cleared of him and his unceasing resistance, their scoundrelly trade would be an easy matter.

"Use all your influence, Lydia," the old father would say, "to urge him never to seize the ill-gotten timber or destroy their whisky, unless he has other Indian wardens with him. They'll kill him if they can, those white men. They have been heard to threaten."

For some time this very thing had been crowding its truth about his wife's daily life. Threatening and anonymous letters had more than once been received by her husband—letters that said he would be "put out of the way" unless he stopped interfering in the liquor trade. There was no ignoring the fact that danger was growing daily, that the fervent young chief was allowing his zeal to overcome his caution, was hazarding his life for the protection of his people against a crying evil. Once a writer of these unsigned letters threatened to burn his house down in the dead of night, another to maim his horses and cattle, others to "do away" with him. His crusade was being waged under the weight of a cross that was beginning to fall on his loyal wife, and to overshadow his children. Then one night the blow fell. Blind with blood, crushed and broken, he staggered and reeled home, unaided, unassisted, and in excruciating torture. Nine white men had attacked him from behind in a border village a mile from his home, where he had gone to intercept a load of whisky that was being hauled into the Indian Reserve. Eight of those lawbreakers circled about him, while the ninth struck him from behind with a leaden plumb attached to an elastic throw-string. The deadly thing crushed in his skull; he dropped where he stood, as if shot. Then brutal boots kicked his face, his head, his back, and, with curses, his assailants left him—for dead.

With a vitality born of generations of warriors, he regained consciousness, staggered the mile to his own gate, where he met a friend, who, with extreme concern, began to assist him into his home. But he refused the helping arm with, "No, I go alone; it would alarm Lydia if I could not walk alone." These, with the few words he spoke as he entered the kitchen, where his wife was overseeing old Milly get the evening meal, were the last intelligent words he spoke for many a day.

"Lydia, they've hurt me at last," he said, gently.

She turned at the sound of his strained voice. A thousand emotions overwhelmed her at the terrifying sight before her. Love, fear, horror, all broke forth from her lips in a sharp, hysterical cry, but above this cry sounded the gay laughter of the children who were playing in the next room, their shrill young voices raised in merriment over some new sport. In a second the mother-heart asserted itself. Their young eyes must not see this ghastly thing.

"Milly!" she cried to the devoted Indian servant, "help Chief George." Then dashing into the next room, she half sobbed, "Children, children! hush, oh, hush! Poor father—"

She never finished the sentence. With a turn of her arm she swept them all into the drawing-room, closed the door, and flew back to her patriot husband.

For weeks and weeks he lay fighting death as only a determined man can—his upper jaw broken on both sides, his lower jaw splintered on one side, his skull so crushed that to the end of his days a silver dollar could quite easily be laid flat in the cavity, a jagged and deep hole in his back, and injuries about the knees and leg bones. And all these weeks Lydia hovered above his pillow, night and day, nursing, tending, helping, cheering. What effort it cost her to be bright and smiling no tongue can tell, for her woman's heart saw that this was but the beginning of the end. She saw it when in his delirium he raved to get better, to be allowed to get up and go on with the fight; saw that his spirit never rested, for fear that, now he was temporarily inactive, the whisky dealers would have their way. She knew then that she must school herself to endure this thing again; that she must never ask him to give up his life work, never be less courageous than he, though that courage would mean never a peaceful moment to her when he was outside their own home.

Mr. Evans was a great comfort to her during those terrible weeks. Hour after hour he would sit beside the injured man, never speaking or moving, only watching quietly, while Lydia barely snatched the necessary sleep a nurse must have, or attended to the essential needs of the children, who, however, were jealously cared for by faithful Milly. During those times the children never spoke except in whispers, their rigid Indian-English training in self-effacement and obedience being now of untold value.

But love and nursing and bravery all counted in the end, and one day George Mansion walked downstairs, the doctor's arm on one side, Lydia's on the other. He immediately asked for his pistol and his dagger, cleaned the one, oiled and sharpened the other, and said, "I'll be ready for them again in a month's time."

But while he lay injured his influential white friends and the Government at Ottawa had not been idle. The lawless creature who dealt those unmerited blows was tried, convicted and sent to Kingston Penitentiary for seven years. So one enemy was out of the way for the time being. It was at this time that advancing success lost him another antagonist, who was placed almost in the rank of an ally.

George Mansion was a guest of the bishop of his diocese, as he was a lay delegate accompanying Mr. Evans to the Anglican Synod. The chief's work had reached other ears than those of the Government at Ottawa, and the bishop was making much of the patriot, when in the See House itself an old clergyman approached him with outstretched hand and the words, "I would like you to call bygones just bygones."

"I don't believe I have the honor of knowing you, sir," replied the Indian, with a puzzled but gracious look.

"I am your wife's brother-in-law," said the old clergyman, "the man who would not allow her to be married from my house—that is, married to *you*."

The Indian bit his lip and instinctively stepped backward. Added to his ancestral creed of never forgiving such injury, came a rush of memory—the backward-surging picture of his homeless little sweetheart and all that she had endured. Then came the memory of his dead mother's teaching—teaching she had learned from her own mother, and she in turn from her mother: "Always forget yourself for *old* people, always honor the *old*."

Instantly George Mansion arose—arose above the prejudices of his blood, above the traditions of his race, arose to the highest plane a man can reach—the memory of his mother's teaching.

"I would hardly be here as a lay delegate of my church were I not willing to let bygones be bygones," he said, simply, and laid his hand in that of the old clergyman, about whose eyes there was moisture, perhaps because this opportunity for peacemaking had come so tardily.

★ ★ ★ ★ ★

The little family of "Grand Mansions" were now growing to very "big childhood," and the inevitable day came when Lydia's heart must bear the wrench of having her firstborn say good-bye to take his college course. She was not the type of mother who would keep the boy at home because of the heartache the good-byes must bring, but the parting was certainly a hard one, and she watched his going with a sense of loss that was almost greater than her pride in him. He had given evidence of the most remarkable musical talent. He played classical airs even before he knew a note, and both his parents were in determined unison about this talent being cultivated. The following year the oldest daughter also entered college, having had a governess at home for a year, as some preparation. But these changes brought no difference into the home, save that George Mansion's arm grew stronger daily in combat against the old foe. Then came the second attack of the enemy, when six white men beset him from behind, again knocking him insensible, with a heavy blue beech hand-spike. They broke his hand and three ribs, knocked out his teeth, injured his side and head; then seizing his pistol, shot at him, the ball fortunately not reaching a vital spot. As his senses swam he felt them drag his poor maimed body into the middle of the road, so it would appear as if horses had trampled him, then he heard them say, "*This* time the devil is dead." But hours afterwards he again arose, again walked home, five interminable miles, again greeted his ever watchful and anxious wife with, "Lydia, they've hurt me once more." Then came weeks of renewed suffering, of renewed care and nursing, of renewed vitality, and at last of conquered health.

These two terrible illnesses seemed to raise Lydia into a peculiar, half-protecting attitude towards him. In many ways she "mothered" him almost as though he were her son—he who had always been the leader, and so strong and self-reliant. After this, when he went forth on his crusades, she watched his going with the haunting fear with which one would watch a child wandering on the edge of a chasm. She waited on him when he returned, served him with the tenderness with which one serves a cripple or a baby. Once he caught her arm, as she carried to him a cup of broth, after he had spent wearisome hours at the same old battle, and turning towards her, said softly: "You are like my mother used to be to me." She did not ask him in what way—she knew—and carried broth to him when next he came home half exhausted. Gradually he now gathered about him a little force of zealous Indians who became enthusiastic to take up arms with him against the whisky dealers. He took greater precautions in his work, for the growing mist of haunting anxiety in Lydia's eyes began to call to him that there were other claims than those of the nation. His splendid zeal had brought her many a sleepless night, when she knew he was scouring the forests for hidden supplies of the forbidden merchandise, and that a whole army of desperadoes would not deter him from fulfilling his duty of destroying it. He felt, rather than saw, that she never bade him good-bye but that she was prepared not to see him again alive. Added to this he began to suffer as she did—to find that in his good-byes was the fear of never seeing her again. He, who had always been so fearless, was now afraid of the day when he should not return and she would be once more alone.

So he let his younger and eager followers do some of the battling, though he never relaxed his vigilance, never took off his armor, so to speak. But now he spent long days and quiet nights with Lydia and his children. They entertained many guests, for the young people were vigorous and laughter-loving, and George and Lydia never grew old, never grew weary, never grew commonplace. All the year round guests came to the hospitable country house—men and women of culture, of learning, of artistic tastes, of congenial habits. Scientists, authors, artists, all made their pilgrimages to this unique household, where refinement and much luxury, and always a glad welcome from the chief and his English wife, made their visits long remembered. And in some way or other, as their children grew up, those two seemed to come closer together once more. They walked among the trees they had once loved in those first bridal days, they rested by the river shore, they wandered over the broad meadows and bypaths of the old estate, they laughed together frequently like children, and always and ever talked of and acted for the good of the Indian people who were so unquestionably the greatest interest in their lives, outside their own children. But one day, when the beautiful estate he was always so proud of was getting ready to smile under the suns of spring, he left her just when she needed him most, for their boys had plunged forward into the world of business in the large cities, and she wanted a strong arm to lean on. It was the only time he failed to respond to her devoted nursing, but now she could not bring him back from the river's brink, as she had so often done before. Cold had settled in all the broken places of his poor body, and he slipped away from her, a sacrifice to his fight against evil on the altar of his nation's good. In his feverish wanderings he returned to the tongue of his childhood, the beautiful, dulcet Mohawk. Then recollecting and commanding himself, he would weakly apologize to Lydia with: "I forgot; I thought it was my mother," and almost his last words were, "It must be by my mother's side," meaning his resting-place. So his valiant spirit went fearlessly forth.

★ ★ ★ ★ ★

"Do you ever think, dear," said Lydia to her youngest child, some years later, "that you are writing the poetry that always lived in an unexpressed state here in my breast?"

"No, Marmee," answered the girl, who was beginning to mount the ladder of literature, "I never knew you wanted to *write* poetry, although I knew you loved it."

"Indeed, I did," answered the mother, "but I never could find expression for it. I was made just to sing, I often think, but I never had the courage to sing in public. But I did want to write poetry, and now you, dear, are doing it for me. How proud your father would have been of you!"

"Oh, he knows! I'm sure he knows all that I have written," answered the girl, with the sublime faith that youth has in its own convictions. "And if you like my verses, Marmee, I am sure he does, for he knows."

"Perhaps," murmured the older woman. "I often feel that he is very near to us. I never have felt that he is really gone very far away from me."

"Poor little Marmee!" the girl would say to herself. "She misses him yet. I believe she will always miss him."

Which was the truth. She saw constantly his likeness in all her children, bits of his character, shades of his disposition, reflections of his gifts and talents, hints of his bravery, and she always spoke of these with a commending air, as though they were characteristics to be cultivated, to be valued and fostered.

At first her fear of leaving her children, even to join him, was evident, she so believed in a mother's care and love being a necessity to a child. She had sadly missed it all out of her own strange life, and she felt she *must* live until this youngest daughter grew to be a woman. Perhaps this desire, this mother-love, kept her longer beside her children than she would have stayed without it, for the years rolled on, and her hair whitened, her once springing step halted a little, the glorious blue of her English eyes grew very dreamy, and tender, and wistful. Was she seeing the great Hereafter unfold itself before her as her steps drew nearer and nearer?

And one night the Great Messenger knocked softly at her door, and with a sweet, gentle sigh she turned and followed where he led—joining gladly the father of her children in the land that holds both whites and Indians as one.

And the daughter who writes the verses her mother always felt, but found no words to express, never puts a last line to a story, or a sweet cadence into a poem, but she says to herself as she holds her mother's memory within her heart:

"She knows—she knows."

6. "Heroic Indian Mothers" (1908)

[Here Johnson explains the marriage and motherhood rituals of the Iroquois. Johnson argues that Iroquois mothers display heroism by suppressing their maternal instinct for the sake of their children's well-being. The story first appeared in *Mother's Magazine* in September 1908.]

There are many national customs and obligations which the Iroquois mother is called upon to bear that are positive tests of heroic spirit—instances which the white mother could hardly understand, and certainly would not sympathize with, yet which tend wonderfully towards the building of a child's character, and the development of the best and bravest that is in him.

From the hour that her marriage invitations are issued, the would-be matron is instructed by the older women of her tribe as to her coming position as wife, and probable motherhood. The wedding "invitations" are primitively unique, consisting of a single grain of corn taken from a red ear. These grains are carried by some member of her immediate family, who calls personally upon the favored friends and relatives of both bride and groom, and sits for a time talking and probably smoking. No mention whatever is made of the coming marriage, but upon leave-taking the caller places, without comment, the little red kernel upon some table or bench near the door, just as a calling card would be left by a lady in "civilized" circles in making her afternoon visits. As that entire section of the Indian Reserve has already learned through the medium of much banter, teasing and gossip, the date of the prearranged marriage, the difficulties of naming time and place, through the seemingly inadequate red grain, are simplified. The wedding festivities invariably occupy two or three days, the ceremony itself being brief enough, but the dancing and feasting lasting through day and dark, until the lavish supply of good things is completely exhausted. It is very beautiful and impressive—this dignified marriage ceremony of the old-time pagan Iroquois. Before all the assembled guests, who count as witnesses to their vow, the two young people arise, walk slowly and seriously to the end of the lodge, and, standing side by side, join hands, and declare audibly that they each shall live only for each other and with each other while time and life last. There is a primal stateliness in its sincerity and artlessness, and the breaking of this marriage vow is a most infrequent occurrence among the pagans. But while in every nation and clime there must always be instances of wedded infelicity, the moral code of the pagan red man is exceedingly strict, and one of the unpardonable crimes against one's own self-respect is that of a husband and wife continuing to live as such when all sentiment, affection and *mutual* attraction is dead.

Under these conditions, decency and the pagan Decalogue[1] demand that the couple separate, but neither of them is ever known to remarry during the lifetime of the first chosen mate. The Indian law concerning the division of property in event of separation is immutable. Everything *inside* the house belongs to the woman, everything *outside* the house to the man. Thus the farm, grain, cattle, horses, barns, etc., revert to the man. The house, with all its furniture, cook stove, clothing, bedding, stored meats, foods, and, most important of all, *the children*, become the absolute property of the wife. All Indians holding that children are closer to the mother, are more her right and heritage than of the father, this reasonable law excludes much of the trouble that may otherwise follow upon unhappy conditions. There is no wrangling, no litigation, no kidnaping of babies or heirs. The little people bereft of a father's care may always sleep within the cuddling band of their own mother's elbow, without fear of being snatched from her side.

But fortunately these conditions rarely prevail. Indian mar-

---

1 Ten Commandments.

riages, particularly in the "uncivilized state," are proverbially happy. It is only when the conflicting results of attempting to emulate the white man's ways enter into the forest lodge, that domestic difficulties arise. Extravagance, social rivalry, whisky, love of display—these are what strike at the roots of Indian family felicity, and the little brown bride who so courageously stands beside her husband and utters the simple marriage vow before her father's guests, has but few misgivings regarding the coming years. Nevertheless she keeps among her personal treasures a "love-charm" consisting of two tiny carved figures bound closely together with pliable straps of buckskin, and between the figures, just above the hearts, is sprinkled a rare and mystical powder, given to her by the "Medicine Man." While these figures remain thus, and in her possession, her own little heart tells itself that infidelity cannot enter her home.

Before her first wee baby arrives, the older women of the tribe visit her, and the wise Medicine Men bring the "Maternity Mask," hanging it to the wall above her couch, while they chant weird incantations in a soft, soothing tone. The "Maternity Mask" is either carved in wood, or made of corn husks, and represents a woman's face, with the face of a baby tucked beneath the chin. It is one of the most important of the Medicine Man's possessions, has probably done duty for many generations, and is, without doubt, one of the most potent bits of abiding witchcraft practiced by the pagans of to-day. Its presence gives the expectant mother every confidence; its absence would cause her untold anxiety and fretting, albeit the strange, grotesque thing but hangs above her head where she cannot even see it.

Girl babies are always welcome to the Iroquois mother, who knows well how dear the tribesmen hold their womankind, notwithstanding all that has been written and said to the contrary.

In ancient days, before the advent of the paleface, a woman captive was held for far higher ransom than a man, it mattered not how great a chief or warrior he might be. To redeem the most insignificant woman captive, her tribe must offer, at the very least, nine wampum belts, the most priceless possession of the Iroquois, while the greatest leader of men in battles could be ransomed for seven belts. Thus, the young Iroquois mother smiles in pride at her girl baby, for the enemies of her people would hold this wee thing at higher value than a stalwart boy.

But when a baby son does come, the gentle mother knows that sixteen years, to a day, hence, her heart must steel itself against suffering, against even sympathy, for the honor of that boy's name, for on his sixteenth birthday he must undergo the national test of bravery, or forever be shamed as a disgrace to his household. He must go without a mouthful of food for three consecutive days and nights. It is during this supreme test of her son's warrior blood that the Indian mother must call all her resources of self-command into action. To watch her half-grown boy going foodless hour by hour, to know of his gnawing hunger, to see his covetous eyes lingering on the wholesome dishes her own deft hand has fashioned, to smother down in her mother-heart the almost irresistible desire and temptation to smuggle a surreptitious morsel, to withhold the little dainty that he loves, to know that growing torture is creeping nearer and nearer to him as time crawls slowly on, and, worst of all, that perhaps, through some fleeting moment of his weakness, he may cry out desperately for the merest mouthful; to hearken to her boy's begging, when food lies near at hand in opulent profusion, *then* to resist, to deny him, to perhaps struggle with him in order to snatch away what his momentary collapse of will has led him to seize—*that* is heroic motherhood, strangling her own maternal inclinations and sympathies, shutting her suffering eyes to his agony, all because of his future welfare and standing among the men of his race. If he were to fail, he is disgraced for all time. Never may he rank on a footing with his father; he must even bear the gibes and sneers of his fellows. But she knows well that if he comes through the ordeal courageously, valiantly, the close of the third day will see him standing beside the wise and aged counselors, having won the proud titles of "brave" and "warrior," with the right to look his forest world straight in the face and say, "I too am a man and a fighter."

And while this is the greatest pride and honor, it is also the supremest test of all her years of motherhood, although once, long ago, when they—her boys and girls—were very little, she had the dagger enter her heart in the seemingly innocent guise of a single porcupine quill.

The ears of both her boys and girls must be pierced, for the national adornment of earrings marks them as well-bred and well-born.

The tip of a porcupine quill is inserted very *slightly* into the lobe of each ear, the "operation" usually being conducted by a Medicine Man. The peculiar "fishhook" formation of the quill tends to make it "work" through the flesh, which sometimes takes a week's time. The process is exceedingly painful, as the writer well knows from personal experience. Festers form, and occasionally cause a species of blood-poisoning, but the quill labors persistently through, making its exit finally on the further side of the lobe, and leaving a clean, round, flesh perforation through which the gaudy ornament is eventually suspended.

Many a tiny, copper-colored child implores (with bravely mastered tears) the gentle mother to release it from this torturing quill, but the aching mother-heart must answer "No." Her nation demands these things, her offspring must comply. If she weakly yielded to their supplications, perhaps the day would arrive when these same children would carry sore hearts in their brave young breasts, because of her momentary weakness. She must be brave, as she desires them to be brave, and her reward, as well as theirs, will come when the people of her race shall say with admiration, "What splendid sons, what womanly daughters, what glorious Indian offspring, this woman has given birth to!"

7. "Forty-Five Miles on the Grand" (1892)

[Here Johnson shares her experience canoeing on the Grand River, which runs through the Six Nations Reserve where she grew up. Johnson demonstrates that her family has played a part in making the history of Canada when she recounts her father's friendship with inventor Alexander Graham Bell (1847–1922). The article first appeared in the *Brantford Expositor* in December 1892. The Bell family home at Tutela Heights, near Brantford, is now an historic site.]

Ontario boasts many a beautiful inland river, whose waters fret shores historically famous and naturally picturesque, but the royal little stream that laughs and slumbers alternately through the south-western counties, that tosses its current wildly about rocky coast and midstream boulder, that hurls itself into spray, whirlpool and rapid, then, tired and silent, slips into dark, still pools and long, yellow sand reaches—Ah! Who would not know it was The Grand River? with its romantic forests, its legend-thronged hills, its wide and storied flats, its tradition-fraught valleys? This was the great domain of that most powerful of North American nations, the Iroquois, who, after joining their forces and fortunes with Britain, subsequent to the American war of independence, received as indemnity the vast tract of country lying within the limits of six miles bordering on either side of the Grand from its source to its mouth, although, with all the alleged wealth of this ancient people, they count to-day as their sole landed possessions only a few thousand acres, but a small portion of which fronts on the waters that are inseparably linked with the red man and his traditions. In olden days, when the industrious beaver dammed the creeks, and bears haunted the almost impenetrable forests, when the shy red deer stole lightly down to slake its thirst in the crystal stream, and only the Indian's moccasined foot left its imprint along the shore, the Grand was a narrow, turbulent, forest watercourse, abounding in fish of all kinds, and navigable only by the birch bark canoe and the old, native 'dug-out,' which even to-day may be seen in many unbridged, ferryless localities, especially along the Iroquois reserve tracts. But for many a by-gone year the Grand has been a broad, semi-sluggish stretch of water, owing to many mills and their requisite dams backing the water into the wide, still stretches for miles up stream, above which many ripples and rills of the erstwhile rapids sing and purl to the birch-crowned banks, like souvenirs of the long ago, and although these rapids cannot boast the fascination of danger, or the charm of peril, their rollicking laughter is a delight to the canoeist's ear, and their devious, boulder-fraught course a test of his paddle's skill. The canoeist who has not 'run' the Grand, who has never pitched canvas on its lovely shores, who has never hoisted a sail to its treacherous and coquettish winds, scarcely deserves the name, and he certainly has a future sporting ground rife with surprises and delights, which is well worth a long trip to traverse.

Canoeing has sprung into marvellous popularity in Canada within the last five years, and, apart from the great sporting cen-tres, there exist no clubs of more active organization than those of Galt and Brantford, on the Grand. A stretch of some thirty-five miles of water lies between these points, and a lovelier run cannot be found in the Province. It can be covered in a few hours, for the rapids follow each other thick and fast, and the stern paddler must keep pretty wide awake, or his craft will come to grief in the twinkling of an eye, on one of the myriad rock shelves, or tiny, innocent-looking boulders that throng the river bed.

One warm June morning two of us made the run in a little, cruising Peterbo'[1] that we had shipped by rail across country the previous day. Our taut little craft slipped between the rocky shores upon which the slumbering old town of Galt crowds its grey stone houses, and in the fourth of an hour we had left streets and buildings and people behind the rolling hills and pasture

---

1   The Peterborough Canoe Company was founded in 1892 and be-came famous for its wooden canoes; Johnson is referring to one of their models here.

lands, and were dancing along on the sunny breast of the Grand that very soon changed its shores from green country sides and meadow lands, to wild, cedar-crested banks, where shy birds hushed their song at the sound of our voices, and where pathless woods and underbrush stretched along the very water's edge.

A few miles of placid water, on the surface of which our paddles dipped audibly, and then the 'waking of waves amid stream, a visibly accelerated movement of shores slipping astern, a soft whisper of bows cutting rapidly through hurrying waters, and then, O, sweetest of all music, the far-off laughter of a rapid, rollicking and scampering among its stones. Nearer, nearer it came; the ripple grew into a roar, the sweet, wild laughter arose into boisterous, tempestuous merriment, and in another moment we swirled round a bend, dashing headlong into a tossing, twirling mass of waters that fretted and fumed themselves into eddies and whirlpools and showers of pearly spray, with a petulance that defied restraint.

Without a word we gripped our paddles with fingers like iron, I heard the hurried plunge of the stern blade, and with the knowledge of the pliant wrist and mighty muscle that was master of rapid, paddle and Peterboro', and which had piloted me through many a more dangerous run than this, I knelt steady and straight, while we bounded through, swerving one moment to the right to escape a boulder, then next, running to the left to avoid a shoal. More than once I thought we were over, but that sturdy little canoe never failed us, bringing up at the foot of the rapid with scarcely a quart of water shipped, but with two breathless, wind-blown, spray-showered people, kneeling fore and aft, and wearing expressions of mingled surprise and triumph. And this was but the beginning of the end; following closely, came rapid after rapid, with a quarter mile breathing space between, until eleven of these noisy, frolicsome fellows had linked themselves into one long chain, covering seven miles, and then, in apparently utter weariness, the waters sank to slumber in great, deep pools, sluggish and currentless as a lagoon.

We paddled on, disturbing great cranes that rose on indolent wings, flapped lazily by, and settled once more in the marshes when we had passed. Only the voices of the land-locked springs, trickling their way to the river, and the quaint cry of the sandpipers scurrying along shore arose on the warm June air, until the stream, jealous of these rivals, laughed out once more into the rapids and natural dams, the shooting of which drenched us to the throats. But with all their quarrelling and tempestuous fury they failed to overthrow our basswood, and the sole complaint we had against them was that they were not dangerous and frequent enough to suit our venturesome spirits.

We slipped very slowly into Brantford, for many waste waters, dams and mill races take the life out of the stream above the town. But if it lacks character above, it certainly regains its natural temper and tone, as it whirls away from the little city, like a steed broken loose from chafing harness, and whatever bondage it suffers to serve the good townsfolk, is but a tonic and stimulant to further vivacity, and rejuvenates all its upstream vitality. The river takes a huge loop here, forming so perfect a horseshoe that at the end of eleven miles, it is only two and a half across country to the point you started from. A short portage brings you to the canal, up which you paddle with perfect ease, having performed the extraordinary feat of running more than thirteen miles, bringing up at the starting point with not a paddle stroke against stream. This is the favourite run of the Brantford Canoe Club, who invade the river three times each summer, with flags waving, club colours flying, and each little craft laden down with fantastic devices in Chinese lanterns and torch effects. The flotilla musters fifty-five strong, and probably no club in Canada claims a more interesting or historic route, for an annual cruise.

The city lies scarcely a mile astern, before the lovely ridge of hills known as Tutela Heights outline their crests against the sky. They were the old-time haunts of the now extinct Indian tribe, whose language even is comparatively a dead one. There remains but one old woman, living on the Six Nations Reserve, twenty miles down stream, who speaks this forgotten tongue, and, were it not for the indefatigable zeal and study manifested by Mr Horatio Hale, the eminent Indianologist,[1] this quaint dialect would have remained forever unrecorded.

In the midst of these hills that have many a time echoed the eerie death cry that told of up-stream murders and bloodshed; when the red man only lived and hunted and died, before the curtain dropped on that wild wood scene, and the action changed amid other stage settings, there stands an old-fashioned white frame cottage, with faded green shutters, a wide verandah, and a drowsy air of yesterday hanging about its eaves and half-neglected gardens. It was for many years the home

---

1 Horatio Hale (1817–96), an ethnologist and lawyer, worked with Johnson's father, her grandfather, John "Smoke" Johnson (Sakayengwaraton), and other chiefs to record Iroquois languages, oral culture, and ceremonies.

of Alexander Graham Bell,[1] of telephone fame and from this house to Brantford, two and a half miles distant, the trial wire was stretched. When a little child I often heard my father relate this story of the initial performance over this unperfected wire that was to grow with years into a necessity more important than at that time they even dared to hope. The young scientist, anxious, but confident, had bidden a number of guests to dine at the quaint Bell homestead, and to participate in the pleasure of the experiment.

Young Graham and my father personally tacked much of the wire, with non-conducting staples to the fences and trees between the Heights and the city, spending much of the afternoon at the work. Succeeding the dinner came the experiment, which was very satisfactory, the operator in the city being able to distinguish the voices of each guest, until my father was requested to speak in Mohawk.

"Can't hear," said the city operator.

The greeting was repeated.

"Something's wrong," said the city man.

Another Mohawk sentence from my father.

"What's that?" from the city.

More Mohawk.

City man, "Oh! I say professor, you might have invited me, how many cases did you open?"

A wild roar of laughter from "The Heights," and young Graham's voice over my father's shoulder "You've insulted the chief." Apologies from the city man, and general amusement at both ends of the line. With what horror the simple-minded old Tutelas would have regarded that bewitched bit of wire that carried the human voice across those silent hills of theirs, that have nurtured the greatness of race, and the power of intellect. A century ago the Tutela roved here in the pride of heritage and health, a century hence, and who shall say what the world will not owe to this gifted young pale face whose feet have wandered through many days among those heights and valleys? The redman's doom has overtaken the Tutela, the white man has overtaken his ambition, and to-day both race and genius are unknown to the beautiful hills that alone remain unchanging and unchanged, lifting forever their purple heads, while the river purls and whispers a ceaseless lullaby about their feet.

---

1 Alexander Graham Bell, inventor of the telephone, did much of his work at his home near Brantford.

A few miles further down stream, and the spire of the "Old Mohawk" church[1] looks somberly out through the trees. Probably no church in America has been more frequently written up than this century-old building. A long and exhaustive write-up has already appeared in these columns, so it may be here sufficient to mention that it was built especially for the Mohawks in Brant's time. The Bible, law, silver communion service, bell, and British coat-of-arms being presented by Queen Ann, many years prior to its erection.

One more notable spot to pass, and the paddles of the cruisers redip in home waters. To the right, low and level stretch "the fields and meadows of Bow Park" the model stock farm of the province. Some of the cattle on these lands have a world-wide reputation, and as the gorgeous fleet sails past, the brilliant flags and lanterns are stared at in wonderment by meek-eyed Jerseys and robust Holsteins, a single one of which is worth more bank notes than all the graceful craft put together.

But the gay canoeists care little for past histories of nations, for genius, for stock farms. To them the rapids are dearer than yesterday's romance; they love laughter more than money. And when the portage is made, and they begin their grand triumphal entry into town, when the old lagoon banks are thronged with spectators who watch with eager eyes the torches and fireworks, when the rollicking choruses are started, and the sluggish canal is converted into a bit of Venice dropped down into the new world, the quiet old river is left far behind, left to its hills and its twilights, to its long winding, through flats and marshes and forests, past village and town and the lonely reserve of the Iroquois; on, on, until with irresistible longing, it is lost in the great hungry arms of Lake Erie.

8. "A Brother Chief" (1892)

[Here Johnson describes the initiation of Prince Arthur (1850–1942), third son of Queen Victoria, and Duke of Connaught and Strathern, into the Six Nations council of chiefs. Johnson illuminates the long-standing relationship between the Iroquois people and British royalty and calls for the brotherhood of the nations. The article first appeared in *Weekly Detroit Free Press* on 12 May 1892.]

---

1 Her Majesty's Royal Chapel of the Mohawks, built in 1785, is the oldest building in Ontario and a National Historic Site.

Inaccessible as is the haughty Iroquois, there are instances when he unbends with the most exquisite condescension from his rigid tribal ordinances, and confers both honor and favor where worth merits the distinction. His keen insight into national and individual character seldom deceives him; it has been too often whetted by the white man's grinding stone of greed and injustice to lack an edge. There are few who meet the North American Indians disinterestedly; if native life is studied at all it is generally for gain. The researches made in archaeology and ethnology benefit not the subjects studied. The scholar but strengthens his own mental acquirements, just as the trade fattens his pocketbook. But there are to this class of self-seekers some noble and welcome exceptions, who are not only practically sympathetic regarding the rights of a royal humanity, but who are doing their utmost to show the world how the good old Indian character when unsullied by contamination with the vices of their white brethren, breathes nobility, romance and beauty, as forest pines in their native grandeur exhale a wild, stimulating perfume.

There is no nation in this world more tenacious of their birthrights—and of all heritages, chieftainship ranks the highest. The "titled" families, exclusive and conservative for centuries, renew in each generation their claims to a peerage, the accession of which has never been weakened by the intermixture of race or blood. The Iroquois Chief possesses a purer pedigree, a "bluer" blood, than any hand, British or French, that ever planted the Red, White and Blue in his territory.

But there are rare instances where this rite of chieftainship has been conferred upon outsiders, and the one I have in my memory is the occasion when one of England's young princes received this most exalted honor that his mother's Indian subjects could bestow. The Duke of Connaught, who was cheered by all "Canada from sea to sea" two years ago,[1] has for twenty years been possessed of the right to sit among the hereditary chiefs in the great council and to have a voice in the administration of the affairs of the Six Nations.

Twenty years ago! My childish recollection of the ceremony consists of such rude outlines that I fear they would make but a very unfinished sketch if reproduced unaided, but this old yellow newspaper bearing the date of October 2, 1869, will be admirable reference, and has the additional magic of having once been the

---

1   The Duke of Connaught and his wife visited all of Canada's major cities in 1890. Here Johnson alludes to Canada's motto, "From sea to sea."

property of the prince himself, and was sent to one of his favorite Mohawks with the direction written in the old-fashioned manner, on the wide white space near a big capital lettered heading. The ink is beginning to fade, but the writing, which is by the same pen as the little message inscribed on the inner margin, is still clear, with the firm English curve in its lettering, well known as that of the genial Arthur.

How he has changed since that day when some strong arm lifted me up to the windows and a kindly old gentleman took sufficient interest in my childish curiosity to tell me which was "the prince." I cannot recall what I expected to see; what I did see was a slender, pale-featured, delicate-looking lad, garmented in a plain suit of gray tweed and an unpretentious black felt hat, which he lifted bashfully to the crowd that cheered with that strange wild, eerie intonation that only Indian throats can give.

The very memory of that cheer thrills me now as I fancy a bugle call must thrill a warhorse. I see again those grand old Iroquois chiefs in their savage dress, their copper-colored faces dashed with red and black paint, their only head covering a tuft of eagle plumes that waved and swayed with each motion of the wearer's head, their metal tomahawks that gleamed in the yellow sunlight, fascinating the eyes of the boyish prince as the warriors crowded near, eager to clasp his hand and to tell him in broken, almost unintelligible English how loyal they were to his "great mother" and how well they remembered his brother, the Prince of Wales.

But my childish eyes watched only two people in that vast gathering, the pale young prince and the dark, military-looking chief that rode beside him. How proud my little heart was of that rider! How well I knew those square, Napoleonic shoulders, that beautiful buckskin costume, those brilliant silver medals and ornaments, that dainty, though deadly, scalping knife, and well-worn tomahawk, how familiar was that flaunting crest of ostrich plumes that, waving, fell almost to the shoulders over which was flung the red broadcloth "blanket" that contrasted so vividly with the jet-black pony arching its head so proudly—for had not the queen's son just patted its glossy flanks and praised the royal little horse for its beauty?

Then my ears caught the sound of the deer-foot rattles ornamenting my rider's ankles. Ah! me, how the latent germs of nationality will well up even in a child's sentimentality. The jangle of those rattles that kept such perfect time with each determined little step of the pony, flew to my head like reddest wine.

I leaned far out of the window and peered down into the savage-visaged throng.

"Will he look up?" I cried to my mother, but she was too eagerly watching that pair to reply, and a clear, proud light crept into her blue English eyes when she saw "our" chief dismount, toss off the scarlet blanket, spread it on the green as a carpet, conduct the young prince to a place of honor upon it, take from his own shoulders a magnificent sash of Indian workmanship in beads, moose hair and porcupine quills, and laying it across young royalty's shoulder tie it in a loose knot beneath his arm.

Then stepped on to that scarlet carpeting one, rich in years and renown, one whose privilege it was to adopt the young Britisher into the Iroquois nation, one who had been the speaker of the council for forty years, who was called "the Mohawk Warbler," because of his exquisite language—a veritable Indian Ruskin.[1] That splendid old veteran fought bravely for the British flag in the long ago, so with pardonable pride he took the prince's hand within his own, and the strange, solemn rites commenced.

My ears have heard some of nature's loveliest songs—the wild splash of the rapids in great rivers as they leap over broken rocks and cascade in murmuring eddies away to the sea; the hushed melancholy of winds in the forest pines away up in Northern Canada; the torturing loneliness that midnight airs breathe, when flapped through the pinions of migrating night birds, and one is conscious of the far-offness of any human habitation—but those sounds cannot equal the wild, strange euphony that fell from the lips of the veteran chief as he chanted the formula of that ordinance. Hand in hand with the scion of English royalty he walked to and fro, his low, monotonous tones, eerie and strange as a wild bird's call, his song supplemented from time to time by manifestations of approval from his confederate chiefs.

In accordance with the ancient rules the novitiate was presented with some strings of white wampum by the owner of the scarlet "blanket," with these words:

"As beads are pure, so we trust your life will be an honor to the tribe to which you belong, as the clear sky proves a happiness to many. Your name, 'Kavakoudge,' will represent the flying sun, the great sun that tramps from morning till night

---

1 John "Smoke" Johnson was renowned for his eloquence; one of his nicknames was "The Mohawk Warbler." He is compared here to John Ruskin (1819–1900), noted British art critic and social activist, whose lectures and published works were immensely popular.

on the vast dominions of your great mother. In giving you this name we trust your path through life may be bright and clear as the sun's brightest rays. It will represent the progress of the sun in its daily course under the guidance of the Great Spirit, and put us in memory of your journey from the far east to see us. You have traveled with the sun toward us, and as the sun does, flying, and lighting the world in its course. Our people are devoted to her majesty's throne. [Loud indications of assent.] We always rely on the kindness of Great Britain and believe in her and in her people. We wish you prosperity in this world."

His royal highness hesitated for a moment, then with gaining confidence replied: "I am much touched by the kind speech which you have just delivered, and I feel particularly happy to be made one of your tribe. Most sincerely do I thank you for your kind and affectionate mention of my mother and for all your loyal expressions toward her."

The prince was then lustily cheered as a Six Nation Indian, and this old newspaper says "He took to his new decoration kindly, and for one who already wears the ribbon of the garter,[1] appeared to enjoy it."

Ah, well! That all happened long, long ago, but he did not forget his redskin brothers when he returned to old England, for his beautiful gifts—portraits of the queen, the prince consort and himself—are to-day the most honored and cherished treasures in the Council House of the Six Nations.

Well, he came to Canada again two summers ago, came with his noble wife, and was received from coast to coast by "loyal hearts and true."[2] But I doubt if in the latter days he found a moment or a people more interesting than when he stood among the chiefs, braves and warriors that were to confer upon him the most ancient honor that America could offer. And on this latter occasion, when the whole atmosphere rang with cheers, there was one who crept quietly into an unpretentious parlor. She resurrected from a quaint birch bark basket an old yellow newspaper upon whose margin was written "With kind regards from your brother chief—Arthur," who looked longingly at an old buckskin coat with its tarnished silver medals, at a rusty tomahawk that lay on a British-red broadcloth— at some purple wampum belts and deerfoot anklets, but there is no

---

1 The Most Noble Order of the Garter has been bestowed at the British Sovereign's pleasure since 1348.

2 The phrase may come from an 1894 Christmas carol by J.B. Gray.

one to wear them. The warrior rider, with many others who gave the war-whoop that day more than twenty years ago, has

> "Sailed into the dusk of the evening
> In the glory of the sunset
> To the islands of the blessed
> To the land of the hereafter!"[1]

9. "The Brotherhood" (1910)

[In this story, a Mohawk man tells a white youth about the last revenge killing carried out before British law came to Canada. The story was originally published in *Boys' World* on 1 January 1910.]

"What is the silver chain for, Queetah?" asked the boy, lifting the tomahawk and running the curious links between his thumb and fingers. "I never saw one before."

The Mohawk smiled. "That is because few tomahawks content themselves with times of peace. While war lives, you will never see a silver chain worn by an Iroquois, nor will you see it on anything he possesses," he answered.

"Then it is the badge of peace?" questioned the boy.

"The badge of peace—yes," replied Queetah.

It was a unique weapon which the boy fingered so curiously. The tomahawk itself was shaped like a slender axe, and wrought of beaten copper, with a half-inch edge of gleaming steel cleverly welded on, forming a deadly blade. At the butt end of the axe was a delicately shaped pipe bowl, carved and chased with heads of animals, coiling serpents and odd conventional figures, totems of the once mighty owner, whose war cry had echoed through the lake lands and forests more than a century ago. The handle was but eighteen inches long, a smooth polished stem of curled maple, the beauty of the natural wood heightened by a dark strip of color that wound with measured, even sweeps from tip to base like a ribbon. Queetah had long ago told the boy how that rich spiral decoration was made—how the old Indians wound the wood with strips of wet buckskin, then burnt the exposed wood sufficiently to

---

1 Johnson selects a few lines from the end of *The Song of Hiawatha*, by Henry Wadsworth Longfellow (1807–82), to refer to her father.

color it. The beautiful white coils were the portions protected by the hide from the flame and smoke.

Inlaid in this handle were strange designs of dull-beaten silver, cubes and circles and innumerable hearts, the national symbol of the Mohawks. At the extreme end was a small, flat metal mouthpiece, for this strange weapon was a combination of sun and shadow; it held within itself the unique capabilities of being a tomahawk, the most savage instrument in Indian warfare, and also a peace pipe, that most beautiful of all Indian treasures.

"It is so strange," said the boy, fingering the weapon lovingly. "Your people are the most terrible on the warpath of all the nations in the world, yet they seem to think more of that word 'peace,' and to honor it more, than all of us put together. Why, you even make silver chains for emblems of peace, like this," and he tangled his slim fingers in the links that looped from the lower angle of the steel edge to the handle.

"Yes," replied Queetah, "we value peace; it is a holy word to the red man, perhaps because it is so little with us, because we know its face so slightly. The face of peace has no fiery stripes of color, no streaks of the deadly black and red, the war paints of the fighting Mohawks. It is a face of silver, like this chain, and when it smiles upon us, we wash the black and red from off our cheeks, and smoke this pipe as a sign of brotherhood with all men."

"Brotherhood with all men," mused the boy, aloud. "We palefaces have no such times, Queetah. Some of us are always at war. If we are not fighting here, we are fighting beyond the great salt seas. I wish we had more of your ways, Queetah—your Indian ways. I wish we could link a silver chain around the world; we think we are the ones to teach, but I believe you could teach us much. Will you not teach me now? Tell me the story of this tomahawk. I may learn something from it—something of Indian war, peace and brotherhood."

"The story is yours to hear," said the Mohawk, "if you would see how peace grows out of deeds of blood, as the blue iris grows from the blackness of the swamp; but it is the flower that the sun loves, not the roots, buried in the darkness, from which the blossom springs. So we of the red race say that the sun shines on peace alone, not the black depths beneath it."

The Mohawk paused and locked his hands about his knees, while the boy stretched himself at full length and stared up at the far sky beyond the interlacing branches overhead. He loved to lie thus, listening to the quaint tales of olden days that Queetah had stored up in his wonderful treasure-house of memory. Everything the Indian possessed had associated with it some wild tale of early Canadian history, some strange half-forgotten Indian custom or legend, so he listened now to the story of the last time that the ancient Indian law of "a life for a life" was carried out in the beautiful Province of Ontario, while the low, even voice of the Mohawk described the historical event, giving to the tale the Indian term for the word "peace," which means "the silver chain that does not tarnish."

"This was the tomahawk of my grandsire, who had won his eagle plume by right of great bravery. For had he not at your age—just fifteen years—stood the great national test of starving for three days and three nights without a whimper? Did not this make him a warrior, with the right to sit among the old men of his tribe, and to flaunt his eagle plume in the face of his enemy? Ok-wa-ho was his name; it means 'The Wolf,' and young as he was, like the wolf he could snarl and show his fangs. His older brother was the chief, tall and terrible, with the scowl of thunder on his brow and the gleaming fork of lightning in his eyes. This chief thought never of council fires or pipes or hunting or fishing, he troubled not about joining the other young men in their sports of lacrosse or snow-snake, or bowl-and-beans; to him there was nothing in life but the warpath, no song but the war cry, no color but the war paint. Daily he sharpened his scalping knife, daily he polished his tomahawk, daily feathered and poisoned his arrows, daily he sought enemies, taunted them, insulted them, braved them and conquered them; while his young brother, Ok-wa-ho, rested in their lodge listening to the wisdom of the old men, learning their laws and longing for peace. Once Ok-wa-ho had said, 'My brother, stay with us, wash from thy cheeks the black and scarlet; thy tomahawk has two ends: one is an edge, dyed often in blood, but show us that thou hast not forgotten how to use the other end—fill thy pipe.'

"'Little brother,' replied the chief, 'thou art yet but a stripling boy; smoke, then, the peace pipe, but it is not for me.'

"Ok-wa-ho felt this to be an insult. It was a taunt on his bravery. He squared his boyish shoulders, and, lifting his narrow chin, flung back the answer, 'I, too, can use both ends, the edge as well as the pipe.' The great chief laughed. 'That is right, Little Brother, and some day the tribe will ask you to show them how well you can use the edge. I shall not always be victor; some day I shall fall, and my enemy will place his foot on my throat and voice the war cry of victory, just as I have done these many days. Hast thou sat among the wise men of our people long enough to learn what thou must do then—when the enemy laughs over my body?'

"'Yes,' replied the boy, 'I am thy nearest of kin. Indian law demands that I alone must avenge thy death. Thy murderer must die, and die by no hand but mine. It is the law.'

"'It is the law,' echoed the chief. 'I can trust you to carry it out, eh, Little Brother?'

"'You can trust me, no matter how great a giant thy enemy may be,' answered the boy.

"'Thy words are as thy name,' smiled the chief. 'Thou art indeed worthy of thy eagle plume. Thou art a true Ok-wa-ho.' Then placing his scalping knife in its sheath at his belt he lifted his palm to his lips, a long, strange, quivering yell rent the forest trails—a yell of defiance, of mastery, of challenge; his feet were upon the warpath once more.

"That night, while the campfires yet glowed and flickered, painting the forest with black shadows, against which curled the smoke from many pipe bowls, a long, strange, haunting note came faintly down on the wings of the water—the dark river whispering past bore on its deep currents the awful sound of the Death Cry.

"'Some mighty one has fallen,' said the old men. 'The victor is voicing his triumph from far upstream.' Then as the hours slipped by, a runner came up the forest trail, chanting the solemn song of the departed. As he neared the campfires he ceased his song, and in its place gave once again the curdling horror of the Death Cry.

"'Who is the victor? Who the fallen brave?' cried the old men.

"'Thy chief this hour hunts buffalo in the happy hunting grounds, while his enemy, Black Star, of the Bear Clan, sings the war song of the Great Unconquered,' replied the runner.

"'Ah, ha!' replied the old men. 'Ok-wa-ho here is next of kin, but this stripling boy is too young, too small, to face and fight Black Star. But the law is that no other hand but his may avenge his brother's death. So our great dead chief must sleep—sleep while his murderer sings and taunts us with his freedom.'

"'Not so!' cried the young Ok-wa-ho. 'I shall face Black Star. I shall obey the law of my people. My hand is small but strong, my aim is sure, my heart is brave, and my vengeance will be swift.'

"Before the older men could stay him he was away, but first he snatched the silver chain from off his tomahawk, emptied the bowl of tobacco, destroyed all the emblems of peace, and turned his back upon the council fire. All night long he scoured the forest for his brother's slayer, all night long he flung from his boyish lips the dreaded war cry of the avenger, and when day broke he drank from the waters of the river, and followed the trail that led to the lodge of his mighty enemy. Outside the door sat Black Star of the Bear Clan; astride a fallen tree he lounged arrogantly; his hands, still red with last night's horrors, were feathering arrows. His savage face curled into a sneer as the boy neared him. Then a long, taunting laugh broke over the dawn, and he jeered:

"'So, pretty maiden-boy, what hast thou to do with the Great Unconquered?'

"'I am the brother of thy victim,' said Ok-wa-ho, as he slipped his tomahawk from his belt, placing it on the low bark roof of the lodge, in case he needed a second weapon.

"'The Avenger, eh?' scoffed Black Star, mockingly.

"'The Avenger—yes,' repeated the boy. Then walking deliberately up to the savage warrior, he placed his left hand on the other's shoulder, and, facing him squarely, said: 'I am here to carry out the law of our people; because I am young, it does not mean that I must not obey the rules of older and wiser men. Will you fight me now? I demand it.'

"The other sneered. 'Fight *you*?' he said disdainfully. 'I do not fight babies or women. Thou hast a woman's wrist, a baby's fingers. They could not swing a tomahawk.'

"'No?' the boy sneered. 'Perhaps thou art right, but they can plunge a knife. Did thou not lend my brother a knife last night? Yes? Then I have come to return it.' There was a flash of steel, a wild death cry, and Ok-wa-ho's knife was buried to the hilt in the heart of Black Star of the Bear Clan.'"

Queetah ceased speaking, for the paleface boy, lying at his feet, had shuddered and locked his teeth at the gruesome tale.

"But, Queetah," he said, after a long pause, "I thought this was a story of peace, of 'the silver chain that does not tarnish.'"

"It is," replied the Indian. "You shall hear how peace was born out of that black deed—listen:

"When Black Star of the Bear Clan lay dead at his feet, the centuries of fighting blood surged up in the boy's whole body. He placed his moccasined foot on the throat of the conquered, flung back his head, and gave the long, wild Mohawk war cry of victory. Far off that cry reached the ears of the older men, smoking about their council fire.

"'It is Ok-wa-ho's voice,' they said proudly, 'and it is the cry of victory. We may never hear that cry again, for the white man's law and rule begins to-day.' Which was true, for after that the Mohawks came under the governmental laws of Canada. It was the last time the red man's native law of justice, of 'blood for blood,' was ever enacted in Ontario. This is history—Canadian history—not merely a tale of horror with which to pass this winter afternoon." Again Queetah ceased speaking, and again the boy persisted.

"But the silver chain?"

With a dreamy, far-away look the Indian continued:

"One never uses an avenging knife again. The blade even must not be wiped; it is a dark deed, even to an Indian's soul, and the knife must be buried on the dark side of a tree—the north side, where the sun never shines, where the moss grows thickest. Ok-wa-ho buried his blood-stained knife, slipping it blade downwards beneath the moss, took his unused tomahawk, and returned to his people. 'The red man's law is ended,' he said.

"'Yes, we must be as white men now,' replied the older men, sadly.

"That night Ok-wa-ho beat into this handle these small silver hearts. They are the badge of brotherhood with all men. The next day white men came, explaining the new rule that must hold sway in the forest. 'If there is bloodshed among you,' they said, 'the laws of Canada will punish the evil-doer. Put up your knives and tomahawks, and be at peace.'

"And as the years went on and on, these ancient Indian customs all dropped far into the past. Only one thing remained to remind Ok-wa-ho of his barbarous, boyish deed: it was the top branch of a tall tree waving above its fellows. As he fished and paddled peacefully miles up the river, he could see that treetop, and his heart never forgot what was lying at its roots. He grew old, old, until he reached the age of eighty-nine, but the tree-top still waved and the roots still held their secret.

"He came to me then. I was but a boy myself, but his grandson, and he loved me. He told me this strange tale, adding: 'Queetah, my feet must soon travel up the long trail. I would know what peace is like before I go on the journey—come, we will unearth the knife.' I followed where he led. We found the weapon three feet down in the earth, where the years had weighted it. In places the steel was still bright, but in others dark patches of rust covered the scarlet of Black Star's blood, [Fact.][1] fresh seventy-three years before.

"'It is yours,' said Ok-wa-ho, placing it in my hand. 'See, the sun shines on it; perhaps that will lessen the darkness of the deed, but I obeyed the Indian law. Seventy-three years this knife has lain buried. [Fact.] It was the last law, the last law.'

---

1 Johnson bases this story on an experience recounted by her father, which she also tells in a less dramatic version in her interview with Garth Grafton (see Appendix A1).

"That night Ok-wa-ho began to hammer and beat and mold these silver links. When they were finished he welded them firmly to the tomahawk, and, just before he went up the long, long trail, he gave it to me, saying, 'This blade has never tasted blood, it will never have dark spots on it like those on the knife. The silver chain does not tarnish, for it means peace, and brotherhood of all men.'"

Queetah's voice ceased. The tale was ended.

"And peace has reigned ever since?" asked the boy, still looking at the far-off sky through the branches overhead.

"Peace has reigned ever since," replied Queetah. "The Mohawks and the palefaces are brothers, under one law. That was the last Avenging Knife. It is Canadian history."

10. "The Death Cry" (1888)

Moonless the skies, unlit the forest way,
Black hangs the night o'er northern Canada.
Parting the silence comes the hoot of owls,
A stray fox barks—afar some strange dog howls,
In such forebodings crouches death—
                          A knife
Uplifted in the crisis of hot strife
Has drunk vermillion draughts, its hostile blow
Has stilled the hostile blood of some dark foe,
Noiseless the victor through the midnight creeps
Toward the forest stream which silent sleeps—
Leans he low down above the snake-like flood,
To tell his world that law is blood for blood,
Bold from his parted lips the death-cry leaps
Adown the waters, icily it sweeps,
Weird, strange and chilling, awfulest of cries
That on distant darkness floats—then dies,
The Mohawk listens! all is still as death,
Aye, death itself seems dead—once more that breath
Curdles the air with savage eloquence,
Vibrating through the forest black and dense,
One moment more of gloom, ghostlike and drear,
Then the red warrior's catlike, listening ear
Catches a seeming echo—a reply
From miles adown the stream—his wild death-cry
Has floated with the waters, and 'tis passed
From mouth to mouth, the deed is known at last.

Unmoved he hears the far off eerie wail,
Then turns to take again the midnight trail,
He parts the boughs—bends low his eagle plume
And merges in the depths of forest gloom.

11. "As Red Men Die" (1890)

Captive! Is there a hell to him like this?
A taunt more galling than the Huron's hiss?
He—proud and scornful, he—who laughed at law,
He—scion of the deadly Iroquois,
He—the bloodthirsty, he—the Mohawk chief,
He—who despises pain and sneers at grief,
Here in the hated Huron's vicious clutch,
That even captive he disdains to touch!

Captive! But *never* conquered; Mohawk brave
Stoops not to be to *any* man a slave;
Least, to the puny tribe his soul abhors,
The tribe whose wigwams sprinkle Simcoe's shores.
With scowling brow he stands and courage high,
Watching with haughty and defiant eye
His captors, as they council o'er his fate,
Or strive his boldness to intimidate.
Then fling they unto him the choice;

                              "Wilt thou
Walk o'er the bed of fire that waits thee now—
Walk with uncovered feet upon the coals,
Until thou reach the ghostly Land of Souls,
And, with thy Mohawk death-song please our ear?
Or wilt thou with the women rest thee here?"

His eyes flash like an eagle's, and his hands
Clench at the insult. Like a god he stands.
"Prepare the fire!" he scornfully demands.
He knoweth not that this same jeering band
Will bite the dust—will lick the Mohawk's hand;
Will kneel and cower at the Mohawk's feet;
Will shrink when Mohawk war drums wildly beat.

His death will be avenged with hideous hate
By Iroquois, swift to annihilate

His vile detested captors, that now flaunt
Their war clubs in his face with sneer and taunt,
Not thinking, soon that reeking, red, and raw,
Their scalps will deck the belts of Iroquois.

The path of coals outstretches, white with heat,
A forest fir's length—ready for his feet.
Unflinching as a rock he steps along
The burning mass, and sings his wild war song;
Sings, as he sang when once he used to roam
Throughout the forests of his southern home,
Where, down the Genesee, the water roars,
Where gentle Mohawk purls between its shores,
Songs, that of exploit and of prowess tell;
Songs of the Iroquois invincible.

Up the long trail of fire he boasting goes,
Dancing a war dance to defy his foes.
His flesh is scorched, his muscles burn and shrink,
But still he dances to death's awful brink.
The eagle plume that crests his haughty head
Will *never* droop until his heart be dead.
Slower and slower yet his footstep swings,
Wilder and wilder still his death-song rings,
Fiercer and fiercer through the forest bounds
His voice that leaps to Happier Hunting Grounds.
One savage yell—

Then loyal to his race,
He bends to death—but *never* to disgrace.

12. "The Avenger" (1892)

A starless night:
               Thickened with deeds of doom
The black stream serpent-like slips through the gloom
Choked with a Mohawk's blood that trickles slow
From out a well nigh pulseless heart, laid low
By tribal hate and discord—giving rise
To hostile feuds and violent jealousies
'Twas but a moment's work.

The Cherokee
Meets with his Mohawk foe; the enmity
Inherited through ages fires the palm
Of each red hand, they face—

A meaning calm
With venom gorged—then on the night is flung
The deadliest yell that e'er left Indian tongue—
Like wild-cats raged, concurrently they spring,
With tomahawks athirst and glittering;
They close—they struggle—then they leap apart,
Hate as a hell burns madness in each heart.
Some strategy—a crafty, rival strife,
Then parts the darkness to a gleaming knife;
A treacherous manoeuvre—

On the shore
The Mohawk lifeless lies. The feud is o'er.

Exultingly, the Cherokee now stands,
Appeased his hate, avenged his reeking hands;
With foot upon his writhing victim's throat
He backward flings his head—one long, strange note
Leaves his thin lips—then up to Heaven's height
His war-whoop pierces through the fateful night.

Leagues off, the death-cry 'roused from sleep a son
Of the same sire as is the murdered one,
Nearest of kindred, Indian law demands
The dead must be avenged but by his hands.
The hours drift by—another midnight gloom
Curdles and cringes 'neath impending doom;
With trick of stealth a Mohawk lad slips o'er
The trail—till near a fire-illumed lodge door
He sees a man, a sinewy, ruthless scion
Of Western blood (inhuman as a lion).

The boy's step breaks
The brittle twigs—the red giant starts, awakes,
Then springs erect to meet th' unflinching eye
Of one so youthful, by whose hand to die
Is ignominy—shame—affront—disgrace.
He winces at the insult he, his race

Must take from tribes who tauntingly employ
T'avenge their wrong this fearless stripling boy.
To fate, he offers no resistance; he
Well knows that naught can shatter the decree,
That naught averts the iron Indian law
Of blood for blood, among the Iroquois,
Knows their retaliation firm and fell
Would hound him to the very depths of hell.
Boldly the youth confronts his monstrous foe,
Before whom nations quail—his eyes aglow
With hate and triumph as he hisses through
Locked teeth, "Last night thou lendest a knife unto
My brother; come I now O! Cherokee,
To give thy bloody weapon back to thee."
An evil curse—a flash of steel—

      A leap—
A thrust above the heart, well aimed and deep,
Plunged to its very hilt in blood, the blade,
While vengeance gloating yells!

      The debt is paid.

13. "Her Majesty's Guest" (1913)

[First published in *The Moccasin Maker* (1910); for more on the events that prompted this story, see "My Mother," above.]

★ ★ ★ ★ ★

[Author's Note.—The "Onondaga Jam" occurred late in the seventies, and this tale is founded upon actual incidents in the life of the author's father, who was Forest Warden on the Indian Reserve.]

I have never been a good man, but then I have never pretended to be one, and perhaps that at least will count in my favor in the day when the great dividends are declared.

I have been what is called "well brought up" and I would give some years of my life to possess now the money spent on my education; how I came to drop from what I should have been to what I am would scarcely interest anyone—if indeed I were capable of detailing the process, which I am not. I suppose I just rolled leisurely down hill like many another fellow.

My friends, however, still credit me with one virtue; that is an absolute respect for my neighbor's wife, a feeling which, however, does not extend to his dollars. His money is mine if I can get it, and to do myself justice I prefer getting it from him honestly, at least without sufficient dishonesty to place me behind prison bars.

Some experience has taught me that when a man is reduced to getting his living, as I do, by side issues and small deals, there is no better locality for him to operate than around the borders of some Indian Reserve.

The pagan Indian is an unsuspicious fool. You can do him up right and left. The Christian Indian is as sharp as a fox, and with a little gloved handling he will always go in with you on a few lumber and illicit whiskey deals, which means that you have the confidence of his brethren and their dollars at the same time.

I had outwitted the law for six years. I had smuggled more liquor into the Indian Bush on the Grand River Reserve and drawn more timber out of it to the Hamilton and Brantford markets than any forty dealers put together. Gradually, the law thinned the whole lot out—all but me; but I was slippery as an eel and my bottles of whiskey went on, and my loads of ties and timber came off, until every officer and preacher in the place got up and demanded an inspection.

The Government at Ottawa awoke, stretched, yawned, then printed some flaring posters and stuck them around the border villages. The posters were headed by a big print of the British Coat of Arms, and some large type beneath announced terrible fines and heavy imprisonments for anyone caught hauling Indian timber off the Reserve, or hauling whiskey on to it. Then the Government rubbed its fat palms together, settled itself in its easy chair, and snored again.

I? Oh, I went on with my operations.

And at Christmas time Tom Barrett arrived on the scene. Not much of an event, you'd say if you saw him, still less if you heard him. According to himself, he knew everything and could do everything in the known world; he was just twenty-two and as obnoxiously fresh a thing as ever boasted itself before older men.

He was the old missionary's son and had come up from college at Montreal to help his father preach salvation to the Indians on Sundays, and to swagger around week-days in his brand new clerical-cut coat and white tie.

He enjoyed what is called, I believe, "deacon's orders." They tell me he was recently "priested," to use their straight English Church term, and is now parson of a swell city church. Well! they can have him. I'll never split on him, but I could tell them some things about Tom Barrett that would soil his surplice[1]—at least in my opinion, but you never can be sure when even religious people will make a hero out of a rogue.

The first time I ever saw him he came into "Jake's" one night, quite late. We were knocked clean dumb. "Jake's" isn't the place you would count on seeing a clerical-cut coat in.

It's not a thoroughly disreputable place, for Jake has a decent enough Indian wife; but he happens also to have a cellar which has a hard name for illicit-whiskey supplies, though never once has the law, in its numerous and unannounced visits to the shanty, ever succeeded in discovering barrel or bottle. I consider myself a pretty smart man, but Jake is cleverer than I am.

When young Barrett came in that night, there was a clatter of hiding cups. "Hello, boys," he said, and sat down wearily opposite me, leaning his arms on the table between us like one utterly done out.

Jake, it seemed, had the distinction of knowing him; so he said kind of friendly-like,

"Hello, parson—sick?"

"Sick? Sick nothing," said Barrett, "except sick to death of this place. And don't 'parson' me! I'm 'parson' on Sundays; the rest of the six days I'm Tom Barrett—Tom, if you like."

We were dead silent. For myself, I thought the fellow clean crazy; but the next moment he had turned half around, and with a quick, soft, coaxing movement, for all the world like a woman, he slipped his arm around Jake's shoulders, and said, "Say, Jake, don't let the fellows mind me." Then in a lower tone—"What have you got to drink?"

Jake went white-looking and began to talk of some cider he'd got in the cellar; but Barrett interrupted with, "Look here, Jake, just drop that rot; I know all about *you*." He tipped a half wink at the rest of us, but laid his fingers across his lips. "Come, old man," he wheedled like a girl, "you don't know what it is to be dragged away from college and buried alive in this Indian bush. The governor's good enough, you know—treats me white and all that—but you know what he is on whiskey. I tell you I've got a throat as long and dry as a fence rail—"

No one spoke.

"You'll save my life if you do," he added, crushing a bank note into Jake's hand.

Jake looked at me. The same thought flashed on us both; if we could get this church student on our side—Well! Things would

---

1 The white over-garment worn in Christian religious services; here the reference is to the fact that Tom Barrett is an ordained priest of the Anglican Church.

be easy enough and public suspicion never touch us. Jake turned, resurrected the hidden cups, and went down cellar.

"You're Dan McLeod, aren't you?" suggested Barrett, leaning across the table and looking sharply at me.

"That's me," I said in turn, and sized him up. I didn't like his face; it was the undeniable face of a liar—small, uncertain eyes, set together close like those of a fox, a thin nose, a narrow, womanish chin that accorded with his girlish actions of coaxing, and a mouth I didn't quite understand.

Jake had come up with the bottle, but before he could put it on the table Barrett snatched it like a starving dog would a hunk of meat.

He peered at the label, squinting his foxy eyes, then laughed up at Jake.

"I hope you don't sell the Indians *this*," he said, tapping the capsule.

No, Jake never sold a drop of whiskey to Indians,—the law, you know, was very strict and—

"Oh, I don't care whatever else you sell them," said Barrett, "but their red throats would never appreciate fine twelve-year-old[1] like this. Come, boys."

We came.

"So you're Dan McLeod," he continued after the first long pull, "I've heard about you, too. You've got a deck of cards in your pocket—haven't you? Let's have a game."

I looked at him, and though, as I said in the beginning, I'm not a good man, I felt honestly sorry for the old missionary and his wife at that moment.

"It's no use," said the boy, reading my hesitation. "I've broken loose. I must have a slice of the old college life, just for to-night."

I decided the half-cut of Indian blood on his mother's side was showing itself; it was just enough to give Tom a good red flavoring and a rare taste for gaming and liquor.

We played until daylight, when Barrett said he must make his sneak home, and reaching for his wide-brimmed, soft felt preacher's hat, left—having pocketed twenty-six of our good dollars, swallowed unnumbered cups of twelve-year-old and won the combined respect of everyone at Jake's.

The next Sunday Jake went to church out of curiosity. He said Tom Barrett "officiated" in a surplice as white as snow and with a face as sinless as your mother's. He preached most eloquently against the terrible evil of the illicit liquor trade, and implored

---

1 The number of years that the whiskey has been aged.

his Indian flock to resist this greatest of all pitfalls. Jake even seemed impressed as he told us.

But Tom Barrett's "breaking loose for once" was like any other man's. Night after night saw him at Jake's, though he never played to win after that first game. As the weeks went on, he got anxious-looking; his clerical coat began to grow seedy, his white ties uncared for; he lost his fresh, cheeky talk, and the climax came late in March when one night I found him at Jake's sitting alone, his face bowed down on the table above his folded arms, and something so disheartened in his attitude that I felt sorry for the boy. Perhaps it was that I was in trouble myself that day; my biggest "deal" of the season had been scented by the officers and the chances were they would come on and seize the five barrels of whiskey I had been as many weeks smuggling into the Reserve. However it was, I put my hand on his shoulder, and told him to brace up, asking at the same time what was wrong.

"Money," he answered, looking up with kind of haggard eyes. "Dan, I must have money. City bills, college debts—everything has rolled up against me. I daren't tell the governor, and he couldn't help me anyway, and I can't go back for another term owing every man in my class." He looked suicidal. And then I made the plunge I'd been thinking on all day.

"Would a hundred dollars be any good to you?" I eyed him hard as I said it, and sat down in my usual place, opposite him.

"Good?" he exclaimed, half rising. "It would be an eternal godsend." His foxy eyes glittered. I thought I detected greed in them; perhaps it was only relief.

I told him it was his if he would only help me, and making sure we were quite alone, I ran off a hurried account of my "deal," then proposed that he should "accidentally" meet the officers near the border, ring in with them as a parson would be likely to do, tell them he suspicioned the whiskey was directly at the opposite side of the Reserve to where I really had stored it, get them wild-goose chasing miles away, and give me a chance to clear the stuff and myself as well; in addition to the hundred I would give him twenty per cent. on the entire deal. He changed color and the sweat stood out on his forehead.

"One hundred dollars this time to-morrow night," I said. He didn't move. "And twenty per cent. One hundred dollars this time to-morrow night," I repeated.

He began to weaken. I lit my pipe and looked indifferent, though I knew I was a lost man if he refused—and informed. Suddenly he stretched his hand across the table, impulsively, and closed it over mine. I knew I had him solid then.

"Dan," he choked up, "it's a terrible thing for a divinity student to do; but—" his fingers tightened nervously. "I'm with you!" Then in a moment, "Find some whiskey, Dan. I'm done up."

He soon got braced enough to ask me who was in the deal, and what timber we expected to trade for. When I told him Lige Smith and Jack Jackson were going to help me, he looked scared and asked me if I thought they would split on him. He was so excited I thought him cowardly, but the poor devil had reason enough, I supposed, to want to keep the transaction from the ears of his father, or worse still—the bishop. He seemed easier when I assured him the boys were square, and immensely gratified at the news that I had already traded six quarts of the stuff for over a hundred dollars' worth of cordwood.

"We'll never get it across the river to the markets," he said dolefully. "I came over this morning in a canoe. Ice is all out."

"What about the Onondaga Jam?" I said. He winked.

"That'll do. I'd forgotten it," he answered, and chirped up right away like a kid.

But I hadn't forgotten the Jam. It had been a regular gold-mine to me all that open winter, when the ice froze and thawed every week and finally jammed itself clean to the river bottom in the throat of the bend up at Onondaga, and the next day the thermometer fell to eleven degrees below zero, freezing it into a solid block that bridged the river for traffic, and saved my falling fortunes.

"And where's the whiskey hidden?" he asked after awhile.

"No you don't," I laughed. "Parson or pal, no man living knows or will know where it is till he helps me haul it away. I'll trust none of you."

"I'm not a thief," he pouted.

"No," I said, "but you're blasted hard up, and I don't intend to place temptation in your way."

He laughed good-naturedly and turned the subject aside just as Lige Smith and Jack Jackson came in with an unusual companion that put a stop to all further talk. Women were never seen at night time around Jake's; even his wife was invisible, and I got a sort of shock when I saw old Cayuga Joe's girl, Elizabeth, following at the boys' heels. It had been raining and the girl, a full blood Cayuga, shivered in the damp and crouched beside the stove.

Tom Barrett started when he saw her. His color rose and he began to mark up the table with his thumb nail. I could see he felt his fix. The girl—Indian right through—showed no surprise at seeing him there, but that did not mean she would keep her mouth shut about it next day, Tom was undoubtedly *discovered*.

Notwithstanding her unwelcome presence, however, Jackson managed to whisper to me that the Forest Warden and his officers were alive and bound for the Reserve the following day. But it didn't worry me worth a cent; I knew we were safe as a church with Tom Barrett's clerical coat in our midst. He was coming over to our corner now.

"That hundred's right on the dead square, Dan?" he asked anxiously, taking my arm and moving to the window.

I took a roll of bank notes from my trousers' pocket and with my back to the gang counted out ten tens. I always carry a good wad with me with a view to convenience if I have to make a hurried exit from the scene of my operations.

He shook his head and stood away. "Not till I've earned it, McLeod."

What fools very young men make of themselves sometimes. The girl arose, folding her damp shawl over her head, and made towards the door; but he intercepted her, saying it was late and as their ways lay in the same direction, he would take her home. She shot a quick glance at him and went out. Some little uneasy action of his caught my notice. In a second my suspicions were aroused; the meeting had been arranged, and I knew from what I had seen him to be that the girl was doomed.

It was all very well for me to do up Cayuga Joe—he was the Indian whose hundred dollars' worth of cordwood I owned in lieu of six quarts of bad whiskey—but his women-folks were entitled to be respected at least while I was around. I looked at my watch; it was past midnight. I suddenly got boiling hot clean through.

"Look here, Tom Barrett," I said, "I ain't a saint, as everybody knows; but if you don't treat that girl right, you'll have to square it up with me, d'you understand?"

He threw me a nasty look. "Keep your gallantry for some occasion when it's needed, Dan McLeod," he sneered, and with a laugh I didn't like, he followed the girl out into the rain.

I walked some distance behind them for two miles. When they reached her father's house and went in, I watched her through the small uncurtained window put something on the fire to cook, then arouse her mother, who even at that late hour sat beside the stove smoking a clay pipe. The old woman had apparently met with some accident; her head and shoulders were bound up, and she seemed in pain. Barrett talked with her considerably and once when I caught sight of his face, it was devilish with some black passion I did not recognize. Although I felt sure the girl was now all right for the night, there was something about this meeting I didn't like; so I lay around until just daylight when Jackson and Lige Smith came through the bush as pre-arranged should I not return to Jake's.

It was not long before Elizabeth and Tom came out again and entered a thick little bush behind the shanty. Lige lifted the axe off the woodpile with a knowing look, and we all three followed silently. I was surprised to find it a well beaten and equally well concealed trail. All my suspicions returned. I knew now that Barrett was a bad lot all round, and as soon as I had quit using him and his coat, I made up my mind to rid my quarters of him; fortunately I knew enough about him to use that knowledge as a whip-lash.

We followed them for something over a mile, when—heaven and hell! The trail opened abruptly on the clearing where lay my recently acquired cordwood with my five barrels of whiskey concealed in its midst.

The girl strode forward, and with the strength of a man, pitched down a dozen sticks with lightning speed.

"There!" she cried, turning to Tom. "There you find him— you find him whiskey. You say you spill. No more my father he's drunk all day, he beat my mother."

I stepped out.

"So, Tom Barrett," I said, "you've played the d——d sneak and hunted it out!"

He fairly jumped at the sound of my voice; then he got white as paper, and then—something came into his face that I never saw before. It was a look like his father's, the old missionary.

"Yes, McLeod," he answered. "And I've hunted *you* out. It's cost me the loss of a whole term at college and a considerable amount of self-respect, but I've got my finger on you now!"

The whole infernal trick burst right in on my intelligence. If I had had a revolver, he would have been a dead man; but border traders nowadays are not desperadoes with bowie knives and hip pockets—

"You surely don't mean to split on me?" I asked.

"I surely don't mean to do anything else," he cheeked back.

"Then, Tom Barrett," I sputtered, raging, "you're the dirtiest cad and the foulest liar that ever drew the breath of life."

"I dare say I am," he said smoothly. Then with rising anger he advanced, peering into my face with his foxy eyes. "And I'll tell you right here, Dan McLeod, I'd be a hundred times a cad, and a thousand times a liar to save the souls and bodies of our Indians from going to hell, through your cursed whiskey."

I have always been a brave man, but I confess I felt childishly scared before the wild, mesmeric power of his eyes. I was unable to move a finger, but I blurted out boastfully: "If it wasn't for your preacher's hat and coat I'd send your sneaking soul to Kingdom Come, right here!"

Instantly he hauled off his coat and tie and stood with clenched fists while his strange eyes fairly spat green fire.

"Now," he fumed, "I've discarded my cloth, Dan McLeod. You've got to deal with a man now, not with a minister."

To save my immortal soul I can't tell why I couldn't stir. I only know that everything seemed to drop out of sight except his two little blazing eyes. I stood like a fool, queered, dead queered right through.

He turned politely to the girl. "You may go, Elizabeth," he said, "and thank you for your assistance." The girl turned and went up the trail without a word.

With the agility of a cat he sprang on to the wood-pile, pitched off enough cordwood to expose my entire "cellar"; then going across to Lige, he coolly took the axe out of his hand. His face was white and set, but his voice was natural enough as he said:

"Now, gentlemen, whoever cares to interrupt me will get the blade of this axe buried in his brain, as heaven is my witness."

I didn't even curse as he split the five barrels into slivers and my well-fought-for whiskey soaked into the slush. Once he lifted his head and looked at me, and the mouth I didn't understand revealed itself; there was something about it like a young Napoleon's.

I never hated a man in my life as I hated Tom Barrett then. That I daren't resist him made it worse. I watched him finish his caddish job, throw down the axe, take his coat over his arm, and leave the clearing without a word.

But no sooner was he out of sight than my devilish temper broke out, and I cursed and blasphemed for half an hour. I'd have his blood if it cost my neck a rope, and that too before he could inform on us. The boys were with me, of course, poor sort of dogs with no grit of their own, and with the axe as my only weapon we left the bush and ran towards the river.

I fairly yelled at my good luck as I reached the high bank. There, a few rods down shore, beside the open water sat Tom Barrett, calling something out to his folks across the river, and from upstream came the deafening thunder of the Onondaga Jam that, loosened by the rain, was shouldering its terrific force downwards with the strength of a million drunken demons.

We had him like a rat in a trap, but his foxy eyes had seen us. He sprang to his feet, hesitated for a fraction of a moment, saw the murder in our faces, then did what any man but a fool would have done—ran.

We were hot on his heels. Fifty yards distant an old dug-out lay hauled up. He ran it down into the water, stared wildly at the oncoming jam, then at us, sprang into the canoe and grabbed the paddle.

I was murderously mad. I wheeled the axe above my shoulder and let fly at him. It missed his head by three inches.

He was paddling for dear life now, and, our last chance gone, we stood riveted to the spot, watching him. On the bluff across the river stood his half-blood mother, the raw March wind whipping her skirts about her knees; but her strained, ashen face showed she never felt its chill. Below with his feet almost in the rapidly rising water, stood the old missionary, his scant grey hair blowing across his eyes that seemed to look out into eternity—amid stream Tom, paddling with the desperation of death, his head turning every second with the alertness of an animal to gauge the approaching ice-shove.

Even I wished him life then. Twice I thought him caught in the crush, but he was out of it like an arrow, and in another moment he had leapt ashore while above the roar of the grinding jam I heard him cry out with a strange exultation:

"Father, I've succeeded. I have had to be a scoundrel and a cad, but I've trapped them at last!"

He staggered forward then, sobbing like a child, and the old man's arms closed round him, just as two heavy jaws of ice snatched the dug-out, hurled it off shore and splintered it to atoms.

Well! I had made a bad blunder, which I attempted to rectify by reaching Buffalo that night; but Tom Barrett had won the game. I was arrested at Fort Erie, handcuffed, jailed, tried, convicted of attempted assault and illicit whiskey-trading on the Grand River Indian Reserve—and spent the next five years in Kingston Penitentiary, the guest of Her Most Gracious Majesty Queen Victoria.

14. "A Pagan in Saint Paul's Cathedral" (1906)

Iroquois Poetess' Impressions in London's Cathedral

[Johnson compares the scene of Christian devotion in the cathedral to the religious rituals of the Iroquois people, arguing that each method of worship is as valid as the other. The story first appeared in the London *Daily Express* on 3 August 1906 and included this note: "The visit of the three Red Indian chiefs to London gives the following article by Tekahionwake, the Iroquois poetess, an additional topical interest." The note refers to Chiefs

Joe Capilano (Squamish), Charley Isipaymilt (Cowichan), and Basil David (Shuswap / Secwepemc), in London to discuss land questions with King Edward VII.]

It is a far cry from a wigwam to Westminster, from a prairie trail to the Tower Bridge, and London looks a strange place to the Red Indian whose eyes still see the myriad forest trees, even as they gaze across the Strand, and whose feet still feel the clinging moccasin even among the scores of clicking heels that hurry along the thoroughfares of this camping-ground of the paleface.[1]

So this is the place where dwells the Great White Father, ruler of many lands, lodges, and tribes, in the hollow of whose hands is the peace that rests between the once hostile red man and white. They call him the King of England, but to us, the powerful Iroquois nation of the north, he is always the "Great White Father." For once he came to us in our far-off Canadian reserves, and with his own hand fastened decorations and medals on the buckskin coats of our oldest chiefs, just because they and their fathers used their tomahawks in battle in the cause of England.

So I, one of his loyal allies, have come to see his camp, known to the white man as London, his council which the whites call his Parliament, where his sachems and chiefs make the laws of his tribes, and to see his wigwam, known to the palefaces as Buckingham Palace, but to the red man as the "Tepee of the Great White Father." And this is what I see:—

WHAT THE INDIAN SEES

Lifting toward the sky are vast buildings of stone, not the same kind of stone from which my forefathers fashioned their carven pipes and corn-pounders, but a grayer, grimier rock that would not take the polish we give by fingers dipped in sturgeon oil, and long days of friction with fine sand and deer-hide.

I stand outside the great palace wigwam, the huge council-house by the river. My seeing eyes may mark them, but my heart's eyes are looking beyond all this wonderment, back to

---

1 Westminster is an area of London that contains many landmarks, including Buckingham Palace and the Palace of Westminster, where Parliament meets. The Strand is the City of Westminster's major thoroughfare. Tower Bridge crosses the Thames near the Tower of London, another historic castle.

the land I have left behind me. I picture the tepees by the far Saskatchewan; there the tent poles, too, are lifting skyward, and the smoke ascending through them from the smouldering fires within curls softly on the summer air. Against the blurred sweep of horizon other camps etch their outlines, other bands of red men with their herds of wild cattle have sought the river lands. I hear the untamed hoofs thundering up the prairie trail.

But the prairie sounds are slipping away, and my ears catch other voices that rise above the ceaseless throb about me—voices that are clear, high, and calling; they float across the city like the music of a thousand birds of passage beating their wings through the night, crying and murmuring plaintively as they journey northward. They are the voices of St. Paul's[1] calling, calling me—St. Paul's where the paleface worships the Great Spirit, and through whose portals he hopes to reach the happy hunting grounds.

THE GREAT SPIRIT

As I entered its doorways it seemed to me to be the everlasting abiding-place of the white man's Great Spirit.

The music brooded everywhere. It beat in my ears like the far-off cadences of the Sault Ste. Marie rapids, that rise and leap and throb—like a storm hurling through the fir forest—like the distant rising of an Indian war-song; it swept up those mighty archways until the gray dome above me faded, and in its place the stars came out to look down, not on these paleface kneeling worshippers, but on a band of stalwart, sinewy, copper-coloured devotees, my own people in my own land, who also assembled to do honour to the Manitou of all nations.[2]

The deep-throated organ and the boy's voices were gone; I heard instead the melancholy incantations of our own pagan religionists. The beautiful dignity of our great sacrificial rites seemed to settle about me, to enwrap me in its garment of solemnity and primitive stateliness.

---

1 St. Paul's Cathedral is the seat of the Anglican Bishop of London, designed by Sir Christopher Wren and built after the Great Fire of London destroyed its predecessor in 1666.
2 "Manitou" means "life force" or "spirit" in the Algonquian languages such as Cree and Ojibwe.

BEAT OF THE DRUM

The atmosphere pulsed with the beat of the Indian drum, the eerie penetrations of the turtle rattle that set the time of the dancers' feet. Dance? It is not a dance, that marvellously slow, serpentine-like figure with the soft swish, swish of moccasined feet, and the faint jingling of elks'-teeth bracelets, keeping rhythm with every footfall. It is not a dance, but an invocation of motion. Why may we not worship with the graceful movement of our feet?[1] The paleface worships by moving his lips and tongue; the difference is but slight.

The altar-lights of St. Paul's glowed for me no more. In their place flared the camp fires of the Onondaga "long-house," and the resinous scent of the burning pine drifted across the fetid London air. I saw the tall, copper-skinned fire-keeper of the Iroquois council enter, the circle of light flung fitfully against the black surrounding woods. I have seen their white bishops, but none so regal, so august as he. His garb of fringed buckskin and ermine was no more grotesque than the vestments worn by the white preachers in high places; he did not carry a book or a shining golden symbol, but from his splendid shoulders was suspended a pure white lifeless dog.

Into the red flame the strong hands gently lowered it, scores of reverent, blanketed figures stood silent, awed, for it is the highest, holiest festival of the year. Then the wild, strange chant arose—the great pagan ritual was being intoned by the fire-keeper, his weird, monotonous tones voicing this formula:

"The Great Spirit desires no human sacrifice, but we, His children, must give to Him that which is nearest our hearts and nearest our lives. Only the spotless and stainless can enter into His presence, only that which is purified by fire. So—this white dog—a member of our household, a co-habitant of our wigwam, and on the smoke that arises from the purging fires will arise also the thanksgivings of all those who desire that the Great Spirit in His happy hunting grounds will forever smoke His pipe of peace, for peace is between Him and His children for all time."[2]

---

1 Many ceremonies were banned between 1885 and 1951.
2 Johnson is describing the traditional White Dog ceremony. In her *Memoirs*, Evelyn H.C. Johnson recounts being taken to see this ceremony when she was a child. It is still performed as part of the midwinter rites, although a basket covered with ribbons has replaced the dog.

The mournful voice ceases. Again the hollow pulsing of the Indian drum, the purring, flexible step of cushioned feet. I lift my head, which has been bowed on the chair before me. It is St. Paul's after all—and the clear boy-voices rise above the rich echoes of the organ.

15. "We-hro's Sacrifice" (1907)

[An Onondaga boy sacrifices his pet so that his community can carry out its yearly ceremony. The story was first published in *Boys' World* on 19 January 1907.]

We-hro was a small Onondaga Indian boy, a good-looking, black-eyed little chap with as pagan a heart as ever beat under a copper-colored skin. His father and grandfathers were pagans. His ancestors for a thousand years back, and yet a thousand years back of that, had been pagans, and We-hro, with the pride of his religion and his race, would not have turned from the faith of his fathers for all the world. But the world, as he knew it, consisted entirely of the Great Indian Reserve, that lay on the banks of the beautiful Grand River, sixty miles west of the great Canadian city of Toronto.

Now, the boys that read this tale must not confuse a pagan with a heathen. The heathen nations that worship idols are terribly pitied and despised by the pagan Indians, who are worshippers of "The Great Spirit," a kind and loving God, who, they say, will reward them by giving them happy hunting grounds to live in after they die; that is, if they live good, honest, upright lives in this world.

We-hro would have scowled blackly if anyone had dared to name him a heathen. He thoroughly ignored the little Delaware boys, whose fathers worshipped idols fifty years ago, and on all the feast days and dance days he would accompany his parents to the "Longhouse" (which was their church), and take his little part in the religious festivities. He could remember well as a tiny child being carried in his mother's blanket "pick-a-back," while she dropped into the soft swinging movement of the dance, for We-hro's people did not worship their "Great Spirit" with hymns of praise and lowly prayers, the way the Christian Indians did. We-hro's people worshipped their God by dancing beautiful, soft, dignified steps, with no noisy clicking heels to annoy one, but only the velvety shuffle of the moccasined feet, the weird beat of the Indian drums, the mournful chanting of the old chiefs, keeping time with the throb of their devoted hearts.

Then, when he grew too big to be carried, he was allowed to clasp his mother's hand, and himself learn the pretty steps, following his father, who danced ahead, dressed in full costume of scarlet cloth and buckskin, with gay beads and bear claws about his neck, and wonderful carven silver ornaments, massive and solid, decorating his shirt and leggings. We-hro loved the tawny fringes and the hammered silver quite as much as a white lady loves diamonds and pearls; he loved to see his father's face painted in fierce reds, yellows and blacks, but most of all he loved the unvarying chuck-a, chuck-a, chuck-a of the great mud-turtle rattles that the "musicians" skilfully beat upon the benches before them. Oh, he was a thorough little pagan, was We-hro! His loves and his hates were as decided as his comical but stately step in the dance of his ancestors' religion. Those were great days for the small Onondaga boy. His father taught him to shape axe-handles, to curve lacrosse sticks, to weave their deer-sinew netting, to tan skins, to plant corn, to model arrows and—most difficult of all—to "feather" them, to "season" bows, to chop trees, to burn, hollow, fashion and "man" a dugout canoe, to use the paddle, to gauge the wind and current of that treacherous Grand River, to learn wild cries to decoy bird and beast for food. Oh, little pagan We-hro had his life filled to overflowing with much that the civilized white boy would give all his dimes and dollars to know. And it was then that the great day came, the marvellous day when We-hro discovered his second self, his playmate, his loyal, unselfish, loving friend—his underbred, unwashed, hungry, vagabond dog, born white and spotless, but begrimed by contact with the world, the mud, and the white man's hovel.

It happened this way:

We-hro was cleaning his father's dugout canoe, after a night of fish spearing. The soot, the scales, the fire ashes, the mud—all had to be "swabbed" out at the river's brink by means of much water and an Indian "slat" broom. We-hro was up to his little ears in work, when suddenly, above him, on the river road, he heard the coarse voice and thundering whipfalls of a man urging and beating his horse—a white man, for no Indian used such language, no Indian beat an animal that served him. We-hro looked up. Stuck in the mud of the river road was a huge wagon, grain-filled. The driver, purple of face, was whaling the poor team, and shouting to a cringing little drab-white dog, of fox-terrier lineage, to "Get out of there or I'll—!" The horses were dragging and tugging. The little dog, terrified, was sneaking off with tail between its hind legs. Then the brutal driver's whip came down, curling its lash about the dog's thin body, forcing from the little speechless brute a howl of agony. Then We-hro spoke—spoke in all the English he knew.

"Bad! bad! You die some day—you! You hurt that dog. White man's God, he no like you. Indian's Great Spirit, he not let you shoot in happy hunting grounds. You die some day—you *bad!*"

"Well, if I *am* bad I'm no pagan Indian Hottentot like you!"[1] yelled the angry driver. "Take the dog, and begone!"

"Me no Hottentot," said We-hro, slowly. "Me Onondaga, all right. Me take dog"; and from that hour the poor little white cur and the copper-colored little boy were friends for all time.

★ ★ ★ ★ ★

The Superintendent of Indian Affairs was taking his periodical drive about the Reserve when he chanced to meet old "Ten-Canoes," We-hro's father. The superintendent was a very important person. He was a great white gentleman, who lived in the city of Brantford, fifteen miles away. He was a kindly, handsome man, who loved and honored every Indian on the Grand River Reserve. He had a genial smile, a warm handshake, so when he stopped his horse and greeted the old pagan, Ten-Canoes smiled too.

"Ah, Ten-Canoes!" cried the superintendent, "a great man told me he was coming to see your people—a big man, none less than Great Black-Coat, the bishop of the Anglican Church. He thinks you are a bad lot, because you are pagans; he wonders why it is that you have never turned Christian. Some of the missionaries have told him you pagans are no good, so the great man wants to come and see for himself. He wants to see some of your religious dances—the 'Dance of the White Dog,' if you will have him; he wants to see if it is really *bad.*"

---

1 Hottentot, a derogatory name the Dutch gave to the Khoikhoi people of southern Africa, was borrowed into English.

Ten-Canoes laughed. "I welcome him," he said, earnestly, "Welcome the 'Great Black-Coat.' I honor him, though I do not think as he does. He is a good man, a just man; I welcome him, bid him come."

Thus was his lordship, the Bishop, invited to see the great pagan Onondaga "Festival of the White Dog."

But what was *this* that happened?

Never yet had a February moon waned but that the powerful Onondaga tribe had offered the burnt "Sacrifice of the White Dog," that most devout of all native rites. But now, search as they might, not a single spotlessly white dog could be found. No other animal would do. It was the law of this great Indian tribe that no other burnt sacrifice could possibly be offered than the strangled body of a white dog.

We-hro heard all the great chiefs talking of it all. He listened to plans for searching the entire Reserve for a dog, and the following morning he arose at dawn, took his own pet dog down to the river and washed him as he had seen white men wash their sheep. Then out of the water dashed the gay little animal, yelping and barking in play, rolling in the snow, tearing madly about, and finally rushing off towards the log house which was We-hro's home and scratching at the door to get in by the warm fire to dry his shaggy coat. Oh! what an ache that coat caused in We-hro's heart. From a dull drab grey, the dog's hair had washed pure white, not a spot or a blemish on it, and in an agony of grief the little pagan boy realized that through his own action he had endangered the life of his dog friend; that should his father and his father's friends see that small white terrier, they would take it away for the nation's sacrifice.

Stumbling and panting and breathless, We-hro hurried after his pet, and, seizing the dog in his arms, he wrapped his own shabby coat about the trembling, half-dry creature, and carried him to where the cedars grew thick at the back of the house. Crouched in their shadows he hugged his treasured companion, thinking with horror of the hour when the blow would surely fall.

For days the boy kept his dog in the shelter of the cedars, tied up tightly with an old rope, and sleeping in a warm raccoon skin, which We-hro smuggled away from his own simple bed. The dog contented himself with what little food We-hro managed to carry to him, but the hiding could not keep up forever, and one dark, dreaded day We-hro's father came into the house and sat smoking in silence for many minutes. When at last he spoke, he said:

"We-hro, your dog is known to me. I have seen him, white as the snow that fell last night. It is the law that someone must always suffer for the good of the people. We-hro, would you have the great 'Black-Coat,' the great white preacher, come to see our beautiful ceremony, and would you have the great Onondaga tribe fail to show the white man how we worship our ancient Great Spirit? Would you have us fail to burn the sacrifice? Or will you give your white dog for the honor of our people?"

The world is full of heroes, but at that moment it held none greater than the little pagan boy, who crushed down his grief and battled back his tears as he answered:

"Father, you are old and honored and wise. For you and for my people alone would I give the dog."

At last the wonderful Dance Day arrived. His lordship, the Bishop of the Anglican Church, drove down from the city of Brantford; with him the Superintendent of Indian Affairs, and a man who understood both the English and the Onondaga languages. Long before they reached the "Longhouse" they could hear the wild beat of the drum, could count the beats of the dance rattles, could distinguish the half-sad chant of the worshippers. The kind face of the great bishop was very grave. It pained his gentle old heart to know that this great tribe of Indians were pagans—savages, as he thought—but when he entered that plain log building that the Onondagas held as their church, he took off his hat with the beautiful reverence all great men pay to other great men's religion, and he stood bareheaded while old Ten-Canoes chanted forth this speech:

"Oh, brothers of mine! We welcome the white man's friend, the great 'Black-Coat,' to this, our solemn worship. We offer to the red man's God—the Great Spirit—a burnt offering. We do not think that anything save what is pure and faithful and without blemish can go into the sight of the Great Spirit. Therefore do we offer this dog, pure as we hope our spirits are, that the God of the red man may accept it with our devotion, knowing that we, too, would gladly be as spotless as this sacrifice."

Then was a dog carried in dead, and beautifully decorated with wampum, beads and porcupine embroidery. Oh! so mercifully dead and out of pain, gently strangled by reverent fingers, for an Indian is never unkind to an animal. And far over in a corner of the room was a little brown figure, twisted with agony, choking back the sobs and tears—for was he not taught that tears were for babies alone, and not for boys that grew up into warriors?

"Oh, my dog! my dog!" he muttered. "They have taken you away from me, but it was for the honor of my father and of my own people."

The great Anglican bishop turned at that moment, and, catching the sight of suffering on little We-hro's face, said aloud to the man who spoke both languages:

"That little boy over there seems in torture. Can I do anything for him, do you think?"

"That little boy," replied the man who spoke both languages, "is the son of the great Onondaga chief. No white dog could be found for this ceremony but his. This dog was his pet, but for the honor of his father and of his tribe he has given up his pet as a sacrifice."

For a moment the great Anglican bishop was blinded by his own tears. Then he walked slowly across the wide log building and laid his white hand tenderly on the head of the little Onondaga boy. His kindly old eyes closed, and his lips moved—noiselessly, for a space, then he said aloud:

"Oh, that the white boys of my great city church knew and practiced half as much of self-denial as has this little pagan Indian lad, who has given up his heart's dearest because his father and the honor of his people required it."

16. "The Happy Hunting Grounds" (1889)

Into the rose gold westland, its yellow prairies roll,
World of the bison's freedom, home of the Indian's soul.
Roll out, O seas! in sunlight bathed,
Your plains wind-tossed, and grass enswathed.

Farther than vision ranges, farther than eagles fly,
Stretches the land of beauty, arches the perfect sky,
Hemm'd through the purple mists afar
By peaks that gleam like star on star.

Fringing the prairie billows, fretting horizon's line,
Darkly green are slumb'ring wildernesses of pine,
Sleeping until the zephyrs throng
To kiss their silence into song.

Whispers freighted with odour swinging into the air,
Russet needles as censers swing to an altar, where
The angels' songs are less divine
Than duo sung twixt breeze and pine.

Laughing into the forest, dimples a mountain stream,
Pure as the airs above it, soft as a summer dream,
O! Lethean[1] spring thou'rt only found
In this ideal hunting ground.

Surely the great Hereafter cannot be more than this,
Surely we'll see that country after Time's farewell kiss.
Who would his lovely faith condole?
Who envies not the Red-skin's soul,

Sailing into the cloud land, sailing into the sun,
Into the crimson portals ajar when life is done?
O! dear dead race, my spirit too
Would fain sail westward unto you.

---

1 In classical Greek mythology, Lethe was the river of forgetfulness, one of the five rivers of Hades.

II. THE PLAINS AND THE SECOND RIEL RESISTANCE

II. *The Plains and the Second Riel Resistance*

[Johnson and her family keenly followed events on the Plains during the second Riel Resistance; her brother Beverly "relinquished his family's traditional support for the Conservative party when John A. Macdonald's government brutally suppressed the starving prairie tribes during the Northwest Rebellions of 1885" (Strong-Boag and Gerson 52). Like all Canadians in the east, Johnson was dependent for the most part on extremely biased newspaper reports for her impressions of Riel and accounts of events. Her sympathy for Riel was limited, but in "A Cry from an Indian Wife," she shares the widespread assumption, now questioned, that Poundmaker / Pîhtokahanapiwiyin and Big Bear / Mistahimuskwa were allied with the Métis. They were both convicted of treason in trials that have been described as travesties of justice. Recent histories take into account both the breaking of treaties by the government and the fearful reaction of settlers and officials who had been primed to fight by constant talk of an "Indian war."]

1. "A Cry from an Indian Wife" (1895)

[Johnson revised the poem to enhance its effect between its first publication in *The Week* in 1885 and its publication in *The White Wampum* in 1895 (Gerson and Strong-Boag 292). The first version did not include the last four lines as in the version below, skipping the dramatic assertion "By right, by birth, we Indians own these lands!", instead going from "win the glories of the war" to these lines:

> O! heart o'erfraught—O! nation lying low—
> God, and fair Canada have willed it so.]

My forest brave, my Red-skin love, farewell;
We may not meet to-morrow; who can tell
What mighty ills befall our little band,
Or what you'll suffer from the white man's hand?
Here is your knife! I thought 'twas sheathed for aye.
No roaming bison calls for it to-day;

No hide of prairie cattle will it maim;
The plains are bare, it seeks a nobler game:
'Twill drink the life-blood of a soldier host.
Go; rise and strike, no matter what the cost.
Yet stay. Revolt not at the Union Jack,
Nor raise Thy hand against this stripling pack
Of white-faced warriors, marching West to quell
Our fallen tribe that rises to rebel.
They all are young and beautiful and good;
Curse to the war that drinks their harmless blood.
Curse to the fate that brought them from the East
To be our chiefs—to make our nation least
That breathes the air of this vast continent.
Still their new rule and council is well meant.
They but forget we Indians owned the land
From ocean unto ocean; that they stand
Upon a soil that centuries agone
Was our sole kingdom and our right alone.
They never think how they would feel to-day,
If some great nation came from far away,
Wresting their country from their hapless braves,
Giving what they gave us—but wars and graves.
Then go and strike for liberty and life,
And bring back honour to your Indian wife.
Your wife? Ah, what of that, who cares for me?
Who pities my poor love and agony?
What white-robed priest prays for your safety here,
As prayer is said for every volunteer
That swells the ranks that Canada sends out?
Who prays for vict'ry for the Indian scout?
Who prays for our poor nation lying low?
None—therefore take your tomahawk and go.
My heart may break and burn into its core,
But I am strong to bid you go to war.
Yet stay, my heart is not the only one
That grieves the loss of husband and of son;
Think of the mothers o'er the inland seas;
Think of the pale-faced maiden on her knees;
One pleads her God to guard some sweet-faced child
That marches on toward the North-West wild.
The other prays to shield her love from harm,
To strengthen his young, proud uplifted arm.
Ah, how her white face quivers thus to think,

Your tomahawk his life's best blood will drink.
She never thinks of my wild aching breast,
Nor prays for your dark face and eagle crest
Endangered by a thousand rifle balls,
My heart the target if my warrior falls.
O! coward self I hesitate no more;
Go forth, and win the glories of the war.
Go forth, nor bend to greed of white men's hands,
By right, by birth we Indians own these lands,
Though starved, crushed, plundered, lies our nation low...
Perhaps the white man's God has willed it so.

2. "Wolverine" (1893)

"Yes, sir, it's quite a story, though you won't believe it's true,
But such things happened often when I lived beyond the Soo."[1]
And the trapper tilted back his chair and filled his pipe anew.

"I ain't thought of it neither fer this many 'n many a day,
Although it used to haunt me in the years that's slid away,
The years I spent a-trappin' for the good old Hudson's Bay.

"Wild? You bet, 'twas wild then, an' few an' far between
The squatters' shacks, for whites was scarce as furs when things is
    green,
An' only reds an' 'Hudson's' men was all the folk I seen.

"No. Them old Indyans ain't so bad, not if you treat 'em square.
Why, I lived in amongst 'em all the winters I was there,
An' I never lost a copper, an' I never lost a hair.

"But I'd have lost my life the time that you've heard tell about;
I don't think I'd be settin' here, but dead beyond a doubt,
If that there Indyan 'Wolverine' jest hadn't helped me out.

"'Twas freshet time, 'way back, as long as sixty-six or eight,
An' I was comin' to the Post that year a kind of late,
For beaver had been plentiful, and trappin' had been great.

---

1 Sault Ste. Marie is nicknamed "the Soo," a mispronunciation of the
   French word "Sault" (pronounced "so").

"One day I had been settin' traps along a bit of wood,
An' night was catchin' up to me jest faster 'an it should,
When all at once I heard a sound that curdled up my blood.

"It was the howl of famished wolves—I didn't stop to think
But jest lit out across for home as quick as you could wink,
But when I reached the river's edge I brought up at the brink.

"That mornin' I had crossed the stream straight on a sheet of ice
An' now, God help me! There it was, churned up an' cracked to dice,
The flood went boiling past—I stood like one shut in a vice.

"No way ahead, no path aback, trapped like a rat ashore,
With naught but death to follow, and with naught but death afore;
The howl of hungry wolves aback—ahead, the torrent's roar.

"An' then—a voice, an Indyan voice, that called out clear and clean,
'Take Indyan's horse, I run like deer, wolf can't catch Wolverine.'
I says, 'Thank Heaven.' There stood the chief I'd nicknamed Wolverine.

"I leapt on that there horse, an' then jest like a coward fled,
An' left that Indyan standin' there alone, as good as dead,
With the wolves a-howlin' at his back, the swollen stream ahead.

"I don't know how them Indyans dodge from death the way they do,
You won't believe it, sir, but what I'm tellin' you is true,
But that there chap was 'round next day as sound as me or you.

"He came to get his horse, but not a cent he'd take from me.
Yes, sir, you're right, the Indyans now ain't like they used to be;
We've got 'em sharpened up a bit an' *now* they'll take a fee.

"No, sir, you're wrong, they ain't no 'dogs.' I'm not through tellin' yet;
You'll take that name right back again, or else jest out you get!
You'll take that name right back when you hear all this yarn, I bet.

"It happened that same autumn, when some Whites was comin' in,
I heard the old Red River carts a-kickin' up a din,
So I went over to their camp to see an English skin.

"They said, 'They'd had an awful scare from Injuns,' an' they swore
That savages had come around the very night before
A-brandishing their tomahawks an' painted up for war.

"But when their plucky Englishmen had put a bit of lead
Right through the heart of one of them, an' rolled him over, dead,
The other cowards said that they had come in peace instead.

"That they (the Whites) had lost some stores, from off their little pack,
An' that the Red they peppered dead had followed up their track,
Because he'd found the packages an' came to *give them back.*

"'Oh!' they said, 'they were quite sorry, but it wasn't like as if
They had killed a decent Whiteman by mistake or in a tiff,
It was only some old Injun dog that lay there stark an' stiff.'

"I said, 'You are the meanest dogs that ever yet I seen,'
Then I rolled the body over as it lay out on the green;
I peered into the face—My God! 'twas poor old Wolverine."

3. "Silhouette" (1894)

[In this and the next poems, Johnson recounts the starvation on the plains caused by the near-extinction of the buffalo. The Canadian government used the desperation of the plains nations to enact the numbered treaties; government officials did not provide promised food, leading to the Frog Lake Massacre in 1885, where the refusal of an Indian agent to release food led to the killing of nine settlers before Big Bear could intervene. Poundmaker's advance on Battleford, seen as an attack, was an attempt to ask for access to the food stored in the fort. Debate still continues over the extent to which these leaders saw themselves as part of Louis Riel's second resistance.]

The sky-line melts from russet into blue,
Unbroken the horizon, saving where
A wreath of smoke curls up the far, thin air,
And points the distant lodges of the Sioux.

Etched where the lands and cloudlands touch and die
A solitary Indian tepee stands,
The only habitation of these lands,
That roll their magnitude from sky to sky.

The tent poles lift and loom in thin relief,
The upward floating smoke ascends between,
And near the open doorway, gaunt and lean,
And shadow-like, there stands an Indian Chief.

With eyes that lost their lustre long ago,
With visage fixed and stern as fate's decree,
He looks towards the empty west, to see
The never-coming herd of buffalo.

Only the bones that bleach upon the plains,
Only the fleshless skeletons that lie
In ghastly nakedness and silence, cry
Out mutely that naught else to him remains.

4. "The Cattle Thief" (1894)

They were coming across the prairie, they were galloping hard
    and fast;
For the eyes of those desperate riders had sighted their man at last—
Sighted him off to Eastward, where the Cree encampment lay,
Where the cotton woods fringed the river, miles and miles away.
Mistake him? Never! Mistake him? the famous Eagle Chief!
That terror to all the settlers, that desperate Cattle Thief—
That monstrous, fearless Indian, who lorded it over the plain,
Who thieved and raided, and scouted, who rode like a hurricane!
But they've tracked him across the prairie; they've followed him
    hard and fast;
For those desperate English settlers have sighted their man at last.

Up they wheeled to the tepees, all their British blood aflame,
Bent on bullets and bloodshed, bent on bringing down their game;
But they searched in vain for the Cattle Thief: that lion had left his lair,
And they cursed like a troop of demons—for the women alone
    were there.
"The sneaking Indian coward," they hissed; "he hides while yet he can;
He'll come in the night for cattle, but he's scared to face a *man*."
"Never!" and up from the cotton woods rang the voice of Eagle Chief;
And right out into the open stepped, unarmed, the Cattle Thief.
Was that the game they had coveted? Scarce fifty years had rolled
Over that fleshless, hungry frame, starved to the bone and old;
Over that wrinkled, tawny skin, unfed by the warmth of blood.
Over those hungry, hollow eyes that glared for the sight of food.

He turned, like a hunted lion: "I know not fear," said he;
And the words outleapt from his shrunken lips in the language of
    the Cree.
"I'll fight you, white-skins, one by one, till I kill you all," he said;

But the threat was scarcely uttered, ere a dozen balls of lead
Whizzed through the air about him like a shower of metal rain,
And the gaunt old Indian Cattle Thief dropped dead on the open
  plain.
And that band of cursing settlers gave one triumphant yell,
And rushed like a pack of demons on the body that writhed and fell.
"Cut the fiend up into inches, throw his carcass on the plain;
Let the wolves eat the cursed Indian, he'd have treated us the
  same."
A dozen hands responded, a dozen knives gleamed high,
But the first stroke was arrested by a woman's strange, wild cry.
And out into the open, with a courage past belief,
She dashed, and spread her blanket o'er the corpse of the Cattle Thief;
And the words outleapt from her shrunken lips in the language
  of the Cree,
"If you mean to touch that body, you must cut your way through *me*."
And that band of cursing settlers dropped backward one by one,
For they knew that an Indian woman roused, was a woman to let
  alone.
And then she raved in a frenzy that they scarcely understood,
Raved of the wrongs she had suffered since her earliest babyhood:
"Stand back, stand back, you white-skins, touch that dead man
  to your shame;
You have stolen my father's spirit, but his body I only claim.
You have killed him, but you shall not dare to touch him now he's
  dead.
You have cursed, and called him a Cattle Thief, though you
  robbed him first of bread—
Robbed him and robbed my people—look there, at that shrunk-
  en face,
Starved with a hollow hunger, we owe to you and your race.
What have you left to us of land, what have you left of game,
What have you brought but evil, and curses since you came?
How have you paid us for our game? how paid us for our land?
By a *book*, to save our souls from the sins you brought in your other
  hand.
Go back with your new religion, we never have understood
Your robbing an Indian's *body*, and mocking his *soul* with food.
Go back with your new religion, and find—if find you can—
The *honest* man you have ever made from out a *starving* man.
You say your cattle are not ours, your meat is not our meat;
When *you* pay for the land you live in, *we'll* pay for the meat we eat.
Give back our land and our country, give back our herds of game;

Give back the furs and the forests that were ours before you
  came;
Give back the peace and the plenty. Then come with your new
  belief,
And blame, if you dare, the hunger that *drove* him to be a thief."

5. "A Request" (1886)

[Author's note: To the noble society known as "The Woman's
Auxiliary of Missions of the Church of England in Canada,"—who are doing their utmost in the good work of sending
Missionaries to the Crees and Blackfeet—the following lines are
respectfully and gratefully inscribed.]

Beyond the boundaries of all our mighty inland lakes,
Beyond the old Red River shore, where Manitoba breaks
Into the far and fair North-west its limitless extent,
Last year with cannon, shot, and shell the British soldier went.
Full many a city flocked to bid her gallant boys good-bye,
Cheer after cheer went ringing out, and flags were flaunted high;
And well indeed those warriors fought, and surely well they bled,
And surely well some sleep to-day within their silent bed.
Perhaps a soldier's medals are of greater honour when
He wins them at the cost of his own fellow-countrymen—
'Tis not my place to question if their laurel wreath still thrives,
If its fragrance is of Indian blood, its glory Indian lives.
I only know some heart still waits with pulse that beats and burns
For footsteps of the boy who left but nevermore returns,
Another heart still dwells beyond thy banks, Saskatchewan—
O Indian mother, list'ning for the coming of your son
Who left his home a year ago to fight the Volunteers,
To meet his death from British guns, his death-song British cheers.
For you I speak to-day, and ask some noble, faithful hands,
To send another band of men to meet you in your lands.
Not as last year these gallant hearts as dogs of war will go,
No swords within their hands, no cause to bring the after-glow
Of blush to Canada's fair cheek, for none can say as then:
"She treats her Indian wards as foes." No! These are different men,
Their strength is not in rank and file, no martial host they lead,
Their mission is the cross of Christ, their arms the Christian creed.
Instead of helmet round their head, a halo shines afar,
'Twill light your prairie pathway up more than the flash of war.
Seek not to find upon this band a coat of crimson glow—

God grant their hands will spotless be as their own robes of snow,
O men who go on missions to the North-west Indian lands,
The thorns may pierce your foreheads and the cross may bruise
  your hands,
For though the goal seems far away, reward seems vague and dim—
If ye Christianise the least of them, "Ye do it unto Him,"
And, perhaps, beyond the river brink the waves of death have
  laved,
The jewels in your crown will be the Indian souls you've saved.

6. "The Indian Corn Planter" (1897)

He needs must leave the trapping and the chase,[1]
  For mating game his arrows ne'er despoil,
And from the hunter's heaven turn his face,
  To wring some promise from the dormant soil.
He needs must leave the lodge that wintered him,
  The enervating fires, the blanket bed—
The women's dulcet voices, for the grim
  Realities of labouring for bread.
So goes he forth beneath the planter's moon
  With sack of seed that pledges large increase,
His simple pagan faith knows night and noon,
  Heat, cold, seedtime and harvest shall not cease.
And yielding to his needs, this honest sod,
  Brown as the hand that tills it, moist with rain,
Teeming with ripe fulfilment, true as God,
  With fostering richness, mothers every grain.

7. "The Haunting Thaw" (1907)

[First published in the *Canadian Magazine* in May 1907, this
story is set in the land allocated to the Hudson's Bay Company
in 1670 and sold to Canada in 1870.]

For three minutes the trader had been peering keenly at the
sky. Then his eyes lowered, sweeping the horizon with a sharp

---

1 Because of the destruction of the buffalo herds, treaties included
  farm implements and farm instructors so that the plains peoples
  could support themselves. Here Johnson describes the transition as
  possible without conversion to Christianity or the loss of Indigenous traditions.

discernment that would not admit of self-deception.

"Peter!" he called.

Peter Blackhawk came to the door, though he only came to that insistent voice when it suited him.

"Peter," repeated the trader crisply, yet with something of deference in his tone, "we can't wait another hour for Louis. He should have been here with that pack of stone-marten[1] a week ago. There is a thaw threatening and we can't wait." Then almost pleadingly: "Can we, Peter?"

"No, Mr. McKenzie. I am afraid it will be hard to make Edmonton as it is," answered the Indian.

"You have *got to* make Edmonton, or you and I will lose two thousand dollars apiece. Do you know that, Peter?"

The words *got to* lacked the tone of authority. The trader could never bully this Indian.

"Then I'll make it," acquiesced Peter, with the pleasantness born of independence. "The dogs are fit, and I have got the mink and beaver ready, and a few—"

"How many mink skins?" demanded the trader.

"Sixteen hundred."

"Not bad, not bad. They're the primest skins that ever went out of the north, and the price gone up sky-high. Not a bad pack, Peter."

The strain on the trader's face relaxed. "But we must get them to the market, or they're fur, just plain fur, not money."

The Indian scanned the horizon. "I'll start in an hour, if you say don't wait for Louis and the stone-marten."

"Then don't wait for Louis and his d——d stone-marten," jerked the trader, and turned on his heel with a curse at the threatening thaw.

Within the hour Mr. McKenzie was shaking hands with the Indian.

"Got everything, Peter?" he asked genially, now that the dog-train was really off. "Everything? Plenty of Muck-a-muck,[2] tobac, dog-fish, matches, everything?"

"Everything," said Peter Blackhawk, knotting his scarlet sash about the waist of his buffalo coat. "Plenty of everything but

---

1 The stone or beech marten is native to Europe; this is a reference to the American marten, a weasel still widely trapped for its fur in North America.

2 "Food" or "plenty to eat" in Chinook Jargon, a lingua franca spoken mainly on the Pacific coast from Alaska to northern California during the fur trade.

time." He shook his head gravely. "I'm starting too late in the season, I will have to work them too hard," he added, turning towards the dogs, which were plaintively yapping to be away, their noses raised snuffing into the wind, the chime of their saddle bells responding to every impatient twist of their wolfish bodies. Another hitch to the scarlet sash, an alert, quick glance at huskies and pack-sled, then—"Good-bye, Mr. McKenzie."

"Good-bye, Peter, my boy."

The red and the white palms met and the dog-train hit the trail.

An hour later the trader came to the door and looked out. Far against the southern horizon a black speck blurred the monotonous sweep of snows and sky. "He'll make it all right," he assured himself. "He'll beat the thaw if any one can. But, d—m him, he wouldn't have gone if he didn't want to. You can't boss those Iroquois."

Swinging into the southward trail towards the rim of civilisation, Peter Blackhawk was saying to himself, "I'll beat the thaw if any one can; but I wouldn't have come if I didn't want to. Those d——d traders can't boss an Iroquois," which only goes to show that absolute harmony existed between those two men, trader and train-dog driver though they were.

Blackhawk had come from the far east with three score of his tribesmen on the first Red River Expedition. Voyageurs they were of a rare and desirable type, hardy, energetic, lithe, indomitable, as distinct from the western tribes as the poles from the tropics. Few of them had returned with Wolseley.[1] The lure of the buffalo chase proved stronger than the call of their cradle lands. In the northern foothills they made their great camps, mixing with no other people, the exclusive, conservative habits of their forefathers still strong upon them. And young Blackhawk had grown into manhood, learned in the wisdom of the great Six Nations Indians of the east, and in the acquired craft and cult of the native-born plainsman of the west. McKenzie considered him the most valuable man, white or red, in all the Northwest Territories.

---

1 The Red River Expedition under Colonel Garnet Wolseley was sent out by Prime Minister John A. Macdonald to put down the first Riel Resistance in 1870. The United States, which had territorial designs on the west, refused permission to travel in its territory, so 1,000 men trekked through hundreds of miles of wilderness. The Iroquois were invited to join the expedition for their canoeing ability. Riel negotiated the entry of Manitoba into Confederation, but at the price of his exile to the US and the scattering of his followers. Wolseley later invited 61 Iroquois to join his expedition down the Nile to relieve Major-General Gordon at Khartoum in 1884–85.

The third night out something disturbed Blackhawk in his sleep, and his head burrowed up from his sleeping bag. It was the heavy hour before dawn. The dogs lay sleeping, exhausted by their over-mileage of the previous day. The gray-white night lay around, soundless, motionless. What had awakened Blackhawk? His tense ears seemed to acquire sight as well as hearing. Then across his senses came the nearing doom—the honk, honk of wild geese V-ing their way along the shadow trail of the night sky. He heard the rush of their wings above, then again their heralding honk as they waned into the north. They were the death-knell of winter. Blackhawk whistled to his dogs.

"Soft snow after sunrise, boys," he said aloud, after the manner of men who face the trail without human companionship. "We must travel at night after this, when sundown means hard surfaces."

The dogs stretched sulkily. They devoured their fish, while the man brewed coffee of cognac strength to fortify himself against limited sleep and increased action.

When the sun looked up above the rim of the white north, its gold was warm as well as dazzling. The snow ceased to drift under the keen night wind. The hummocks grew packed and sodden. The dogs slipped in their even trot, their feet wet and their flanks sweating. Peter put up his whip and prepared to stay until nightfall. He could not deceive himself. The snow was going and Edmonton dozens of leagues away! But with sunset the biting frost returned. The south outstretched before him, smooth, glassy, frozen hard; it was the hour of action for man and beast. Again the north became draped with an inverted crescent of silvery fringes that trembled into delicate pink, deep rose, inflammable crimson, and finally shifting into a poisonous purple, with high lights of cold, freezing cold, blue.

"God's lanterns,"[1] whispered Peter. "He must mean me to make Edmonton. I cannot miss the trail with those northern lights ablaze."

And night after night it was so, until one morning came a soft, feathery Chinook[2] wind, the first real proclamation that spring was at his heels. That day gray geese in numberless flocks fishtailed the sky. As Blackhawk passed each succeeding slough,

---

1 The aurora borealis, or northern lights.
2 Its name derived from the same Columbia River tribe whose language forms a large part of Chinook Jargon, the chinook is a strong warming wind most common in southern Alberta, where it has raised temperatures by as much as 41 degrees Celsius in a few hours.

scores of brown muskrats crouched in the sunshine on the thin ice at the doors of their humped-up houses.

That night for the first time the Indian lashed the dogs, feeling in his heart the lash of his partner's tongue. Again hanging in the north were "God's lanterns," but the invisible spirit of the coming thaw urged him on like a whip. At night he could feel its fingers clutching at the sled, balking its speed. He could see its shadowy presence ahead in the trail obstructing the course of the dogs, weighting their feet with its leaden warmth. It began to trail beside him, to mock and jeer at him, to speed neck and neck with him hour after hour. In the daytime it outstripped him, throwing up uncovered tufts of grass and black earth in the trail, so that the sled could not carry and the dogs almost bleated like sheep in their exhaustion. At night he distanced it, flying across the newly-frozen crusty snow and sloughs.

But the haunting thaw was on his track, coming nearer and nearer now even in the night time. It was tracing lines on his forehead, painting worry in his eyes. It was thinning the limbs and emptying the bellies of his dogs. It was whispering, then speaking, then shouting the word "Failure" at him. And that night a thin sickle of moon was born with its frequent change of weather. Snow fell, spongy, wet stuff. Once more the dog-train made time, and late the next afternoon, up the slush and mud of the main street in Edmonton trudged a weary-footed Indian, the sole alert thing about him being the shrewd bright eyes that snapped something of triumph to the casual greetings of acquaintances. At his heels lagged a train of four huskie dogs, cadaverous, inert, spent, their red tongues dripping, their sides palpitating, dragging the fur pack as if it were a load of lead.

But when the great fur-buyer greeted Blackhawk with a thousand questions, Peter had but four words to say, and he said them fifty times that night: "I beat the thaw."

And when the sickle moon arose, round and ripened, Peter turned his back on the southern trail, facing once more God's lanterns of the north. This time the dogs trotted free of burden, and Peter took his ease astride a cayuse[1] which had already begun to shed the long ragged coat it had grown for self-protection against the winter cold, leaving but the rich dark fuzz beneath, soon to be bleached buckskin colour by the hot Alberta sunshine. The little people of the prairies were thinking of spring gar-

---

1 A small sturdy horse, sometimes taken from wild herds.

ments; the rabbit and weasel were discarding their snowy coats for jackets of russet; the white owl was abandoning his ermine robe, calling through the night for darker, obscuring feathers; the wary lynx, which had grown huge, mat-like showshoes of fur about his feet last November, was replacing these articles, useful only for winter prowling, with his usual summer footwear of soft, silent padding.

For the third time that day Trader McKenzie came to the door and looked out. Then once more far against the southern horizon, a black speck blurred the monotonous sweep of prairie grass and sky.

"Peter," he yelled, and taking a key from his leathern fob, unlocked a door that swung clear of the wall. From behind it he took a black bottle, ripped off the capsule, pulled the cork and set it on the table with two large horn cups.

They did not say much as they met and clasped hands, palm to palm, red and white. But McKenzie spoke: "Did you beat the thaw?"

"Beat it by driving like hell. Sold every pelt at the top-notch price—here's the credit."

For an instant the two men eyed the paper with a gratification utterly devoid of greed. Then the Scot's hand reached for the bottle.

The horn cups were spilling full as each man raised one to his lips.

Then McKenzie said with some emotion: "Bully for you, Peter. Here's ho!"

"Ho," said Peter.

III. DREAMS, RIVERS, AND WINDS

III. Dreams, Rivers, and Winds

[Johnson's fame was attached to her lyric ability, marked by the inclusion of "At the Ferry" and "Shadow River" in W.D. Lighthall's *Songs of the Great Dominion* (1889), an important early anthology. Her sense of humour is often overlooked. In "His Majesty, the West Wind" she makes fun of her own famous "The Song My Paddle Sings."]

1. "At the Ferry" (1886)

We are waiting in the nightfall by the river's placid rim,
Summer silence all about us, save where swallows' pinions skim
The still grey waters sharply, and the widening circles reach,
With faintest, stillest music, the white gravel on the beach.
The sun has set long, long ago. Against the pearly sky
Elm branches lift their etching up in arches slight and high.
Behind us stands the forest, with its black and lonely pines;
Before us, like a silver thread, the old Grand River winds.
Far down its banks the village lights are creeping one by one;
Far up above, with holy torch, the evening star looks down.

Amid the listening stillness, you and I have silent grown,
Waiting for the river ferry,—waiting in the dusk alone.
At last we hear an eager step, sweet silence reigns no more;
'Tis a barefoot, sun-burnt little boy upon the other shore.
To lift the heavy chain, then turn the rusty old cog-wheel;
And the water-logged old ferry-boat moves slowly from the brink,
Breaking all the star's reflections with the waves that rise and sink;
While the water drippings gently form the rising, falling chains,
Is the only interruption to the quiet that remains
To lull us into golden dreams, to charm our cares away
With its Lethean waters flowing 'neath the bridge of yesterday.
Oh! the day was calm and tender, but the night is calmer still,
As we go aboard the ferry, where we stand and dream, until
We cross the sleeping river, with its restful whisperings,
And peace falls, like a feather from some pressing angel's wings.

2. "The Song My Paddle Sings" (1892)

West wind, blow from your prairie nest,
Blow from the mountains, blow from the west
The sail is idle, the sailor too;
O! wind of the west, we wait for you.
Blow, blow!
I have wooed you so,
But never a favour you bestow.
You rock your cradle the hills between,
But scorn to notice my white lateen.

I stow the sail, unship the mast:
I wooed you long but my wooing's past;
My paddle will lull you into rest.
O! drowsy wind of the drowsy west,
Sleep, sleep,
By your mountain steep,
Or down where the prairie grasses sweep!
Now fold in slumber your laggard wings,
For soft is the song my paddle sings.

August is laughing across the sky,
Laughing while paddle, canoe and I,
Drift, drift,
Where the hills uplift
On either side of the current swift.

The river rolls in its rocky bed;
My paddle is plying its way ahead;
Dip, dip,
While the waters flip
In foam as over their breast we slip.

And oh, the river runs swifter now;
The eddies circle about my bow.
Swirl, swirl!
How the ripples curl
In many a dangerous pool awhirl!

And forward far the rapids roar,
Fretting their margin for evermore.
Dash, dash,

With a mighty crash,
They seethe, and boil, and bound, and splash.

Be strong, O paddle! be brave, canoe!
The reckless waves you must plunge into.
Reel, reel.
On your trembling keel,
But never a fear my craft will feel.

We've raced the rapid, we're far ahead!
The river slips through its silent bed.
Sway, sway,
As the bubbles spray
And fall in tinkling tunes away.

And up on the hills against the sky,
A fir tree rocking its lullaby,
Swings, swings,
Its emerald wings,
Swelling the song that my paddle sings.

3. "His Majesty, the West Wind" (1894)

Once in a fit of mental aberration
I wrote some stanzas to the western wind,
A very stupid, maudlin invocation
That into ears of audiences I've dinned.

A song about a sail, canoe and paddle,
Recited I, in sailor flannels dressed,
And when they heard it would skiddadle,
Particularly those who had been west.

For they, alas, had knowledge. I was striving
To write of something I had never known,
That I had ne'er experienced—the driving
Of western winds across a prairie blown.

I never thought when grinding out those stanzas,
I'd live to swallow pecks of prairie dust,
That I'd deny my old extravaganzas,
And wish his Majesty distinctly—cussed.

4. "Shadow River" (1889)

Muskoka

A stream of tender gladness,
Of filmy sun, and opal tinted skies;
Of warm midsummer air that lightly lies
In mystic rings,
Where softly swings
The music of a thousand wings
That almost tones to sadness.

Midway 'twixt earth and heaven,
A bubble in the pearly air, I seem
To float upon the sapphire floor, a dream
Of clouds of snow,
Above, below,
Drift with my drifting, dim and slow,
As twilight drifts to even.

The little fern-leaf, bending
Upon the brink, its green reflection greets,
And kisses soft the shadow that it meets
With touch so fine,
The border line
The keenest vision can't define;
So perfect is the blending.

The far, fir trees that cover
The brownish hills with needles green and gold,
The arching elms o'erhead, vinegrown and old,
Repictured are
Beneath me far,
Where not a ripple moves to mar
Shades underneath, or over.

Mine is the undertone;
The beauty, strength, and power of the land
Will never stir or bend at my command;
But all the shade
Is marred or made,
If I but dip my paddle blade;
And it is mine alone.

O! pathless world of seeming!
O! pathless life of mine whose deep ideal
Is more my own than ever was the real.
For others Fame
And Love's red flame,
And yellow gold: I only claim
The shadows and the dreaming.

5. "Kicking Horse River" (1894)

It does not care for grandeur,
    And it does not care for state,
It flips its little fingers
    In the very face of fate;
And when its course is thwarted
    Its current set at bay,
It just kicks up its saucy heels
    And takes another way.

It laughs among the monarchs,
    It giggles at the kings.
It dances in the gorges,
    While a comic song it sings;
It ripples into waterfalls,
    It tipples into spray,
And when they raise their eyebrows up
    It—takes another way.

It does not care a button
    For the granite or the rocks.
It never gets discouraged,
    For it's never in a box.
When mountains contradict it,
    And canyons have their say,
It kicks a little higher,
    And takes another way.

6. "Moonset" (1894)

Idles the night wind through the dreaming firs,
That waking murmur low,
As some lost melody returning stirs
The love of long ago;

And though the far, cool distance, zephyr-fanned,
The moon is sinking into shadow-land.

The troubled night-bird, calling plaintively,
Wanders on restless wing;
The cedars, chanting vespers to the sea,
Awaiting its answer,
That comes in wash of waves along the strand,
The while the moon slips into shadow-land.

O! soft responsive voices of the night
I join your minstrelsy,
And call across the fading silver light
As something calls to me;
I may not all your meaning understand,
But I have touched your soul in shadow-land.

IV. WOMEN AND CHILDREN

IV. Women and Children

[As a Mohawk, Johnson was familiar with powerful women like her paternal grandmother, Helen Martin Johnson; at a time when Canadian women were expected to be submissive to men, an expectation reflected in their inability to vote and in the marriage laws that converted any property they had into their husband's, she wrote against the stereotypes of the sexually promiscuous "squaw." She also wrote about marriages that succumbed to the widespread disapproval of "mixed" marriages, as well as relationships that survived this social pressure, like that of her parents.]

1. "A Strong Race Opinion: On the Indian Girl in Modern Fiction" (1892)

[In this essay, Johnson attacks the dominant stereotype of the "Indian maiden" and argues that writers should educate themselves about Indigenous peoples, rather than simply repeat the usual platitudes. Her references reveal her wide knowledge of Indigenous activism and of works about and by Native Americans published on both sides of the border. This essay was first published in the *Toronto Sunday Globe* on 22 May 1892.]

Every race in the world enjoys its own peculiar characteristics, but it scarcely follows that every individual of a nation must possess these prescribed singularities, or otherwise forfeit in the eyes of the world their nationality. Individual personality is one of the most charming things to be met with, either in a flesh and blood existence, or upon the pages of fiction, and it matters little to what race an author's heroine belongs, if he makes her character distinct, unique and natural.

The American book heroine of today is vari-coloured as to personality and action. The author does not consider it necessary to the development of her character, and the plot of the story to insist upon her having American-coloured eyes, an American carriage, an American voice, American motives, and an American mode of dying; he allows her to evolve an individuality ungoverned by nationalisms—but the outcome of impulse and nature and a general womanishness.

Not so the Indian girl in modern fiction, the author permits her character no such spontaneity, she must not be one of womankind at large, neither must she have an originality, a singularity that is not definitely "Indian." I quote "Indian" as there seems to be an impression amongst authors that such a thing as tribal distinction does not exist amongst the North American aborigines.

The term "Indian" signifies about as much as the term "European," but I cannot recall ever having read a story where the heroine was described as "a European." The Indian girl we meet in cold type, however, is rarely distressed by having to belong to any tribe, or to reflect any tribal characteristics. She is merely a wholesome sort of mixture of any band existing between the Mic Macs of Gaspe and the Kwaw-Kewlths of British Columbia,[1] yet strange to say, that notwithstanding the numerous tribes, with their aggregate numbers reaching more than 122,000 souls in Canada alone, our Canadian authors can cull from this huge revenue of character, but one Indian girl, and stranger still that this lonely little heroine never had a prototype in breathing flesh-and-blood existence!

It is a deplorable fact, but there is only one of her. The story-writer who can create a new kind of Indian girl, or better still portray a "real live" Indian girl who will do something in Canadian literature that has never been done, but once. The general author gives the reader the impression that he has concocted the plot, created his characters, arranged his action, and at the last moment has been seized with the idea that the regulation Indian maiden will make a very harmonious background whereon to paint his pen picture, that, he, never having met this interesting individual, stretches forth his hand to his library shelves, grasps the first Canadian novelist he sees, reads up his subject, and duplicates it in his own work.

After a half dozen writers have done this, the reader might as well leave the tale unread as far as the interest touches upon the Indian character, for an unvarying experience tells him that this convenient personage will repeat herself with monotonous accuracy. He knows what she did and how she died in other romances by other romancers, and she will do and die likewise in his (she always does die, and one feels relieved that it is so, for she is too unhealthy and too unnatural to live).

The rendition of herself and her doings gains no variety in the pens of manifold authors, and the last thing that they will

---

1 Mic Macs, from eastern Canada, now refer to themselves
as Mi'kmaq; often the West Coast nations that form the
Kwakwaka'wakw were referred to by the name of one of them, the
Kwakiutl or Kwagulth, which Johnson does here.

ever think of will be to study "The Indian Girl" from life, for the being we read of is the offspring of the writer's imagination and never existed outside the book covers that her name decorates. Yes, there is only one of her, and her name is "Winona."

Once or twice she has borne another appellation, but it always has a "Winona" sound about it.[1] Even Charles Mair, in that masterpiece of Canadian-Indian romances, "Tecumseh," could not resist "Winona."[2]

We meet her as a Shawnee, as a Sioux, as a Huron, and then, her tribe unnamed, in the vicinity of Brockville.

She is never dignified by being permitted to own a surname, although, extraordinary to note, her father is always a chief, and had he ever existed, would doubtless have been as conservative as his contemporaries about the usual significance that his people attach to family name and lineage.

In addition to this most glaring error this surnameless creation is possessed with a suicidal mania. Her unhappy, self-sacrificing life becomes such a burden to both herself and the author that this is the only means by which they can extricate themselves from a lamentable tangle, though, as a matter of fact suicide is an evil positively unknown among Indians. To-day there may be rare instances where a man crazed by liquor might destroy his own life, but in the periods from whence "Winona's" character is sketched self-destruction was unheard of. This seems to be a fallacy which the best American writers have fallen a prey to. Even Helen Hunt Jackson, in her powerful and beautiful romance of "Ramona,"[3] has weakened her work deplorably by having no less than three Indians suicide while maddened by their national wrongs and personal grief.

The hardest fortune that the Indian girl of fiction meets with is the inevitable doom that shadows her love affairs. She is always desperately in love with the young white hero, who in turn is grateful to her for services rendered the garrison in general and

---

1 Winona is the name the Lakota (Sioux) traditionally gave to their first-born daughters; it was popularized by Longfellow's *Song of Hiawatha*, where Hiawatha's mother is named Winona.
2 Charles Mair (1838–1927), *Tecumseh: A Drama* (Toronto: Hunter, Rose, 1886).
3 Helen Hunt Jackson (1830–85) was inspired by the Ponca activist Standing Bear (c. 1829–1908) to take on the Native American cause. *Ramona* (1884), which described the mistreatment of the Native Americans of Southern California by the federal government, became a bestseller.

himself in particular during red days of war. In short, she is so much wrapped up in him that she is treacherous to her own people, tells falsehoods to her father and the other chiefs of her tribe, and otherwise makes herself detestable and dishonourable. Of course, this white hero never marries her! Will some critic who understands human nature, and particularly the nature of authors, please tell the reading public why marriage with the Indian girl is so despised in books and so general in real life? Will this good farseeing critic also tell us why the book-made Indian makes all the love advances to the white gentleman, though the real wild Indian girl (by the way, we are never given any stories of educated girls, though there are many such throughout Canada) is the most retiring, reticent, noncommittal being in existence!

Captain Richardson, in that inimitable novel, "Wacousta," scarcely goes as far in this particular as his followers.[1]

To be sure he has his Indian heroine madly in love with young de Haldimar, a passion which it goes without saying he does not reciprocate, but which he plays upon to the extent of making her a traitor to Pontiac inasmuch as she betrays the secret of one of the cleverest intrigues of war known in the history of America, namely, the scheme to capture Fort Detroit through the means of an exhibition game of lacrosse. In addition to this de Haldimar makes a cat's paw of the girl, using her as a means of communication between his fiancee and himself, and so the excellent author permits his Indian girl to get herself despised by her own nation and disliked by the reader. Unnecessary to state, that as usual the gallant white marries his fair lady, whom the poor little red girl has assisted him to recover.

Then comes another era in Canadian-Indian fiction, wherein G. Mercer Adam and A. Ethelwyn Wetherald have given us the semi-historic novel "An Algonquin Maiden."[2]

The former's masterly touch can be recognized on every page he has written; but the outcome of the combined pens is the same old story. We find "Wanda" violently in love with

1 *Wacousta, or The Prophecy: A Tale of the Canadas* (London, 1832) by John Richardson, who grew up on the Detroit frontier and, like Johnson's grandfather, fought in the War of 1812 alongside Tecumseh. Johnson's father admired the novel. See Project Gutenberg for an online version under the title *Wacousta: A Tale of the Pontiac Conspiracy,* the American edition published in 1851.

2 *An Algonquin Maiden: A Romance of the Early Days of Upper Canada*, by G. Mercer Adams and A. Ethelwyn Wetherald (Toronto: Briggs, 1886).

Edward MacLeod, she makes all the overtures, conducts herself disgracefully, assists him to a reunion with his fair-skinned love, Helene; then betakes herself to a boat, rows out into the lake in a thunderstorm, chants her own death-song, and is drowned.

But, notwithstanding all this, the authors have given us something exceedingly unique and novel as regards their red heroine. They have sketched us a wild Indian girl who kisses. They, however, forgot to tell us where she learned this pleasant fashion of emotional expression; though two such prominent authors who have given so much time to the study of Indian customs and character, must certainly have noticed the entire ignorance of kissing that is universal among the Aborigines. A wild Indian never kisses; mothers never kiss their children even, nor lovers their sweethearts, husbands their wives. It is something absolutely unknown, unpractised.

But "Wanda" was one of the few book Indian girls who had an individuality and was not hampered with being obliged to continually be national first and natural afterwards. No, she was not national; she did things and said things about as un-Indian like as Bret Harte's "M'liss:"[1] in fact, her action generally resembles "M'liss" more than anything else; for "Wanda's" character has the peculiarity of being created more by the dramatis personae in the play than by the authors themselves. For example: Helene speaks of her as a "low, untutored savage," and Rose is guilty of remarking that she is "a coarse, ignorant woman, whom you cannot admire, whom it would be impossible for you to respect"; and these comments are both sadly truthful, one cannot love or admire a heroine that grubs in the mud like a turtle, climbs trees like a raccoon, and tears and soils her gowns like a madwoman.

Then the young hero describes her upon two occasions as a "beautiful little brute." Poor little Wanda! not only is she non-descript and ill-starred, but as usual the authors take away her love, her life, and last and most terrible of all, her reputation; for they permit a crowd of men-friends of the hero to call her a "squaw,"and neither hero nor authors deny that she is a "squaw." It is almost too sad when so much prejudice exists against the Indians, that any one should write an Indian heroine with such glaring accusations against her virtue, and no contradictory statements either from writer, hero, or circumstance. "Wanda" had without doubt the saddest, unsunniest, unequal life ever given to Canadian readers.

---

1   "M'liss: An Idyll of Red Mountain," a short story by American writer Bret Harte (1836–1902), was published in 1860 and collected in *The Luck of the Roaring Camp and Other Sketches* (1870).

Jessie M. Freeland has written a pretty tale published in *The Week*; it is called "Winona's Tryst,"[1] but Oh! grim fatality, here again our Indian girl duplicates her former self. "Winona" is the unhappy victim of violent love for Hugh Gordon, which he does not appreciate or return. She assists him, serves him, saves him in the usual "dumb animal" style of book Indians. She manages by self abnegation, danger, and many heartaches to restore him to the arms of Rose McTavish, who of course he has loved and longed for all through the story. Then "Winona" secures the time honoured canoe, paddles out into the lake and drowns herself.

But Miss Freeland closes this pathetic little story with one of the simplest, truest, strongest paragraphs that a Canadian pen has ever written, it is the salvation of the otherwise threadbare development of plot. Hugh Gordon speaks, "I solemnly pledge myself in memory of Winona to do something to help her unfortunate nation. The rightful owners of the soil, dispossessed and driven back inch by inch over their native prairies by their French and English conquerors; and he kept his word."

Charles Mair has enriched Canadian Indian literature perhaps more than any of our authors, in his magnificent drama, "Tecumseh." The character of the grand old chief himself is most powerfully and accurately drawn. Mair has not fallen into that unattractive fashion of making his Indians "assent with a grunt"—or look with "eyes of dog-like fidelity" or to appear "very grave, very dignified, and not very immaculately clean." Mair avoids the usual commonplaces used in describing Indians by those who have never met or mixed with them. His drama bears upon every page evidence of long study and life with the people whom he has written of so carefully, so truthfully.

As for his heroine, what portrayal of Indian character has ever been more faithful than that of "Iena." Oh! happy inspiration vouchsafed to the author of "Tecumseh" he has invented a novelty in fiction—a white man who deserves, wins and reciprocates the Indian maiden's love—who says, as she dies on his bosom, while the bullet meant for him stills and tears her heart.

> "Silent for ever! Oh, my girl! my girl!
> Those rich eyes melt; those lips are sunwarm still—
> They look like life, yet have no semblant voice.
> Millions of creatures throngs and multitudes

1 Jessie M. Freeland, "Winona's Tryst," *The Week* (6 February 1891), 155–57.

Of heartless beings, flaunt upon the earth,
There's room enough for them, but thou, dull fate—
Thou cold and partial tender of life's field,
That pluck'st the flower, and leav'st the weed to thrive—
Thou had'st not room for her! Oh, I must seek
A way out of the rack—I need not live,
* * * * but she is dead—
And love is left upon the earth to starve,
My object's gone, and I am but a shell,
A husk, and empty case, or anything
What may be kicked about the world."

After perusing this refreshing white Indian drama the reader has but one regret, that Mair did not let "Iena" live. She is the one "book" Indian girl that has Indian life, Indian character, Indian beauty, but the inevitable doom of death could not be stayed even by Mair's sensitive Indian-loving pen. No, the Indian girl must die, and with the exception of "Iena" her heart's blood must stain every page of fiction whereon she appears. One learns to love Lefroy, the poet painter; he never abuses by coarse language and derisive epithets his little Indian love, "Iena" accepts delicately and sweetly his overtures, Lefroy prizes nobly and honourably her devotion. Oh! Lefroy, where is your fellowman in fiction? "Iena," where is your prototype? Alas, for all the other pale-faced lovers, they are indifferent, almost brutal creations, and as for the red skin girls that love them, they are all fawn eyed, unnatural, unmaidenly idiots and both are merely imaginary make-shifts to help out romances, that would be immeasurably improved by their absence.

Perhaps, sometimes an Indian romance may be written by someone who will be clever enough to portray national character without ever having come in contact with it. Such things have been done, for are we not told that Tom Moore had never set foot in Persia before he wrote Lalla Rookh[1] and those who best know what they affirm declare that remarkable poem as a faithful and accurate delineation of Oriental scenery, life and character. But such things are rare, half of our authors who write up Indian stuff have never been on an Indian reserve in their lives, have never met a "real live" Redman, have never even read Parkman,

---

1 *Lalla Rookh* (1817), the popular "Oriental romance" by Thomas Moore (1779–1852).

Schoolcraft or Catlin;[1] what wonder that their conception of a people that they are ignorant of, save by heresay, is dwarfed, erroneous and delusive.

And here follows the thought—do authors who write Indian romances love the nation they endeavour successfully or unsuccessfully to describe? Do they, like Tecumseh, say, "And I, who love your nation, which is just, when deeds deserve it," or is the Indian introduced into literature but to lend a dash of vivid colouring to an otherwise tame and sombre picture of colonial life: it looks suspiciously like the latter reason, or why should the Indian always get beaten in the battles of romances, or the Indian girl get inevitably the cold shoulder in the wars of love?

Surely the Redman has lost enough, has suffered enough without additional losses and sorrows being heaped upon him in romance. There are many combats he has won in history from the extinction of the Jesuit Fathers at Lake Simcoe to Cut Knife Creek.[2]

There are many girls who have placed dainty red feet figuratively upon the white man's neck from the days of Pocahontas to those of little 'Bright Eyes,' who captured all Washington a few seasons ago.[3] Let us not only hear, but read something of

---

1 Francis Parkman (1823–93) wrote many volumes of early North American history; Henry Rowe Schoolcraft (1793–1864), an American explorer, ethnologist, and bureaucrat, married Jane Johnston, the daughter of a Scots-Irish fur trader and a high-ranking Ojibwe woman (see Appendix B1). He based some of his many publications on Native Americans on her stories or translations. George Catlin (1796–1892) journeyed west five times to paint the Indigenous peoples of the Plains, beginning in the 1830s.

2 Between 1647 and 1649, during a period of renewed Iroquois-Huron warfare, the Iroquois destroyed Jesuit missions set up to convert the Huron (Wendat) people. In 1649, Iroquois warriors tortured and killed a group of Huron converts and missionaries, including Jean de Brébeuf, who was canonized in 1930. This event has inspired several works of literature, including E.J. Pratt's poem *Brébeuf and His Brethren* (1941) and Joseph Boyden's novel *The Orenda* (2013). The Battle of Cut Knife Creek (1885) took place during the second Riel Resistance, after an encampment of Cree and Assiniboine people was attacked by a Canadian force led by Colonel Otter. After six hours of fighting, when Otter's men were retreating, Poundmaker, a Plains Cree chief, convinced the Indigenous forces to let them go.

3 Susette La Flesche (1854–1903), an activist journalist and writer; her Omaha name, Inshata Theumba, translates as "Bright Eyes." See Appendix B4.

the North American Indian "besting" some one at least once in a decade, and above all things let the Indian girl of fiction develop from the "doglike," "fawnlike," "deer-footed," "fire-eyed," "crouching," "submissive" book heroine into something of the quiet, sweet womanly woman she is, if wild, or the everyday, natural, laughing girl she is, if cultivated and educated; let her be natural, even if the author is not competent to give her tribal characteristics.

2. "A Red Girl's Reasoning" (1893)

[This story illuminates the controversy around "country marriages" between European fur traders and First Nations women, performed without clergy or by Indigenous rites and ceremony and thus according to "the custom of the country," or, in French, *à la façon du pays*. The story was originally published in Montreal's *Dominion Illustrated* in February 1893.]

"Be pretty good to her, Charlie, my boy, or she'll balk sure as shooting." That was what old Jimmy Robinson said to his brand new son-in-law, while they waited for the bride to reappear.

"Oh! you bet, there's no danger of much else. I'll be good to her, help me Heaven," replied Charlie McDonald, brightly.

"Yes, of course you will," answered the old man, "but don't you forget, there's a good big bit of her mother in her, and," closing his left eye significantly, "you don't understand these Indians as I do."

"But I'm just as fond of them, Mr. Robinson," Charlie said assertively, "and I get on with them too, now, don't I?"

"Yes, pretty well for a town boy; but when you have lived forty years among these people, as I have done; when you have had your wife as long as I have had mine—for there's no getting over it, Christine's disposition is as native as her mother's, every bit—and perhaps when you've owned for eighteen years a daughter as dutiful, as loving, as fearless, and, alas! as obstinate as that little piece you are stealing away from me to-day—I tell you, youngster, you'll know more than you know now. It is kindness for kindness, bullet for bullet, blood for blood. Remember, what you are, she will be," and the old Hudson Bay trader scrutinized Charlie McDonald's face like a detective.

It was a happy, fair face, good to look at, with a certain ripple of dimples somewhere about the mouth, and eyes that laughed out the very sunniness of their owner's soul. There was not a severe nor yet a weak line anywhere. He was a well-meaning young fellow, happily dispositioned, and a great favorite with the tribe at Robinson's Post, whither he had gone in the service of the Department of Agriculture, to assist the local agent through the tedium of a long census-taking.

As a boy he had had the Indian relic-hunting craze, as a youth he had studied Indian archaeology and folk-lore, as a man he consummated his predilections for Indianology, by loving, winning and marrying the quiet little daughter of the English trader, who himself had married a native woman twenty years ago. The country was all backwoods, and the Post miles and miles from even the semblance of civilization, and the lonely young Englishman's heart had gone out to the girl who, apart from speaking a very few words of English, was utterly uncivilized and uncultured, but had withal that marvellously innate refinement so universally possessed by the higher tribes of North American Indians.

Like all her race, observant, intuitive, having a horror of ridicule, consequently quick at acquirement and teachable in mental and social habits, she had developed from absolute pagan indifference into a sweet, elderly Christian woman, whose broken English, quiet manner, and still handsome copper-colored face, were the joy of old Robinson's declining years.

He had given their daughter Christine all the advantages of his own learning—which, if truthfully told, was not universal; but the girl had a fair common education, and the native adaptability to progress.

She belonged to neither and still to both types of the cultured Indian. The solemn, silent, almost heavy manner of the one so commingled with the gesticulating Frenchiness and vivacity of the other, that one unfamiliar with native Canadian life would find it difficult to determine her nationality.

She looked very pretty to Charles McDonald's loving eyes, as she reappeared in the doorway, holding her mother's hand and saying some happy words of farewell. Personally she looked much the same as her sisters, all Canada through, who are the offspring of red and white parentage—olive-complexioned, gray-eyed, black-haired, with figure slight and delicate, and the wistful, unfathomable expression in her whole face that turns one so heart-sick as they glance at the young Indians of to-day—it is the forerunner too frequently of "the white man's disease," consumption—but McDonald was pathetically in love, and thought her the most beautiful woman he had ever seen in his life.

There had not been much of a wedding ceremony. The priest had cantered through the service in Latin, pronounced the benediction in English, and congratulated the "happy couple" in Indian, as a compliment to the assembled tribe in the little amateur structure that did service at the post as a sanctuary.

But the knot was tied as firmly and indissolubly as if all Charlie McDonald's swell city friends had crushed themselves up against the chancel to congratulate him, and in his heart he was deeply thankful to escape the flower-pelting, white gloves, rice-throwing, and ponderous stupidity of a breakfast, and indeed all the regulation gimcracks of the usual marriage celebrations, and it was with a hand trembling with absolute happiness that he assisted his little Indian wife into the old muddy buckboard that, hitched to an underbred-looking pony, was to convey them over the first stages of their journey. Then came more adieus, some hand-clasping, old Jimmy Robinson looking very serious just at the last, Mrs. Jimmy, stout, stolid, betraying nothing of visible emotion, and then the pony, rough-shod and shaggy, trudged on, while mutual hand-waves were kept up until the old Hudson Bay Post dropped out of sight, and the buckboard with its lightsome load of hearts deliriously happy, jogged on over the uneven trail.

★ ★ ★ ★ ★

She was "all the rage" that winter at the provincial capital. The men called her a "deuced fine little woman." The ladies said she was "just the sweetest wildflower." Whereas she was really but an ordinary, pale, dark girl who spoke slowly and with a strong accent, who danced fairly well, sang acceptably, and never stirred outside the door without her husband.

Charlie was proud of her; he was proud that she had "taken" so well among his friends, proud that she bore herself so complacently in the drawing-rooms of the wives of pompous Government officials, but doubly proud of her almost abject devotion to him. If ever human being was worshipped that being was Charlie McDonald; it could scarcely have been otherwise, for the almost godlike strength of his passion for that little wife of his would have mastered and melted a far more invincible citadel than an already affectionate woman's heart.

Favorites socially, McDonald and his wife went everywhere. In fashionable circles she was "new"—a potent charm to acquire popularity, and the little velvet-clad figure was always the centre of interest among all the women in the room. She always dressed in velvet. No woman in Canada, has she but the faintest dash of native blood in her veins, but loves velvets and silks. As beef to the Englishman, wine to the Frenchman, fads to the Yankee, so are velvet and silk to the Indian girl, be she wild as prairie grass, be she on the borders of civilization, or, having stepped within its boundary, mounted the steps of culture even under its superficial heights.

"Such a dolling little appil blossom," said the wife of a local M.P.,[1] who brushed up her etiquette and English once a year at Ottawa. "Does she always laugh so sweetly, and gobble you up with those great big gray eyes of her, when you are togetheah at home, Mr. McDonald? If so, I should think youah pooah brothah would feel himself terrible *de trop.*"[2]

He laughed lightly. "Yes, Mrs. Stuart, there are not two of Christie; she is the same at home and abroad, and as for Joe, he doesn't mind us a bit; he's no end fond of her."

"I'm very glad he is. I always fancied he did not care for her, d'you know."

If ever a blunt woman existed it was Mrs. Stuart. She really meant nothing, but her remark bothered Charlie. He was fond of his brother, and jealous for Christie's popularity. So that night when he and Joe were having a pipe, he said:

"I've never asked you yet what you thought of her, Joe." A brief pause, then Joe spoke. "I'm glad she loves you."

"Why?"

"Because that girl has but two possibilities regarding humanity—love or hate."

"Humph! Does she love or hate *you?*"

"Ask her."

"You talk bosh. If she hated you, you'd get out. If she loved you I'd *make* you get out."

Joe McDonald whistled a little, then laughed.

"Now that we are on the subject, I might as well ask—honestly, old man, wouldn't you and Christie prefer keeping house alone to having me always around?"

"Nonsense, sheer nonsense. Why, thunder, man, Christie's no end fond of you, and as for me—you surely don't want assurances from me?"

"No, but I often think a young couple—"

---

1 Member of Parliament.
2 "Too much" (French), superfluous; she means that Joe should feel that he is intruding on the newly married couple's privacy.

"Young couple be blowed! After a while when they want you and your old surveying chains, and spindle-legged tripod tele-scope kickshaws, farther west, I venture to say the little woman will cry her eyes out—won't you, Christie?" This last in a higher tone, as through clouds of tobacco smoke he caught sight of his wife passing the doorway.

She entered. "Oh, no, I would not cry; I never do cry, but I would be heart-sore to lose you Joe, and apart from that"—a little wickedly—"you may come in handy for an exchange some day, as Charlie does always say when he hoards up duplicate relics."

"Are Charlie and I duplicates?"

"Well—not exactly"—her head a little to one side, and eyeing them both merrily, while she slipped softly on to the arm of her husband's chair—"but, in the event of Charlie's failing me"—everyone laughed then. The "some day" that she spoke of was nearer than they thought. It came about in this wise.

There was a dance at the Lieutenant-Governor's, and the world and his wife were there. The nobs were in great feather that night, particularly the women, who flaunted about in new gowns and much splendor. Christie McDonald had a new gown also, but wore it with the utmost unconcern, and if she heard any of the flattering remarks made about her she at least appeared to disregard them.

"I never dreamed you could wear blue so splendidly," said Captain Logan, as they sat out a dance together.

"Indeed she can, though," interposed Mrs. Stuart, halting in one of her gracious sweeps down the room with her husband's private secretary.

"Don't shout so, captain. I can hear every sentence you uttah—of course Mrs. McDonald can wear blue—she has a morning gown of cadet blue that she is a picture in."

"You are both very kind," said Christie. "I like blue; it is the color of all the Hudson's Bay posts, and the factor's residence is always decorated in blue."[1]

"Is it really? How interesting—do tell us some more of your old home, Mrs. McDonald; you so seldom speak of your life at the post, and we fellows so often wish to hear of it all," said Logan eagerly.

"Why do you not ask me of it, then?"

"Well—er, I'm sure I don't know; I'm fully interested in the Ind—in your people—your mother's people, I mean, but it al-ways seems so personal, I suppose; and—a—a—"

1 A factor is the chief trader of a Hudson's Bay Company post.

"Perhaps you are, like all other white people, afraid to mention my nationality to me."

The captain winced and Mrs. Stuart laughed uneasily. Joe McDonald was not far off, and he was listening, and chuckling, and saying to himself, "That's you, Christie, lay 'em out; it won't hurt 'em to know how they appear once in a while."

"Well, Captain Logan," she was saying, "what is it you would like to hear—of my people, or my parents, or myself?"

"All, all, my dear," cried Mrs. Stuart clamorously. "I'll speak for him—tell us of yourself and your mother—your father is delightful, I am sure—but then he is only an ordinary Englishman, not half as interesting as a foreigner, or—or, perhaps I should say, a native."

Christie laughed. "Yes," she said, "my father often teases my mother now about how *very* native she was when he married her; then, how could she have been otherwise? She did not know a word of English, and there was not another English-speaking person besides my father and his two companions within sixty miles."

"Two companions, eh? one a Catholic priest and the other a wine merchant, I suppose, and with your father in the Hudson Bay, they were good representatives of the pioneers in the New World," remarked Logan, waggishly.

"Oh, no, they were all Hudson Bay men. There were no rumsellers and no missionaries in that part of the country then."

Mrs. Stuart looked puzzled. "No *missionaries*?" she repeated with an odd intonation.

Christie's insight was quick. There was a peculiar expression of interrogation in the eyes of her listeners, and the girl's blood leapt angrily up into her temples as she said hurriedly, "I know what you mean; I know what you are thinking. You were wondering how my parents were married—"

"Well—er, my dear, it seems peculiar—if there was no priest, and no magistrate, why—a—" Mrs. Stuart paused awkwardly.

"The marriage was performed by Indian rites," said Christie.

"Oh, do tell me about it; is the ceremony very interesting and quaint—are your chieftains anything like Buddhist priests?" It was Logan who spoke.

"Why, no," said the girl in amazement at that gentleman's ignorance. "There is no ceremony at all, save a feast. The two people just agree to live only with and for each other, and the man takes his wife to his home, just as you do. There is no ritual to bind them; they need none; an Indian's word was his law in those days, you know."

Mrs. Stuart stepped backwards. "Ah!" was all she said.

Logan removed his eye-glass and stared blankly at Christie. "And did McDonald marry you in this singular fashion?" He questioned.

"Oh, no, we were married by Father O'Leary. Why do you ask?"

"Because if he had, I'd have blown his brain out to-morrow."

Mrs. Stuart's partner, who had hitherto been silent, coughed and began to twirl his cuff stud nervously, but nobody took any notice of him. Christie had risen, slowly, ominously—risen, with the dignity and pride of an empress.

"Captain Logan," she said, "what do you dare to say to me? What do you dare to mean? Do you presume to think it would not have been lawful for Charlie to marry me according to my people's rites? Do you for one instant dare to question that my parents were not as legally—"

"Don't, dear, don't," interrupted Mrs. Stuart hurriedly; "it is bad enough now, goodness knows; don't make—" Then she broke off blindly. Christie's eyes glared at the mumbling woman, at her uneasy partner, at the horrified captain. Then they rested on the McDonald brothers, who stood within earshot, Joe's face scarlet, her husband's white as ashes, with something in his eyes she had never seen before. It was Joe who saved the situation. Stepping quickly across towards his sister-in-law, he offered her his arm, saying, "The next dance is ours, I think, Christie."

Then Logan pulled himself together, and attempted to carry Mrs. Stuart off for the waltz, but for once in her life that lady had lost her head. "It is shocking!" she said, "outrageously shocking! I wonder if they told Mr. McDonald before he married her!" Then looking hurriedly round, she too saw the young husband's face—and knew that they had not.

"Humph! deuced nice kettle of fish—and poor old Charlie has always thought so much of honorable birth."

Logan thought he spoke in an undertone, but "poor old Charlie" heard him. He followed his wife and brother across the room. "Joe," he said, "will you see that a trap[1] is called?" Then to Christie, "Joe will see that you get home all right." He wheeled on his heel then and left the ball-room.

Joe *did* see.

He tucked a poor, shivering, pallid little woman into a cab, and wound her bare throat up in the scarlet velvet cloak that was hanging uselessly over her arm. She crouched down beside him, saying, "I

---

1 A light carriage pulled by a pony or horse.

am so cold, Joe; I am so cold," but she did not seem to know enough to wrap herself up. Joe felt all through this long drive that nothing this side of Heaven would be so good as to die, and he was glad when the little voice at his elbow said, "What is he so angry at, Joe?"

"I don't know exactly, dear," he said gently, "but I think it was what you said about this Indian marriage."

"But why should I not have said it? Is there anything wrong about it?" she asked pitifully.

"Nothing, that I can see—there was no other way; but Charlie is very angry, and you must be brave and forgiving with him, Christie, dear."

"But I did never see him like that before, did you?"

"Once."

"When?"

"Oh, at college, one day, a boy tore his prayer book in half, and threw it into the grate, just to be mean, you know. Our mother had given it to him at his confirmation."

"And did he look so?"

"About, but it all blew over in a day—Charlie's tempers are short and brisk. Just don't take any notice of him; run off to bed, and he'll have forgotten it by the morning."

They reached home at last. Christie said goodnight quietly, going directly to her room. Joe went to his room also, filled a pipe and smoked for an hour. Across the passage he could hear her slippered feet pacing up and down, up and down the length of her apartment. There was something panther-like in those restless footfalls, a meaning velvetyness that made him shiver, and again he wished he were dead—or elsewhere.

After a time the hall door opened, and someone came upstairs, along the passage, and to the little woman's room. As he entered, she turned and faced him.

"Christie," he said harshly, "do you know what you have done?"

"Yes," taking a step nearer him, her whole soul springing up into her eyes, "I have angered you, Charlie, and—"

"Angered me? You have disgraced me; and, moreover, you have disgraced yourself and both your parents."

"*Disgraced*?"

"Yes, *disgraced*; you have literally declared to the whole city that your father and mother were never married, and that you are the child of—what shall we call it—love? certainly not legality."

Across the hallway sat Joe McDonald, his blood freezing; but it leapt into every vein like fire at the awful anguish in the little voice that cried simply, "Oh! Charlie!"

"How could you do it, how could you do it, Christie, without shame either for yourself or for me, let alone your parents?"

The voice was like an angry demon's—not a trace was there in it of the yellow-haired, blue-eyed, laughing-lipped boy who had driven away so gaily to the dance five hours before.

"Shame? Why should I be ashamed of the rites of my people any more than you should be ashamed of the customs of yours—of a marriage more sacred and holy than half of your white man's mockeries."

It was the voice of another nature in the girl—the love and the pleading were dead in it.

"Do you mean to tell me, Charlie—you who have studied my race and their laws for years—do you mean to tell me that, because there was no priest and no magistrate, my mother was not married? Do you mean to say that all my forefathers, for hundreds of years back, have been illegally born? If so, you blacken my ancestry beyond—beyond—beyond all reason."

"No, Christie, I would not be so brutal as that; but your father and mother live in more civilized times. Father O'Leary has been at the post for nearly twenty years. Why was not your father straight enough to have the ceremony performed when he *did* get the chance?"

The girl turned upon him with the face of a fury. "Do you suppose," she almost hissed, "that my mother would be married according to your *white* rites after she had been five years a wife, and I had been born in the meantime? No, a thousand times I say, *no*. When the priest came with his notions of Christianizing, and talked to them of re-marriage by the Church, my mother arose and said, 'Never—never—I have never had but this one husband; he has had none but me for wife, and to have you re-marry us would be to say as much to the whole world as that we had never been married before. [Fact.] You go away; *I* do not ask that *your* people be re-married; talk not so to me. I *am* married, and you or the Church cannot do or undo it.'"

"Your father was a fool not to insist upon the law, and so was the priest."

"Law? *My* people have *no* priest, and my nation cringes not to law. Our priest is purity, and our law is honor. Priest? Was there a *priest* at the most holy marriage known to humanity—that stainless marriage whose offspring is the God you white men told my pagan mother of?"

"Christie—you are *worse* than blasphemous; such a profane

remark shows how little you understand the sanctity of the Christian faith—"

"I know what I *do* understand; it is that you are hating me because I told some of the beautiful customs of my people to Mrs. Stuart and those men."

"Pooh! who cares for them? It is not them; the trouble is they won't keep their mouths shut. Logan's a cad and will toss the whole tale about at the club to-morrow night; and as for the Stuart woman, I'd like to know how I'm going to take you to Ottawa for presentation and the opening,[1] while she is blabbing the whole miserable scandal in every drawing-room, and I'll be pointed out as a romantic fool, and you—as worse; I *can't* understand why your father didn't tell me before we were married; I at least might have warned you never to mention it." Something of recklessness rang up through his voice, just as the panther-likeness crept up from her footsteps and couched herself in hers. She spoke in tones quiet, soft, deadly.

"Before we were married! Oh! Charlie, would it have—made—any—difference?"

"God knows," he said, throwing himself into a chair, his blonde hair rumpled and wet. It was the only boyish thing about him now.

She walked towards him, then halted in the centre of the room. "Charlie McDonald," she said, and it was as if a stone had spoken, "look up." He raised his head, startled by her tone. There was a threat in her eyes that, had his rage been less courageous, his pride less bitterly wounded, would have cowed him.

"There was no such time as that before our marriage, for we *are not married now.* Stop," she said, outstretching her palms against him as he sprang to his feet, "I tell you we are not married. Why should I recognize the rites of your nation when you do not acknowledge the rites of mine? According to your own words, my parents should have gone through your church ceremony as well as through an Indian contract; according to *my* words, *we* should go through an Indian contract as well as through a church marriage. If their union is illegal, so is ours. If you think my father is living in dishonor with my mother, my people will think I am living in dishonor with you. How do I know when another nation will come and conquer you as you white men conquered us? And

---

1 Here Charlie refers to the opening of Parliament, which is followed by the presentation of invited guests to the governor general. This event also begins the "season" of high-society balls.

they will have another marriage rite to perform, and they will tell us another truth, that you are not my husband, that you are but disgracing and dishonoring me, that you are keeping me here, not as your wife, but as your—your—*squaw*."

The terrible word had never passed her lips before, and the blood stained her face to her very temples. She snatched off her wedding ring and tossed it across the room, saying scornfully, "That thing is as empty to me as the Indian rites to you."

He caught her by the wrists; his small white teeth were locked tightly, his blue eyes blazed into hers.

"Christine, do you dare doubt my honor towards you? *you*, whom I should have died for; do you *dare* to think I have kept you here, not as my wife, but—"

"Oh, God! You are hurting me; you are breaking my arm," she gasped.

The door was flung open, and Joe McDonald's sinewy hands clinched like vices on his brother's shoulders.

"Charlie, you're mad, mad as the devil. Let go of her this minute."

The girl staggered backwards as the iron fingers loosed her wrists. "Oh! Joe," she cried, "I am not his wife, and he says I am born—nameless."

"Here," said Joe, shoving his brother towards the door. "Go downstairs till you can collect your senses. If ever a being acted like an infernal fool, you're the man."

The young husband looked from one to the other, dazed by his wife's insult, abandoned to a fit of ridiculously childish temper. Blind as he was with passion, he remembered long afterwards seeing them standing there, his brother's face darkened with a scowl of anger—his wife, clad in the mockery of her ball dress, her scarlet velvet cloak half covering her bare brown neck and arms, her eyes like flames of fire, her face like a piece of sculptured graystone.

Without a word he flung himself furiously from the room, and immediately afterwards they heard the heavy hall door bang behind him.

"Can I do anything for you, Christie?" asked her brother-in-law calmly.

"No, thank you—unless—I think I would like a drink of water, please."

He brought her up a goblet filled with wine; her hand did not even tremble as she took it. As for Joe, a demon arose in his soul as he noticed she kept her wrists covered.

"Do you think he will come back?" she said.

"Oh, yes, of course; he'll be all right in the morning. Now go to bed like a good little girl, and—and, I say, Christie, you can call me if you want anything; I'll be right here, you know."

"Thank you, Joe; you are kind—and good."

He returned then to his apartment. His pipe was out, but he picked up a newspaper instead, threw himself into an armchair, and in a half-hour was in the land of dreams.

When Charlie came home in the morning, after a six-mile walk into the country and back again, his foolish anger was dead and buried. Logan's "Poor old Charlie" did not ring so distinctly in his ears. Mrs. Stuart's horrified expression had faded considerably from his recollection. He thought only of that surprisingly tall, dark girl, whose eyes looked like coals, whose voice pierced him like a flint-tipped arrow. Ah, well, they would never quarrel again like that, he told himself. She loved him so, and would forgive him after he had talked quietly to her, and told her what an ass he was. She was simple-minded and awfully ignorant to pitch those old Indian laws at him in her fury, but he could not blame her; oh, no, he could not for one moment blame her. He had been terribly severe and unreasonable, and the horrid McDonald temper had got the better of him; and he loved her so. Oh! He loved her so! She would surely feel that, and forgive him, and—He went straight to his wife's room. The blue velvet evening dress lay on the chair into which he had thrown himself when he doomed his life's happiness by those two words, "God knows." A bunch of dead daffodils and her slippers were on the floor, everything—but Christie.

He went to his brother's bedroom door.

"Joe," he called, rapping nervously thereon; "Joe, wake up; where's Christie, d'you know?"

"Good Lord, no," gasped that youth, springing out of his armchair and opening the door. As he did so a note fell from off the handle. Charlie's face blanched to his very hair while Joe read aloud, his voice weakening at every word:—

"DEAR OLD JOE,—I went into your room at daylight to get that picture of the Post on your bookshelves. I hope you do not mind, but I kissed your hair while your slept; it was so curly, and yellow, and soft, just like his. Good-bye, Joe.

"CHRISTIE."

And when Joe looked into his brother's face and saw the anguish settle in those laughing blue eyes, the despair that drove the dimples away from that almost girlish mouth; when he realized that this boy was but four-and-twenty years old, and that all his future was perhaps darkened and shadowed for ever, a great, deep sorrow arose in his heart, and he forgot all things, all but the agony that rang up through the voice of the fair, handsome lad as he staggered forward, crying, "Oh! Joe—what shall I do—what shall I do!"

★ ★ ★ ★ ★

It was months and months before he found her, but during all that time he had never known a hopeless moment; discouraged he often was, but despondent, never. The sunniness of his ever-boyish heart radiated with warmth that would have flooded a much deeper gloom than that which settled within his eager young life. Suffer? ah! yes, he suffered, not with locked teeth and stony stoicism, not with the masterful self-command, the reserve, the conquered bitterness of the still-water sort of nature, that is supposed to run to such depths. He tried to be bright, and his sweet old boyish self. He would laugh sometimes in a pitiful, pathetic fashion. He took to petting dogs, looking into their large, solemn eyes with his wistful, questioning blue ones; he would kiss them, as women sometimes do, and call them "dear old fellow," in tones that had tears; and once in the course of his travels while at a little way-station, he discovered a huge St. Bernard imprisoned by some mischance in an empty freight car; the animal was nearly dead from starvation, and it seemed to salve his own sick heart to rescue back the dog's life. Nobody claimed the big starving creature, the train hands knew nothing of its owner, and gladly handed it over to its deliverer. "Hudson," he called it, and afterwards when Joe McDonald would relate the story of his brother's life he invariably terminated it with, "And I really believe that big lumbering brute saved him." From what, he was never to say.

But all things end, and he heard of her at last. She had never returned to the Post, as he at first thought she would, but had gone to the little town of B——, in Ontario, where she was making her living at embroidery and plain sewing.

The September sun had set redly when at last he reached the outskirts of the town, opened up the wicket gate, and walked up the weedy, unkept path leading to the cottage where she lodged.

Even through the twilight, he could see her there, leaning on the rail of the verandah—oddly enough she had about her shoulders the scarlet velvet cloak she wore when he had flung himself so madly from the room that night.

The moment the lad saw her his heart swelled with a sudden heat, burning moisture leapt into his eyes, and clogged his long, boyish lashes. He bounded up the steps—"Christie," he said, and the word scorched his lips like audible flame.

She turned to him, and for a second stood magnetized by his passionately wistful face; her peculiar grayish eyes seemed to drink the very life of his unquenchable love, though the tears that suddenly sprang into his seemed to absorb every pulse in his body through those hungry, pleading eyes of his that had, oh! so often been blinded by her kisses when once her whole world lay in their blue depths.

"You will come back to me, Christie, my wife? My wife, you will let me love you again?"

She gave a singular little gasp, and shook her head. "Don't, oh! don't," he cried piteously. "You will come to me, dear? it is all such a bitter mistake—I did not understand. Oh! Christie, I did not understand, and you'll forgive me, and love me again, won't you—won't you?"

"No," said the girl with quick, indrawn breath.

He dashed the back of his hand across his wet eyelids. His lips were growing numb, and he bungled over the monosyllable "Why?"

"I do not like you," she answered quietly.

"God! Oh! God, what is there left?"

She did not appear to hear the heart-break in his voice; she stood like one wrapped in sombre thought; no blaze, no tear, nothing in her eyes; no hardness, no tenderness about her mouth. The wind was blowing her cloak aside, and the only visible human life in her whole body was once when he spoke the muscles of her brown arm seemed to contract.

"But, darling, you are mine—*mine*—we are husband and wife! Oh, heaven, you *must* love me, and you *must* come to me again."

"You cannot *make* me come," said the icy voice, "neither church, nor law, nor even"—and the voice softened—"nor even love can make a slave of a red girl."

"Heaven forbid it," he faltered. "No, Christie, I will never claim you without your love. What reunion would that be? But oh, Christie, you are lying to me, you are lying to yourself, you are lying to heaven."

She did not move. If only he could touch her he felt as sure of her yielding as he felt sure there was a hereafter. The memory of the times when he had but to lay his hand on her hair to call a most passionate response from her filled his heart with a torture that choked all words before they reached his lips; at the thought of those days he forgot she was unapproachable, forgot how forbidding were her eyes, how stony her lips. Flinging himself forward, his knee on the chair at her side, his face pressed hardly in the folds of the cloak on her shoulder, he clasped his arms about her with a boyish petulance, saying, "Christie, Christie, my little girl wife, I love you, I love you, and you are killing me."

She quivered from head to foot as his fair, wavy hair brushed her neck, his despairing face sank lower until his cheek, hot as fire, rested on the cool, olive flesh of her arm. A warm moisture oozed up through her skin, and as he felt its glow he looked up. Her teeth, white and cold, were locked over her under lip, and her eyes were as grey stones.

Not murderers alone know the agony of a death sentence.

"Is it all useless? all useless, dear?" he said, with lips starving for hers.

"All useless," she repeated. "I have no love for you now. You forfeited me and my heart months ago, when you said *those two words.*"

His arms fell away from her wearily, he arose mechanically, he placed his little gray checked cap on the back of his yellow curls, the old-time laughter was dead in the blue eyes that now looked scared and haunted, the boyishness and the dimples crept away for ever from the lips that quivered like a child's; he turned from her, but she had looked once into his face as the Law Giver must have looked at the land of Canaan outspread at his feet. She watched him go down the long path and through the picket gate, she watched the big yellowish dog that had waited for him lumber up on to its feet—stretch—then follow him. She was conscious of but two things, the vengeful lie in her soul, and a little space on her arm that his wet lashes had brushed.

★ ★ ★ ★ ★

It was hours afterwards when he reached his room. He had said nothing, done nothing—what use were words or deeds? Old Jimmy Robinson was right; she had "balked" sure enough.

What a bare, hotelish room it was! He tossed off his coat and sat for ten minutes looking blankly at the sputtering gas jet. Then his whole life, desolate as a desert, loomed up before him with appalling distinctness. Throwing himself on the floor beside his bed, with clasped hands and arms outstretched on the white counterpane, he sobbed. "Oh! God, dear God, I thought you loved me; I thought you'd let me have her again, but you must be tired of me, tired of loving me too. I've nothing left now, nothing! it doesn't seem that I even have you to-night."

He lifted his face then, for his dog, big and clumsy and yellow, was licking at his sleeve.

3. "Dawendine" (1895)

There's a spirit on the river, there's a ghost upon the shore,
They are chanting, they are singing through the starlight
    evermore,
As they steal amid the silence,
    And the shadows of the shore.

You can hear them when the Northern candles light the
    Northern sky,
Those pale, uncertain candle flames, that shiver, dart and die,
Those dead men's icy finger tips,
    Athwart the Northern sky.

You can hear the ringing war-cry of a long-forgotten brave
Echo through the midnight forest, echo o'er the midnight
    wave,
And the Northern lanterns tremble
    At the war-cry of that brave.

And you hear a voice responding, but in soft and tender song;
It is Dawendine's spirit singing, singing all night long;
And the whisper of the night wind
    Bears afar her Spirit song.

And the wailing pine trees murmur with their voice attuned
    to hers,
Murmur when they 'rouse from slumber as the night wind
    through them stirs;
And you listen to their legend,
    And their voices blend with hers.

There was feud and there was bloodshed near the river by the hill;
And Dawendine listened, while her very heart stood still:
Would her kinsman or her lover
    Be the victim by the hill?

Who would be the great unconquered? who come boasting how
    he dealt
Death? and show his rival's scalplock fresh and bleeding at
    his belt.
Who would say, "O Dawendine!
    Look upon the death I dealt?"

And she listens, listens, listens—till a war-cry rends the night,
Cry of her victorious lover, monarch he of all the height;
And his triumph wakes the horrors,
    Kills the silence of the night.

Heart of her! it throbs so madly, then lies freezing in her breast,
For the icy hand of death has chilled the brother she loved best;
And her lover dealt the death-blow;
    And her heart dies in her breast.

And she hears her mother saying, "Take thy belt of wampum
    white;
Go unto yon evil savage while he glories on the height;
Sing and sue for peace between us:
    At his feet lay wampum white.

"Lest thy kinsmen all may perish, all thy brothers and thy sire
Fall before his mighty hatred as the forest falls to fire;
Take thy wampum pale and peaceful,
    Save thy brothers, save thy sire."

And the girl arises softly, softly slips toward the shore;
Loves she well the murdered brother, loves his hated foeman
    more,
Loves, and longs to give the wampum;
    And she meets him on the shore.

"Peace," she sings, "O mighty victor, Peace! I bring thee
    wampum white.
Sheathe thy knife whose blade has tasted my young kinsman's
    blood to-night

Ere it drink to slake its thirsting,
    I have brought thee wampum white."

Answers he, "O Dawendine! I will let thy kinsmen be,
I accept thy belt of wampum; but my hate demands for me
That they give their fairest treasure,
    Ere I let thy kinsmen be.

"Dawendine, for thy singing, for thy suing, war shall cease;
For thy name, which speaks of dawning, Thou shalt be the
    dawn of peace;
For thine eyes whose purple shadows tell of dawn,
    My hate shall cease.

"Dawendine, Child of Dawning, hateful are thy kin to me;
Red my fingers with their heart blood, but my heart is red
    for thee:
Dawendine, Child of Dawning,
    Wilt thou fail or follow me?"

And her kinsmen still are waiting her returning from the
    night,
Waiting, waiting for her coming with her belt of wampum white;
But forgetting all, she follows,
    Where he leads through day or night.

There's a spirit on the river, there's a ghost upon the shore,
And they sing of love and loving through the starlight
    evermore,
As they steal amid the silence,
    And the shadows of the shore.

4. "Ojistoh" (1895)

I am Ojistoh, I am she, the wife
Of him whose name breathes bravery and life
And courage to the tribe that calls him chief
I am Ojistoh, his white star, and he
Is land, and lake, and sky—and soul to me.

Ah! But they hated him, those Huron braves,
Him who had flung their warriors into graves,
He who had crushed them underneath his heel,
Whose arm was iron, and whose heart was steel
To all—save me, Ojistoh, chosen wife
Of my great Mohawk, white star of his life.

Ah! but they hated him, and councilled long
With subtle witchcraft how to work him wrong;
How to avenge their dead, and strike him where
His pride was highest, and his fame most fair.
Their hearts grew weak as women at his name:
They dared no war-path since my Mohawk came
With ashen bow, and flinten arrow-head
To pierce their craven bodies; but their dead
Must be avenged. Avenged? They dared not walk
In day and meet his deadly tomahawk;
They dared not face his fearless scalping knife;
So—Niyoh!¹—then they thought of me, his wife.

O! evil, evil face of them they sent
With evil Huron speech: "would I consent
To take of wealth? be queen of all their tribe?
Have wampum ermine?" Back I flung the bribe
Into their teeth, and said, "While I have life
Know this—Ojistoh is the Mohawk's wife."

Wah! how we struggled! But their arms were strong.
They flung me on their pony's back, with thong
Round ankle, wrist, and shoulder. Then upleapt
The one I hated most: his eye he swept
Over my misery, and sneering said,
"Thus, fair Ojistoh, we avenge our dead."

And we two rode, rode as a sea wind-chased,
I, bound with buckskin to his hated waist,
He, sneering, laughing, jeering, while he lashed
The horse to foam, as on and on we dashed.
Plunging through creek and river, bush and trail,
On, on we galloped like a northern gale.
At last, his distant Huron fires aflame
We saw, and nearer, nearer still we came.

---

1 [Johnson's note:] God, in the Mohawk language.

I, bound behind him in the captive's place,
Scarcely could see the outline of his face.
I smiled and laid my cheek against his back:
"Loose thou my hands," I said. "This pace let slack.
Forget we now that thou and I are foes.
I like thee well, and wish to clasp thee close;
I like the courage of thine eye and brow;
I like thee better than my Mohawk now."

He cut the cords; we ceased our maddened haste.
I wound my arms around his tawny waist;
My hand crept up the buckskin of his belt;
His knife hilt in my burning hand I felt;
One hand caressed his cheek, the other drew
The weapon softly—"I love you, love you,"
I whispered, "I love you as my life."
And—buried in his back his scalping knife.

Ha! how I rode, rode as a sea wind-chased,
Back to my Mohawk and my home. I lashed
That horse to foam, as on and on I dashed.
Plunging through creek and river, bush and trail,
On, on I galloped like a northern gale.
And then my distant Mohawk's fires aflame
I saw, as nearer, nearer still I came,
My hands all wet, stained with a life's red dye,
But pure my soul, pure as those stars on high—
"My Mohawk's pure white star, Ojistoh, still am I."

5. "The Derelict" (1896)

[A young Anglican missionary falls in love with a woman whose
father is English and mother Chippewa. He saves her good name,
but in doing so violates the sanctity of a death-bed confession.
The story was first published in *Massey's Magazine* in December
1896.]

Cragstone had committed what his world called a crime—an
inexcusable offence that caused him to be shunned by society
and estranged from his father's house. He had proved a failure.

Not one of his whole family connections could say unto the
others, "I told you so," when he turned out badly.

They had all predicted that he was born for great things, then to discover that they had over-estimated him was irritating, it told against their discernment, it was unflattering, and they thought him inconsiderate.

So, in addition to his failure, Cragstone had to face the fact that he had made himself unpopular among his kin.

As a boy he had been the pride of his family, as a youth, its hope of fame and fortune; he was clever, handsome, inventive, original, everything that society and his kind admired, but he criminally fooled them and their expectation, and they never forgave him for it.

He had dabbled in music, literature, law, everything—always with semi-success and brilliant promise; he had even tried the stage, playing the Provinces for an entire season; then, ultimately sinking into mediocrity in all these occupations, he returned to London, a hopelessly useless, a pitiably gifted man. His chilly little aristocratic mother always spoke of him as "poor, dear Charles." His brothers, clubmen all, graciously alluded to him with, "deuced hard luck, poor Charlie." His father never mentioned his name.

Then he went into "The Church," sailed for Canada, idled about for a few weeks, when one of the great colonial bishops, not knowing what else to do with him, packed him off north as a missionary to the Indians.

And, after four years of disheartening labor amongst a semi-civilized people, came this girl Lydia into his life. This girl of the mixed parentage, the English father, who had been swept northward with the rush of lumber trading, the Chippewa mother, who had been tossed to his arms by the tide of circumstances. The girl was a strange composition of both, a type of mixed blood, pale, dark, slender, with the slim hands, the marvellously beautiful teeth of her mother's people, the ambition, the small tender mouth, the utter fearlessness of the English race. But the strange, laughless eyes, the silent step, the hard sense of honor, proclaimed her far more the daughter of red blood than of white.

And, with the perversity of his kind, Cragstone loved her; he meant to marry her because he knew that he should not. What a monstrous thing it would be if he did! He, the shepherd of this half-civilized flock, the modern John Baptist; he, the voice of the great Anglican Church crying in this wilderness, how could he wed with this Indian girl who had been a common serving-maid in a house in Penetanguishene, and been dismissed therefrom with an accusation of theft that she could never prove untrue? How could he bring this reproach upon the Church? Why, the marriage would have no precedent; and yet he loved her, loved her sweet, silent ways, her listening attitudes, her clear, brown, consumptive-suggesting skin. She was the only thing in all the irksome mission life that had responded to him, had encouraged him to struggle anew for the spiritual welfare of this poor red race. Of course, in Penetanguishene they had told him she was irreclaimable, a thief, with ready lies to cover her crimes; for that very reason he felt tender towards her, she was so sinful, so pathetically human.

He could have mastered himself, perhaps, had she not responded, had he not seen the laughless eyes laugh alone for him, had she not once when a momentary insanity possessed them both confessed in words her love for him as he had done to her. But now? Well, now only this horrible tale of theft and untruth hung between them like a veil; now even with his arms locked about her, his eyes drowned in hers, his ears caught the whispers of calumny, his thoughts were perforated with the horror of his Bishop's censure, and these things rushed between his soul and hers, like some bridgeless deep he might not cross, and so his lonely life went on.

And then one night his sweet humanity, his grand, strong love rose up, battled with him, and conquered. He cast his pharisaical ideas, and the Church's "I am better than thou," aside forever; he would go now, to-night, he would ask her to be his wife, to have and to hold from this day forward, for better, for worse, for—

A shadow fell across the doorway of his simple home; it was August Beaver, the trapper, with the urgent request that he would come across to French Island at once, for old "Medicine" Joe was there, dying, and wished to see the minister. At another time Cragstone would have felt sympathetic, now he was only irritated; he wanted to find Lydia, to look in her laughless eyes, to feel her fingers in his hair, to tell her he did not care if she were a hundred times a thief, that he loved her, loved her, loved her, and he would marry her despite the Church, despite—

"Joe, he's near dead, you come now?" broke in August's voice. Cragstone turned impatiently, got his prayer-book, followed the trapper, took his place in the canoe, and paddled in silence up the bay.

The moon arose, large, limpid, flooding the cabin with a wondrous light, and making more wan the features of a dying man, whose fever-wasted form lay on some lynx skins on the floor.

Cragstone was reading from the Book of Common Prayer the

exquisite service of the Visitation of the Sick.[1] Outside, the loons clanged up the waterways, the herons called across the islands, but no human things ventured up the wilds. Inside, the sick man lay, beside him August Beaver holding a rude lantern, while Cragstone's matchless voice repeated the Anglican formula. A spasm, an uplifted hand, and Cragstone paused. Was the end coming even before a benediction? But the dying man was addressing Beaver in Chippewa, whispering and choking out the words in his death struggle.

"He says he's bad man," spoke Beaver. A horrible, humorous sensation swept over Cragstone; he hated himself for it, but at college he had always ridiculed death-bed confessions; but in a second that feeling had vanished, he bent his handsome, fair face above the copper-colored countenance of the dying man. "Joe," he said, with that ineffable tenderness that had always drawn human hearts to him; "Joe, tell me before I pronounce the Absolution, how you have been 'bad'?"

"I steal three times," came the answer. "Oncet horses, two of them from farmer near Barrie. Oncet twenty fox-skins at North Bay; station man he in jail for those fox-skins now. Oncet gold watch from doctor at Penetanguishene."

The prayer-book rattled from Cragstone's hands and fell to the floor.

"Tell me about this watch," he mumbled. "How did you come to do it?"

"I liffe at the doctor's; I take care his horse, long time; old River's girl, Lydia, she work there too; they say she steal it; I sell to trader, the doctor he nefer know, he think Lydia."

Cragstone was white to the lips. "Joe," he faltered, "you are dying; do you regret this sin, are you sorry?"

An indistinct "yes" was all; death was claiming him rapidly.

But a great, white, purified love had swept over the young clergyman. The girl he worshipped could never now be a reproach to his calling, she was proved blameless as a baby, and out of his great human love arose the divine calling, the Christ-like sense of forgiveness, the God-like forgetfulness of injury and suffering done to his and to him, and once more his soft, rich voice broke the stillness of the Northern night, as the Anglican absolution of the dying fell from his lips in merciful tenderness:

"O Lord Jesus Christ, who hath left power to His Church to

---

1 This rite of the Anglican Church contains prayers, blessings, and
   an exhortation to confess and receive absolution.

absolve all sinners who truly repent and believe in Him, of His great mercy forgive thee thine offences, and by His authority committed to me I absolve thee from all thy sins in the name of the Father, and of the Son, and of the Holy Ghost. Amen."

Beaver was holding the lantern close to the penitent's face; Cragstone, kneeling beside him, saw that the end had come already, and, after making the sign of the Cross on the dead Indian's forehead, the young priest arose and went silently out into the night.

★ ★ ★ ★ ★

The sun was slipping down into the far horizon, fretted by the inimitable wonder of islands that throng the Georgian Bay; the blood-colored skies, the purpling clouds, the extravagant beauty of a Northern sunset hung in the west like the trailing robes of royalty, soundless in their flaring, their fading; soundless as the unbroken wilds which lay bathed in the loneliness of a dying day.

But on the color-flooded shore stood two, blind to the purple, the scarlet, the gold, blind to all else save the tense straining of the other's eyes; deaf to nature's unsung anthem, hearing only the other's voice. Cragstone stood transfixed with consternation. The memory of the past week of unutterable joy lay blasted with the awfulness of this moment, the memory of even that first day—when he had stood with his arms about her, had told her how he had declared her reclaimed name far and wide, how even Penetanguishene knew now that she had suffered blamelessly, how his own heart throbbed suffocatingly with the honor, the delight of being the poor means through which she had been righted in the accusing eyes of their little world, and that now she would be his wife, his sweet, helping wife, and she had been great enough not to remind him that he had not asked her to be his wife until her name was proved blameless, and he was great enough not to make excuse of the resolve he had set out upon just when August Beaver came to turn the current of his life.

But he had other eyes to face to-night, eyes that blurred the past, that burned themselves into his being—the condemning, justly and righteously indignant eyes of his Bishop—while his numb heart, rather than his ears, listened to the words that fell from the prelate's lips like curses on his soul, like the door that would shut him forever outside the holy place.

"What have you done, you pretended servant of the living God? What use is this you have made of your Holy Orders? You hear the confessions of a dying man, you absolve and you bless him, and come away from the poor dead thief to shout his crimes in the ears of the world, to dishonor him, to be a discredit to your calling. Who could trust again such a man as you have proved to be—faithless to himself, faithless to his Church, faithless to his God?"

But Cragstone was on the sands at his accuser's feet. "Oh! my Lord," he cried, "I meant only to save the name of a poor, mistrusted girl, selfishly, perhaps, but I would have done the same thing just for humanity's sake had it been another to whom injustice was done."

"Your plea of justice is worse than weak; to save the good name of the living is it just to rob the dead?"

The Bishop's voice was like iron.

"I did not realize I was a priest, I only knew I was a *man*," and with these words Cragstone arose and looked fearlessly, even proudly, at the one who stood his judge.

"Is it not better, my Lord, to serve the living than the dead?"

"And bring reproach upon your Church?" said the Bishop, sternly.

It was the first thought Cragstone ever had of his official crime; he staggered under the horror of it, and the little, dark, silent figure, that had followed them unseen, realized in her hiding amid the shadows that the man who had lifted her into the light was himself being thrust down into irremediable darkness. But Cragstone only saw the Bishop looking at him as from a supreme height, he only felt the final stinging lash in the words: "When a man disregards the most sacred offices of his God, he will hardly reverence the claims of justice of a simple woman who knows not his world, and if he so easily flings his God away for a woman, just so easily will he fling her away for other gods."

And Lydia, with eyes that blazed like flame, watched the Bishop turn and walk frigidly up the sands, his indignation against this outrager of the Church declaring itself in every footfall.

Cragstone flung himself down, burying his face in his hands. What a wreck he had made of life! He saw his future, loveless, for no woman would trust him now; even the one whose name he had saved would probably be more unforgiving than the Church; it was the way with women when a man abandoned God and honor for them; and this nameless but blackest of sins, this falsity to one poor dying sinner, would stand between him and heaven forever, though through that very crime he had saved a fellow being. Where was the justice of it?

The purple had died from out the western sky, the waters of the Georgian Bay lay colorless at his feet, night was covering the world and stealing with inky blackness into his soul.

She crept out of her hiding-place, and, coming, gently touched his tumbled fair hair; but he shrank from her, crying: "Lydia, my girl, my girl, I am not for a good woman now! I, who thought you an outcast, a thief, not worthy to be my wife, to-night I am not an outcast of man alone, but of God."

But what cared she for his official crimes? She was a woman. Her arms were about him, her lips on his; and he who had, until now, been a portless derelict, who had vainly sought a haven in art, an anchorage in the service of God, had drifted at last into the world's most sheltered harbor—a woman's love.

But, of course, the Bishop took away his gown.[1]

6. "The Pilot of the Plains" (1891)

"False," they said, "thy Pale-face lover, from the land of waking
    morn;
Rise and wed thy Redskin wooer, nobler warrior ne'er was born;
Cease thy watching, cease thy dreaming,
    Show the white thine Indian scorn."

Thus they taunted her, declaring, "He remembers naught of
    thee:
Likely some white maid he wooeth, far beyond the inland sea."
But she answered ever kindly,
    "He will come again to me,"

Till the dusk of Indian summer crept athwart the western skies;
But a deeper dusk was burning in her dark and dreaming eyes,
As she scanned the rolling prairie,
    Where the foothills fall, and rise.

Till the autumn came and vanished, till the season of the rains,
Till the western world lay fettered in midwinter's crystal chains,
Still she listened for his coming,
    Still she watched the distant plains.

Then a night with nor'land tempest, nor'land snows a-swirling
    fast,
Out upon the pathless prairie came the Pale-face through the
    blast,
Calling, calling, "Yakonwita,
    I am coming, love, at last."

---

1   That is, Cragstone was "defrocked" and no longer able to act as a priest.

Hovered night above, about him, dark its wings and cold and
   dread;
Never unto trail or tepee were his straying footsteps led;
Till benumbed, he sank, and pillowed
      On the drifting snows his head,

Saying, "O! my Yakonwita call me, call me, be my guide
To the lodge beyond the prairie—for I vowed ere winter died
I would come again, beloved;
      I would claim my Indian bride."

"Yakonwita, Yakonwita!" Oh, the dreariness that strains
Through the voice that calling, quivers, till a whisper but
   remains,
"Yakonwita, Yakonwita,
      I am lost upon the plains."

But the Silent Spirit hushed him, lulled him as he cried anew,
"Save me, save me! O! beloved, I am Pale but I am true.
Yakonwita, Yakonwita,
      I am dying, love, for you."

Leagues afar, across the prairie, she had risen from her bed,
Roused her kinsmen from their slumber: "He has come
   tonight," she said.
"I can hear him calling, calling;
      But his voice is as the dead.

"Listen!" and they sat all silent, while the tempest louder grew,
And a spirit-voice called faintly, "I am dying, love, for you."
Then they wailed, "O! Yakonwita.
      He was Pale, but he was true."

Wrapped she then her ermine round her, stepped without the
   tepee door,
Saying, "I must follow, follow, though he call for evermore,
Yakonwita, Yakonwita";
      And they never saw her more.

Late at night, say Indian hunters, when the starlight clouds or
   wanes,
Far away they see a maiden, misty as the autumn rains,
Guiding with her lamp of moonlight
      Hunters lost upon the plains.

7. "Lullaby of the Iroquois" (1896)

Little brown baby-bird, lapped in your nest,
    Wrapped in your nest,
    Strapped in your nest,
Your straight little cradle-board rocks you to rest;
    Its hands are your nest,
    Its bands are your nest;
It swings from the down-bending branch of the oak;
You watch the camp flame, and the curling gray smoke;
But, oh, for your pretty black eyes sleep is best,—
Little brown baby of mine, go to rest.

Little brown baby-bird swinging to sleep,
    Winging to sleep,
    Singing to sleep,
Your wonder-black eyes that so wide open keep,
    Shielding their sleep,
    Unyielding to sleep,
The heron is homing, the plover is still,
The night-owl calls from his haunt on the hill,
Afar the fox barks, afar the stars peep,—
Little brown baby of mine, go to sleep.

8. "The Corn Husker" (1896)

Hard by the Indian lodges, where the bush
    Breaks in a clearing, through ill-fashioned fields,
She comes to labour, when the first still hush
    Of autumn follows large and recent yields.

Age in her fingers, hunger in her face,
    Her shoulders stooped with weight of work and years,
But rich in tawny coloring of her race,
    She comes a-field to strip the purple ears.

And all her thoughts are with the days gone by,
    Ere might's injustice banished from their lands
Her people, that to-day unheeded lie,
    Like the dead husks that rustle through her hands.

V. RESIDENTIAL SCHOOL

V. Residential School

[As Johnson's writing here reveals, she saw residential schooling as bad for children, families, and communities. From Confederation on, the Canadian policy was aimed at "civilizing" Indigenous people by separating their children from their families and punishing them for speaking their languages (see Appendix D1). In 1920 a revision to the Indian Act made it compulsory for Status Indians to attend either day or residential school.[1] Although many Indigenous people were eager to have their children educated, and often the stated ideals for the schools were lofty, in practice the girls spent most of their time doing laundry, cleaning, and preparing meals while the boys were trained in trades or worked on the farm that fed the students. Inadequate funding, low standards, and poor regulation meant that often the food they raised was sold for staff salaries, and the children, crowded, overworked, and undernourished, became prey to diseases, particularly tuberculosis. Worse, they were often humiliated, beaten, and sexually abused by teachers and staff. Separated from their parents, children returned home unable to speak their language or follow the traditional ways of their people. Few spoke openly about their experiences until recently.]

1. "As It Was in the Beginning" (1899)

[The title is a phrase from the Anglican creed: "As it was in the beginning, is now, and ever shall be." This story concerns a young Cree woman, separated from her family and taken into Christian mission school as a child. It first appeared in *Saturday Night*'s Christmas Number, 1899.]

They account for it by the fact that I am a Redskin, but I am something else, too—I am a woman.

I remember the first time I saw him. He came up the trail with some Hudson's Bay trappers, and they stopped at the door of my father's tepee. He seemed even then, fourteen years ago, an old man; his hair seemed just as thin and white, his hands just as

---

1 See *Honouring the Truth, Reconciling for the Future. Summary of the Final Report of the Truth and Reconciliation Commission of Canada*, 2015.

trembling and fleshless as they were a month since, when I saw him for what I pray his God is the last time.

My father sat in the tepee, polishing buffalo horns and smoking; my mother, wrapped in her blanket, crouched over her quill-work, on the buffalo-skin at his side; I was lounging at the doorway, idling, watching, as I always watched, the thin, distant line of sky and prairie; wondering, as I always wondered, what lay beyond it. Then he came, this gentle old man with his white hair and thin, pale face. He wore a long black coat, which I now know was the sign of his office, and he carried a black leather-covered book, which, in all the years I have known him, I have never seen him without.

The trappers explained to my father who he was, the Great Teacher, the heart's Medicine Man, the "Blackcoat" we had heard of, who brought peace where there was war, and the magic of whose black book brought greater things than all the Happy Hunting Grounds of our ancestors.

He told us many things that day, for he could speak the Cree tongue, and my father listened, and listened, and when at last they left us, my father said for him to come and sit within the tepee again.

He came, all the time he came, and my father welcomed him, but my mother always sat in silence at work with the quills; my mother never liked the Great "Blackcoat."

His stories fascinated me. I used to listen intently to the tale of the strange new place he called "heaven," of the gold crown, of the white dress, of the great music; and then he would tell of that other strange place—hell. My father and I hated it; we feared it, we dreamt of it, we trembled at it. Oh, if the "Blackcoat" would only cease to talk of it! Now I know he saw its effect upon us, and he used it as a whip to lash us into his new religion, but even then my mother must have known, for each time he left the tepee she would watch him going slowly away across the prairie; then when he was disappearing into the far horizon she would laugh scornfully, and say:

"If the white man made this Blackcoat's hell, let him go to it. It is for the man who found it first. No hell for Indians, just Happy Hunting Grounds. Blackcoat can't scare me."

And then, after weeks had passed, one day as he stood at the tepee door he laid his white, old hand on my head and said to my father: "Give me this little girl, chief. Let me take her to the mission school; let me keep her, and teach her of the great God and His eternal heaven. She will grow to be a noble woman, and return perhaps to bring her people to the Christ."

My mother's eyes snapped. "No," she said. It was the first

word she ever spoke to the "Blackcoat." My father sat and smoked. At the end of a half-hour he said:

"I am an old man, Blackcoat. I shall not leave the God of my fathers. I like not your strange God's ways—all of them. I like not His two new places for me when I am dead. Take the child, Blackcoat, and save her from hell."

★ ★ ★ ★ ★

The first grief of my life was when we reached the mission. They took my buckskin dress off, saying I was now a little Christian girl and must dress like all the white people at the mission. Oh, how I hated that stiff new calico dress and those leather shoes. But, little as I was, I said nothing, only thought of the time when I should be grown, and do as my mother did, and wear the buckskins and the blanket. My next serious grief was when I began to speak the English, that they forbade me to use any Cree words whatever. The rule of the school was that any child heard using its native tongue must get a slight punishment. I never understood it, I cannot understand it now, why the use of my dear Cree tongue could be a matter for correction or an action deserving punishment.

She was strict, the matron of the school, but only justly so, for she had a heart and a face like her brother's, the "Blackcoat." I had long since ceased to call him that. The trappers at the post called him "St. Paul," because, they told me, of his self-sacrificing life, his kindly deeds, his rarely beautiful old face; so I, too, called him "St. Paul," thought oftener "Father Paul," though he never liked the latter title, for he was a Protestant. But as I was his pet, his darling of the whole school, he let me speak of him as I would, knowing it was but my heart speaking in love. His sister was a widow, and mother to a laughing yellow-haired boy of about my own age, who was my constant playmate and who taught me much of English in his own childish way. I used to be fond of this child, just as I was fond of his mother and of his uncle, my "Father Paul," but as my girlhood passed away, as womanhood came upon me, I got strangely wearied of them all; I longed, oh, God, how I longed for the old wild life! It came with my womanhood, with my years.

What mattered it to me now that they had taught me all their ways?—their tricks of dress, their reading, their writing, their books. What mattered it that "Father Paul" loved me, that the traders at the post called me pretty, that I was a pet of all, from the factor to the poorest trapper in the service? I wanted my own people, my own old life, my blood called out for it, but they always said I must not return to my father's tepee. I heard them talk amongst themselves of keeping me away from pagan influences; they told each other that if I returned to the prairies, the tepees, I would degenerate, slip back to paganism, as other girls had done; marry, perhaps, with a pagan—and all their years of labor and teaching would be lost.

I said nothing, but I waited. And then one night the feeling overcame me. I was in the Hudson's Bay store when an Indian came in from the north with a large pack of buckskin. As they unrolled it a dash of its insinuating odor filled the store. I went over and leaned above the skins a second, then buried my face in them, swallowing, drinking the fragrance of them, that went to my head like wine. Oh, the wild wonder of that wood-smoked tan, the subtilty of it, the untamed smell of it! I drank it into my lungs, my innermost being was saturated with it, till my mind reeled and my heart seemed twisted with a physical agony. My childhood recollections rushed upon me, devoured me. I left the store in a strange, calm frenzy, and going rapidly to the mission house I confronted my Father Paul and demanded to be allowed to go "home," if only for a day. He received the request with the same refusal and the same gentle sigh that I had so often been greeted with, but this time the desire, the smoke-tan, the heart-ache, never lessened.

Night after night I would steal away by myself and go to the border of the village to watch the sun set in the foothills, to gaze at the far line of sky and prairie, to long and long for my father's lodge. And Laurence—always Laurence—my fair-haired, laughing, child playmate, would come calling and calling for me: "Esther, where are you? We miss you; come in, Esther, come in with me." And if I did not turn at once to him and follow, he would come and place his strong hands on my shoulders and laugh into my eyes and say, "Truant, truant, Esther; can't *we* make you happy?"

My old childhood playmate had vanished years ago. He was a tall, slender young man now, handsome as a young chief, but with laughing blue eyes, and always those yellow curls about his temples. He was my solace in my half-exile, my comrade, my brother, until one night it was, "Esther, Esther, can't *I* make you happy?"

I did not answer him; only looked out across the plains and thought of the tepees. He came close, close. He locked his arms about me, and with my face pressed up to his throat he stood silent. I felt the blood from my heart sweep to my very finger-tips. I loved him. O God, how I loved him! In a wild, blind instant it all came, just because he held me so and was whispering brokenly,

"Don't leave me, don't leave me, Esther; *my* Esther, my child-love, my playmate, my girl-comrade, my little Cree sweetheart, will you go away to your people, or stay, stay for me, for my arms, as I have you now?"

No more, no more the tepees; no more the wild stretch of prairie, the intoxicating fragrance of the smoke-tanned buckskin; no more the bed of buffalo hide, the soft, silent moccasin; no more the dark faces of my people, the dulcet cadence of the sweet Cree tongue—only this man, this fair, proud, tender man who held me in his arms, in his heart. My soul prayed his great white God, in that moment, that He would let me have only this. It was twilight when we re-entered the mission gate. We were both excited, feverish. Father Paul was reading evening prayers in the large room beyond the hallway; his soft, saint-like voice stole beyond the doors, like a benediction upon us. I went noiselessly upstairs to my own room and sat there undisturbed for hours.

The clock downstairs struck one, startling me from my dreams of happiness, and at the same moment a flash of light attracted me. My room was in an angle of the building, and my window looked almost directly down into those of Father Paul's study, into which at that instant he was entering, carrying a lamp. "Why, Laurence," I heard him exclaim, "what are you doing here? I thought, my boy, you were in bed hours ago."

"No, uncle, not in bed, but in dreamland," replied Laurence, arising from the window, where evidently he, too, had spent the night hours as I had done.

Father Paul fumbled about a moment, found his large black book, which for once he seemed to have got separated from, and was turning to leave, when the curious circumstance of Laurence being there at so unusual an hour seemed to strike him anew. "Better go to sleep, my son," he said simply, then added curiously, "Has anything occurred to keep you up?"

Then Laurence spoke: "No, uncle, only—only, I'm happy, that's all."

Father Paul stood irresolute. Then: "It is—?"

"Esther," said Laurence quietly, but he was at the old man's side, his hand was on the bent old shoulder, his eyes proud and appealing. Father Paul set the lamp on the table, but, as usual, one hand held that black book, the great text of his life. His face was paler than I had ever seen it—graver.

"Tell me of it," he requested.

I leaned far out of my window and watched them both. I listened with my very heart, for Laurence was telling him of me, of his love, of the new-found joy of that night.

"You have said nothing of marriage to her?" asked Father Paul.

"Well—no; but she surely understands that—"

"Did you speak of *marriage*?" repeated Father Paul, with a harsh ring in his voice that was new to me.

"No, uncle, but—"

"Very well, then, very well."

There was a brief silence. Laurence stood staring at the old man as though he were a stranger; he watched him push a large chair up to the table, slowly seat himself; then mechanically following his movements, he dropped on to a lounge. The old man's head bent low, but his eyes were bright and strangely fascinating. He began:

"Laurence, my boy, your future is the dearest thing to me of all earthly interests. Why you *can't* marry this girl—no, no, sit, sit until I have finished," he added, with raised voice, as Laurence sprang up, remonstrating. "I have long since decided that you marry well; for instance, the Hudson's Bay factor's daughter."[1]

Laurence broke into a fresh, rollicking laugh. "What, uncle," he said, "little Ida McIntosh? Marry that little yellow-haired fluff ball, that kitten, that pretty little dolly?"

"Stop," said Father Paul. Then with a low, soft persuasiveness, "She is *white*, Laurence."

My lover started. "Why, uncle, what do you mean?" he faltered.

"Only this, my son: poor Esther comes of uncertain blood; would it do for you—the missionary's nephew, and adopted son, you might say—to marry the daughter of a pagan Indian? Her mother is hopelessly uncivilized; her father has a dash of French somewhere—half-breed, you know, my boy, half-breed." Then, with still lower tone and half-shut, crafty eyes, he added: "The blood is a bad, bad mixture, *you* know that; you know, too, that I am very fond of the girl, poor dear Esther. I have tried to separate her from evil pagan influences; she is the daughter of the Church; I want her to have no other parent; but you never can tell what lurks in a caged animal that has once been wild. My whole heart is with the Indian people, my son; my whole heart, my whole life, has been devoted to

---

1 The chief trading officer in a Hudson's Bay Company trading post was called a factor.

bringing them to Christ, *but it is a different thing to marry with one of them.*"

His small old eyes were riveted on Laurence like a hawk's on a rat. My heart lay like ice in my bosom.

Laurence, speechless and white, stared at him breathlessly.

"Go away somewhere," the old man was urging; "to Winnipeg, Toronto, Montreal; forget her, then come back to Ida McIntosh. A union of the Church and Hudson's Bay will mean great things, and may ultimately result in my life's ambition, the civilization of this entire tribe, that we have worked so long to bring to God."

I listened, sitting like one frozen. Could those words have been uttered by my venerable teacher, by him whom I revered as I would one of the saints in his own black book? Ah, there was no mistaking it. My white father, my life-long friend who pretended to love me, to care for my happiness, was urging the man I worshipped to forget me, to marry with the factor's daughter—because of what? Of my red skin; my good, old, honest pagan mother; my confiding French-Indian father. In a second all the care, the hollow love he had given me since my childhood, were as things that never existed. I hated that old mission priest as I hated his white man's hell. I hated his long, white hair; I hated his thin, white hands; I hated his body, his soul, his voice, his black book—oh, how I hated the very atmosphere of him.

Laurence sat motionless, his face buried in his hands, but the old man continued, "No, no; not the child of that pagan mother; you can't trust her, my son. What would you do with a wife who might any day break from you to return to her prairies and her buckskins? *You can't trust her.*" His eyes grew smaller, more glittering, more fascinating then, and leaning with an odd, secret sort of movement towards Laurence, he almost whispered, "Think of her silent ways, her noiseless step; the girl glides about like an apparition; her quick fingers, her wild longings—I don't know why, but with all my fondness for her, she reminds me sometimes of a strange—*snake.*"

Laurence shuddered, lifted his face, and said hoarsely: "You're right, uncle; perhaps I'd better not; I'll go away, I'll forget her, and then—well, then—yes, you are right, it *is* a different thing to marry one of them." The old man arose. His feeble fingers still clasped his black book; his soft white hair clung about his forehead like that of an Apostle; his eyes lost their peering, crafty expression; his bent shoulders resumed the dignity of a minister of the living God; he was the picture of what the trader called him—"St. Paul."

"Good-night, son," he said.

"Good-night, uncle, and thank you for bringing me to myself."

They were the last words I ever heard uttered by either that old arch-fiend or his weak, miserable kinsman. Father Paul turned and left the room. I watched his withered hand—the hand I had so often felt resting on my head in holy benedictions—clasp the door-knob, turn it slowly, then, with bowed head and his pale face wrapped in thought, he left the room—left it with the mad venom of my hate pursuing him like the very Evil One he taught me of.

What were his years of kindness and care now? What did I care for his God, his heaven, his hell? He had robbed me of my native faith, of my parents, of my people, of this last, this life of love that would have made a great, good woman of me. God! how I hated him!

I crept to the closet in my dark little room. I felt for the bundle I had not looked at for years—yes, it was there, the buckskin dress I had worn as a little child when they brought me to the mission. I tucked it under my arm and descended the stairs noiselessly. I would look into the study and speak good-bye to Laurence; then I would—

I pushed open the door. He was lying on the couch where a short time previously he had sat, white and speechless, listening to Father Paul. I moved towards him softly. God in heaven, he was already asleep. As I bent over him the fullness of his perfect beauty impressed me for the first time; his slender form, his curving mouth that almost laughed even in sleep, his fair, tossed hair, his smooth, strong-pulsing throat. God! how I loved him!

Then there arose the picture of the factor's daughter. I hated her. I hated her baby face, her yellow hair, her whitish skin. "She shall not marry him," my soul said. "I will kill him first—kill his beautiful body, his lying, false heart." Something in my heart seemed to speak; it said over and over again, "Kill him, kill him; she will never have him then. Kill him. It will break Father Paul's heart and blight his life. He has killed the best of you, of your womanhood; kill *his* best, his pride, his hope—his sister's son, his nephew Laurence." But how? how?

What had that terrible old man said I was like? A *strange snake*. A snake? The idea wound itself about me like the very coils of a serpent. What was this in the beaded bag of my buckskin dress? This little thing rolled in tan that my mother had given me at parting with the words, "Don't touch much, but some time maybe you want it!" Oh! I knew well enough what it was—a small flint arrow-head dipped in the venom of some *strange snake*.

I knelt beside him and laid my hot lips on his hand. I worshipped him, oh, how, how I worshipped him! Then again the vision of *her* baby face, *her* yellow-hair—I scratched his wrist twice with the arrow-tip. A single drop of red blood oozed up; he stirred. I turned the lamp down and slipped out of the room—out of the house.

★ ★ ★ ★ ★

I dream nightly of the horrors of the white man's hell. Why did they teach me of it, only to fling me into it?

Last night as I crouched beside my mother on the buffalo-hide, Dan Henderson, the trapper, came in to smoke with my father. He said old Father Paul was bowed with grief, that with my disappearance I was suspected, but that there was no proof. Was it not merely a snake bite?

They account for it by the fact that I am a Redskin.

They seem to have forgotten I am a woman.

2. "His Sister's Son" (1896)

[Although Johnson recited "His Sister's Son" regularly, no published version has been found. This fragment taken down by an audience member was published in a press clipping from the *Fort Wayne Indiana Gazette*, 25 November 1896.]

For they killed the best that was in me
When they said I must not return
To my father's lodge, to my mother's arms
When my heart would burn—and burn!
For when dead is a daughter's womanhood
There is nothing left that is grand and good.

3. "Little Wolf-Willow" (1907)

[This is a story about a Cree boy who does not let residential school change him and who reconciles his father with the North-West Mounted Police. It was first published in *The Boys' World* on 7 December 1907 and collected in *The Shaganappi* (1913).]

Fig. 3: Chiefs from Crooked Lake: Kahkewistahaw sits in the
middle between Ahtahkakoop (l.) and Mistawasis (r.). Standing:
Louis O'Soup (Saulteaux, l.) and Peter Hourie (Metis translator,
r.). Brantford, ON, 13 October 1886. Prince Albert Historical
Society. PAHS T-503-10

Old Beaver-Tail hated many things, but most of all he hated the North-West Mounted Police. Not that they had ever molested or worried him in his far corner of the Crooked Lakes Indian Reserve,[1] but they stood for the enforcing of the white man's laws, and old Beaver-Tail hated the white man. He would sit for hours together in his big tepee counting his piles of furs, smoking, grumbling and storming at the inroads of the pale-faces on to his lands and hunting grounds. Consequently it was an amazing surprise to everybody when he consented to let his eldest son, Little Wolf-Willow, go away to attend the Indian School in far-off Manitoba. But old Beaver-Tail explained with rare appreciation his reasons for this consent. He said he wished the boy to learn English, so that he would grow up to be a keen, sharp trader, like the men of the Hudson's Bay Company, the white men who were so apt to outwit the redskins in a fur-trad-ing bargain. Thus we see that poor old Beaver-Tail had suffered and been cheated at the hands of the cunning paleface. Little Wolf-Willow was not little, by any means; he was tall, thin, wiry, and quick, a boy of marked intelligence and much ability. He was called Little Wolf-Willow to distinguish him from his grandsire, Big Wolf-Willow by name, whose career as a warrior made him famed throughout half of the great Canadian North-West. Little Wolf-Willow's one idea of life was to grow up and be like his grandfather, the hero of fifty battles against both hostile Indian tribes and invading white settlers; to have nine scalps at his belt, and scars on his face; to wear a crimson-tipped eagle feather in his hair, and to give a war-whoop that would echo

---

1 Crooked Lake Reserves were created in 1881 as part of Treaty 4, on the edge of the Qu'Appelle Valley east of Regina, Saskatchewan. After much pressure from settlers, in 1907 the Canadian govern-ment seized three-quarters of the land and auctioned it off. In 1997, an inquiry concluded that the transfer breached the fiduciary obligations of the government to the Kakewistahaw First Nation, who lost almost all their arable land. Johnson may have based her picture of "Old Beaver Tail" on Kakewistahaw (c. 1810–1906). The chiefs who signed treaties regarded them as sacred and did not join the 1885 Resistance (see Cardinal and Hildebrandt; Stonechild and Waiser). Along with other loyal chiefs, Kakewistahaw was chosen to travel to Brantford, Ontario, for the unveiling of the memorial to Joseph Brant (Thayendanegea) at which Johnson was present.

from lake to lake and plant fear in the hearts of his enemies. But instead of all this splendid life the boy was sent away to the school taught by paleface men and women; to a terrible, far-away, strange school, where he would have to learn a new language and perhaps wear clothes like the white men wore. The superintendent of the school, who had persuaded old Beaver-Tail to let the boy come, brought him out from the Crooked Lakes with several other boys. Most of them could speak a few words of English, but not so Little Wolf-Willow, who arrived from his prairie tepee dressed in buckskin and moccasins, a pretty string of white elks' teeth about his throat, and his long, straight, black hair braided in two plaits, interwoven with bits of rabbit skin. A dull green blanket served as an overcoat, and he wore no hat at all. His face was small, and beautifully tinted a rich, reddish copper color, and his eyes were black, alert, and very shining.

The teachers greeted him very kindly, and he shook hands with them gravely, like a very old man. And from that day onward Little Wolf-Willow shut his heart within himself, and suffered.

In the first place, the white people all looked sick to him—unhealthy, bleached. Then, try as he would, he could not accustom his feet to the stiff leather shoes he was induced to wear. One morning his buckskin coat was missing, and in its place was a nice blue cloth one with gleaming golden buttons. He hated it, but he had to wear it. Then his green blanket disappeared; a warm, heavy overcoat in its place. Then his fringed buckskin "chaps" went; in their place a pair of dreadful grey cloth trousers. Little Wolf-Willow made no comment, but he kept his eyes and ears open, and mastered a few important words of English, which, however, he kept to himself—as yet. And then, one day, when he had worn these hated clothes for a whole month, the superintendent who had brought him away from his father's tepee sent for him to come to his little office. The boy went. The superintendent was so kind and so gentle, and his smile was so true, that the boy had grown somewhat attached to him, so, without fear of anything in the world, the little Cree scholar slipped noiselessly into the room.

"Ah, Little Wolf-Willow," said the superintendent, kindly, "I notice that you are beginning to understand a little English already." The boy smiled, and nodded slightly. "You are very quick and smart, my boy, quick as a lynx, smart as a fox. Now tell me, are you happy here? Do you like the school?" continued Mr. Enderby.

There was a brief silence, then a direct, straight look from the small Cree eyes, and the words, "I like you—me."

Mr. Enderby smiled. "That's good; I like you, too, Little Wolf-Willow. Now tell me, do you like your new clothes?"

"No good," said the boy.

Mr. Enderby looked grave. "But, my boy, that is what you must wear if you are to be educated. Do you know what the word 'education' means? Have you ever heard the teachers or boys here use it?"

"White man, English," came the quick reply.

"That's it; you have described it exactly. To become educated you must try and wear and do what the white people do—like the English, as you say," Mr. Enderby went on. "Now what about your hair? White men don't wear long hair, and you see all the Cree boys in the school have let me cut their hair. Wouldn't you like to be like them?"

"No; hair good," said the boy.

"Well, how about a 'white' name?" asked Mr. Enderby. "The other boys have taken them. Wouldn't you like me to call you John? I'd like to."

"Me Wolf-Willow, same grandfather," came in tones of pronounced decision.

"Very well, Little Wolf-Willow, you must do as you like, you know; but you said when you came in that you liked me, and I like you very much. Perhaps some day you will do these things to please me." Then Mr. Enderby added softly to himself, "It will all come in time. It is pretty hard to ask any boy to give up his language, his clothes, his customs, his old-time way of living, his name, even the church of his fathers. I must have patience, patience?"

"You speak?" asked the boy.

"Just to myself," said Mr. Enderby.

"I speak," said the little Indian, standing up and looking fearlessly into the superintendent's face. "I speak. I keep hair, good. I keep name Wolf-Willow, good. I keep skin Indian color. I not white man's skin. English skin no good. My skin best, good."

Mr. Enderby laughed. "No, no, Little Wolf-Willow, we won't try to change the color of your skin," he said.

"No good try. I keep skin, better skin than white man. I keep skin, me." And the next instant he was gone.

Miss Watson, the matron, appeared at the door. "What have you done to Little Wolf-Willow?" she asked in surprise. "Why, he is careering down the hall at a breakneck speed."

"I believe the child thought I was going to skin him, to make a white boy out of him," laughed Mr. Enderby.

"Poor little chap! I expect you wanted to cut off his hair," said Miss Watson, "and perhaps call him Tom, Dick, Harry, or some such name."

"I did," answered the superintendent. "The other boys have all come to it."

"Yes, I know they have," agreed Miss Watson, "but there is something about that boy that makes me think that you'll never get his hair or his name away from him."

And she was right. They never did.

It was six years before Little Wolf-Willow again entered the door of his father's tepee. He returned to the Crooked Lakes speaking English fluently, and with the excellent appointment of interpreter for the Government Indian Agent. The instant his father saw him, the alert Cree eye noted the uncut hair. Nothing could have so pleased old Beaver-Tail. He had held for years a fear in his heart that the school would utterly rob him of his boy. Little Wolf-Willow's mother arose from preparing an antelope stew for supper. She looked up into her son's face. When he left he had not been as high as her ear tips. With the wonderful intuition of mothers the world over, she knew at the first glance that they had not made him into a white man. Years seemed to roll from her face. She had been so fearful lest he should not come back to their old prairie life.

"Rest here," she said, in the gentle Cree tongue. "Rest here, Little Wolf-Willow; it is your home."

The boy himself had been almost afraid to come. He had grown accustomed to sleeping in a house, in a bed, to wearing shoes, to eating the white man's food; but the blood of the prairies leaped in his veins at the sight of the great tepee, with its dry sod floor spread with wolf-skins and ancient buffalo hides. He flung himself on to the furs and the grass, his fingers threading themselves through the buckskin fringes that adorned old Beaver-Tail's leggings.

"Father," he cried out, in the quaint Cree tongue, "father, sire of my own, I have learned the best the white man had to give, but they have not changed me, or my heart, any more than they could change the copper tint of my skin."

Old Beaver-Tail fairly chuckled, then replied, between pipe puffs, "Some of our Cree boys go to school. They learn the white man's ways, and they are of no more use to their people. They cannot trap for furs, nor scout, nor hunt, nor find a prairie trail. You are wiser than that, Little Wolf-Willow. You are smarter than when you left us, but you return to us, the old people of your tribe, just the same—just the same as your father and grandfather."

"Not quite the same," replied the boy, cautiously, "for, father, I do not now hate the North-West Mounted Police."

For answer, old Beaver-Tail snarled like a husky dog. "You'll hate them again when you live here long enough!" he muttered. "And if you have any friends among them, keep those friends distant, beyond the rim of the horizon. I will not have their scarlet coats showing here."

Wisely, the boy did not reply, and that night, rolled in coyote skins, he slept like a little child once more on the floor of his father's tepee.

For many months after that he travelled about the great prairies, visiting with the Government Indian Agent many distant camps and Cree lodges. He always rode astride a sturdy little buckskin-colored cayuse. Like most Indian boys, he was a splendid horseman, steady in his seat, swift of eye, and sure of every prairie trail in all Saskatchewan. He always wore a strange mixture of civilized and savage clothes—fringed buckskin "chaps," beaded moccasins, a blue flannel shirt, a scarlet silk handkerchief knotted around his throat, a wide-brimmed cowboy hat with a rattlesnake skin as a hatband, and two magnificent bracelets of ivory elks' teeth. His braided hair, his young, clean, thin, dark face, his fearless riding, began to be known far and wide. The men of the Hudson's Bay Company trusted him. The North-West Mounted Police loved him. The white traders admired him. But, most of all, he stood fast in the affection of his own Indian people. They never forgot the fact that, had he wished, he could have stayed with the white people altogether, that he was equal to them in English education, but he did not choose to do so—he was one of their own for all time.

But one dreadful night Corporal Manan of the North-West Mounted Police rode into barracks at Regina with a serious, worried face. He reported immediately to his captain. "A bad business, captain," he said, coming to attention, "a very bad business, sir. I have reports from old 'Scotty' McIntyre's ranch up north that young Wolf-Willow, that we all know so well, has been caught rustling cattle—cut out two calves, sir, and—well, he's stolen them, sir, and old Scotty is after him with a shot-gun."

"Too bad, too bad!" said the captain, with genuine concern. "Young Wolf-Willow gone wrong! I can hardly believe it. How old is he, Corporal?"

"About sixteen or seventeen, I should say, sir."

"Too bad!" again said the captain. "Well educated; fine boy, too. What good has it done him? It seems these Indians *will* cut up. Education seems to only make them worse, Corporal. He'll feel arrest less from you than most of us. You'll have to go. Start early, at daylight, and bring him in to prison when you return."

"*I?*" fairly shouted Corporal Manan. "*I* arrest young Wolf-Willow? No, sir! You'll have to get another policeman."

"You'll do as you receive orders," blurted the captain, then added more graciously, "Why, Manan, don't you see how much better it is to arrest him? Scotty is after him with a shotgun, and he'll kill the boy on sight. Wolf-Willow is safest here. You leave at daylight, and bring him in, if you have to handcuff him to do it."

Corporal Manan spent a miserable night. Never had a task been so odious to him. He loved the bright, handsome Cree boy, and his heart was sore that he had gone wrong, after giving such promise of a fine, useful manhood. But the white settlers' cattle must be protected, and orders were orders—a soldier must obey his superior officer. So, at daybreak, the fastest horse in the service was saddled, and Corporal Manan was hard on the trail of the young Cree thief.

But Little Wolf-Willow knew nothing of all this. Far away up the northern plains a terrible bit of news had come to him. At the Hudson's Bay post he had been told that his old grandfather had been caught stealing cattle, that the North-West Mounted Police were after him, that they would surely capture him and put him in Regina jail. The boy was horrified. His own old grandfather a thief! He knew that old warrior well enough—knew that he was innocent of intentional crime; knew that, should the scarlet-coated police give chase, the old Indian would never understand, but would probably fire and kill the man who attempted to arrest him. The boy knew that with his own perfect knowledge of English, he could explain everything away if only he could be at his grandfather's in time, or else intercept the police before they should arrest him. His grandfather would shoot; the boy knew it. Then there would be bloodshed added to theft. But Big Wolf-Willow's lodge was ninety miles distant, and it was the middle of a long, severe winter. What was to be done? One thing only—he, Little Wolf-Willow, must ride, ride, ride! He must not waste an hour, or the prison at Regina would have his grandfather, and perhaps a gallant soldier of the king would meet his death doing his duty.

Thrusting a pouch of pemmican into his shirt front, and fastening his buckskin coat tightly across his chest, he flung himself on to his wiry little cayuse, faced about to the north-east, and struck the trail for the lodges of his own people. Then began the longest, most terrible ride of his life. Afterwards, when he became a man, he often felt that he lived through years and years during that ninety-mile journey. On all sides of him stretched the blinding white, snow-covered prairie. Not a tree, not an object to mark the trail. The wind blew straight and level directly down from the Arctic zone, icy, cutting, numbing. It whistled past his ears, pricking and stinging his face like a whiplash. The cold, yellow sunlight on the snow blinded him, like a light flashed from a mirror. Not a human habitation, not a living thing, lay in his path. Night came, with countless stars and a joyous crescent of Northern Lights hanging low in the sky, and the intense, still cold that haunts the prairie country. He grudged the hours of rest he must give his horse, pitying the poor beast for its lack of food and water, but compelled to urge it on and on. After what seemed a lifetime of hardship, both boy and beast began to weaken. The irresistible sleepiness that forebodes freezing began to overcome Little Wolf-Willow. Utter exhaustion was sapping the strength of the cayuse. But they blundered on, mile after mile, both with the pluck of the prairies in their red blood; colder, slower, wearier, they became. Little Wolf-Willow's head was whirling, his brain thickening, his fingers clutching aimlessly. The bridle reins slipped from his hands. Hunger, thirst, cold, exhaustion, overpowered both horse and rider. The animal stumbled once, twice, then fell like a dead weight.

★ ★ ★ ★ ★

At daybreak, Corporal Manan, hot on the pursuit of the supposed young cattle thief, rode up the freezing trail, headed for the north-east. A mile ahead of him he saw what he thought was a dead steer which the coyotes had probably killed and were eating. As he galloped nearer he saw it was a horse. An exclamation escaped his lips. Then, slipping from his own mount, stiff and half frozen himself, he bent pityingly above the dead animal that lay with the slender body of an Indian hugging up to it for warmth.

"Poor little chap!" choked the Corporal. "Poor Little Wolf-Willow! Death's got him now, I'm afraid, and that's worse than the Mounted Police."

Then the soldier knelt down, and for two long hours rubbed with snow and his own fur cap the thin, frozen face and hands of the almost lifeless boy. He rolled the lithe young body about, pounding it and beating it, until consciousness returned, and the boy opened his eyes dully.

"That's better," said the Corporal. "Now, my lad, it's for home!" Then he stripped himself of his own great-coat, wrapped it snugly about the young Indian, and, placing the boy on his own horse, he trudged ahead on foot—five, ten, fifteen miles of it, the boy but half conscious and freezing, the man tramping ahead, footsore, chilled through, and troubled, the horse with hanging head and lagging step—a strange trio to enter the Indian camp.

From far off old Beaver-Tail had seen the approaching bit of hated scarlet—the tunic worn by the North-West Mounted Police—but he made no comment as Corporal Manan lifted in his strong arms the still figure from the saddle, and, carrying it into the tepee, laid it beside the fire on the warm wolf skins and buffalo hides. It took much heat and nourishment before Little Wolf-Willow was able to interpret the story from the Cree tongue into English, then back again into Cree, and so be the go-between for the Corporal and old Beaver-Tail. "Yes, my grandfather, Big Wolf-Willow, is here," said the boy, his dark eyes looking fearlessly into the Corporal's blue ones. "He's here, as you see, and I suppose you will have to arrest him. He acknowledges he took the cattle. He was poor, hungry, starving. You see, Corporal, he cannot speak English, and he does not understand the white men or their laws. He says for me to tell you that the white men came and stole all our buffaloes, the millions of beautiful animals that supplied us with hides to make our tepees, furs to dress in, meat to eat, fat to keep us warm; so he thought it no harm to take two small calves when he was hungry. He asks if anyone arrested and punished the white men who took all his buffaloes, and, if not, why should he be arrested and punished for doing far less wrong than the wrong done by the white man?"

"But—but—" stammered Corporal Manan, "I'm not after *him*. It is *you* I was told to arrest."

"Oh, why didn't I know? Why didn't I know it was I you were after?" cried the boy. "I would have let you take me, handcuff me, anything, for I understand, but he does not."

Corporal Manan stood up, shaking his shoulders as a big dog shakes after a plunge. Then he spoke: "Little Wolf-Willow, can you ever forgive us all for thinking you were a cattle-thief? When I think of your grandfather's story of the millions of buffaloes he has lost, and those two paltry calves he took for food, I make no arrests here. My captain must do what he thinks best."

"And you saved me from freezing to death, and brought me

home on your own horse, when you were sent out to take me to prison!" muttered the boy, turning to his soldier friend with admiration.

But old Beaver-Tail interrupted. He arose, held out his hand towards the once hated scarlet-coated figure, and spoke the first words he had ever voiced in English. They were, "North-West Mounted Police, good man, he. Beaver-Tail's friend."

VI. THE WEST COAST

VI. The West Coast

[Johnson travelled to the west coast several times during her performing career. When she spent a month there in the summer of 1908, Chief Joe Capilano, whom she had met in London in 1906, went to the Hotel Vancouver to welcome her. After one more year of touring, she settled there for good in 1909, moving into an apartment on Howe Street, quickly making new friends and connecting with old ones. Here she began writing for *Boys' World* and *Mother's Magazine*, both published in Elgin, Illinois. She also placed in Vancouver's *Daily Province* the stories that Chief Capilano and his wife, Mary Agnes, had told her. Several women's organizations in the city invited her to speak and later supported her in her last illness.

Johnson often used words from Chinook Jargon (also called Chinook Wawa) in her work. It was a trade language (also called a pidgin) widely used in the Pacific Northwest by all ethnic groups until around 1920, particularly in canneries, logging camps and mills, and other worksites. It contains words from many Indigenous languages, as well as English and French. Some words have moved into British Columbia English and even beyond.]

1. "The Potlatch" (1910)

["The Potlatch" tells the story of a boy from Vancouver Island who dreams of going to the mainland and finally gets a chance to prove himself at a Squamish potlatch. The story was published for the first time in *Boys' World* on 8 October 1910. The potlatch, an important ceremony for many tribes of British Columbia, was banned by the Canadian federal government from 1885 until 1951. Missionaries and officials saw it as a scene of moral disorder rather than a system for sharing wealth, settling disputes, and regulating family and intertribal relationships. The words in this story that Johnson translates are Chinook Jargon.]

Fig. 4: Potlatch at Alert Bay (Kwakiutl), 1890s. Photo: William Halliday. Vancouver Public Library. VPL #8664

Young Ta-la-pus sat on the highest point of rock that lifted itself on the coast at the edge of his father's Reserve. At his feet stretched the Straits of Georgia, and far across the mists of the salt Pacific waters he watched the sun rise seemingly out of the mainland that someone had told him stretched eastward thousands of miles, where another ocean, called the Atlantic, washed its far-off shore, for Ta-la-pus lived on Vancouver Island, and all his little life had been spent in wishing and longing to set his small, moccasined feet on that vast mainland that the old men talked of, and the young men visited year in and year out. But never yet had he been taken across the wide, blue Straits, for he was only eleven years old, and he had two very big brothers who always accompanied their father, old chief Mowitch, on his journeyings, for they were good fishermen, and could help in the salmon catch, and bring good chicamin (money) home to buy supplies for the winter. Sometimes these big brothers would tease him and say, "What can you expect? Your name is Ta-la-pus, which means a prairie wolf. What has a prairie wolf to do with crossing great waters? He cannot swim, as some other animals can. Our parents gave us better names, 'Chet-woot,' the bear, who swims well, and 'Lapool,' the water fowl, whose home is on the waters, whose feet are webbed, and who floats even while he sleeps. No, our young brother, Ta-la-pus, the prairie wolf, was never meant to cross the great salt Straits."

Then little Ta-la-pus would creep away to his lonely rock, trying to still the ache in his heart and forcing back the tears from his eyes. Prairie wolves must not cry like little girl babies—and sometimes when his heart was sorest, a clear, dazzlingly bright day would dawn, and far, far off he could see the blur of the mainland coast, resting on the sea like an enormous island. Then he would tell himself that, no matter what his name was, some day he would cross to that great, far country, whose snow-crowned mountain peaks he could just see merging into the distant clouds.

Then, late in the summer, there came one marvellous night, when his father and brother returned from the sockeye salmon fishing, with news that set the entire Indian village talking far into the early morning. A great Squamish chief on the mainland was going to give a Potlatch. He had been preparing for it for weeks. He had enjoyed a very fortunate fishing season, was a generous-hearted man, and was prepared to spend ten thousand dollars[1] in gifts and entertainment for his friends and all the poor of the various neighboring tribes.

Chief Mowitch and all his family were invited, and great rejoicing and anticipation were enjoyed over their salmon suppers that night.

"You and the boys go," said his wife. "Perhaps you will be lucky and bring home chicamin and blankets. The old men say the winter will be cold. Grey geese were going south yesterday, three weeks earlier than last year. Yes, we will need blankets when the ollalies (berries) are ripe in October. I shall stay at home, until the babies are older. Yes, you and the boys go."

"Yes," responded the chief. "It would never do for us to miss a great Squamish Potlatch. We must go."

Then the elder son, Chet-woot, spoke joyously:

"And, mama,[2] we may bring back great riches, and even if the cold does come while we are away, our little brother, Ta-la-pus, will care for you and the babies. He'll carry water and bring all the wood for your warmth."

The father looked smilingly at Ta-la-pus, but the boy's eyes, great and dark, and hungry for the far mainland, for the great feasts he had heard so much of, were fastened in begging, pleading seriousness on his father's face. Suddenly a whim seized the old chief's fancy.

"Ta-la-pus," he said, "you look as if you would like to go, too. Do you want to take part in the Potlatch?"

Instantly Chet-woot objected. "Papa, he could never go, he's too young. They may ask him to dance for them. He can't dance. Then perhaps they would never ask us."

The chief scowled. He was ruler in his own lodge, and allowed no interference from anyone.

"Besides," continued Chet-woot, "there would be no one to fetch wood for mama and the babies."

"Yes, there would be someone," said the chief, his eyes snapping fiercely. "*You* would be here to help your mama."

"I?" exclaimed the young man. "But how can I, when I shall be at the Potlatch? I go to *all* the Potlatches."

"So much more reason that you stay home this once and care for your mama and baby sisters, and you *shall* stay. Lapool and little Ta-la-pus will go with me. It is time the boy saw something

---

1 [Johnson's note:] Fact. This amount has frequently been given away.

2 [Johnson's note:] The Chinook for father and mother is "papa" and "mama," adopted from the English language.

of the other tribes. Yes, I'll take Lapool and Ta-la-pus, and there is no change to my word when it is once spoken."

Chet-woot sat like one stunned, but an Indian son knows better than to argue with his father. But the great, dark eyes of little Ta-la-pus glowed like embers of fire, his young heart leaped joyously. At last, at last, he was to set foot in the country of his dreams—the far, blue, mountain-circled mainland.

All that week his mother worked day and night on a fine new native costume for him to wear on the great occasion. There were trousers of buckskin fringed down each side, a shirt of buckskin, beaded and beautified by shell ornaments, a necklace of the bones of a rare fish, strung together like little beads on deer sinew, ear-rings of pink and green pearl from the inner part of the shells of a bivalve, neat moccasins, and solid silver, carven bracelets.

She was working on a headdress consisting of a single red fox-tail and eagle feathers, when he came and stood beside her.

"Mama," he said, "there is a prairie wolf skin you cover the babies with while they sleep. Would you let me have it this once, if they would not be cold without it?"

"They will never be cold," she smiled, "for I can use an extra blanket over them. I only use it because I started to when you were the only baby I had, and it was your name, so I covered you with it at night."

"And I want to cover myself with it now," he explained, "its head as my headdress, its front paws about my neck, its thick fur and tail trailing behind me as I dance."

"So you are going to dance, my little Ta-la-pus?" she answered proudly. "But how is that, when you do not yet know our great tribal dances?"

"I have made one of my own, and a song, too," he said, shyly.

She caught him to her, smoothing the hair back from his dark forehead. "That is right," she half whispered, for she felt he did not want anyone but herself to know his boyish secret. "Always make things for yourself, don't depend on others, try what you can do alone. Yes, you may take the skin of the prairie wolf. I will give it to you for all time—it is yours."

That night his father also laid in his hands a gift. It was a soft, pliable belt, woven of the white, peeled roots of the cedar, dyed brilliantly, and worked into a magnificent design.

"Your great-grandmother made it," said the chief. "Wear it on your first journey into the larger world than this island, and do nothing in all your life that would make her regret, were she alive, to see it round your waist."

So little Ta-la-pus set forth with his father and brother, well equipped for the great Potlatch, and the meeting of many from half a score of tribes.

They crossed the Straits on a white man's steamer, a wonderful sight to Ta-la-pus, who had never been aboard any larger boat than his father's fishing smack and their own high-bowed, gracefully-curved canoe. In and out among the islands of the great gulf the steamer wound, bringing them nearer, ever nearer to the mainland. Misty and shadowy, Vancouver Island dropped astern, until at last they steamed into harbor, where a crowd of happy-faced Squamish Indians greeted them, stowed them away in canoes, paddled a bit up coast, then sighted the great, glancing fires that were lighting up the grey of oncoming night—fires of celebration and welcome to all the scores of guests who were to partake of the lavish hospitality of the great Squamish chief.

As he stepped from the great canoe, Ta-la-pus thought he felt a strange thrill pass through the soles of his feet. They had touched the mainland of the vast continent of North America for the first time; his feet seemed to become sensitive, soft, furry, cushioned like those of a wild animal. Then, all at once, a strange inspiration seized him. Why not try to make his footsteps "pad" like the noiseless paws of a prairie wolf? "pad" in the little. dance he had invented, instead of "shuffling" in his moccasins, as all the grown men did? He made up his mind that when he was alone in his tent he would practise it, but just now the great Squamish chief was coming towards them with outstretched greeting hands, and presently he was patting little Ta-la-pus on the shoulder, and saying, "Oh, ho, my good Tillicum Mowitch, I am glad you have brought this boy. I have a son of the same size. They will play together, and perhaps this Tenas Tyee (Little Chief) will dance for me some night."

"My brother does not dance our tribal dances," began Lapool, but Ta-la-pus spoke up bravely.

"Thank you, O Great Tyee (Chief), I shall dance when you ask me." His father and brother both stared at him in amazement. Then Chief Mowitch laughed, and said, "If he says he will dance, he will do it. He never promises what he cannot do, but I did not know he could do the steps. Ah! he is a little hoolool (mouse) this boy of mine; he keeps very quiet, and does not boast what he can do."

Little Ta-la-pus was wonderfully encouraged by his father's notice of him and his words of praise. Never before had he seemed so close to manhood, for, being the youngest boy of the family, he had but little companionship with any at home except his mother and the little sisters that now seemed so far behind him in their island home. All that evening the old chiefs and the stalwart young braves were gravely shaking hands with his father, his brother Lapool, and himself, welcoming them to the great festival and saying pleasant things about peace and brotherhood prevailing between the various tribes instead of war and bloodshed, as in the olden times. It was late when the great supper of boiled salmon was over, and the immense bonfires began to blaze on the shore where the falling tides of the Pacific left the beaches dry and pebbly. The young men stretched themselves on the cool sands, and the old men lighted their peace pipes, and talked of the days when they hunted the mountain sheep and black bear on these very heights overlooking the sea. Ta-la-pus listened to everything. He could learn so much from the older men, and hour by hour he gained confidence. No more he thought of his dance with fear and shyness, for all these people were kindly and hospitable even to a boy of eleven. At midnight there was another feast, this time of clams, and luscious crabs, with much steaming black tea. Then came the great Squamish chief, saying more welcoming words, and inviting his guests to begin their tribal dances. Ta-la-pus never forgot the brilliant sight that he looked on for the next few hours. Scores of young men and women went through the most graceful figures of beautiful dances, their shell ornaments jingling merrily in perfect time to each twist and turn of their bodies. The wild music from the beat of Indian drums and shell "rattles" arose weirdly, half sadly, drifting up the mountain heights, until it lost itself in the timber line of giant firs that crested the summits. The red blaze from the camp fires flitted and flickered across the supple figures that circled around, in and out between the three hundred canoes beached on the sands, and the smoke-tipped tents and log lodges beyond the reach of tide water. Above it all a million stars shone down from the cloudless heavens of a perfect British Columbian night. After a while little Ta-la-pus fell asleep, and when he awoke, dawn was just breaking. Someone had covered him with a beautiful, white, new blanket, and as his young eyes opened they looked straight into the kindly face of the great Squamish chief.

"We are all aweary, 'Tenas Tyee' (Little Chief)," he said. "The dancers are tired, and we shall all sleep until the sun reaches midday, but my guests cry for one more dance before sunrise. Will you dance for us, oh, little Ta-la-pus?"

The boy sprang up, every muscle and sinew and nerve on the alert. The moment of his triumph or failure had come.

"You have made me, even a boy like me, very welcome, O Great Tyee," he said, standing erect as an arrow, with his slender, dark chin raised manfully. "I have eaten of your kloshe muck-a-muck (very good food), and it has made my heart and my feet very skookum (strong). I shall do my best to dance and please you." The boy was already dressed in the brilliant buckskin costume his mother had spent so many hours in making, and his precious wolfskin was flung over his arm. The great Squamish chief now took him by the hand and led him towards the blazing fires round which the tired dancers, the old men and women, sat in huge circles where the chill of dawn could not penetrate. "One more dance, then we sleep," said the chief to the great circle of spectators. "This Tenas Tyee will do his best to amuse us."

Then Ta-la-pus felt the chief's hand unclasp, and he realized that he was standing absolutely alone before a great crowd of strangers, and that every eye was upon him.

"Oh, my brother," he whispered, smoothing the prairie wolf skin, "help me to be like you, help me to be worthy of your name." Then he pulled the wolf's head over his own, twisted the fore legs about his throat, and stepped into the great circle of sand between the crouching multitude and the fires.

Stealthily he began to pick his way in the full red flare from the flames. He heard many voices whispering, "Tenas," "Tenas," meaning "He is little, he is young," but his step only grew more stealthy, until he "padded" into a strange, silent trot in exact imitation of a prairie wolf. As he swung the second time round the fires, his young voice arose, in a thin, wild, wonderful barking tone, so weird and wolf-like that half the spectators leaped up to their knees, or feet, the better to watch and listen. Another moment, and he was putting his chant into words.

"They call me Ta-la-pus, the prairie-wolf,
    And wild and free am I.
I cannot swim like Eh-ko-lie, the whale,
    Nor like the eagle, Chack-chack, can I fly.
    I cannot talk as does the great Ty-ee,
    Nor like the o-tel-agh[1] shine in the sky.
I am but Ta-la-pus, the prairie-wolf,
    And wild and free am I."

---

1 [Johnson's note:] Sun.

With every word, every step, he became more like the wolf he was describing. Across his chanting and his "padding" in the sand came murmurs from the crowd. He could hear "Tenas, tenas," "To-ke-tie Tenas" (pretty boy), "Skookum-tanse," (good strong dance). Then at last, "Ow," "Ow" meaning "Our young brother." On and on went Ta-la-pus. The wolf feeling crept into his legs, his soft young feet, his clutching fingers, his wonderful dark eyes that now gleamed red and lustrous in the firelight. He was as one inspired, giving a beautiful and marvellous portrait of the wild vagabonds of the plains. For fully ten minutes he circled and sang, then suddenly crouched on his haunches, then, lifting his head, he turned to the east, his young throat voiced one long, strange note, wolf-like he howled to the rising sun, which at that moment looked over the crest of the mountains, its first golden shaft falling full upon his face.

His chant and his strange wolf-dance were ended. Then one loud clamor arose from the crowd. "Tenas Tyee," "Tenas Tyee," they shouted, and Ta-la-pus knew that he had not failed. But the great Squamish chief was beside him.

"Tillicums,"[1] he said, facing the crowd, "this boy has danced no tribal dance learned from his people or his parents. This is his own dance, which he has made to deserve his name. He shall get the first gifts of our great Potlatch. Go," he added, to one of the young men, "bring ten dollars of the white man's chicamin (money), and ten new blankets as white as that snow on the mountain top."

The crowd was delighted. They approved the boy and rejoiced to see the real Potlatch was begun. When the blankets were piled up beside him they reached to the top of Ta-la-pus' head. Then the chief put ten dollars in the boy's hand with the simple words, "I am glad to give it. You won it well, my Tenas Tyee."

That was the beginning of a great week of games, feasting and tribal dances, but not a night passed but the participants called for the wild "wolf-dance" of the little boy from the island. When the Potlatch was over, old Chief Mowitch and Lapool and Ta-la-pus returned to Vancouver Island, but no more the boy sat alone on the isolated rock, watching the mainland through a mist of yearning. He had set foot in the wider world, he had won his name, and now honored it, instead of hating it, as in the old days when his brothers taunted him, for the great Squamish chief, in bidding good-bye to him, had said: "Little Ta-la-pus, remember

1 Friends, my people.

a name means much to a man. You despised your name, but you have made it great and honorable by your own act, your own courage. Keep that name honorable, little Ta-la-pus; it will be worth far more to you than many blankets or much of the white man's chicamin."

2. "Catharine of the Crow's Nest" (1910)

[Crow's Nest Pass is a pass through the Rocky Mountains on the southern Alberta–British Columbia border; the CPR rail line through this pass was built during 1897 and 1898. The story was first published in *Mother's Magazine* in December 1910.]

The great transcontinental railway had been in running order for years before the managers thereof decided to build a second line across the Rocky Mountains. But "passes" are few and far between in those gigantic fastnesses, and the fearless explorers, followed by the equally fearless surveyors, were many a toilsome month conquering the heights, depths and dangers of the "Crow's Nest Pass."

Eastward stretched the gloriously fertile plains of southern "Sunny Alberta," westward lay the limpid blue of the vast and indescribably beautiful Kootenay Lakes, but between these two arose a barrier of miles and miles of granite and stone and rock, over and through which a railway must be constructed. Tunnels, bridges, grades must be bored, built and blasted out. It was the work of science, endurance and indomitable courage. The summers in the canyons were seething hot, the winters in the mountains perishingly cold, with apparently inexhaustible snow clouds circling forever about the rugged peaks—snows in which many a good, honest laborer was lost until the eagles and vultures came with the April thaws, and wheeled slowly above the pulseless sleeper, if indeed the wolves and mountain lions had permitted him to lie thus long unmolested. Those were rough and rugged days, through which equally rough and rugged men served and suffered to find foundations whereon to lay those two threads of steel that now cling like a cobweb to the walls of the wonderful "gap" known as Crow's Nest Pass.

Work progressed steadily, and before winter set in construction camps were built far into "the gap," the furthermost one being close to the base of a majestic mountain, which was also named "The Crow's Nest." It arose beyond the camp with almost overwhelming immensity. Dense forests of Douglas fir and bull pines shouldered their way up one-third of its height, but above the timber line the shaggy, bald rock reared itself thousands of feet skyward, desolate, austere and deserted by all living things; not even the sure-footed mountain goat travelled up those frowning, precipitous heights; no bird rested its wing in that frozen altitude. The mountain arose, distinct, alone, isolated, the most imperial monarch of all that regal Pass.

The construction gang called it "Old Baldy," for after working some months around its base, it began to grow into their lives. Not so, however, with the head engineer from Montreal, who regarded it always with baleful eye, and half laughingly, half seriously, called it his "Jonah."

"Not a thing has gone right since we worked in sight of that old monster," he was heard to say frequently; and it did seem as if there were some truth in it. There had been deaths, accidents and illness among the men. Once, owing to transportation difficulties, the rations were short for days, and the men were in rebellious spirit in consequence. Twice whiskey had been smuggled in, to the utter demoralization of the camp; and one morning, as a last straw, "Cookee" had nearly severed his left hand from his arm with a meat axe. Young Wingate, the head engineer, and Mr. Brown, the foreman, took counsel together. For the three meals of that day they tried three different men out of the gang as "cookees." No one could eat the atrocious food they manufactured. Then Brown bethought himself. "There's an Indian woman living up the canyon that can cook like a French chef," he announced, after a day of unspeakable gnawing beneath his belt. "How about getting her? I've tasted pork and beans at her shack, and flapjacks, and—"

"Get her! get her!" clamored Wingate. "Even if she poisons us, it's better than starving. I'll ride over to-night and offer her big wages."

"How about her staying here?" asked Brown. "The boys are pretty rough and lawless at times, you know."

"Get the axe men to build her a good, roomy shack—the best logs in the place. We'll give her a lock and key for it, and you, Brown, report the very first incivility to her that you hear of," said Wingate crisply.

That evening Mr. Wingate himself rode over to the canyon; it was a good mile, and the trail was rough in the extreme. He did not dismount when he reached the lonely log lodge, but rapping on the door with the butt of his quirt, he awaited its opening. There was some slight stirring about inside before this occurred; then the door slowly opened, and she stood before him—a rather tall woman, clad in buckskin garments, with a rug made of coyote skins about her shoulders; she wore the beaded leggings and moccasins of her race, and her hair, jet black, hung in ragged plaits about her dark face, from which mournful eyes looked out at the young Montrealer.

Yes, she would go for the wages he offered, she said in halting English; she would come to-morrow at daybreak; she would cook their breakfast.

"Better come to-night," he urged. "The men get down the grade to work very early; breakfast must be on time."

"I be on time," she replied. "I sleep here this night, every night. I not sleep in camp."

Then he told her of the shack he had ordered and that was even now being built.

She shook her head. "I sleep here every night," she reiterated.

Wingate had met many Indians in his time, so dropped the subject, knowing full well that persuasion or argument would be utterly useless.

"All right," he said; "you must do as you like; only remember, an early breakfast to-morrow."

"I 'member," she replied.

He had ridden some twenty yards, when he turned to call back: "Oh, what's your name, please?"

"Catharine," she answered, simply.

"Thank you," he said, and, touching his hat lightly, rode down towards the canyon. Just as he was dipping over its rim he looked back. She was still standing in the doorway, and above and about her were the purple shadows, the awful solitude, of Crow's Nest Mountain.

★ ★ ★ ★ ★

Catharine had been cooking at the camp for weeks. The meals were good, the men respected her, and she went her way to and from her shack at the canyon as regularly as the world went around. The autumn slipped by, and the nipping frosts of early winter and the depths of early snows were already daily occurrences. The big group of solid log shacks that formed the construction camp were all made weather-tight against the long mountain winter. Trails were beginning to be blocked, streams to freeze, and "Old Baldy," already wore a canopy of snow that reached down to the timber line.

"Catharine," spoke young Wingate, one morning, when the clouds hung low and a soft snow fell, packing heavily on the selfsame snows of the previous night, "you had better make up your mind to occupy the shack here. You won't be able to go to your home much longer now at night; it gets dark so early, and the snows are too heavy."

"I go home at night," she repeated.

"But you can't all winter," he exclaimed. "If there was one single horse we could spare from the grade work, I'd see you got it for your journeys, but there isn't. We're terribly short now; every animal in the Pass is overworked as it is. You'd better not try going home any more."

"I go home at night," she repeated.

Wingate frowned impatiently; then in afterthought he smiled. "All right, Catharine," he said, "but I warn you. You'll have a search-party out after you some dark morning, and you know it won't be pleasant to be lost in the snows up that canyon."

"But I go home, night-time," she persisted, and that ended the controversy.

But the catastrophe he predicted was inevitable. Morning after morning he would open the door of the shack he occupied with the other officials, and, looking up the white wastes through the gray-blue dawn, he would watch the distances with an anxiety that meant more than a consideration for his breakfast. The woman interested him. She was so silent, so capable, so stubborn. What was behind all this strength of character? What had given that depth of mournfulness to her eyes? Often he had surprised her watching him, with an odd longing in her face; it was something of the expression he could remember his mother wore when she looked at him long, long ago. It was a vague, haunting look that always brought back the one great tragedy of his life—a tragedy he was even now working night and day at his chosen profession to obliterate from his memory, lest he should be forever unmanned—forever a prey to melancholy.

He was still a young man, but when little more than a boy he had married, and for two years was transcendently happy. Then came the cry of "Kootenay Gold" ringing throughout Canada—of the untold wealth of Kootenay mines.[1] Like thousands of others he followed the beckoning of that yellow finger, taking his young wife and baby daughter West with him. The little town of Nelson, crouching on its beautiful hills, its feet laved by

---

1   The first Kootenay gold rush began in 1864; by the late nineteenth century, most of the gold coming from Canada was mined in the region.

the waters of Kootenay Lake, was then in its first robust, active infancy. Here he settled, going out alone on long prospecting expeditions; sometimes he was away a week, sometimes a month, with the lure of the gold forever in his veins, but the laughter of his child, the love of his wife, forever in his heart. Then—the day of that awful home-coming! For three weeks the fascination of searching for the golden pay-streak had held him in the mountains. No one could find him when it happened, and now all they could tell him was the story of an upturned canoe found drifting on the lake, of a woman's light summer shawl caught in the thwarts, of a child's little silken bonnet washed ashore. [Fact.] The great-hearted men of the West had done their utmost in the search that followed. Miners, missionaries, prospectors, Indians, settlers, gamblers, outlaws, had one and all turned out, for they liked young Wingate, and they adored his loving wife and dainty child. But the search was useless. The wild shores of Kootenay Lake alone held the secret of their resting-place.

Young Wingate faced the East once more. There was but one thing to do with his life—*work*, work, WORK; and the harder, the more difficult, that work, the better. It was this very difficulty that made the engineering on the Crow's Nest Pass so attractive to him. So here he was building grades, blasting tunnels, with Catharine's mournful eyes following him daily, as if she divined something of that long-ago sorrow that had shadowed his almost boyish life.

He liked the woman, and his liking quickened his eye to her hardships, his ear to the hint of lagging weariness in her footsteps; so he was the first to notice it the morning she stumped into the cook-house, her feet bound up in furs, her face drawn in agony.

"Catharine," he exclaimed, "your feet have been frozen!"

She looked like a culprit, but answered: "Not much; I get lose in storm las' night."

"I thought this would happen," he said, indignantly. "After this you sleep here."

"I sleep home," she said, doggedly.

"I won't have it," he declared. "I'll cook for the men myself first."

"All right," she replied. "You cookee; I go home—me."

That night there was a terrible storm. The wind howled down the throat of the Pass, and the snow fell like bales of sheep's wool, blanketing the trails and drifting into the railroad cuts until they attained their original level. But after she had cooked supper Catharine started for home as usual. The only unusual thing about it was that the next morning she did not return. It was Sunday, the men's day "off." Wingate ate no breakfast, but after swallowing some strong tea he turned to the foreman. "Mr. Brown, will you come with me to try and hunt up Catharine?" he asked.

"Yes, if we can get beyond the door," assented Brown. "But I doubt if we can make the canyon, sir."

"We'll have a try at it, anyway," said the young engineer. "I almost doubt myself if she made it last night."

"She's a stubborn woman," commented Brown.

"And has her own reasons for it, I suppose," replied Wingate. "But that has nothing to do with her being lost or frozen. If something had not happened I'm sure she would have come to-day, notwithstanding I scolded her yesterday, and told her I'd rather cook myself than let her run such risks. How will we go, Mr. Brown; horses or snowshoes?"

"Shoes," said the foreman decidedly. "That snow'll be above the middle of the biggest horse in the outfit."

So they set forth on their tramp up the slopes, peering right and left as they went for any indication of the absent woman. Wingate's old grief was knocking at his heart once more. A woman lost in the appalling vastness of this great Western land was entering into his life again. It took them a full hour to go that mile, although both were experts on the shoes, but as they reached the rim of the canyon they were rewarded by seeing a thin blue streak of smoke curling up from her lodge "chimney." Wingate sat down in the snows weakly. The relief had unmanned him.

"I didn't know how much I cared," he said, "until I knew she was safe. She looks at me as my mother used to; her eyes are like mother's, and I loved my mother."

It was a simple, direct speech, but Brown caught its pathos.

"She's a good woman," he blurted out, as they trudged along towards the shack. They knocked on the door. There was no reply. Then just as Wingate suggested forcing it in case she were ill and lying helpless within, a long, low call from the edge of the canyon startled them. They turned and had not followed the direction from which the sound came more than a few yards when they met her coming towards them on snowshoes; in her arms she bore a few faggots, and her face, though smileless, was very welcoming.

She opened the door, bidding them enter. It was quite warm inside, and the air of simple comfort derived from crude benches, tables and shelves, assured them that she had not suffered. Near the fire was drawn a rough home-built couch, and on it lay in heaped disorder a pile of gray blankets. As the two men warmed their hands at the grateful blaze, the blankets stirred. Then a small hand crept out and a small arm tossed the covers a little aside.

"*Catharine*," exclaimed Wingate, "have you a child here?"

"Yes," she said simply.

"How long is it that you have had it here?" he demanded.

"Since before I work at your camp," she replied.

"Whew!" said the foreman, "I now understand why she came home nights."

"To think I never guessed it!" murmured Wingate. Then to Catharine: "Why didn't you bring it into camp and keep it there day and night with you, instead of taking these dangerous tramps night and morning?"

"It is a girl child," she answered.

"Well what of it?" he asked impatiently.

"Your camp no place for girl child," she replied, looking directly at him. "Your men they rough, they get whisky sometimes. They fight. They speak bad words, what you call *swear*. I not want her hear that. I not want her see whisky man."

"Oh, Brown!" said Wingate, turning to his companion. "What a reproach! What a reproach! Here our gang is—the vanguard of the highest civilization, but unfit for association with a little Indian child!"

Brown stood speechless, although in his rough, honest mind he was going over a list of those very "swears" she objected to, but they were mentally directed at the whole outfit of his ruffianly construction gang. He was silently swearing at them for their own shortcomings in that very thing.

The child on the couch stirred again. This time the firelight fell full across the little arm. Wingate stared at it, then his eyes widened. He looked at the woman, then back at the bare arm. It was the arm of a *white* child.

"Catharine, was your husband *white*?" he asked, in a voice that betrayed anxiety.

"I got no husban'," she replied, somewhat defiantly.

"Then—" he began, but his voice faltered.

She came and stood between him and the couch.

Something of the look of a she-panther came into her face, her figure, her attitude. Her eyes lost their mournfulness and blazed a black-red at him. Her whole body seemed ready to spring.

"You not touch the girl child!" she half snarled. "I not let you touch her; she *mine*, though I have no husban'!"

"I don't want to touch her, Catharine," he said gently, trying to pacify her. "Believe me, I don't want to touch her."

The woman's whole being changed. A thousand mother-lights gleamed from her eyes, a thousand measures of mother-love stormed at her heart. She stepped close, very close to him and laid her small brown hand on his, then drawing him nearer to her said: "Yes you *do* want to touch her; you not speak truth when you say 'no.' You *do* want to touch her!" With a rapid movement she flung back the blankets, then slipping her bare arm about him she bent his form until he was looking straight into the child's face—a face the living miniature of his own! His eyes, his hair, his small kindly mouth, his fair, perfect skin. He staggered erect.

"Catharine! what does it mean? What does it mean?" he cried hoarsely.

"*Your child—*" she half questioned, half affirmed.

"Mine? Mine?" he called, without human understanding in his voice. "Oh, Catharine! Where did you get her?"

"The shores of Kootenay Lake," she answered.

"Was—was—she *alone*?" he cried.

The woman looked away, slowly shaking her head, and her voice was very gentle as she replied: "No, she alive a little, but *the other*, whose arms 'round her, she not alive; my people, the Kootenay Indians, and I—we—we bury that other."

For a moment there was a speaking silence, the young Wingate, with the blessed realization that half his world had been saved for him, flung himself on his knees, and, with his arms locked about the little girl, was calling:

"Margie! Margie! Papa's little Margie girl! Do you remember papa? Oh, Margie! Do you? Do you?"

Something dawned in the child's eyes—something akin to a far-off memory. For a moment she looked wonderingly at him, then put her hand up to his forehead and gently pulled a lock of his fair hair that always curled there—an old trick of hers. Then she looked down at his vest pocket, slowly pulled out his watch and held it to her ear. The next minute her arms slipped round his neck.

"Papa," she said, "papa been away from Margie a long time."

Young Wingate was sobbing. He had not noticed that the big, rough foreman had gone out of the shack with tear-dimmed eyes, and had quietly closed the door behind him.

★ ★ ★ ★ ★

It was evening before Wingate got all the story from Catharine, for she was slow of speech, and found it hard to explain her feelings. But Brown, who had returned alone to the camp in the morning, now came back, packing an immense bundle of all the tinned delicacies he could find, which, truth to tell, were few. He knew some words in Kootenay, and led Catharine on to reveal the strange history that sounded like some tale from fairyland. It appeared that the reason Catharine did not attempt to go to the camp that morning was that Margie was not well, so she would not leave her, but in her heart of hearts she knew young Wingate would come searching to her lodge. She loved the child as only an Indian woman can love an adopted child. She longed for him to come when she found Margie was ill, yet dreaded that coming from the depths of her soul. She dreaded the hour he would see the child and take it away. For the moment she looked upon his face, the night he rode over to engage her to cook, months ago, she had known he was Margie's father. The little thing was the perfect mirror of him, and Catharine's strange wild heart rejoiced to find him, yet hid the child from him for very fear of losing it out of her own life.

After finding it almost dead in its dead mother's arms on the shore, the Indians had given it to Catharine for the reason that she could speak some English. They were only a passing band of Kootenays, and as they journeyed on and on, week in and week out, they finally came to Crow's Nest Mountain. Here the child fell ill, so they built Catharine a log shack, and left her with plenty of food, sufficient to last until the railway gang had worked that far up the Pass, when more food would be available. When she had finished the strange history, Wingate looked at her long and lovingly.

"Catharine," he said, "you were almost going to fight me once to-day. You stood between the couch and me like a panther. What changed you so that you led me to my baby girl yourself?"

"I make one last fight to keep her," she said, haltingly. "She mine so long, I want her; I want her till I die. Then I think many times I see your face at camp. It look like sky when sun does not shine—all cloud, no smile, no laugh. I know you think of your baby then. Then I watch you many times. Then after while my heart is sick for you, like you are my own boy, like I am your own mother. I hate see no sun in your face. I think I not good mother to you; if I was good mother I would give you your child; make the sun come in your face. To-day I make last fight to keep the child. She's mine so long, I want her till I die. Then somet'ing in my heart say, 'He's like son to you, as if he your own boy; make him glad—happy. Oh, ver' glad! Be like his own mother. Find him his baby.'"

"Bless the mother heart of her!" growled the big foreman, frowning to keep his face from twitching.

It was twilight when they mounted the horses one of the men had brought up for them to ride home on, Wingate with his treasure-child hugged tightly in his arms. Words were powerless to thank the woman who had saved half his world for him. His voice choked when he tried, but she understood, and her woman's heart was very, very full.

Just as they reached the rim of the canyon Wingate turned and looked back. His arms tightened about little Margie as his eyes rested on Catharine—as once before she was standing in the doorway, alone; alone, and above and about her were the purple shadows, the awful solitude of Crow's Nest Mountain.

"Brown!" he called. "Hold on, Brown! I can't do it! I can't leave her like that!"

He wheeled his horse about and, plunging back through the snow, rode again to her door. Her eyes radiated as she looked at him. Years had been wiped from his face since the morning. He was a laughing boy once more.

"You are right," he said, "I cannot keep my little girl in that rough camp. You said it was no place for a girl child. You are right. I will send her into Calgary until my survey is over. Catharine, will you go with her, take care of her, nurse her, guard her for me? You said I was as your own son; will you be that good mother to me that you want to be? Will you do this for your white boy?"

He had never seen her smile before. A moment ago her heart had been breaking, but now she knew with a great gladness that she was not only going to keep and care for Margie, but that this laughing boy would be as a son to her for all time. No wonder Catharine of the Crow's Nest smiled!

3. "Hoolool of the Totem Poles" (1911)

[In this story, a mother who refuses to sell her family's ancestral totem pole discovers a creative way to support herself and her son. The Haida began making tourist art out of argillite (what Johnson calls "black slate") in the early nineteenth century. The story first appeared in the pages of *Mother's Magazine* in February 1911.]

Fig 5: Three children at Friendly Cove (Nuuchahmulth), 1930s. Photo: Associated Screen News. Vancouver Public Library. VPL #13441

The upcoast people called her "Hoolool," which means "The Mouse" in the Chinook tongue. For was she not silent as the small, grey creature that depended on its own bright eyes and busy little feet to secure a living?

The fishermen and prospectors had almost forgotten the time when she had not lived alone with her little son, "Tenas," for although Big Joe, her husband, had been dead but four years, time travels slowly north of Queen Charlotte Sound, and four years on the "Upper Coast" drag themselves more leisurely than twelve at the mouth of the Fraser River. Big Joe had left her with but three precious possessions—"Tenas," their boy, the warm, roomy firwood house of the thrifty Pacific Coast Indian build, and the great Totem Pole that loomed outside at its northwestern corner like a guardian of her welfare and the undeniable hallmark of their child's honorable ancestry and unblemished lineage.

After Big Joe died Hoolool would have been anchorless without that Totem Pole. Its extraordinary carving, its crude but clever coloring, its massed figures of animals, birds and humans, all designed and carved out of the solid trunk of a single tree, meant a thousand times more to her than it did to the travellers who, in their great "Klondike rush,"[1] thronged the decks of the northern-bound steamboats; than it did even to those curio-hunters who despoil the Indian lodges of their ancient wares, leaving their white man's coin in lieu of old silver bracelets and rare carvings in black slate or finely woven cedar-root baskets.

Many times was she offered money for it, but Hoolool would merely shake her head, and, with a half smile, turn away, giving no reason for her refusal.

"The woman is like a mouse," those would-be purchasers would say, so "Hoolool" she became, even to her little son, who called her the quaint word as a white child would call its mother a pet name; and she in turn called the little boy "Tenas," which means "Youngness"—the young spring, the young day, the young moon—and he was all these blessed things to her. But all the old-timers knew well why she would never part with the Totem Pole.

"No use to coax her," they would tell the curio-hunters. "It is to her what your family crest is to you. Would you sell your *crest?*"

So year after year the greedy-eyed collectors would go away empty-handed, their coin in their pockets, and Hoolool's silent refusal in their memories.

---

1 The Klondike gold rush lasted from 1896 to 1899.

Yet how terribly she really needed their money she alone knew. To be sure, she had her own firewood in the forest that crept almost to her door, and in good seasons the salmon fishing was a great help. She caught and smoked and dried this precious food, stowing it away for use through the long winter months; but life was a continual struggle, and Tenas was yet too young to help her in the battle.

Sometimes when the silver coins were very, very scarce, when her shoulders ached with the cold, and her lips longed for tea and her mouth for bread, when the smoked salmon revolted her, and her thin garments grew thinner, she would go out and stand gazing at the Totem Pole, and think of the great pile of coin that the last "collector" had offered for it—a pile of coin that would fill all her needs until Tenas was old enough to help her, to take his father's place at the hunting, the fishing, and above all, in the logging camps up the coast.

"I would sell it to-day if they came," she would murmur. "I would not be strong enough to refuse, to say no."

Then Tenas, knowing her desperate thoughts, would slip, mouse-like, beside her and say:

"Hoolool, you are looking with love on our great Totem Pole—with love, as you always do. It means that I shall be a great man some day, does it not, Hoolool?"

Then the treachery of her thoughts would roll across her heart like a crushing weight, and she knew that no thirst for tea, no hunger for flour-bread, no shivering in thin garments, would ever drive her to part with it. For the grotesque, carven thing was the very birthright of her boy. Every figure, hewn with infinite patience by his sire's, his grandsire's, his great-grandsire's, hands meant the very history from which sprang the source of red blood in his young veins, the birth of each generation, its deeds of valor, its achievements, its honors, its undeniable right to the family name.

Should Tenas grow to youth, manhood, old age, and have no Totem Pole to point to as a credential of being the honorable son of a long line of honorable sons? Never! She would suffer in silence, like the little grey, hungry Hoolool that scampered across the bare floors of her firwood shack in the chill night hours, but her boy must have his birthright. And so the great pole stood unmoved, baring its grinning figures to the storms, the suns, the grey rains of the Pacific Coast, but by its very presence it was keeping these tempests from entering the heart of the lonely woman at its feet.

It was the year that spring came unusually early, weeks earlier than the oldest Indian recalled its ever having come before.

March brought the wild geese honking northward, and great flocks of snow-white swans came daily out of the southern horizon to sail overhead and lose themselves along the Upper Coast, for it was mating and nesting time, and the heat of the south had driven them early from its broad lagoons.

Every evening Tenas would roll himself in his blanket bed, while he chatted about the migrating birds, and longed for the time when he would be a great hunter, able to shoot the game as they flitted southward with their large families in September.

"*Then*, Hoolool, we will have something better to eat than the smoked salmon," he would say.

"Yes, little loved one," she would reply, "and you are growing so fast, so big, that the time will not be long now before you can hunt down the wild birds for your Hoolool to eat, eh, little Spring Eyes? But now you must go to sleep; perhaps you will dream of the great flocks of the fat, young, grey geese you are to get us for food."

"I'll tell you if I do; I'll tell you in the morning if I dream of the little geese," he would reply, his voice trailing away into dreamland as his eyes blinked themselves to sleep.

"Hoolool, I *did* dream last night," he told her one early April day, when he awoke dewy-eyed and bird-like from a long night's rest. "But it was not of the bands of grey geese; it was of our great Totem Pole."

"Did it speak to you in your dreams, little April Eyes?" she asked, playfully.

"No-o," he hesitated, "it did not really *speak*, but it showed me something strange. Do you think it will come true, Hoolool?" His dark, questioning eyes were pathetic in appeal. He *did* want it to come true.

"Tell your Hoolool," she replied indulgently, "and perhaps she can decide if the dream will come true."

"You know how I longed to dream of the great flocks of young geese flying southward in September," he said, longingly, his little thin elbows propped each on one of her knees, his small, dark chin in his hands, his wonderful eyes shadowy with the fairy dreams of childhood. "But the flocks I saw were not flying grey geese, that make such fat eating, but around the foot of our Totem Pole I saw flocks and flocks of little tenas Totem Poles, hundreds of them. They were not *half* as high as I am. They were just baby ones you could take in your hand, Hoolool. Could you take my knife the trader gave me and make me one just like our big one? Only make it little, young—oh, *very* tenas—that I can carry it about with me. I'll paint it. Will you make me one, Hoolool?"

The woman sat still, a peculiar stillness that came of half fear, half unutterable relief, and wholly of inspiration. Then she caught up the boy, and her arms clung about him as if they would never release him.

"I know little of the white man's God," she murmured, "except that He is good, but I know that the Great Tyee (god) of the West is surely good. One of them has sent you this dream, my little April Eyes."

"Perhaps the Great Tyee and the white man's God are the same," the child said, innocent of expressing a wonderful truth. "*You* have two names—'Marna' (mother, in the Chinook) and 'Hoolool'—yet you are the same. Maybe it's that way with the two Great Tyees, the white man's and ours. But why should they send me dreams of flocks of baby Totem Poles?"

"Because Hoolool will make *you* one to-day, and then flocks and flocks of tenas poles for the men with the silver coins. I cannot sell them our great one, but I can make many small ones like it. Oh! they will buy the little totems, and the great one will stand as the pride of your manhood and the honor of your old age." Her voice rang with the hope of the future, the confidence of years of difficulty overcome.

Before many hours had passed, she and the child had scoured the nearby edges of the forest for woods that were dried, seasoned, and yet solid. They had carried armfuls back to the fir shack, and the work of carving had begun. The woman sat by the fire hour after hour—the fire that burned in primitive fashion in the centre of the shack, stoveless and hearthless, its ascending smoke curling up through an aperture in the roof, its red flames flickering and fading, leaping and lighting the work that even her unaccustomed fingers developed with wonderful accuracy in miniature of the Totem Pole at the north-west corner outside. By nightfall it was completed, and by the fitful firelight Tenas painted and stained its huddled figures in the black, orange, crimson and green that tribal custom made law. The warmth of the burning cedar knots dried the paints and pigments, until their acrid fragrance filled the little room, and the child's eyelids drooped sleepily, and in a delightful happiness he once more snuggled into his blanket bed, the baby Totem Pole hugged to his little heart. But his mother sat far into the night, her busy fingers at work on the realization of her child's dream. She was determined to fashion his dream-flock of "young" totems which would bring to them both more of fat eating than many bands of grey geese flying southward. The night wore on, and she left her task only to rebuild the fire and to cover with an extra blanket the little form of her sleeping boy. Finally she, too, slept, but briefly, for daybreak found her again at her quaint occupation, and the following nightfall brought no change. A week drifted by, and one morning, far down the Sound, the whistle of a coming steamer startled both boy and woman into brisk action. The little flock of Totem Poles now numbered nine, and hastily gathering them together in one of her cherished cedar-root baskets she clasped the child's hand, and they made their way to the landing-stage.

When she returned an hour later, her basket was empty, and her kerchief filled with silver coins.

On the deck of the steamer one of the ship's officers was talking to a little group of delighted tourists who were comparing their miniature purchases with the giant Totem Pole in the distance.

"*You* are lucky," said the officer. "I know people who have tried for years to buy the big Pole from her, but it was always 'No' with her—just a shake of her head, and you might as well try to buy the moon. It's for that little boy of hers she's keeping it, though she could have sold it for hundreds of good dollars twenty times over."

That all happened eleven years ago, and last summer when I journeyed far north of Queen Charlotte Sound, as the steamer reached a certain landing I saw a giant Totem Pole with a well-built frame house at its base. It was standing considerably away from the shore, but its newness was apparent, for on its roof, busily engaged at shingling, was an agile Indian youth of some seventeen years.

"That youngster built that house all by himself," volunteered one of the ship's officers at my elbow. "He is a born carpenter, and gets all the work he can do. He has supported his mother in comfort for two years, and he isn't full grown yet."

"Who is he?" I asked, with keen interest.

"His name is Tenas," replied the officer. "His mother is a splendid woman. 'Hoolool,' they call her. She is quite the best carver of Totem Poles on the North Coast."

4. "The Tenas Klootchman"[1] (1911)

["Tenas Klootchman" tells the story of a Coast Salish woman and her search for motherhood. The story originally appeared on the pages of *Mother's Magazine* in August 1911.]

---

1   [Johnson's note:] In Chinook language "Tenas Klootchman" means "girl baby."

This story came to me from the lips of Maarda herself. It was hard to realize, while looking at her placid and happy face, that Maarda had ever been a mother of sorrows, but the healing of a wounded heart oftentimes leaves a light like that of a benediction on a receptive face, and Maarda's countenance held something greater than beauty, something more like lovableness, than any other quality.

We sat together on the deck of the little steamer throughout the long violet twilight, that seems loath to leave the channels and rocky shores of the Upper Pacific in June time. We had dropped easily into conversation, for nothing so readily helps one to an introduction as does the friendly atmosphere of the extreme West, and I had paved the way by greeting her in the Chinook, to which she responded with a sincere and friendly handclasp.

Dinner on the small coast-wise steamers is almost a function. It is the turning-point of the day, and is served English fashion, in the evening. The passengers "dress" a little for it, eat the meal leisurely and with relish. People who perhaps have exchanged no conversation during the day, now relax, and fraternize with their fellow men and women.

I purposely secured a seat at the dining-table beside Maarda. Even she had gone through a simple "dressing" for dinner, having smoothed her satiny black hair, knotted a brilliant silk handkerchief about her throat, and laid aside her large, heavy plaid shawl, revealing a fine delaine[1] gown of green, bordered with two flat rows of black silk velvet ribbon. That silk velvet ribbon, and the fashion in which it was applied, would have bespoken her nationality, even had her dark copper-colored face failed to do so.

The average Indian woman adores silk and velvet, and will have none of cotton, and these decorations must be in symmetrical rows, not designs. She holds that the fabric is in itself excellent enough. Why twist it and cut it into figures that would only make it less lovely?

We chatted a little during dinner. Maarda told me that she and her husband lived at the Squamish River, some thirty-five miles north of Vancouver City, but when I asked if they had any children, she did not reply, but almost instantly called my attention to a passing vessel seen through the porthole. I took the hint, and said no more of family matters, but talked of the fishing and the prospects of a good sockeye run this season.

---

1 Delaine is a fine fabric of wool, or wool and cotton.

Afterwards, however, while I stood alone on deck watching the sun set over the rim of the Pacific, I felt a feathery touch on my arm. I turned to see Maarda, once more enveloped in her shawl, and holding two deck stools. She beckoned with a quick uplift of her chin, and said,

"We'll sit together here, with no one about us, and I'll tell you of the child." And this was her story:

She was the most beautiful little Tenas Klootchman a mother could wish for, bright, laughing, pretty as a spring flower, but—just as frail. Such tiny hands, such buds of feet! One felt that they must never take her out of her cradle basket for fear that, like a flower stem, she would snap asunder and her little head droop like a blossom.

But Maarda's skilful fingers had woven and plaited and colored the daintiest cradle basket in the entire river district for this little woodland daughter. She had fished long and late with her husband, so that the canner's money would purchase silk "blankets" to enwrap her treasure; she had beaded cradle bands to strap the wee body securely in its cosy resting-nest. Ah, it was such a basket, fit for an English princess to sleep in! Everything about it was fine, soft, delicate, and everything born of her mother-love.

So, for weeks, for even months, the little Tenas Klootchman laughed and smiled, waked and slept, dreamed and dimpled in her pretty playhouse. Then one day, in the hot, dry summer, there was no smile. The dimples did not play. The little flower paled, the small face grew smaller, the tiny hands tinier; and one morning, when the birds awoke in the forests of the Squamish, the eyes of the little Tenas Klootchman remained closed.

They put her to sleep under the giant cedars, the lulling, singing firs, the whispering pines that must now be her lullaby, instead of her mother's voice crooning the child-songs of the Pacific, that tell of baby foxes and gamboling baby wolves and bright-eyed baby birds. Nothing remained to Maarda but an empty little cradle basket, but smoothly-folded silken "blankets," but disused beaded bands. Often at nightfall she would stand alone, and watch the sun dip into the far waters, leaving the world as gray and colorless as her own life; she would outstretch her arms—pitifully empty arms—towards the west, and beneath her voice again croon the lullabies of the Pacific, telling of the baby foxes, the soft, furry baby wolves, and the little downy fledglings in the nests. Once in an agony of loneliness she sang these things aloud, but her husband heard her, and his face turned gray and drawn, and her soul told her she must not be heard again singing these things aloud.

And one evening a little steamer came into harbor. Many Indians came ashore from it, as the fishing season had begun. Among others was a young woman over whose face the finger of illness had traced shadows and lines of suffering. In her arms she held a baby, a beautiful, chubby, round-faced, healthy child that seemed too heavy for her wasted form to support. She looked about her wistfully, evidently seeking a face that was not there, and as the steamer pulled out of the harbor, she sat down weakly on the wharf, laid the child across her lap, and buried her face in her hands. Maarda touched her shoulder.

"Who do you look for?" she asked.

"For my brother Luke 'Alaska,'" replied the woman. "I am ill, my husband is dead, my brother will take care of me; he's a good man."

"Luke 'Alaska,'" said Maarda. What had she heard of Luke "Alaska"? Why, of course, he was one of the men her own husband had taken a hundred miles up the coast as axeman on a surveying party, but she dared not tell this sick woman. She only said: "You had better come with me. My husband is away, but in a day of two he will be able to get news to your brother. I'll take care of you till they come."

The woman arose gratefully, then swayed unsteadily under the weight of the child. Maarda's arms were flung out, yearningly, longingly, towards the baby.

"Where is your cradle basket to carry him in?" she asked, looking about among the boxes and bales of merchandise the steamer had left on the wharf.

"I have no cradle basket. I was too weak to make one, too poor to buy one. I have *nothing*," said the woman.

"Then let me carry him," said Maarda. "It's quite a walk to my place; he's too heavy for you."

The woman yielded the child gratefully, saying, "It's not a boy, but a Tenas Klootchman."

Maarda could hardly believe her senses. That splendid, sturdy, plump, big baby a Tenas Klootchman! For a moment her heart surged with bitterness. Why had her own little girl been so frail, so flower-like? But with the touch of that warm baby body, the bitterness faded. She walked slowly, fitting her steps to those of the sick woman, and jealously lengthening the time wherein she could hold and hug the baby in her yearning arms.

The woman was almost exhausted when they reached Maarda's home, but strong tea and hot, wholesome food revived her; but fever burned brightly in her cheeks and eyes. The woman was very ill, extremely ill. Maarda said, "You must go to bed, and as soon as you are there, I will take the canoe and go for a doctor. It is two or three miles, but you stay resting, and I'll bring him. We will put the Tenas Klootchman beside you in—" she hesitated. Her glance travelled up to the wall above, where a beautiful empty cradle basket hung, with folded silken "blankets" and disused beaded bands.

The woman's gaze followed hers, a light of beautiful understanding pierced the fever glare of her eyes, she stretched out her hot hand protestingly, and said, "Don't put her in—that. Keep that, it is yours. She is used to being rolled only in my shawl."

But Maarda had already lifted the basket down, and was tenderly arranging the wrappings. Suddenly her hands halted, she seemed to see a wee flower face looking up to her like the blossom of a russet-brown pansy. She turned abruptly, and, going to the door, looked out speechlessly on the stretch of sea and sky glimmering through the tree trunks.

For a time she stood. Then across the silence broke the little murmuring sound of the baby half crooning, half crying, indoors, the little cradleless baby that, homeless, had entered her home. Maarda returned, and, lifting the basket, again arranged the wrappings. "The Tenas Klootchman shall have this cradle," she said, gently. The sick woman turned her face to the wall and sobbed.

It was growing dark when Maarda left her guests, and entered her canoe on the quest for a doctor. The clouds hung low, and a fine, slanting rain fell, from which she protected herself as best she could with a shawl about her shoulders, crossed in front, with each end tucked into her belt beneath her arms—Indian-fashion. Around rocks and boulders, headlands and crags, she paddled, her little craft riding the waves like a cork, but pitching and plunging with every stroke. By and by the wind veered, and blew head on, and now and again she shipped water; her skirts began dragging heavily about her wet ankles, and her moccasins were drenched. The wind increased, and she discarded her shawl to afford greater freedom to her arm-play. The rain drove and slanted across her shoulders and head, and her thick hair was dripping with sea moisture and the downpour.

Sometimes she thought of beaching the canoe and seeking shelter until daylight. Then she again saw those fever-haunted eyes of the stranger who was within her gates, again heard the half wail of the Tenas Klootchman in her own baby's cradle basket, and at the sound she turned her back on the possible safety of shelter, and forged ahead.

It was a wearied woman who finally knocked at the doctor's door and bade him hasten. But his strong man's arm found the return journey comparatively easy paddling. The wind helped him, and Maarda also plied her bow paddle, frequently urging him to hasten.

It was dawn when they entered her home. The sick woman moaned, and the child fretted for food. The doctor bent above his patient, shaking his head ruefully as Maarda built the fire, and attended to the child's needs before she gave thought to changing her drenched garments. All day she attended her charges, cooked, toiled, watched, forgetting her night of storm and sleeplessness in the greater anxieties of ministering to others. The doctor came and went between her home and the village, but always with that solemn headshake, that spoke so much more forcibly than words.

"She shall not die!" declared Maarda. "The Tenas Klootchman needs her, she shall not die!" But the woman grew feebler daily, her eyes grew brighter, her cheeks burned with deeper scarlet.

"We must fight for it now," said the doctor. And Maarda and he fought the dread enemy hour after hour, day after day.

Bereft of its mother's care, the Tenas Klootchman turned to Maarda, laughed to her, crowed to her, until her lonely heart embraced the child as a still evening embraces a tempestuous day. Once she had a long, terrible fight with herself. She had begun to feel her ownership in the little thing, had begun to regard it as her right to tend and pet it. Her heart called out for it; and she wanted it for her very own. She began to feel a savage, tigerish joy in thinking—aye, *knowing* that it really would belong to her and to her alone soon—very soon.

When this sensation first revealed itself to her, the doctor was there—had even told her the woman could not recover. Maarda's gloriously womanly soul was horrified at itself. She left the doctor in charge, and went to the shore, fighting out this outrageous gladness, strangling it—killing it.

She returned, a sanctified being, with every faculty in her body, every sympathy of her heart, every energy of her mind devoted to bringing this woman back from the jaws of death. She greeted the end of it all with a sorrowing, half-breaking heart, for she had learned to love the woman she had envied, and to weep for the little child who lay so helplessly against her unselfish heart.

A beautifully lucid half-hour came to the fever-stricken one just before the Call to the Great Beyond!

"Maarda," she said, "you have been a good Tillicum to me, and I can give you nothing for all your care, your kindness—unless—" Her eyes wandered to her child peacefully sleeping in the delicately-woven basket. Maarda saw the look, her heart leaped with a great joy. Did the woman wish to give the child to her? She dared not ask for it. Suppose Luke "Alaska" wanted it. His wife loved children, though she had four of her own in their home far inland. Then the sick woman spoke:

"Your cradle basket and your heart were empty before I came. Will you keep my Tenas Klootchman as your own?—to fill them both again?"

Maarda promised. "Mine was a Tenas Klootchman, too," she said.

"Then I will go to her, and be her mother, wherever she is, in the Spirit Islands they tell us of," said the woman. "We will be but exchanging our babies, after all."

When morning dawned, the woman did not awake.

★ ★ ★ ★ ★

Maarda had finished her story, but the recollections had saddened her eyes, and for a time we both sat on the deck in the violet twilight without exchanging a word.

"Then the little Tenas Klootchman is yours now?" I asked.

A sudden radiance suffused her face, all trace of melancholy vanished. She fairly scintillated happiness.

"Mine!" she said. "All mine! Luke 'Alaska' and his wife said she was more mine than theirs, that I must keep her as my own. My husband rejoiced to see the cradle basket filled, and to hear me laugh as I used to."

"How I should like to see the baby!" I began.

"You shall," she interrupted. Then with a proud, half-roguish expression, she added:

"She is so strong, so well, so heavy; she sleeps a great deal, and wakes laughing and hungry."

As night fell, an ancient Indian woman came up the

companion-way. In her arms she carried a beautifully-woven basket cradle, within which nestled a round-cheeked, smiling-eyes baby. Across its little forehead hung locks of black, straight hair, and its sturdy limbs were vainly endeavoring to free themselves from the lacing of the "blankets." Maarda took the basket, with an expression on her face that was transfiguring.

"Yes, this is my little Tenas Klootchman," she said, as she unlaced the bands, then lifted the plump little creature out on to her lap.

Soon afterwards the steamer touched an obscure little harbor, and Maarda, who was to join her husband there, left me, with a happy good-night. As she was going below, she faltered, and turned back to me. "I think sometimes," she said, quietly, "the Great Spirit thought my baby would feel motherless in the far Spirit Islands, so He gave her the woman I nursed for a mother; and He knew I was childless, and He gave me this child for my daughter. Do you think I am right? Do you understand?"

"Yes," I said, "I think you are right, and I understand."

Once more she smiled radiantly, and turning, descended the companionway. I caught a last glimpse of her on the wharf. She was greeting her husband, her face a mirror of happiness. About the delicately-woven basket cradle she had half pulled her heavy plaid shawl, beneath which the two rows of black velvet ribbon bordering her skirt proclaimed once more her nationality.

5. "A Squamish Legend of Napoleon" (1910)

[This is the story of a lost talisman that once belonged to a Squamish warrior and that later decided the fate of Napoleon Bonaparte. The story first appeared in the *Saturday Magazine* of the *Province* (Vancouver) on 29 October 1910. Johnson's father idolized Napoleon; her middle name, Pauline, was after Bonaparte's sister.]

Holding an important place among the majority of curious tales held in veneration by the coast tribes are those of the sea-serpent. The monster appears and reappears with almost monotonous frequency in connection with history, traditions, legends and superstitions; but perhaps the most wonderful part it ever played was in the great drama that held the stage of Europe, and incidentally all the world during the stormy days of the first Napoleon.[1]

Throughout Canada I have never failed to find an amazing knowledge of Napoleon Bonaparte amongst the very old and "uncivilized" Indians. Perhaps they may be unfamiliar with every other historical character from Adam down, but they will all tell you they have heard of the "Great French Fighter," as they call the wonderful little Corsican.

Whether this knowledge was obtained through the fact that our earliest settlers and pioneers were French, or whether Napoleon's almost magical fighting career attracted the Indian mind to the exclusion of lesser warriors, I have never yet decided. But the fact remains that the Indians of our generation are not as familiar with Bonaparte's name as were their fathers and grandfathers, so either the predominance of English-speaking settlers or the thinning of their ancient war-loving blood by modern civilization and peaceful times must, one or the other, account for the younger Indian's ignorance of the Emperor of the French.

In telling me the legend of "The Lost Talisman," my good tillicum, the late Chief Capilano, began the story with the almost amazing question, Had I ever heard of Napoleon Bonaparte? It was some moments before I just caught the name, for his English, always quaint and beautiful, was at times a little halting; but when he said, by way of explanation, "You know big fighter, Frenchman. The English they beat him in big battle," I grasped immediately of whom he spoke.

"What do you know of him?" I asked.

His voice lowered, almost as if he spoke a state secret. "I know how it is that English they beat him."

I have read many historians on this event, but to hear the Squamish version was a novel and absorbing thing. "Yes?" I said—my usual "leading" word to lure him into channels of tradition.

"Yes," he affirmed. Then, still in a half-whisper, he proceeded to tell me that it all happened through the agency of a single joint from the vertebra of a sea-serpent.

In telling me the story of Brockton Point and the valiant boy who killed the monster, he dwelt lightly on the fact that all people

---

1 Napoleon Bonaparte (1769–1821), first emperor of France, was a brilliant military and political leader who controlled most of continental Europe before his final defeat by the British in 1815 at the Battle of Waterloo.

who approach the vicinity of the creature are palsied, both mentally and physically—bewitched, in fact—so that their bones become disjointed and their brains incapable; but to-day he elaborated upon this peculiarity until I harked back to the boy of Brockton Point and asked how it was that his body and brain escaped this affliction.

"He was all good, and had no greed," he replied. "He was proof against all bad things."

I nodded understandingly, and he proceeded to tell me that all successful Indian fighters and warriors carried somewhere about their person a joint of a sea-serpent's vertebra; that the medicine-men threw "the power" about them so that they were not personally affected by this little "charm," but that immediately they approached an enemy the "charm" worked disaster, and victory was assured to the fortunate possessor of the talisman. There was one particularly effective joint that had been treasured and carried by the warriors of a great Squamish family for a century. These warriors had conquered every foe they encountered, until the talisman had become so renowned that the totem-pole of their entire "clan" was remodelled, and the new one crested by the figure of a single joint of a sea-serpent's vertebra.

About this time stories of Napoleon's first great achievements drifted across the seas; not across the land—and just here may be a clue to buried Coast-Indian history, which those who are cleverer at research than I can puzzle over. The chief was most emphatic about the source of Indian knowledge of Napoleon.

"I suppose you heard of him from Quebec, through, perhaps, some of the French priests," I remarked.

"No, no," he contradicted hurriedly. "Not from East; we hear it from over the Pacific from the place they call Russia." But who conveyed the news or by what means it came he could not further enlighten me. But a strange thing happened to the Squamish family about this time. There was a large blood connection, but the only male member living was a very old warrior, the hero of many battles and the possessor of the talisman. On his death-bed his women of three generations gathered about him; his wife, his sisters, his daughters, his granddaughters, but not one man, nor yet a boy of his own blood, stood by to speed his departing warrior spirit to the land of peace and plenty.

"The charm cannot rest in the hands of women," he murmured almost with his last breath. "Women may not war and fight other nations or other tribes; women are for the peaceful lodge and for the leading of little children. They are for holding baby hands, teaching baby feet to walk. No, the charm cannot rest with you, women. I have no brother, no cousin, no son, no grandson, and the charm must not go to a lesser warrior than I. None of our tribe, nor of any tribe on the coast, ever conquered me. The charm must go to one as unconquerable as I have been. When I am dead send it across the great salt chuck, to the victorious 'Frenchman'; they call him Napoleon Bonaparte." They were his last words.

The older women wished to bury the charm with him, but the younger women, inspired with the spirit of their generation, were determined to send it over-seas. "In the grave it will be dead," they argued. "Let it still live on. Let it help some other fighter to greatness and victory."

As if to confirm their decision, the next day a small sealing-vessel anchored in the Inlet. All the men aboard spoke Russian, save two thin, dark, agile sailors, who kept aloof from the crew and conversed in another language. These two came ashore with part of the crew and talked in French with a wandering Hudson's Bay trapper, who often lodged with the Squamish people. Thus the women, who yet mourned over their dead warrior, knew these two strangers to be from the land where the great "Frenchman" was fighting against the world.

Here I interrupted the chief. "How came the Frenchmen in a Russian sealer?" I asked.

"Captives," he replied. "Almost slaves, and hated by their captors, as the majority always hate the few. So the women drew those two Frenchmen apart from the rest and told them the story of the bone of the sea-serpent, urging them to carry it back to their own country and give it to the great 'Frenchman' who was as courageous and as brave as their dead leader.

"The Frenchmen hesitated; the talisman might affect them, they said; might jangle their own brains, so that on their return to Russia they would not have the sagacity to plan an escape to their own country; might disjoint their bodies, so that their feet and hands would be useless, and they would become as weak as children. But the women assured them that the charm only worked its magical powers over a man's enemies, that the ancient medicine-men had 'bewitched' it with this quality. So the Frenchmen took it and promised that if it were in the power of man they would convey it to 'the Emperor.'

"As the crew boarded the sealer, the women watching from the shore observed strange contortions seize many of the men; some fell on the deck; some crouched, shaking as with palsy; some writhed for a moment, then fell limp and seemingly boneless; only the two Frenchmen stood erect and strong and vital—the Squamish talisman had already overcome their foes. As the little sealer set sail up the gulf she was commanded by a crew of two Frenchmen—men who had entered these waters as captives, who were leaving them as conquerors. The palsied Russians were worse than useless, and what became of them the chief could not state; presumably they were flung overboard, and by some trick of a kindly fate the Frenchmen at last reached the coast of France.

"Tradition is so indefinite about their movements subsequent to sailing out of the Inlet that even the ever-romantic and vividly colored imaginations of the Squamish people have never supplied the details of this beautifully childish, yet strangely historical fairy-tale. But the voices of the trumpets of war, the beat of drums throughout Europe heralded back to the wilds of the Pacific Coast forests the intelligence that the great Squamish 'charm' eventually reached the person of Napoleon; that from this time onward his career was one vast victory, that he won battle after battle, conquered nation after nation, and, but for the direst calamity that could befall a warrior, would eventually have been master of the world."

"What was this calamity, Chief?" I asked, amazed at his knowledge of the great historical soldier and strategist.

The chief's voice again lowered to a whisper—his face was almost rigid with intentness as he replied:

"He lost the Squamish charm—lost it just before one great fight with the English people."

I looked at him curiously; he had been telling me the oddest mixture of history and superstition, of intelligence and ignorance, the most whimsically absurd, yet impressive, tale I ever heard from Indian lips.

"What was the name of the great fight—did you ever hear it?" I asked, wondering how much he knew of events which took place at the other side of the world a century agone.

"Yes," he said, carefully, thoughtfully; "I hear the name sometime in London when I there. Railroad station there—same name."

"Was it Waterloo?" I asked.

He nodded quickly, without a shadow of hesitation. "That the one," he replied. "That's it, Waterloo."

Fig. 6: Mary Agnes Capilano, [Líxwelut] (Squamish), date
unknown. Photo Stuart Thompson. Vancouver Public Library.
VPL #2689

6. "The Legend of the Ice Babies" (1911)

[In a lake in the Chilliwack valley, according to this story, two children have been frozen in time to remain forever innocent. "The Legend" was first published in *Mother's Magazine* in November 1911 after the first edition of *Legends of Vancouver* had appeared earlier that year, and it was not included in subsequent editions. Mary Agnes Capilano / Líxwelut (c. 1836–1940), whom Johnson refers to as the Klootchman, told Johnson this story.]

As you journey across Canada from east to west, and have been absorbed in the beauty of the St. Lawrence, the Great Lakes, the prairies, the Rockies, the Selkirks, and finally the fiercely-rugged grandeur of the Fraser River, as you are nearing the rim of the gentle Pacific, you will pass through one of the most fruitful valleys in all the Great Dominion. Orchards and vineyards, gardens and blossoming flowers stretch on every side, and in the misty distance there circles a band of bubbling mountains, and great armies of the giant Douglas firs and cedars that only the Western slope could ever give birth to. Through this valley stretches many a lazy arm of the sea, but there are also to be found several beautiful little fresh-water lakes. One in particular is remarkably lovely. It is small, and the shores so precipitous that the winds seldom ruffle its clear blue-green waters. The majestic old forest tress, the mosses, the trailing vines, the ferns and bracken crowd so closely down to the margin that they are mirrored in the lake in all their rich coloring and exquisite design. In looking on this secluded beauty one instinctively feels the almost sanctity of purity that can be found only in the undefiled forestlands. Nature has not been molested, and the desecrating hand of man has not yet profaned it. A happy chance had taken me along the shores of this perfect little gem, molded in its rocky setting, and one day when the Klootchman and I sat together on the sands watching the Pacific as it slept under an autumn sun, I spoke to her of the little fresh-water jewel up in the Chilliwack valley.

"You have seen it?" she asked with great interest. I nodded.

"I am very glad. We Squamish women love it. The mothers love it most. We call it the Lake of the Ice Babies."

I remarked on the beauty of the name, and then its oddity. "For," I said, "surely it does not freeze there!"

"Yes," she replied, "it always freezes over at least once in the winter, if only for a day. The lake is so still there is no wind now to keep it open from the frost."

I caught the word "now." "Was there ever a wind there?" I ventured, for one must voice his thoughts delicately if one hopes to extract a tradition from my good old reticent Klootchman.

"Yes, once it used to be very stormy, terrible gales would get imprisoned in that cup of the mountains, and they would sweep round and round, lashing up the waters of the lake like a chained wild animal," she answered. Then she added that ever-present pitiful remark: "But that was long ago—before the white man came." It has been the redskin's cry for more than a century, that melancholy "Before the white man came."

Presently she picked up a handful of silver sand, and while she trailed it leisurely from palm to palm, threading it between her thin, dark, fingers, her voice fell into the sonorous monotone, the half whisper, half chant, in which she loved to relate her quaint stories, while I sat beside her sun-bathed and indolent and listened to the

"LEGEND OF THE ICE BABIES"

"There were two of them, two laughing, toddling little children but just released from the bands of their cradle baskets. Girls, both of them, and cousins, of the same age, happy-hearted and playful, and the treasures of their mother's lives. It was a warm, soft day of late autumn, a day like this, when not a leaf stirred, not a wave danced, that the wandering band of Squamish encamped in the bluffs about the little lake, and prepared to stay the night. The men cut branches and built a small lodge. The women gathered firewood and cooked venison and grouse, and the children and babies played about, watching their elders and sometimes replenishing the camp fires. The evening wore on, and with the twilight came a gentle rising wind, that whispered at first through the pines and cedars like a mother singing very softly to her sleeping child. Then the wind-voice grew louder, it began to speak harshly. The song in it died, and the mighty voices of the trees awoke like the war cry of many tribes in battle. The little lake began to heave and toss, then lash itself into a fury; whirlpools circled, waves rose and foamed and fought each other. The gale was shut within the cup of shores and could not release itself.

"In the stir of fitting the camp for the night, and protecting the frail lodge against destruction, the two girl babies were unnoticed, and hand in hand they wandered with halting childish steps to the brink of the shore. Before them the waves rose and fell, frothed and whirled like some playful wild thing, and their little hands longed to grasp the curling eddies, the long lines of combers and breakers. Laughingly the babies slid down the fern-covered banks, and stepped into the shallow waters at the margin, then wandered out over the surface of the lake, frolicking and playing in the tossing waves and whirlpools, but neither little body sank. The small feet skimmed the angry waters like feathers dropped from the wings of some passing bird, for under those dancing innocent feet the Saghalie Tyee had placed the palms of his hands, and the soft baby soles rested and romped in an anchorage greater than the most sheltered harbor in all the vast Pacific coast.

"From the shores their mothers watched them, first in an agony of fear, then with wonder, then with reverence.

"'The great Tyee holds them in his hand,' spoke one with whispered awe.

"'Listen, he speaks.'

"'Will you give these babies to me oh, mothers of the Squamish?' said a voice from above the clouds. 'To me to keep for you, always as babies, always laughing, happy little ones, or will you take them back to yourselves and the shore, to have them grow away from their innocence, their childhood; to have them suffer in heart and body as women must ever suffer, to have them grow ill with age, old with pain and years, and then to die, to leave you lonely, and to go where you may not follow and care for them and love them? Which will you, oh, mothers of the Squamish? If you love yourselves best, you shall have your babies again. If you love your babies most, you will give them to me.'

"And the two mothers answered as one voice: 'Keep them always as babies, always innocent, always happy—take them, oh, Great Tyee, we love them more than we love ourselves!'

"The winds began to sob lower. The waves ceased swirling, the roar of tempestuous waters calmed to whispers, then lulled into perfect tranquility, but the babies still played and laughed on its blue surface. The hands of the Saghalie Tyee still upheld them.

"That night the lake froze from shore to shore. When morning dawned, the two mothers were 'wakened by a voice that spoke very gently, but it came from invisible lips, and they knew it to be a message from the Tyee of the Happy Hunting Grounds. 'The babies are yours forever,' he said, 'although I, the Saghalie Tyee of all men, shall keep them in the hollow of my hands. I have bridged the waters with eternal stillness, for their little bodies are young and tender, their little feet too soft for rough waves, their little hands too frail to battle rough winds. No storm shall ever again fret this lake, no gale churn its surface to fury. I have tempered their little world to their baby needs, and they shall live in shelter for all time. Rise, oh, mother of the Squamish, and look upon your gifts to me, which I shall keep in trust for you forever.'

"The women arose, and creeping to the door of the lodge beheld their babies dancing on the frail, clear ice far out across the lake. They could see the baby smiles, hear the baby laughter, and they knew their mother-hearts would never mourn for their children's lost innocence, or lost babyhood. And each year since that time, when the first frosts of late autumn touch the little lake with a film of ice, the babies come to play and laugh like elves of the air, upon its shining surface. They have never grown older, never grown less innocent. They are pure as the ice their soft, small feet touch with dancing step, and so they will remain for all time."

The silver sands were still filtering between her brown fingers as the Klootchman ended the tale, and I still lay watching the sunlight glint on the lazy Pacific, and wondering if it, too, were not the dancing feet of some long-ago children.

"Do people ever see these ice babies now?" I asked dreamily.

"Only those who are nearing the country of the Great Tyee," she replied. "As one nears that land one becomes again as a little child, one's eyes grow innocent, one's heart trusting, one's life blameless, as they go down the steep shores of age to the quiet, windless, waveless lake where they must rest forever in the hollows of the Great Tyee's hands, for he has kept these pure Ice Babies there for many hundreds of years because he wishes his Indian children to become like them before they cross the lake to the Happy Hunting Grounds on the far shore."

She was silent for a moment, then added: "I am growing old, Tillicum (friend), perhaps I shall see them—soon."

7. "The Lost Lagoon" (1910)

["The Lost Lagoon" was first published in the *Saturday Magazine* of the *Vancouver Daily Province* on 22 October 1910. The Lost Lagoon, a small body of water in Stanley Park in Vancouver, was named after this poem.]

It is dusk on the Lost Lagoon,
And we two dreaming the dusk away,
Beneath the drift of a twilight grey—
Beneath the drowse of an ending day
And the curve of a golden moon.

It is dark in the Lost Lagoon,
And gone are the depths of haunting blue,
The grouping gulls, and the old canoe,
The singing firs, and the dusk and—you,
And gone is the golden moon.

O! lure of the Lost Lagoon—
I dream to-night that my paddle blurs
The purple shade where the seaweed stirs—
I hear the call of the singing firs
In the hush of the golden moon.

Appendix A: On Johnson

[Although the critics and writers whose interactions with and thoughts about Johnson are collected below have faded somewhat from literary history, their attention was important for Johnson's favourable reception in Canada, the United States, and England.]

1. From Garth Grafton / Sara Jeannette Duncan, Interview with E. Pauline Johnson, "Women's World," Toronto *Globe*, 14 October 1886

[Garth Grafton was one of the pen names of Sara Jeannette Duncan (1861–1922), a journalist, travel writer, and novelist who wrote for the Toronto *Globe*, the *Washington Post*, and the Montreal *Gazette*, among other newspapers. She is best known in Canada for her novel *The Imperialist* (1904), which is set in a fictionalized Brantford. She was a high-school classmate of Johnson's at the Brantford Central School. Here she works hard to make Johnson exotic and verges on mocking Johnson's pride in her Mohawk ancestry and her treasured family artifacts.]

Among the braves that gathered together their peaceful and warlike belongings and followed the loyal Brant to Canada so long ago was one Jacob Johnson. His son, "Smoke" Johnson, who died a short time ago, well remembered Brant, and his journeys to Montreal and Quebec, whither the young Johnson used to accompany him and dance before the houses, which novel entertainment was always liberally recognized with tobacco. "Smoke" Johnson married Helen Martin, whose mother was a white girl named Catharine Rollstone, the daughter of a Boston fur trader, who had been abducted by the Indians, brought to Canada, and finally married one of her captors. One of the sons of Smoke and Helen Johnson was the well-known chief of the Six Nations, G.H.M. Johnson, who married an English lady and brought her to "Chief's Wood," a romantic and secluded home in the Indian Reserve upon the Grand River. And the young poetess whose verses on the occasion of the unveiling of the Brant Memorial yesterday provoked such a storm of applause, Miss E. Pauline Johnson, is the late Chief Johnson's daughter. I think that in connection with this "auspicious occasion" you ought to know about Miss Johnson, and I intend that you shall.

I have had the pleasure of her acquaintance for some time, and while it is a privilege that cannot, unfortunately, be extended to the general public, it seems to me that all Canadiennes deserve at least to enjoy it by proxy. I found her at her residence in Brantford's North Ward. You want to know what she is like first, of course.

Well, she is tall and slender and dark, with grey eyes, beautifully clean cut features, black hair, a very sweet smile, and a clear, musical, pleasant voice. She has certainly that highest attribute of beauty, the rare, fine gift of expression. She is charmingly bright in conversation, and has a vivacity of tone and gesture that is almost French.

"And aren't you connected with Brant in some way?" I asked this graceful olive branch of the Iroquois.

"No," she answered. "There is an impression to that effect. We are not related. But my grandfather, who died a little while ago, remembered Brant perfectly. Poor old grandpa! It is such a pity he couldn't have lived to see the unveiling tomorrow."[1]

And then Miss Johnson proceeded to tell me about her romantic family tree.

"Our real name, you know, isn't Johnson," she said, "but Te-ka-hoon-wa-ke," which sounded very much like Tekkahoonwakky. "That means *two wampums*, so if it were not for the baptism of my great grandfather, Jacob Johnson, after Sir William,[2] I shouldn't be Miss Johnson, but Miss Te-ka-hoon-wa-ke."

"Oh," I said, "aren't you glad he was baptized? A wampum is a sort of shell, isn't it?"

"It is a kind of bead," said Miss Johnson. "These cuffs that my brother will wear tomorrow in the dance are covered with them."

The cuff consisted of the beads curiously woven with slender leather thongs. They were very old, and some of the purple and

---

1 John "Smoke" Johnson spoke at the laying of the cornerstone for the monument on 11 August 1886 and died two weeks later. Celebrations for the unveiling of the monument itself took place over two days, 13 and 14 October. Johnson's poem, "'Brant,' A Memorial Ode," was read on 13 October.

2 Sir William Johnson (c. 1715–74) was Superintendent of Indian Affairs for the British between 1756 and his death. He was godfather to Jacob Johnson, E. Pauline Johnson's great-grandfather.

white ornaments were chipped and broken. Miss Johnson said the white ones signified peace and that the arrangements of the designs upon the body of the purple ones were emblematic of the different tribes. Also that the art of making wampum is a lost one, and that the shells are supposed to have come from the Gulf of Mexico.

"And this," she said, showing me a superlatively awful looking instrument, "was given to my father by the Cayugas for political services. It's a tomahawk you see, and a pipe of peace combined," and Miss Johnson drew a whiff of nothing more noxious than the common air through the hollow handle. "This is a scalping knife my father made himself out of a deer's foot. You see the handle is just the polished bone of the deer's leg."

"But don't they—didn't he—I mean, isn't it usual for people who indulge in that kind of amusement to do it with their tomahawks?" I inquired rather delicately, for I wasn't at all sure that their fair descendant would relish this allusion to the peculiarities of her warrior ancestors. My compunctions were unnecessary.

"Oh, no!" she laughed. "It would be very awkward to scalp with a tomahawk. You see, this is the way they do it," and she raised some of her own dusky locks and made a mimic circle around it.

"Really!" I said. "Please don't. I always thought that to scalp a person was to deprive him of his hirsute adornment out and out!"

"I know most people think that," she responded, "but it is only a single lock and the portion of scalp it grows on. I once saw a scarf of several hundred and fifty Indian scalps. It came from one of the Rocky Mountain tribes. These are strings of deer rattles that the Indians wear about their moccasins when they dance, to make music. You see they are just the ends of the cloven hooves strung together. And this rusty knife," she said, "had quite a history." It was a very rusty knife indeed, all brown and yellow with corrosion, and ragged along the edges. I at once professed my desire to hear the history.

"When my father was a very young man, and had just bought Chief's Wood, an old, old Indian came to him one day, and said 'Johnson, I hear you've bought Chief's Wood.' My father said he had. 'When I was a youth,' said the old Indian, 'I was very jealous of another young man of the tribe, and he of me. One night he slew my brother. The next day I went to him, and found him sitting on a bench. I threw him back and said, "Did you lend my brother a knife last night?" He said, "Yes." "Then," I said, "I have come to return it," and I stabbed the young man through the heart. Then I drew out the knife, and carried it, dripping with his blood, to the dark side of the tree before your door, and slipped it under the moss at the roots. It has been there seventy-three years. And all those years I can go nowhere up or down the Grand River without seeing the top of that tree though it was cut down long ago, for I know that the knife lies under it still.'

"So then my father and he went to the stump and dug far down, and there surely enough was the knife. It was the last case of blood atonement, according to the old Indian law, that was known among us."

"Why did he take the dark side of the tree?"

"That was the north side. The Indians have a superstition that a dark deed should have a dark burial."

Then Miss Johnson showed me a veritable idol which had been grinning at me for some time beneath the parlour table, and a queer old carved powder horn, and bullet pouch, that bore the date 1807 and had been taken from a Kentuckian by her grandfather in 1812, and several other relics of fascinating interest [including photographs].... I did not see one of Mr. W.D. Howells,[1] although he might reasonably be suspected to be enshrined there, being a second cousin of Miss Johnson's on her mother's side. I remember that the notable novelist spoke in terms of the liveliest interest of his "Indian cousins" when I met him last winter in Washington. He was innocently proud, he said, of showing their photograph to the Venetians. Miss Johnson's literary work is familiar to all readers of *The Week*[2] in Canada, and to no small public on "the other side." Her poems have a dreamy quality that is very charming, and while she has given us no sustained work as yet, we may doubtless expect it ere long. She writes best of her own people, whom she dearly loves, when her full sympathy with her subject shows in every line. [Here Duncan quotes all of "A Cry from an Indian Wife" and "The Re-interment of Red Jacket"; see pp. 131–33 and 38–40.] These verses, though not especially germane to the present occasion, will suggest to every reader his own estimate of her abilities....

---

1 William Dean Howells (1837–1920), her mother's cousin, was widely known as a realist novelist and editor of *Atlantic Monthly* (1871–81).

2 Johnson published in *The Week* (1883–96), a literary journal that published many major literary figures, including Duncan, Charles G.D. Roberts (1860–1943), Goldwin Smith (1823–1910), and Pelham Edgar (1871–1948).

2. W.D. Lighthall, "Miss E. Pauline Johnson," biographical note, *Songs of the Great Dominion* (London: Walter Scott, 1889), 453

[This note comes from *Songs of the Great Dominion*, an anthology of Canadian literature in which two poems by Johnson appear. The notes at the back of the volume are quite varied in length, and some indicate that the authors provided the information on which the notes were based. W.D. Lighthall (1857–1954) received a law degree from McGill University and practiced in Montreal for 63 years. Active in politics, he also wrote poetry, novels, and works of history and philosophy. His anthology, from which this poem is taken and which included two poems by Johnson, was influential in establishing a national canon for Canadian poetry.]

Miss E. Pauline Johnson is interesting on account of her race as well as her strong and cultured verse. She is of the Mohawks of Brantford. This race, to-day thoroughly civilised, and occupying high positions all over Canada, have had a wonderfully faithful record of unswerving British alliance for over two hundred and twenty years, during which their devoted courage was the factor which decided the predominance of the Anglo-Saxon in North America. They produced Brant and Tecumseh, and the visit of their chiefs to Queen Anne is recorded in the *Spectator*.[1] At the close of the American Revolution they retired with the other loyalists to their present reserves, where they have prospered. Miss Johnson was born at the Johnson estate "Chiefswood," on the Grand River, on 10th March 1862. She was the youngest child of chief G.H.M. Johnson, head-chief of the Mohawks, and of his wife Emily S., youngest daughter of Henry Howells, Bristol, England, thus being a cousin of W.D. Howells the novelist. She writes poetry only,[2] and contributes to the leading Canadian weekly journals and to many American papers. She was educated in childhood at home by a resident governess, then sent to the Brantford Model School; and after leaving school resided at Chiefswood until her father's death in February 1884, when the family went to Brantford, where they now live.

---

1 Four chiefs visited Queen Anne in 1710; three were Mohawk (including Joseph Brant's grandfather), one Mohican. Their portraits by Jan Verelst (1648–1734) are in the National Gallery of Canada, Ottawa.

2 Johnson began to write prose and short fiction after this note was published.

3. Hector Charlesworth, "Miss Pauline Johnson's Poems," *Canadian Magazine* 5.5 (1895): 478–80

[Hector Charlesworth (1872–1945) was a newspaper and magazine editor and arts commentator, best known as assistant editor and then editor of *Saturday Night* (1910–32). Johnson's admirer since his late teens, he provided her with an important outlet for her work, but the pay the magazine offered was low ($3 for "The Song My Paddle Sings," her most famous poem). The reviews of her performances in *Saturday Night* were always glowing.]

For the past five years Miss Pauline Johnson has been the most popular figure in Canadian literature, and in many respects the most prominent one. There is something more or less remarkable in all this, since her prominence and popularity were accomplished merely by a few occasional lyrics in fugitive publications. Recently Miss Johnson has been figuring throughout Canada in a bardic capacity as the reciter of her own works, but her fame was made before such a course became possible. Instances of a poet's achieving actual fame years before he or she has issued a single volume are sufficiently unique to be remarkable, and now that a collection of Miss Johnson's songs is actually between covers we are enabled to realize something of the charm and power and music that had enabled her to achieve her previous importance.

The volume which has just been issued from the greatest warehouse of poetry in the world—the Bodley Head, of Vigo street, London, is rather an austere looking little tome, with its plum-colored cover and its bold device of tomahawk and wampum. The title "White Wampum," and Miss Johnson's Indian sobriquet, "Tekahionwake"—whatever that may mean—add further to the aboriginal atmosphere of the book; but when you open the volume its broad, creamy margins and clear, bright type caress the eye, and you find that the luxurious bibliophile will have something to delight his senses. The title page, with a delightful design by E.H. New,[1] suggestive of mountains and wigwams and pine trees, whets the appetite, and Miss Johnson's dedication, explaining that white wampum symbolizes for an Indian all that is best in him, is particularly happy. All these are small matters compared with the poems themselves, but they are elements in book making that the sensitive reader is coming to demand. The entire get-up of the volume points to the Indian

---

1   Edmund Hort New (1871–1931) was a well-known British illustrator.

element in Miss Johnson's genius. Hers is a red-skinned muse, we are led to believe, and a snatch of introductory verse runs:

"And few to-day remain,
But copper-tinted face and smouldering fire of wilder life,
Were left me by my sire,
To be my proudest claim." [from "The Re-interment of Red Jacket," see pp. 38–40]

Seven ballads of Indian life are set forward as the chief features of the book, and these dealing as they do with dramatic incidents, are necessarily familiar to those readers who have enjoyed Miss Johnson's platform appearances; the sense of novelty and delight comes when we turn over the pages and meet with the introspective lyrics, songs of love and suffering and passion: and these, I think, give Miss Johnson her greatest claim on public attention. The Indian ballads are fresh and stimulating to healthy people with dramatic intelligences, and there is a fine Mohawk barbarity about them, but the softer lyrics strike a more universal note. They have music in them that lingers in one's ear, and sentiment that grows tuneful in one's heart.

As a balladist, Miss Johnson is endowed with the qualities of swiftness and terseness, and is happy in the fact that she is not much of a rhetorician. Her vocabulary is limited at all times, and for this reason she sometimes fails to give the finite expression to her thought, but the deficiency enables her, in her lyrics, to make music with simple words, which have meaning for every one, and in her ballads to avoid platitudes. The clipped, nervous expression of such ballads as "Ojistoh," and "As Red Men Die," is harsh at moments, but when either poem is judged as a whole, it is seen that the atmosphere of cruelty and intensity could be produced only by such means. And Miss Johnson paints a picture masterfully. In "Ojistoh," the Mohawk Judith,[1] who slays her chief's enemy, is living and breathing before your eyes, and in "As Red Men Die," you can almost hear the exultant chant of the brave as he walks to his death along the path of coals. Miss Johnson has a large infusion of Mohawk blood herself, and these

---

1 Judith is an Israelite heroine whose story appears in some versions of the Old Testament. (The Book of Judith is excluded from Protestant versions.) A widow who manages to gain the trust of Holofernes, an enemy leader, she beheads him as he lies in a drunken stupor and returns to her people with his head.

scenes are realities to her imagination. It is the highest praise of her to say that she makes them realities to the imaginations of her readers also; but this Indian enthusiasm of hers is responsible for the defects of some of these ballads. She is a partisan of the red man; his wrongs burn within her, but in reality one cannot put partisan emotions into poetic bottles with success. They turn what should be dramatic into melodrama, and what should be poetic into a polemic. Thus, in "The Cattle Thief," we have a stirring incident stirringly told in part, but falling into mere controversial eloquence at the end. We are stirred to sympathy as we read of the settlers pursuing the starving redskin, and doing him to death, but when the Indian's untutored wife springs from behind some adjacent tree, and, standing over the body of her brave makes a speech that in eloquence and logic is seldom equalled in the House of Commons, we grow skeptical as to the reality of the episode.[1] No one doubts that Miss Johnson has made a truthful statement of the wrongs of her people in these ballads of hers, but she has marred works that are in essence poetic and strong with mere polemics. She has reversed the settler's joke, and with her it would appear that a good pale face is a dead pale face; except in the case of Yakonwita's fair-browed lover. The story of the latter, entitled "The Pilot of the Plains," is a beautiful and moving ballad, and it will be found that in such efforts as "Ojistoh," "the tale of Yakonwita," and "As Red Men Die," which murmur not of Indian wrongs, but sing of Indian deeds, Miss Johnson is at her best. She is a good story-teller and a vivid scene-painter.

From the ballads we pass on to the songs in which Miss Johnson has chronicled her moods, her joys and her sorrows. They are the intimate expression of herself, and the music, and color, and simplicity of them are exquisite. Her methods in versifying are of the most direct and simple nature; there are none of those gyrating rocket flights of passion of which Swinburne[2] has the key, and in which most lyrists strive to emulate him. But in these simple lyrics there are soft intervals and movements and lulls of sound that caress the senses. In the Indian ballads, Miss Johnson shows herself sensitive to the influence of phrase and metre in suggesting the atmosphere

---

1 Since the speaker is the daughter of the "cattle thief," rather than his wife, as stated here, and the poem makes it clear that she makes her speech in Cree, readers might be skeptical about how much time Charlesworth devoted to writing this review.

2 Algernon Charles Swinburne (1837–1909) was an English poet, critic, and verse dramatist.

by mere sound, and again and again in the lyrics which she has written in a minor key, or with a light heart, you find the sound moulding and mysteriously suggesting the thought. "The Song my Paddle Sings," in which the dash of the rapids, the splash of the paddle, and the trembling of the rushing canoe are perfectly conveyed, is the best example of this gift of hers. The mystic invocation of one fasting from sleep ... has the same felicity in phrasing:

"Go, sleep," I say, "before the darkness die,
To one who needs you even more than I;
For I can bear my part alone, but he
Has need of thee."

"His poor tired eyes in vain have sought relief,
His heart more tired still with all its grief;
His pain is deep, while mine is vague and dim,
Go thou to him."

"When thou hast fanned him with thy drowsy wings,
And laid thy lips upon the pulsing strings,
That in his soul with fret and fever burn,
To me return."

These stanzas are from the poem "Fasting," which is, perhaps, the most remarkable and memorable in the book, and not the only one in which Miss Johnson shows mystical tendencies. But never is there a touch of that wretched obscurantism so prevalent in the efforts of Mr. Bliss Carman[1] and some of his imitators. Health and sanity, and earnestness pulse through every line she writes, even though it is sometimes an imperfect line.

I trust that it is no haughty male prejudice that prompts me to say that in poetry, as in all other things, women must find their chief reward for well-doing in the approval of men. Mankind is for womankind, the ultimate court of appeal, and one is giving Miss Johnson the very best of praise, and setting her on a pedestal high above most other feminine wielders of the pen in saying that her songs will meet with the deepest appreciation from all song-loving men. Of how

---

1   Bliss Carman (1861–1929) is one of the four so-called Confederation Poets in Canada, along with his cousin Charles G.D. Roberts, Duncan Campbell Scott (1862–1947), and Archibald Lampman (1861–99). Carman was internationally famous for his aestheticist lyrics promoting a Bohemian lifestyle.

many of the women writers of today could that be said? And yet there never were so many women writing. The fair scribblers pour forth an endless stream of prose and poetry for the edification of their sisters, while to the men it is a mass that is "erotic, neurotic, and tommyrotic."[1] But Miss Johnson by writing as a natural, generous, healthful woman has, already, command over a large and appreciative audience of men who find something lasting and moving in her music.

Lest it should be thought that I have in any way deprecated the value of the Indian element in Miss Johnson's make-up it should be added that our poet has a quality, difficult to define, which is hers alone, and which, since it can be traced to no other source, must be ascribed to the Indian influence. It is a quality of absolute naivete in dealing with natural things. Her songs of the mountains and the streams and the skies are absolutely without self-consciousness; her love lyrics and the utterance she has given to her religious yearnings—these are all permeated with aboriginal simplicity, not once is the note of self-consciousness struck. Sometimes you find a record of a mood that seems at first blush fin-de-siecle, for instance when she writes: "Soulless is all humanity to me to-night."

But as the verse runs on the mood becomes dignified.

"My keenest longing is to be
Alone, alone with God's grey earth that seems
Pulse of my pulse and consort of my dreams."

The red-skinned muse is healthful and simple and earnest; more markedly it is sensuous and musical. This book of "White Wampum" is the record of passions and aspirations that are elemental and vigorous, but the note of womanly tenderness and sadness is there as well. In the lyric "Overlooked" it is there in all its sweetness.

4. Horatio Hale, Review of *The White Wampum, The Critic: A Weekly Review of Literature and the Arts* (4 January 1896): 4–5

[Horatio Hale (1817–96) was a Harvard-educated anthropologist who worked with Johnson's grandfather and father to record

---

1   Tommyrot is a slang expression meaning nonsense; Charlesworth is deriving the phrase "erotic, neurotic, and tommyrotic" from a phrase coined in 1895 to describe contemporary fiction. See "tommyrotic," *OED* 3 (online).

important Iroquois oral traditions. In this review, Hale notes that the readers might be disappointed to encounter the writing of a "well-bred Canadian lady" rather than of a "wild Indian girl." Hale adds that Johnson's "Indian poems" might be disagreeable reading for white Canadians and recommends her nature poetry as more pleasant.]

Miss Johnson's pretty book of poems has a double claim to attention in the facts that the author is partly in blood and largely in feeling a representative of the original "American race," and that she also belongs to that band of notable Canadian poets whose effusions, both in English and in French, have of late years added a special distinction to North American literature. It must be admitted that Miss Johnson's partly Indian origin is in itself rather a drawback than an advantage to her success as a writer, however it may help her reception as a reciter. The first inclination of the reader will be to look in her poems for some distinctive Indian traits, and to be disappointed if these are not strikingly apparent. Her compositions will be judged as those of a "wild Indian girl," and not as those of a well-bred and accomplished young Canadian lady with a dash of Indian blood, such as she really is.

The earlier poems in her book—earlier in place if not in date of composition—certainly show evidences of the author's warm sympathies with her paternal ancestry. "Ojistoh," "The Cattle Thief," "A Cry from an Indian Wife," "Dawendine," and "Wolverine," are full of vindictive vehemence, and the haughty or pathetic resentment which our earliest associations make us expect in Indian utterances. Though natural in a descendant of the wronged, they are not the most agreeable reading for descendants of the wrongers. Yet some of them, and especially "Dawendine," a legend of ghostly lovers, and "Wolverine," a tale of Indian honor and honesty and English suspicion and heartlessness, are really spirited and effective efforts. When we come to the lyrical pieces, which make up the bulk of the volume, and in which the sentiment of race seldom appears, there is much to please all readers. Many passages show that the author is alive to the poetic beauties of Canadian landscape. The reflections in which she occasionally indulges are sometimes original and striking, and her imagery (as in the religious verses entitled "Good Friday") is drawn directly from nature. There is evidence of a good ear for rhythm and rhyme, and of much descriptive power. Among the best things in the volume—which, with its decorative title-page, presents a very neat appearance—are the pen-pictures, such as "The Camper," "Joe," "Shadow River," and "Erie Waters." We have only room for two brief specimens, in the first of which ("Moonset") the author's descriptive talent and turn for reflection are evident:—

[Here all of "Moonset" is quoted (see pp. 151–52) and he concludes with some verses from "The Happy Hunting Grounds" (see pp. 126–27).]

5. "From Wigwam to Concert Platform," *Evening Telegraph* [Dundee], 4 July 1906

[The extent to which the contents of this piece derive from Johnson herself is not clear, but she and her stage partner, Walter McRaye, were certainly working hard to make a success of their expensive tour to London in 1906. Since they had booked Steinway Hall for the evening of 16 July, she needed all the free publicity she could get. In the end, the house filled and the pair used quotations from the complimentary reviews on their publicity material for the rest of their career.]

Red Indian Chief's Daughter.

London is shortly to be entertained by royalty.

Princess Tekahionwake, daughter of the Iroquois chieftain, Onwanonsyshon,[1] ruler of the Six Nations, and sister by adoption of H.R.H. the Duke of Connaught,[2] will appear at the Steinway Hall on the 16th of this month, in recitations from her own works.

Princess Tekahionwake is perhaps better known as Miss Pauline Johnson, and is the first Red Indian to attain literary prominence.

Her book, "The White Wampum," is composed of old Indian legends, poems, and stories, and is held in high esteem by such world-wide authorities as Sir Theodore Watts Dunton and Sir Gilbert Parker.[3]

---

1 One of her father's names, meaning "Lord of the Great House."
2 Johnson describes the adoption ceremony of Prince Arthur, Duke of Connaught (1850–1942), the third son of Queen Victoria, in "A Brother Chief," pp. 93–98 above.
3 See pieces by Seton (Appendix A8), Watts-Dunton (Appendix A9), and Parker (Appendix A7).

In appearance Miss Pauline Johnson shows but little trace of her ancestry. She is a sweet-voiced, merry-faced woman, with any amount of vivacity and "go," and a slight Canadian accent.

Yesterday Miss Johnson exhibited the costume in which she appears at her recitals. It is the full garb of an Indian Princess—a rich buckskin garment covered with the gaudy trappings and ornamentations so beloved of her race.

"Scalping Not At All Barbarous."

To almost every part of her dress some fierce Indian romance attaches. She is especially proud of an American-Indian's scalp, which dangles from her belt.

"You have a mistaken idea here in England," said Miss Johnson, "that scalping is a cruel and barbarous custom, but you must remember that to the Indian his scalps are as a V.C.[1] to the British soldier. Without them he cannot substantiate his boasts of foes fallen by his hand, for the Indians are, above all, a nation of boasters."

Her skirt is covered with silver ornaments, hammered from coins by native silversmiths of her tribe, four of them being made from brooches plundered at the extermination of the Huron tribe and the twenty Jesuit fathers, under whose influence they had come, while from her shoulder hangs the identical scarlet "blanket" used in the initiation of H.R.H. the Duke of Connaught as a chieftain of the tribe, by her father, in the early 'fifties.[2]

Associated with Miss Pauline Johnson in her performances is a talented young Canadian, Mr. Walter McRaye. Miss Johnson bitterly deplores England's seeming indifference to her colonies, and prophesies a day, not far hence, when all too late she [England] will learn to regret her aloofness.

6. Charles Mair, "Pauline Johnson: An Appreciation," *The Moccasin Maker* (Toronto: Briggs, 1913)

[Charles Mair (1838–1927) was a Canadian poet and journalist noted for his nationalism. Johnson admired his historical drama *Tecumseh* (1886), which deals with the War of 1812. He was heav-

---

1   The Victoria Cross, the highest British military honour, awarded for valour in battle. The scalp-lock of warriors was taken as a trophy from dead enemies. The British also took scalps; see Benn 84–85, and Paul.

2   The Duke of Connaught was adopted into the Wolf clan by the Mohawks in 1869, not "the early 'fifties."

ily involved on the Canadian side during the first Riel Resistance (1869–70). Here, Mair praises Johnson as a poet loyal to both her Mohawk nationality and her Canadian citizenship. The author acknowledges the historic double standard of portraying Indigenous peoples of America as murderers, while whitewashing the crimes of the colonists.]

The writer, having contributed a brief "Appreciation" of the late Miss E. Pauline Johnson to the July number of *The Canadian Magazine*, has been asked by the editor of this collection of her hitherto unpublished writings to allow it to be used as a Preface, with such additions or omissions as might seem desirable. He has not yet seen any portion of the book, but quite apart from its merits it is eagerly looked for by Miss Johnson's many friends and admirers as a final memorial of her literary life. It will now be read with an added interest, begot of her painfully sad and untimely end.

In the death of Miss Johnson a poet passed away of undoubted genius; one who wrote with passion, but without extravagance, and upon themes foreign, perhaps, to some of her readers, but, to herself, familiar as the air she breathed.

When her racial poetry first appeared, its effect upon the reader was as that of something abnormal, something new and strange, and certainly unexampled in Canadian verse. For here was a girl whose blood and sympathies were largely drawn from the greatest tribe of the most advanced nation of Indians on the continent, who spoke out, "loud and bold," not for it alone, but for the whole red race, and sang of its glories and its wrongs in strains of poetic fire.

However aloof the sympathies of the ordinary business world may be from the red man's record, even it is moved at times by his fate, and stirred by his persistent, his inevitable romance. For the Indian's record is the background, and not seldom the foreground, of American history, in which his endless contests with the invader were but a counterpart of the unwritten, or recorded, struggles of all primitive time.

In that long strife the bitterest charge against him is his barbarity, which, if all that is alleged is to be believed—and much of it is authentic—constitutes in the annals of pioneer settlement and aggression a chapter of horrors.

But equally vindictive was his enemy, the American frontiersman. Burnings at the stake, scalping, and other savageries, were not confined to the red man. But whilst his are depicted by the interested writers of the time in the most lurid colours, those of the frontiersman, equally barbarous, are too often palliated, or entirely passed by. It is manifestly unjust to characterize a whole people by its worst members. Of such, amongst both Indians and whites, there were not a few; but it is equally unfair to ascribe to a naturally cruel disposition the infuriated red man's reprisals for intolerable wrongs. As a matter of fact, impartial history not seldom leans to the red man's side; for, in his ordinary and peaceful intercourse with the whites, he was, as a rule, both helpful and humane. In the records of early explorers we are told of savages who possessed estimable qualities lamentably lacking in many so-called civilized men. The Illinois, an inland tribe, exhibited such tact, courtesy and self-restraint, in a word, such good manners, that the Jesuit Fathers described them as a community of gentlemen. Such traits, indeed, were natural to the primitive Indian, and gave rise, no doubt, to the much-derided phrase—"The Noble Red Man."

There may be some readers of these lines old enough to remember the great Indians of the plains in times past, who will bear the writer out in saying that such traits were not uncommon down to comparatively recent years. Tatonkanazin the Dahcota, Sapo-Maxika the Blackfoot, Atakakoop the Cree, not to speak of Yellow Quill[1] and others, were noted in their day for their noble features and dignified deportment.

In our history the Indians hold an honoured place, and the average reader need not be told that, at one time, their services were essential to Canada.[2] They appreciated British justice, and their greatest nations produced great men, who, in the hour of need, helped materially to preserve our independence. They failed, however, for manifest reasons, to maintain their own. They had to yield; but, before quitting the stage, they left behind them an abiding memory, and an undying tradition. And, thus, "Romanticism," which will hold its own despite its hostile critics, is their debtor. Their closeness to nature, their picturesque life in the past, their mythical religion, social system and fateful history have begot one of the wide world's "legends," an ideal not wholly

---

1 Mair names major plains leaders: Tatonkanazin (Standing Buffalo the younger) was a Dakota chief; Sapo-Maxica (c. 1830–90) is Crowfoot, a Blackfoot signatory of Treaty 7 in 1877; both Atakakoop (Starblanket; d. 1896), Cree, and Yellow Quill (d. 1910), Plains Ojibway (Saulteaux), signed Treaty 6 in 1876.
2 He refers to the Indigenous groups who supported the British against the Americans in the War of Independence (1776–83) and the War of 1812 (1812–15).

imaginary, which, as a counterpoise to Realism, our literature needs, and probably never shall outgrow.

These references to the Indian character may seem too extended for their place, yet they are *genre* to the writer's subject. For Miss Johnson's mentality was moulded by descent, by ample knowledge of her people's history, admiration of their character, and profound interest in their fate.

Hence the oncoming into the field of letters of a real Indian poet had a significance which, aided by its novelty, was immediately appreciated by all that was best in Canadian culture. Hence, too, and by reason of its strength, her work at once took its fitting place without jar or hindrance; for there are few educated Canadians who do not possess, in some measure, that aboriginal, historic sense which was the very atmosphere of Pauline Johnson's being.

But while "the Indian" was never far from her thoughts, she was a poet, and therefore inevitably winged her way into the world of art, into the realm common to all countries, and to all peoples. Here there was room for her imaginings, endowed, as she was, with power to appeal to the heart, with refinement, delicacy, pathos, and, above all, sincerity; an Idealist who fused the inner and the outer world, and revelled in the unification of scenery and mind.

The delight of genius in the act of composition has been called the keenest of intellectual pleasures; and this was the poet's almost sole reward in Canada a generation ago, when nothing seemed to catch the popular ear but burlesque, or trivial verse. In strange contrast this with a remoter age! In old Upper Canada, in its primitive days, there was no lack of educated men and women, of cultivated pioneers who appreciated art and good literature in all its forms. Even the average immigrant brought his favourite books with him from the Old Land, and cherished a love of reading, which unfortunately was not always inherited by his sons. It was a fit audience, no doubt; but in a period when all alike were engrossed in a stern struggle for existence, the poets, and we know there were some, were forced, like other people, to earn, by labour of hand, their daily bread. Thackeray's "dapper" George is credited with the saying, that, "If beebles will be boets they must starve."[1] If in England their struggle was severe, in

---

1   "Dapper little George" is a description of George II from William
    Makepeace Thackeray's *The Four Georges* (1862). The phrase wide-
    ly credited to him means "if people will be poets they must starve"
    and makes fun of his foreign accent. He was born in Germany, heir
    to the Elector of Hanover.

Canada it was unrelenting; a bald prospect, certainly, which lasted, one is sorry to say, far down in our literary history.

Probably owing to this, and partly through advice, and partly by inclination, Miss Johnson took to the public platform for a living, and certainly justified her choice of a vocation by her admirable performances. They were not sensational, and therefore not over-attractive to the groundling; but to discerners, who thought highly of her art, they seemed the perfection of monologue, graced by a musical voice, and by gesture at once simple and dignified.

As this is an appreciation and a tribute to Miss Johnson's memory rather than a criticism, the writer will touch but lightly upon the more prominent features of her productions. Without being obtrusive, not the least of these is her national pride, for nothing worthier, she thought, could be said of a man than

"That he was born in Canada, beneath the British flag."

In her political creed wavering and uncertainty had no place. She saw our national life from its most salient angles, and, in current phrase, she saw it whole. In common, therefore, with every Canadian poet of eminence, she had no fears for Canada, if she be but true to herself.

Another opinion is not likely to be challenged, viz., that much of her poetry is unique, not only in subject, but also in the sincerity of her treatment of themes so far removed from the common range. Intense feeling distinguishes her Indian poems from all others; they flow from her very veins, and are stamped with the seal of heredity. This strikes one at every reading, and not less their truth to fact, however idealized. Indeed the wildest of them, "Ojistoh" (The White Wampum), is based upon an actual occurrence, though the incident took place on the Western plains, and the heroine was not a Mohawk. The same intensity marks "The Cattle Thief," and "A Cry From an Indian Wife." Begot of her knowledge of the long-suffering of her race, of iniquities in the past and present, they poured red-hot from her inmost heart.

One turns, however, with a sense of relief from those fierce dithyrambics to the beauty and pathos of her other poems. Take, for example, that exquisite piece of music, "The Lullaby of the Iroquois," simple, yet entrancing! Could anything of its kind be more perfect in structure and expression? Or the sweet idyll, "Shadow River," a transmutation of fancy and fact, which ends with her own philosophy:

"O! pathless world of seeming!
O! pathless life of mine whose deep ideal
Is more my own than ever was the real.
For others fame
And Love's red flame,
And yellow gold: I only claim
The shadows and the dreaming."

And this ideality, the hall-mark of her poetry, has a character of its own, a quality which distinguishes it from the general run of subjective verse. Though of the Christian faith, there is yet an almost pagan yearning manifest in her work, which she indubitably drew from her Indian ancestry. That is, she was in constant contact with nature, and saw herself, her every thought and feeling, reflected in the mysterious world around her.

This sense of harmony is indeed the prime motive of her poetry, and therein we discern a brightness, a gleam, however fleeting, of mystic light—

"The light that never was on sea or land,
The consecration and the poet's dream."

A suggestion of her attitude and sense of inter-penetration lurks in this stanza:

"There's a spirit on the river, there's a ghost upon the shore,
And they sing of love and loving through the starlight evermore,
As they steal amid the silence and the shadows of the shore."

And in the following verses this "correspondence" is more distinctly drawn:

"O! soft responsive voices of the night
 I join your minstrelsy,
And call across the fading silver light
As something calls to me;
I may not all your meaning understand,
But I have touched your soul in Shadow Land."

"Sweetness and light"[1] met in Miss Johnson's nature, but free

---

1 A phrase coined by Jonathan Swift (1667–1745) and popularized by critic Matthew Arnold (1822–88) in *Culture and Anarchy* (1869).

from sentimentality; and even a carping critic will find little to cavil at in her productions. If fault should be found with any of them it would probably be with such a narrative as "Wolverine." It "bites," like all her Indian pieces, and conveys a definite meaning. But, written in the conventional slang of the frontier, it jars with her other work, and seems out of form, if not out of place.

However, no poet escapes a break at times, and Miss Johnson's work is not to be judged, like a chain, by its weakest links. Its beauty, its strength, its originality are unmistakable, and although, had she lived, we might have looked for still higher flights of her genius, yet what we possess is beyond price, and fully justifies the feeling, everywhere expressed, that Canada has lost a true poet.

Such a loss may not be thought a serious one by the sordid man who decries poetry as the useless product of an art already in its decay. Should this ever be the case, it would be a monstrous symptom, a symptom that the noblest impulses of the human heart are decaying also. The truth is, as the greatest of English critics, Hazlitt,[1] has told us, that "poetry is an interesting study, for this reason, that it relates to whatever is most interesting in human life. Whoever, therefore, has a contempt for poetry, has a contempt for himself and humanity."

Turning from Miss Johnson's verse to her prose, there is ample evidence that, had she applied herself, she would have taken high rank as a writer of fiction. Her "Legends of Vancouver" is a remarkable book, in which she relates a number of Coast-Indian myths and traditions with unerring insight and literary skill. These legends had a main source in the person of the famous old Chief, Capilano,[2] who, for the first time, revealed them to her in Chinook, or in broken English, and, as reproduced in her rich and harmonious prose, belong emphatically to what has been called "The literature of power." Bound together, so to speak, in the retentive memory of the old Chief, they are authentic legends of his people, and true to the Indian nature. But we find in them, also, something that transcends history. Indefinable forms, earthly and

---

1 William Hazlitt (1778–1830) was a well-known English essayist and literary critic; here Mair quotes from his *Characters of Shakespeare's Plays* (1817).

2 Chief Joe Capilano (Sahp-luk, 1850–1910) was the Squamish chief who led a delegation to London to speak to King Edward VII in 1906 about Indigenous issues. Johnson met him there and they became friends after she moved to Vancouver; she published some of the stories he and his wife told her in the *Saturday Magazine* of the Vancouver *Province*.

unearthly, pass before us in mystical procession, in a world beyond ordinary conception, in which nothing seems impossible.

The origin of the Indian's myths, East or West, cannot be traced, and must ever remain a mystery. But, from his immemorial ceremonies and intense conservatism, we may reasonably infer that many of them have been handed down from father to son, unchanged, from the prehistoric past to the present day; a past contemporary, perhaps, with the mastodon, but certainly far back in the mists of antiquity. The importance of rescuing them from oblivion is plain enough, and therefore the untimely death of Miss Johnson, who was evidently turning with congenital fitness to the task, is doubly to be regretted. For as Mr. Bernard McEnvoy[1] well says in his preface to her "Vancouver Legends," she "has linked the vivid present with the immemorial past.... In the imaginative power that she has brought to these semi-historical Sagas, and in the liquid flow of her rhythmical prose she has shown herself to be a literary worker of whom we may well be proud."

It is believed to be the general wish of Miss Johnson's friends that some tribute of a national and permanent character should be paid to her memory; not indeed to preserve it—her own works will do that—but as a visible mark of public esteem. In this regard, what could be better than a bronze statue of life-size, with such accompanying symbols as would naturally suggest themselves to a competent artist? Vancouver, in which she spent her latter years, the city she loved, and in which she died, is its proper home; and, as to its site, the spot in Stanley Park where she wished her ashes to be laid is surely, of all places, the most appropriate.

But whatever shape, in the opinion of her friends, the memorial should take, it is important, in any case, that it should be worthy of her genius, and a fitting memento of her services to Canadian letters.

7. Gilbert Parker, Introduction, *The Moccasin Maker* (Toronto: Briggs, 1913)

[Gilbert Parker (1862–1932), born near Kingston, Ontario, began his career as a journalist but gained fame as a bestselling novelist, drawing particularly on Canadian themes, particularly those dealing with the history of Quebec. He sat as a Conserva-

---

1   McEnvoy (1842–1932) wrote for the *Province*.

tive MP in the British House of Commons from 1900 to 1918 and was knighted for "his services to Canadian literature" in 1902. He met Johnson in 1894 and supported her thereafter. She reminded him of Lali, the heroine of his own novel, *The Translation of a Savage* (1893).]

The inducement to be sympathetic in writing a preface to a book like this is naturally very great. The authoress was of Indian blood, and lived the life of the Indian on the Iroquois Reserve with her chieftain father and her white mother for many years; and though she had white blood in her veins was insistently and determinedly Indian to the end. She had the full pride of the aboriginal of pure blood, and she was possessed of a vital joy in the legends, history and language of the Indian race from which she came, crossed by good white stock. But though the inducement to be sympathetic in the case of so chivalrous a being who stood by the Indian blood rather than by the white blood in her is great, there is, happily, no necessity for generosity or magnanimity in the case of Pauline Johnson. She was not great, but her work in verse is sure and sincere; and it is alive with the true spirit of poetry. Her skill in mere technique is good, her handling of narrative is notable, and if there is no striking individuality—which might have been expected from her Indian origin—if she was often reminiscent in her manner, metre, form and expression, it only proves her a minor poet and not a Tennyson or a Browning.[1] That she should have done what she did do, devotedly, with an astonishing charm and the delight of inspired labour, makes her life memorable, as it certainly made both life and work beautiful. The pain and suffering which attended the latter part of her life never found its way into her work save through increased sweetness and pensiveness. No shadow of death fell upon her pages. To the last the soul ruled the body to its will. Phenomenon Pauline Johnson was, though to call her a genius would be to place her among the immortals, and no one was more conscious of her limitations than herself. Therefore, it would do her memory poor service to give her a crown instead of a coronet.

Poet she was, lyric and singing and happy, bright-visioned, high-hearted, and with the Indian's passionate love of nature

---

1 Alfred, Lord Tennyson (1809–92) was Poet Laureate of Britain for most of Queen Victoria's reign; Robert Browning (1812–89) overcame an early reputation for difficulty to become another of Britain's leading poets.

thrilling in all she did, even when from the hunting-grounds of poesy she brought back now and then a poor day's capture. She was never without charm in her writing; indeed, mere charm was too often her undoing. She could not be impersonal enough, and therefore could not be great; but she could get very near to human sympathies, to domestic natures, to those who care for pleasant, happy things, to the lovers of the wild.

This is what she has done in this book called "The Moccasin Maker." Here is a good deal that is biographical and autobiographical in its nature; here is the story of her mother's life told with rare graciousness and affection, in language which is never without eloquence; and even when the dialogue makes you feel that the real characters never talked as they do in this monograph, it is still unstilted and somehow really convincing. Touching to a degree is the first chapter, "My Mother," and it, with all the rest of the book, makes one feel that Canadian literature would have been poorer, that something would have been missed from this story of Indian life if this volume had not been written. It is no argument against the book that Pauline Johnson had not learnt the art of short-story writing; she was a poetess, not a writer of fiction; but the incidents described in many of these chapters show that, had she chosen to write fiction instead of verse, and had begun at an early stage in her career to do so, she would have succeeded. Her style is always picturesque, she has a good sense of the salient incident that makes a story, she could give to it the touch of drama, and she is always interesting, even when there is discursiveness, occasional weakness, and when the picture is not well pulled together. The book had to be written; she knew it, and she did it. The book will be read, not for patriotic reasons, not from admiration of work achieved by one of the Indian race; but because it is intrinsically human, interesting and often compelling in narrative and event.

May it be permitted to add one word of personal comment? I never saw Pauline Johnson in her own land, at her own hearthstone, but only in my house in London and at other houses in London, where she brought a breath of the wild; not because she dressed in Indian costume, but because its atmosphere was round her. The feeling of the wild looked out of her eyes, stirred in her gesture, moved in her footstep. I am glad to have known this rare creature who had the courage to be glad of her origin, without defiance, but with an unchanging, if unspoken, insistence. Her native land and the Empire should be glad of her for what she was and for what she stood; her native land and the Empire should be glad of her for the work, interesting, vivid and human, which she has done. It will preserve her memory. In an age growing sordid such fresh spirits as she should be welcomed for what they are, for what they do. This book by Pauline Johnson should be welcomed for what she was and for what it is.

8. Ernest Thompson Seton, "Tekahionwake (Pauline Johnson)," Introduction, *The Shaganappi* (Toronto: Briggs, 1913)

[Ernest Thompson Seton (1860–1946) grew up in Toronto. He studied at the Royal Academy of Arts in London, England, and was well known as a wildlife artist. His *Wild Animals I Have Known* (1898) was a huge popular success. He was one of the founders of the Boy Scouts of America, into which he incorporated what he believed to be "Indian" lore and woodcraft. He first met Johnson shortly after she returned from London in 1894.]

How well I remember my first meeting with Tekahionwake, the Indian girl! I see her yet as she stood in all ways the ideal type of her race, lithe and active, with clean-cut aquiline features, olive-red complexion and long dark hair; but developed by her white-man training so that the shy Indian girl had given place to the alert, resourceful world-woman, at home equally in the salons of the rich and learned or in the stern of the birch canoe, where, with paddle poised, she was in absolute and fearless control, watching, warring and winning against the grim rocks that grinned out of the white rapids to tear the frail craft and mangle its daring rider.

We met at the private view of one of my own pictures. It was a wolf scene, and Tekahionwake, quickly sensing the painter's sympathy with the Wolf, claimed him as a Medicine Brother, for she herself was of the Wolf Clan of the Mohawks. The little silver token she gave me then is not to be gauged or appraised by any craftsman method known to trade.

From that day, twenty odd years ago, our friendship continued to the end, and it is the last sad privilege of brotherhood to write this brief comment on her personality. I do it with a special insight, for I am charged with a message from Tekahionwake herself. "Never let anyone call me a white woman," she said. "There are those who think they pay me a compliment in saying that I am just like a white woman. My aim, my joy, my pride is to sing the glories of my own people. Ours was the race that gave the world its measure of heroism, its standard of physical prowess. Ours was the race that taught the world that avarice veiled by any name is crime. Ours were the people of the blue air and the green woods, and ours the faith that taught men to live without greed and to die without fear. Ours were the fighting men that, man to man—yes, one to three—could meet and win against the world. But for our few numbers, our simple faith that others were as true as we to keep their honor bright and hold as bond inviolable their plighted word, we should have owned America to-day."

If the spirit of Wetamoo, the beautiful woman Sachem, the Boadicea of New England, ever came back, it must have been in Tekahionwake the Mohawk. The fortitude and the eloquence of the Narragansett Chieftainess[1] were born again in the Iroquois maiden; she typified the spirit of her people that flung itself against the advancing tide of white encroachment even as a falcon might fling himself against a horde of crows whose strength was their numbers and whose numbers were without end, so all his wondrous effort was made vain.

"The Riders of the Plains," the "Legends of Vancouver," "Flint and Feather," and the present volume, "Shagganappi," all tell of the spirit that tells them. Love of the blessed life of blue air without gold-lust is felt in the line and the interline, with joy in the beauty of beaver stream, tamarac swamp, shad-bush and drifting cloud, and faith in the creed of her fathers, that saw the Great Spirit in all things and that reverenced Him at all times, and over and above it all the sad note that tells of a proud race, conscious that it has been crushed by numbers, that its day is over and its heritage gone forever.

Oh, reader of the alien race, keep this in mind: remember that no people ever ride the wave's crest unceasingly. The time must come for us to go down, and when it comes may we have the strength to meet our fate with such fortitude and silent dignity as did the Red Man his.

---

1   Wetamoo (d. 1676) was a Wampanoag Confederacy sachem who led her Narragansett people in battle against the Plymouth colonists during King Philip's War (1675–78). She features in the famous captivity narrative of Mary Rowlandson (1682). She drowned fleeing from the colonists, who cut off her head and displayed it on a rod. Boadicea (d. 60 or 61 CE) was queen of a British tribe, the Iceni. She led an ultimately unsuccessful revolt against the Roman occupiers during the reign of Emperor Nero.

"Oh, why have your people forced on me the name of Pauline Johnson?" she said. "Was not my Indian name good enough? Do you think you help us by bidding us forget our blood? by teaching us to cast off all memory of our high ideals and our glorious past? I am an Indian. My pen and my life I devote to the memory of my own people. Forget that I was Pauline Johnson, but remember always that I was Tekahionwake, the Mohawk that humbly aspired to be the saga singer of her people, the bard of the noblest folk the world has ever seen, the sad historian of her own heroic race."

9. From Theodore Watts-Dunton, "In Memoriam: Pauline Johnson," Introduction, *Flint and Feather: Collected Verse* (Toronto: Musson, 1913)

[British critic Theodore Watts-Dunton (1832–1914) reflects on his brief acquaintance with Johnson. In a review of *Songs of the Great Dominion* in the *Athenaeum* (28 September 1889), he had referred to her as "the cultivated daughter of an Indian chief, who is, on account of her descent, the most interesting English poetess now living," following this remark by quoting all of "In the Shadows." He then expresses his "discontent" that the collection had not included more of her poems. Between 1875 and 1898, he was the leading poetry critic for the *Athenaeum* (1828–1921), which published and reviewed some of the greatest names in English literature; Christina Rossetti (1830–94) published her first poems there and Virginia Woolf's (1882–1941) early writing got top billing in the journal. Johnson certainly knew that the boost given to her reputation by these comments and the reprinting of her poem was incalculable. Sir Gilbert Parker introduced them in London in 1906 just after her successful appearance in Steinway Hall, and she visited him the next day.]

I cannot say how deeply it touched me to learn that Pauline Johnson expressed a wish on her death-bed that I, living here in the mother country all these miles away, should write something about her. I was not altogether surprised, however, for her letters to me had long ago shed a golden light upon her peculiar character. She had made herself believe, quite erroneously, that she was largely indebted to me for her success in the literary world. The letters I had from her glowed with this noble passion: the delusion about her indebtedness to me, in spite of all I could say, never left her. She continued to foster and cherish this delusion. Gratitude indeed was with her not a sentiment merely, as with most of us, but a veritable passion. And when we consider how rare a human trait true gratitude is—the one particular characteristic in which the lower animals put us to shame—it can easily be imagined how I was touched to find that this beautiful and grand Canadian girl remained down to the very last moment of her life the impersonation of that most precious of all virtues. I have seen much of my fellow men and women, and I never knew but two other people who displayed gratitude as a passion—indulged in it, I might say, as a luxury—and they were both poets. I can give no higher praise to the "irritable genius." On this account Pauline Johnson will always figure in my memory as one of the noblest minded of the human race.

Circumstances made my personal knowledge of her all too slight. Our spiritual intimacy, however, was very strong, and I hope I shall be pardoned for saying a few words as to how our friendship began. It was at the time of Vancouver's infancy, when the population of the beautiful town of her final adoption was less than a twelfth of what it now is, and less than a fiftieth part of what it is soon going to be.

In 1906 I met her during one of her tours. How well I remember it! She was visiting London in company with Mr. McRaye—making a tour of England—reciting Canadian poetry. And on this occasion Mr. McRaye added to the interest of the entertainment by rendering in a perfectly marvellous way Dr. Drummond's Habitant poems.[1] It was in the Steinway Hall, and the audience was enthusiastic. When, after the performance, my wife and I went into the room behind the stage to congratulate her, I was quite affected by the warm and affectionate greeting that I got from her. With moist eyes she told her friends that she owed her literary success mainly to me.

And now what does the reader suppose that I had done to win all these signs of gratitude? I had simply alluded—briefly alluded—in the London "Athenaeum" some years before, to her genius and her work. Never surely was a reviewer so royally overpaid. Her allusion was to a certain article of mine on Canadian poetry which was written in 1889, and which she had read so assiduously that she might be said to know it by heart: she seemed to remember every word of it.

---

1   William Henry Drummond (1854–1907), who grew up in Montreal, was known for his comic poems in French-Canadian dialect. *The Habitant* (1897) sold 38,000 copies and was read across North America and in Britain.

Now that I shall never see her face again it is with real emotion that I recur to this article and to the occasion of it. Many years ago—nearly a quarter of a century—a beloved friend whom I still mourn, Norman Maccoll, editor of the "Athenaeum," sent me a book called "Songs of the Great Dominion," selected and edited by the poet, William Douw Lighthall. Maccoll knew the deep interest I have always taken in matters relating to Greater Britain, and especially in everything relating to Canada. Even at that time I ventured to prophesy that the great romance of the twentieth century would be the growth of the mighty world-power of Canada, just as the great romance of the nineteenth century had been the inauguration of the nascent power that sprang up among Britain's antipodes. He told me that a leading article for the journal upon some weighty subject was wanted, and asked me whether the book was important enough to be worth a leader. I turned over its pages and soon satisfied myself as to that point. I found the book rich in poetry—true poetry—by poets some of whom have since then come to great and world-wide distinction, all of it breathing, more or less, the atmosphere of Canada: that is to say Anglo-Saxon Canada. But in the writings of one poet alone I came upon a new note—the note of the Red Man's Canada. This was the poet that most interested me—Pauline Johnson. I quoted her lovely canoe song "In the Shadows," which will be found in this volume. I at once sat down and wrote a long article, which could have been ten times as long, upon a subject so suggestive as that of Canadian poetry.

As it was this article of mine which drew this noble woman to me, it has, since her death, assumed an importance in my eyes which it intrinsically does not merit. I might almost say that it has become sacred to me among my fugitive writings: this is why I cannot resist the temptation of making a few extracts from it. It seems to bring the dead poet very close to me. Moreover, it gives me an opportunity of re-saying what I then said of the great place Canadian poetry is destined to hold in the literature of the English-speaking race. I had often before said in the "Athenaeum," and in the "Encyclopaedia Britannica" and elsewhere, that all true poetry—perhaps all true literature—must be a faithful reflex either of the life of man or of the life of Nature.

Well, this article began by remarking that the subject of Colonial verse, and the immense future before the English-speaking poets, is allied to a question that is very great, the adequacy or inadequacy of English poetry—British, American, and Colonial—to the destiny of the race that produces it. The article enunciated the thesis that if the English language should not in the near future contain the finest body of poetry in the world, the time is now upon us when it ought to do so; for no other literature has had that variety of poetic material which is now at the command of English-speaking poets. It pointed out that at the present moment this material comprises much of the riches peculiar to the Old World and all the riches peculiar to the New. It pointed out that in reflecting the life of man the English muse enters into competition with the muse of every other European nation, classic and modern; and that, rich as England undoubtedly is in her own historic associations, she is not so rich as are certain other European countries, where almost every square yard of soil is so suggestive of human associations that it might be made the subject of a poem. To wander alone, through scenes that Homer knew, or through the streets that were hallowed by the footsteps of Dante, is an experience that sends a poetic thrill through the blood. For it is on classic ground only that the Spirit of Antiquity walks. And it went on to ask the question, "If even England, with all her riches of historic and legendary associations, is not so rich in this kind of poetic material as some parts of the European Continent, what shall be said of the new English worlds—Canada, the United States, the Australias, the South African Settlements, etc.?" Histories they have, these new countries—in the development of the human race, in the growth of the great man, Mankind— histories as important, no doubt, as those of Greece, Italy, and Great Britain. Inasmuch, however, as the sweet Spirit of Antiquity knows them not, where is the poet with wings so strong that he can carry them off into the "ampler ether," the "diviner air" where history itself is poetry?

[...]

The article then discussed the main subject of the argument, saying how very different it is when we come to consider poetic art as the reflex of the life of Nature [rather than of the Spirit of Antiquity]. Here the muse of Canada ought to be, and is, so great and strong. It is not in the old countries, it is in the new, that the poet can adequately reflect the life of Nature. It is in them alone that he can confront Nature's face as it is, uncoloured by associations of history and tradition. What Wordsworth tried all his life to do, the poets of Canada, of the Australias, of the Cape, have the opportunity of doing. How many a home-bounded Englishman must yearn for the opportunity now offered by the Canadian Pacific Railway of seeing the great virgin forests and prairies before settlement has made much progress—of seeing them as they existed before even the foot of the Red Man trod them—of seeing them without that physical toil which only a few hardy explorers can undergo. It is hard to realise that he who has not seen the vast unsettled tracts of the British Empire knows Nature only under the same aspect as she has been known by all the poets from Homer to our own day. And when I made the allusion to Pauline Johnson's poems which brought me such reward, I quoted "In the Shadows." The poem fascinated me—it fairly haunted me. I could not get it out of my head; and I remember that I was rather severe on Mr. Lighthall for only giving us two examples of a poet so rare—so full of the spirit of the open air.

Naturally I turned to his introductory remarks to see who Pauline Johnson was. I was not at all surprised to find that she had Indian blood in her veins, but I was surprised and delighted to find that she belonged to a famous Indian family—the Mohawks of Brantford. The Mohawks of Brantford! that splendid race to whose unswerving loyalty during two centuries not only Canada, but the entire British Empire owes a debt that can never be repaid.

After the appearance of my article I got a beautiful letter from Pauline Johnson, and I found that I had been fortunate enough to enrich my life with a new friendship.

And now as to the genius of Pauline Johnson: it was being recognized not only in Canada, but all over the great Continent of the West. Since 1889 I have been following her career with a glow of admiration and sympathy. I have been delighted to find that this success of hers had no damaging effect upon the grand simplicity of her nature. Up to the day of her death her passionate sympathy with the aborigines of Canada never flagged, as shown by such poems as "The Cattle Thief," "The Pilot of the Plains," "As Red Men Die," and many another. During all this time, however, she was cultivating herself in a thousand ways—taking interest in the fine arts, as witness her poem "The Art of Alma-Tadema."[1] Her native power of satire is shown in the lines

---

1 In 1906, Johnson visited the London studio of Lawrence Alma-Tadema (1836–1912), one of the most famous painters of the day, noted for scenes of classical Greece and Rome.

written after Dreyfus was exiled, called "'Give us Barabbas.'"[1] She had also a pretty gift of *vers de société*, as seen in her lines "Your Mirror Frame."

Her death is not only a great loss to those who knew and loved her: it is a great loss to Canadian literature and to the Canadian nation. I must think that she will hold a memorable place among poets in virtue of her descent and also in virtue of the work she has left behind, small as the quantity of that work is. I believe that Canada will, in future times, cherish her memory more and more, for of all Canadian poets she was the most distinctly a daughter of the soil, inasmuch as she inherited the blood of the great primeval race now so rapidly vanishing, and of the greater race that has supplanted it.

In reading the description of the funeral in the "News-Advertiser," I was specially touched by the picture of the large crowd of silent Red Men who lined Georgia Street, and who stood as motionless as statues all through the service, and until the funeral cortege had passed on the way to the cemetery. This must have rendered the funeral the most impressive and picturesque one of any poet that has ever lived.

---

1   Alfred Dreyfus (1859–1935) was a French military officer of Jewish ancestry whose unjust conviction for treason in 1894 (ascribed to anti-Semitism) and the successful campaign to exonerate him became famously known as "the Dreyfus affair," splitting French opinion.

Appendix B: Writings by Women

[Here we collect writings by women—Indigenous, Black, and White—who engage with some of the political and personal issues that also concerned Johnson. Their writing allows us to contextualize her work in the contemporary conversations and issues of the day concerning "the Indian question" and race relations.]

1. Jane Johnston Schoolcraft, "On Leaving My Children John and Jane at School in the Atlantic States, and Preparing to Return to the Interior, New York, March 18, 1839," in Henry Rowe Schoolcraft, *Personal Memoirs of a Residence of Thirty Years with the Indian Tribes on the American Frontiers* (Philadelphia: Lippincott, Grambo, 1851), 632–33

[Jane Johnston Schoolcraft (1800–42) is widely thought of as the first writer of Native American poetry; she wrote in English and Ojibwe. Her Ojibwe name, *Obabaamwewe-giizhigokwe*, translates as "Woman of the Sound that the Stars Make Rushing through the Sky." Her father was a Scots-Irish fur trader and her mother was from an important Ojibwe family; Schoolcraft's maternal grandfather was Waubojeeg (1747–93), a war chief and political leader who also wrote poetry. She married Henry Rowe Schoolcraft in 1823; they had four children, but only two survived to adulthood. We provide first the Ojibwe version, then the translation made by her husband, followed by a modern translation that reveals what a difference translation can make.]

[Untitled]

Nyau nin de nain dum
May kow e yaun in
Ain dah nuk ki yaun
Waus sa wa kom eg
Ain dah nuk ki yaun

Ne dau nis ainse e
Ne gwis is ainse e

Ishe nau gun ug wau
Waus sa wa kom eg

She gwau go sha ween
Ba sho waud e we
Nin zhe ka we yea
Ishe ez han jau yaun
Ain dah nuk ke yaun

Translation by Henry Rowe Schoolcraft

[Henry Rowe Schoolcraft (1793–1864) was a government agent, folklorist, and explorer, known for his prolific writings about Native Americans. He learned Ojibwe from his wife and her father, and translated and popularized Native American legends while freely changing elements of the stories to better fit his literary taste. He labels what follows as a "free translation" of his wife's work. Their children were sent to an elite boarding school where most students were white.]

Ah! When thought reverts to my country so dear,
My heart fills with pleasure, and throbs with a fear:
My country, my country, my own native land,
So lovely in aspect, in features so grand,
Far, far in the West. What are cities to me,
Oh! land of my mother, compared unto thee?

Fair land of the lakes! thou are blest to my sight,
With thy beaming bright waters, and landscapes of light;
The breeze and the murmur, the dash and the roar,
That summer and autumn cast over the shore,
They spring to my thoughts, like the lullaby tongue,
That soothed me to slumber when youthful and young.

One feeling more strongly still binds me to thee,
There roved my forefathers, in liberty free—
There shook they the war lance, and sported the plume,
Ere Europe had cast o'er this country a gloom;
Nor thought they that kingdoms more happy could be,
White lords of a land so resplendent and free.

Yet it is not alone that my country is fair,
And my home and my friends are inviting me there;

While they beckon me onward, my heart is still here,
With my sweet lovely daughter, and bonny boy dear:
And oh! what's the joy that a home can impart,
Removed from the dear ones who cling to my heart.

It is learning that calls them; but tell me, can schools
Repay for my love, or give nature new rules?
They may teach them the lore of the wit and the sage,
To be grave in their youth, and be gay in their age;
But ah! my poor heart, what are schools to thy view,
While severed from children thou lovest so true!

I return to my country, I haste on my way,
For duty commands me, and duty must sway;
Yet I leave the bright land where my little ones dwell,
With a sober regret, and a bitter farewell;
For there I must leave the dear jewels I love,
The dearest of gifts from my Master above.

[Untitled]

[What follows is a modern translation made for *The Sound the Stars Make Rushing Through the Sky: The Writings of Jane Johnston Schoolcraft*, edited by Robert Dale Parker (Philadelphia: U of Pennsylvania P, 2007). The translators are Dennis Jones, Heidi Stark, and James Vukelich.]

As I am thinking
When I find you
My land
Far in the west
My land

My little daughter
My little son
I leave them behind
Far away land

[emphatically] but soon
It is close however
To my home I shall return
That is the way that I am, my being
My land

My land
To my home I shall return
I begin to make my way home
Ahh but I am sad

2. Margaret Fuller, "Governor Everett Receiving the Indian Chiefs, November, 1837," *Summer on the Lakes in 1843* (Boston: Little and Brown, 1844), 185–90

[Margaret Fuller (1810–50) was a journalist, feminist, and poet. Edward Everett (1794–1865), Governor of Massachusetts from 1836–40 and an educator and orator, greeted leaders of the Sauk and Fox nations visiting Boston in 1837 in a style that imitated that of famous Indian orators (Fuller quotes this speech directly after the poem). Fuller edited the transcendentalist journal *The Dial* from 1840–42. The first woman allowed to use the library at Harvard University, she published *Women in the Nineteenth Century* (1845), which became a foundational feminist work. Fuller became the first full-time literary reviewer in the United States, writing for the *New-York Tribune*, with 50,000 readers. Sent to Europe in 1846 as their first female foreign correspondent, she became involved in the failed Italian Revolution led by Guiseppe Mazzini in 1848–49.]

Who says that Poesy is on the wane,
And that the Muses tune their lyres in vain?
'Mid all the treasures of romantic story,
When thought was fresh and fancy in her glory,
Has ever Art found out a richer theme,
More dark a shadow, or more soft a gleam,
Than fall upon the scene, sketched carelessly,
In the newspaper column of to-day?
American romance is somewhat stale.
Talk of the hatchet, and the faces pale,
Wampum and calumets and forests dreary,
Once so attractive, now begins to weary.
Uncas and Magawisca please us still,[1]

---

1 Uncas figures as the eponymous character in James Fenimore Cooper's *Last of the Mohicans* (1826)—although, in fact, the Mohicans are alive and well. Magawisca is a female character in a historical novel by Catherine Maria Sedgewick (1789–1867), *Hope Leslie, or Early Times in Massachusetts* (1827), unusual for its feminist and pro-Native American sentiments.

Unreal, yet idealized with skill;
But every poetaster scribbling witling,
From the majestic oak his stylus whittling,
Has helped to tire us, and to make us fear
The monotone in which so much we hear
Of "stoics of the wood," and "men without a tear."
Yet Nature, ever buoyant, ever young,
If let alone, will sing as erst she sung;
The course of circumstance gives back again
The Picturesque, erewhile pursued in vain;
Shows us the fount of Romance is not wasted—
The lights and shades of contrast not exhausted.
Shorn of his strength, the Samson now must sue
For fragments from the feast his fathers gave,
The Indian dare not claim what is his due,
But as a boon his heritage must crave;
His stately form shall soon be seen no more
Through all his father's land, the Atlantic shore,
Beneath the sun, to *us* so kind, *they* melt,
More heavily each day our rule is felt;
The tale is old,—we do as mortals must:
Might makes right here, but God and Time are just.
So near the drama hastens to its close,
On this last scene awhile your eyes repose;
The polished Greek and Scythian meet again,[1]
The ancient life is lived by modern men—
The savage through our busy cities walks,—
He in his untouched grandeur silent stalks.
Unmoved by all our gaieties and shows,
Wonder nor shame can touch him as he goes;
He gazes on the marvels we have wrought,
But knows the models from whence all was brought;
In God's first temples he has stood so oft,
And listened to the natural organ loft—
Has watched the eagle's flight, the muttering thunder heard,
Art cannot move him to a wondering word;
Perhaps he sees that all this luxury

---

1 The Greek historian Herodotus (c. 484–425 BCE) writes about
 the Scythians, tribes from the Eurasian steppes who were experts at fighting with bows from horseback. Here, the analogy
 aligns the Greeks with the settlers and the Scythians with the
 Indians.

Brings less food to the mind than to the eye;
Perhaps a simple sentiment has brought
More to him than your arts had ever taught.
What are the petty triumphs *Art* has given,
To eyes familiar with the naked heaven?
All has been seen—dock, railroad, and canal,
Fort, market, bridge, college, and arsenal,
Asylum, hospital, and cotton mill,
The theatre, the lighthouse, and the jail.
The Braves each novelty, reflecting, saw,
And now and then growled out the earnest *yaw*.
And now the time is come, 'tis understood,
When, having seen and thought so much, a *talk* may do some good.
A well-dressed mob have thronged the sight to greet,
And motley figures throng the spacious street;
Majestical and calm through all they stride,
Wearing the blanket with a monarch's pride;
The gazers stare and shrug, but can't deny
Their noble forms and blameless symmetry.
If the Great Spirit their morale has slighted,
And wigwam smoke their mental culture blighted,
Yet the physique, at least, perfection reaches,
In wilds where neither Combe nor Spursheim[1] teaches;
Where whispering trees invite man to the chase,
And bounding deer allure him to the race.
Would thou hadst seen it! That dark, stately band,
Whose ancestors enjoyed all this fair land,
Whence they, by force or fraud, were made to flee,
Are brought, the white man's victory to see.
Can kind emotions in their proud hearts glow,
As through these realms, now decked by Art, they go?
The church, the school, the railroad and the mart—
Can these a pleasure to their minds impart?
All once was theirs—earth, ocean, forest, sky—
How can they joy in what now meets the eye?
Not yet Religion has unlocked the soul,
Nor Each has learned to glory in the Whole!
Must they not think, so strange and sad their lot,
That they by the Great Spirit are forgot?

---

1 George Combe (1788–1858) and Johan Gaspar Spurzheim
   (1776–1832) were well-known European phrenologists; both visited
   the United States.

From the far border to which they are driven,
They might look up in trust to the clear heaven;
But *here*—what tales doth every object tell
Where Massasoit sleeps—where Philip fell![1]
We take our turn, and the Philosopher
Sees through the clouds a hand which cannot err,
An unimproving race, with all their graces
And all their vices, must resign their places;
And Human Culture rolls its onward flood
Over the broad plains steeped in Indian blood.
Such thoughts, steady our faith; yet there will rise
Some natural tears into the calmest eyes—
Which gaze where forest princes haughty go,
Made for a gaping crowd a rare show.
But *this* a scene seems where, in courtesy,
The pale face with the forest prince could vie,
For One presided, who, for tact and grace,
In any age had held an honored place,—
In Beauty's own dear day, had shone a polished Phidian vase![2]
Oft have I listened to his accents bland,
And owned the magic of his silvery voice,
In all the graces which life's arts demand,
Delighted by the justness of his choice.
Not his the stream of lavish, fervid thought,—
The rhetoric by passion's magic wrought;
Not his the massive style, the lion port,
Which with the granite class of mind assort;
But, in a range of excellence his own,
With all the charms to soft persuasion known,
Amid our busy people we admire him—"elegant and lone."
He scarce needs words, so exquisite the skill
Which modulates the tones to do his will,
That the mere sound enough would charm the ear,

---

1 Massasoit (c. 1590–1661) was a chief sachem of the Wampanoag
   at the time of the arrival of the Pilgrims on the east coast of North
   America. Philip, also known as Metacomet (c. 1639–76), was the
   Wampanoag leader in the devastating war against the English colonists known as King Philip's War (1675–78).
2 Phidias (480–430 BCE) was a famous Greek sculptor; here the ad-
   jective is used to reference the famous red and black Greek ceramic
   urns decorated with scenes from mythology.

And lap in its Elysium[1] all who hear.
The intellectual paleness of his cheek,
The heavy eyelids and slow, tranquil smile,
The well cut lips from which the graces speak,
Fit him alike to win or to beguile;
Then those words so well chosen, fit, though few,
Their linked sweetness as our thoughts pursue,
We deem them spoken pearls, or radiant diamond dew.
And never yet did I admire the power
Which makes so lustrous every threadbare theme—
Which won for Lafayette[2] one other hour,
And e'en on July Fourth could cast a gleam—
As now, when I behold him play the host,
With all the dignity which red men boast—
With all the courtesy the whites have lost;—
Assume the very hue of savage mind,
Yet in rude accents show the thought refined:—
Assume the naiveté of infant age,
And in such prattle seem still more a sage;
The golden mean with tact unerring seized,[3]
A courtly critic shone, a simple savage pleased;
The stoic of the woods his skill confessed,
As all the Father answered in his breast,
To the sure mark the silver arrow sped,
The man without a tear a tear has shed;
And thou hadst wept, hadst thou been there, to see
How true one sentiment must ever be,
In court or camp, the city or the wild,
To rouse the Father's heart, you need but name his Child.
'Twas a fair scene—and acted well by all;
So here's a health to Indian braves so tall—
Our Governor and Boston people all!

---

1 Elysium, also the Elysian Fields, is the Greek equivalent of
   heaven.
2 The Marquis de Lafayette (1757–1834), a Frenchman, took the
   American side in the Revolutionary War. He became an important leader and close friend of George Washington (1732–99)
   and helped Thomas Jefferson (1743–1826) write the *Declaration
   of the Rights of Man and of the Citizen*. Barely escaping with his
   life after leading moderate forces in the French Revolution, he
   returned to the United States in 1824 for a tour and was greeted
   as a hero.
3 The desirable middle between two extremes.

3. From Sarah Winnemucca, "Domestic and Social Moralities," *Life among the Piutes: Their Wrongs and Claims*, ed. Mrs. Horace Mann (Boston: Putnam's, 1883), ch. 2, 45–57

[Sarah Winnemucca (c. 1844–91), also known by the name Thocmetony, "Shell Flower," was an activist, lecturer, and educator. *Life among the Piutes* is regarded as an important work of both autobiography and ethnography. In this excerpt from Chapter Two, Winnemucca explains the value of women in social life and politics in her community, yet as can be seen here, she also blames colonial violence for destroying the peace women found prior to contact. Her book is regarded as the first by a Native American woman. She gave over 400 speeches in her lifetime advocating for her people. In 1883, Winnemucca opened a school for Paiute children in Nevada; it closed three years later. Paiute is the common modern spelling for the name of this tribe.]

Our children are very carefully taught to be good. Their parents tell them stories, traditions of old times, even of the first mother of the human race; and love stories, stories of giants, and fables; and when they ask if these last stories are true, they answer, "Oh, it is only coyote," which means that they are make-believe stories. Coyote is the name of a mean, crafty little animal, half wolf, half dog, and stands for everything low. It is the greatest term of reproach one Indian has for another. Indians do not swear,—they have no words for swearing till they learn them of white men. The worst they call each is bad or coyote; but they are very sincere with one another, and if they think each other in the wrong they say so.

We are taught to love everybody. We don't need to be taught to love our fathers and mothers. We love them without being told to. Our tenth cousin is as near to us as our first cousin; and we don't marry into our relations. Our young women are not allowed to talk to any young man that is not their cousin, except at the festive dances, when both are dressed in their best clothes, adorned with beads, feathers or shells, and stand alternately in the ring and take hold of hands. These are very pleasant occasions to all the young people.

Many years ago, when my people were happier than they are now, they used to celebrate the Festival of Flowers in the spring. I have been to three of them only in the course of my life.

Oh, with what eagerness we girls used to watch every spring for the time when we could meet with our hearts' delight, the young men, whom in civilized life you call beaux. We would all go in company to see if the flowers we were named for were yet in bloom, for almost all the girls are named for flowers. We talked about them in our wigwams, as if we were the flowers, saying, "Oh, I saw myself to-day in full bloom!" We would talk all the evening in this way in our families with such delight, and such beautiful thoughts of the happy day when we should meet with those who admired us and would help us to sing our flower-songs which we made up as we sang. But we were always sorry for those that were not named after some flower, because we knew they could not join in the flower-songs like ourselves, who were named for flowers of all kinds.

At last one evening came a beautiful voice, which made every girl's heart throb with happiness. It was the chief, and every one hushed to hear what he said to-day. "My dear daughters, we are told that you have seen yourselves in the hills and in the valleys, in full bloom. Five days from to-day your festival day will come. I know every young man's heart stops beating while I am talking. I know how it was with me many years ago. I used to wish the Flower Festival would come every day. Dear young men and young women, you are saying, 'Why put it off five days?' But you all know that is our rule. It gives you time to think, and to show your sweetheart your flower."

All the girls who have flower-names dance along together, and those who have not go together also. Our fathers and mothers and grandfathers and grandmothers make a place for us where we can dance. Each one gathers the flower she is named for, and then all weave them into wreaths and crowns and scarfs, and dress up in them.

Some girls are named for rocks and are called rock-girls, and they find some pretty rocks which they carry; each one such a rock as she is named for, or whatever she is named for. If she cannot, she can take a branch of sage-brush, or a bunch of rye-grass, which have no flower.

They all go marching along, each girl in turn singing of herself; but she is not a girl any more,—she is a flower singing. She sings of herself, and her sweetheart, dancing along by her side, helps her sing the song she makes.

I will repeat what we say of ourselves. "I, Sarah Winnemucca, am a shell-flower, such as I wear on my dress. My name is Thocmetony. I am so beautiful! Who will come and dance with me while I am so beautiful? Oh, come and be happy with me! I shall be beautiful while the earth lasts. Somebody will always admire me; and who will come and be happy with me in the Spirit-land? I shall be beautiful forever there. Yes, I shall be more beautiful than my shell-flower, my Thocmetony! Then, come, oh come, and dance and be happy with me!" The young men sing with us as they dance beside us.

Our parents are waiting for us somewhere to welcome us home. And then we praise the sage-brush and the rye-grass that have no flower, and the pretty rocks that some are named for; and then we present our beautiful flowers to these companions who could carry none. And so all are happy; and that closes the beautiful day.

My people have been so unhappy for a long time they wish now to *disincrease*, instead of multiply. The mothers are afraid to have more children, for fear they shall have daughters, who are not safe even in their mother's presence....

4. Inshata Theamba ("Bright Eyes") / Susette La Flesche, Introduction to William Justin Harsha's *Ploughed Under: The Story of an Indian Chief, Told by Himself* (New York: Fords, Howard and Hulbert, 1881), 3–6

[Inshata Theamba was Susette La Flesche (1854–1903) a translator, journalist, and activist, whose Omaha name means "Bright Eyes." Like Johnson, she was the well-educated daughter of a chief. Her father, Joseph La Flesche, of mixed Ponca and French-Canadian ancestry, was the last head chief of the Omaha selected according to tradition. Susette La Flesche acted as a translator for Standing Bear, a Ponca who successfully argued in US District Court in Omaha that Indians were "persons" under law. After the success of this case in 1879, she, her fiancé Thomas Tibbles, Standing Bear, and her half-brother Francis La Flesche toured the eastern United States, giving lectures supporting rights for Native Americans. Later, she and her husband reported on the Wounded Knee massacre of over 150 Lakota by the US Army in 1890 for the *Omaha Morning World-Herald*. Published anonymously and purporting to be by an "Indian Chief," *Ploughed Under* was, in fact, a novel by a white missionary, William Justin Harsha (1853–1931), who served for fifteen years as the pastor of the First Presbyterian Church of Omaha.]

The white people have tried to solve the "Indian Question" by commencing with the proposition that the Indian is different from all other human beings.

With some he is a peculiar being, surrounded by a halo of romance, who has to be set apart on a reservation as something sacred, who has to be fed, clothed, and taken care of by a guardian or agent, by whom he is not to be allowed to come into contact with his conquerors lest it might degrade him; his conquerors being a people who hold their civilization above that of all others on the earth, because of their perfect freedom and liberty. "The contact of peoples is the best of all education." And this the ward is denied.

With others again he is a savage, a sort of monster without any heart or soul or mind, but whose whole being is full of hatred, ferocity, and blood-thirstiness. They suppose him to have no family affections, no love for his home, none of the sensitive feelings that all other human beings presumably have. This class demand his extermination.

Under the shelter of the conflicting laws imposed by these extreme views, the clever operators of the Indian Ring—not caring what he is, but looking on him for what he has, and the opportunities he affords, as legitimate prey—pounce on him and use him as a means of obtaining contracts, removals, land speculations, and appropriations which are to be stolen. They tear him from his home, disregarding all the rights of his manhood.

Allow an Indian to suggest that the solution of the vexed "Indian Question" is *Citizenship*, with all its attending duties and responsibilities, as well as the privileges of protection under the law, by which the Indian could appeal to the courts, when deprived of life, liberty, or property, as every citizen can, and would be allowed the opportunity to make something of himself, in common with every other citizen. If it were not for the lands which the Indian holds, he would have been a citizen long before the negro;[1] and in this respect his lands have been a curse to him rather than a blessing. But for them, he would have been insignificant in the eyes of this powerful and wealthy nation,

---

1 This argument that Blacks and Indians were rivals for equal rights comes up—with women added to the mix—in Anna Julia Cooper's excerpt "Woman versus the Indian" below (Appendix B5). Despite Inshata Theamba's argument here, Canada, with its relatively small Black population, did not grant voting rights to Status Indians until 1951.

and allowed to live in peace and quietness, without attracting the birds of prey forever hovering over the helpless; then his citizenship would have protected him, as it does any other ordinary human being. As a 'ward,' or extraordinary being, if he is accused of committing a crime, this serves as a pretext for his extermination, and his father, mother, sister, brother, wife, or people are involved in one common ruin; while if he were simply a citizen, he would be individually arrested by the sheriff, and tried in court, and either protected in his innocence or convicted and punished in his guilt. The Indian, as a "ward," or extraordinary being, affords employment to about ten thousand employees in the Indian Bureau with all the salaries attached, as well as innumerable contractors, freighters, and land speculators. He requires also, periodically, immense appropriations to move him from place to place. Imagine a company of Irish immigrants requiring from Congress an appropriation to move them from one part of the country to another! No wonder that the powers-that-be refuse to recognize the Indian as an ordinary human being, but insist that he is taken care of and "protected" by the decisions of the Indian Bureau. In this "land of freedom and liberty" an Indian has to get the permission of an agent before he can either step off his reservation or allow any civilization to enter it and this, under heavy penalty for disobedience. In this land, where the boast is made that all men are "equal before the law," the Indian cannot sue in the courts for his life, liberty, or property, because, forsooth, the Indian is not a "person," as the learned attorney employed by the Secretary of the Interior argued for five hours, when an Indian [Standing Bear] appealed to the writ of *habeas corpus*[1] for his liberty.

The key to this complicated problem is simply to recognize the Indian as a person and a citizen, give him title to his lands, and place him within the jurisdiction of the courts, *as an individual.* It is absurd for a great government like this to say that it cannot manage a little handful of helpless people, who are but an atom in the mass of fifty millions of people, unless they treat them as "wards."

No, the Indian is not an extraordinary being; he is of the race of man, and like others is the creature of his surroundings. If you would know something of what he is, of how his spirit and his

---

1 "You should have the body" (Latin), a legal expression. This principle requires the presence of a detained person in court so that detention can be justified.

disposition are affected by his circumstances, read the record of life—its loves and hates—here set forth. As the hero of this story says, "If those of our race who have been slain by the white man should spring up from the sod as trees, there would be one broad moaning forest from the great river to the sea." The incidents of this tale are based upon easily authenticated facts—most of them, indeed, being matters of official record. The lines are not too deep nor the colors too strong. It would be impossible to exaggerate the sufferings imposed upon my people by the cruel greed of their plunderers. As the author has so graphically depicted, the huge plough of the "Indian system" has run for a hundred years, beam deep, turning down into the darkness of the earth every hope and aspiration which we have cherished. The sod is rich with the blood of human beings of both races. What sort of a harvest, think you, will it yield in the future to the nation whose hand has guided this plough?

5. From Anna Julia Cooper, "Woman versus the Indian," *A Voice from the South, by a Black Woman from the South* (Xenia, OH: Aldine, 1892), 80–126

[Cooper (1858–1964), born enslaved, became a pre-eminent African-American intellectual. In a long and brilliant essay, she argues that women's rights activists have a responsibility to support the cause of all oppressed groups for equality. This excerpt of less than half of the essay gives a sense of how women of colour responded to some of the attitudes of white feminists of the day. The title of the essay is the title of a speech delivered by the Reverend Anna Shaw to the National Women's Council in 1891. Rather than focus on the divisive nature of this speech, Cooper praises Shaw for another more inclusive action. Cooper received a doctorate in history from the Sorbonne in 1924, becoming the fourth African-American woman to obtain this degree. *A Voice from the South* is a foundational work of Black feminism.]

When the National Woman's Council convened at Washington in February 1891, among a number of thoughtful and suggestive papers read by eminent women, was one by the Rev. Anna Shaw,[1] bearing the above title.

---

1   The Reverend Anna Shaw (1847–1919) was a suffragist and Methodist preacher.

That Miss Shaw is broad and just and liberal in principle is proved beyond contradiction. Her noble generosity and womanly firmness are unimpeachable. The unwavering stand taken by herself and Miss Anthony[1] in the subsequent color ripple in Wimodaughsis ought to be sufficient to allay forever any doubts as to the pure gold of these two women.

Of Wimodaughsis (which, being interpreted for the uninitiated, is a woman's culture club whose name is made up of the first few letters of the four words wives, mothers, daughters, and sisters) Miss Shaw is president, and a lady from the Blue Grass State *was* secretary. Pandora's box is opened in the ideal harmony of this modern Eden without an Adam when a colored lady, a teacher in one of our schools, applies for admission to its privileges and opportunities.

The Kentucky secretary, a lady zealous in good works and one who, I can't help imagining, belongs to that estimable class who daily thank the Lord that He made the earth that they may have the job of superintending its rotations, and who really would like to help "elevate" the colored people (in her own way of course and so long as they understand their places) is filled with grief and horror that any persons of Negro extraction should aspire to learn type-writing or languages or to enjoy any other advantages offered in the sacred halls of Wimodaughsis. Indeed, she had not calculated that there were any wives, mothers, daughters, and sisters, except white ones; and she is really convinced that *Whimodaughsis* would sound just as well, and then it need mean just *white mothers, daughters and sisters*. In fact, so far as there is anything in a name, nothing would be lost by omitting for the sake of euphony, from this unique mosaic, the letters that represent wives. *Whiwimodaughsis* might be a little startling, and on the whole wives would better yield to white; since clearly all women are not wives, while surely all wives are daughters. The daughters therefore could represent the wives and this immaculate assembly for propagating liberal and progressive ideas and disseminating a broad and humanizing culture might be spared the painful possibility of the sight of a black man coming in the future to escort from an evening class this solitary cream-colored applicant. Accordingly the Kentucky secretary took the cream-colored applicant aside, and, with emotions befitting such an epoch-making crisis, told her, "as kindly as she could,"

---

1 Susan B. Anthony (1820–1906) was a famous American abolitionist and suffragist.

that colored people were not admitted to the classes, at the same time refunding the money which said cream-colored applicant had paid for lessons in type-writing.

When this little incident came to the knowledge of Miss Shaw, she said firmly and emphatically, NO. As a minister of the gospel and as a Christian woman, she could not lend her influence to such unreasonable and uncharitable discrimination; and she must resign the honor of president of Wimodaughsis if persons were to be proscribed solely on account of their color.

To the honor of the board of managers, be it said, they sustained Miss Shaw; and the Kentucky secretary, and those whom she succeeded in inoculating with her prejudices, resigned.

'Twas only a ripple,—some bewailing of lost opportunity on the part of those who could not or would not seize God's opportunity for broadening and enlarging their own souls—and then the work flowed on as before.

Susan B. Anthony and Anna Shaw are evidently too noble to be held in thrall by the provincialisms of women who seem never to have breathed the atmosphere beyond the confines of their grandfathers' plantations. It is only from the broad plateau of light and love that one can see petty prejudice and narrow priggishness in their true perspective; and it is on this high ground, as I sincerely believe, these two grand women stand.

As leaders in the woman's movement of today, they have need of clearness of vision as well as firmness of soul in adjusting recalcitrant forces, and wheeling into line the thousand and one none-such, never-to-be-modified, won't-be-dictated-to banners of their somewhat mottled array.

[...]

Lately a great national and international movement characteristic of this age and country, a movement based on the inherent right of every soul to its own highest development, I mean the movement making for Woman's full, free, and complete emancipation, has, after much courting, obtained the gracious smile of the Southern woman—I beg her pardon—the Southern *lady*.

She represents blood, and of course could not be expected to leave that out; and firstly and foremostly she must not, in any organization she may deign to grace with her presence, be asked to associate with "these people who were once her slaves."

Now the Southern woman (I may be pardoned, being one myself) was never renowned for her reasoning powers, and it is not surprising that just a little picking will make her logic fall to pieces even here.

In the first place she imagines that because her grandfather had slaves who were black, all the blacks in the world of every shade and tint were once in the position of her slaves. This is as bad as the Irishman who was about to kill a peaceable Jew in the streets of Cork,—having just learned that Jews slew his Redeemer. The black race constitutes one-seventh the known population of the globe; and there are representatives of it here as elsewhere who were never in bondage at any time to any man,—whose blood is as blue and lineage as noble as any, even that of the white lady of the South. That her slaves were black and she despises her slaves, should no more argue antipathy to all dark people and peoples, than that Guiteau,[1] an assassin, was white, and I hate assassins, should make me hate all persons more or less white. The objection shows a want of clear discrimination.

The second fallacy in the objection grows out of the use of an ambiguous middle, as the logicians would call it, or assigning a double signification to the term *"Social equality."*

Civility to the Negro implies social equality. I am opposed to *associating* with dark persons on terms of social equality. Therefore, I abrogate civility to the Negro. This is like

> Light is opposed to darkness.
> Feathers are light.
> Ergo, Feathers are opposed to darkness.

The "social equality" implied by civility to the Negro is a very different thing from forced association with him socially. Indeed it seems to me that the mere application of a little cold common sense would show that uncongenial social environments could by no means be forced on any one. I do not, and cannot be made to associate with all dark persons, simply on the ground that I am dark; and I presume the Southern lady can imagine some whose faces are white, with whom she would no sooner think of chatting unreservedly than, were it possible, with a veritable "darkey." Such things must and will always be left to individual election. No law, human or divine, can legislate for or against them. Like seeks like; and I am sure with the Southern lady's antipathies at their present temperature, she might enter ten thousand organi-

---

1 Charles Julius Guiteau (1841–82) assassinated US president James Garfield in 1881.

zations besprinkled with colored women without being any more deflected by them than by the proximity of a stone. The social equality scare then is all humbug, conscious or unconscious, I know not which. And were it not too bitter a thought to utter here, I might add that the overtures for forced association in the past history of these two races were not made by the manacled black man, nor by *the silent and suffering black woman!*

When I seek food in a public cafe or apply for first-class accommodations on a railway train, I do so because my physical necessities are identical with those of other human beings of like constitution and temperament, and crave satisfaction. I go because I want food, or I want comfort—not because I want association with those who frequent these places; and I can see no more "social equality" in buying lunch at the same restaurant, or riding in a common car, than there is in paying for dry goods at the same counter or walking on the same street.

The social equality which means forced or unbidden association would be as much depreciated and as strenuously opposed by the circle in which I move as by the most hide-bound Southerner in the land. Indeed I have been more than once annoyed by the inquisitive white interviewer, who, with spectacles on nose and pencil and note-book in hand, comes to get some "points" about *"your people."* My "people" are just like other people—indeed, too like for their own good. They hate, they love, they attract and repel, they climb or they grovel, struggle or drift, aspire or despair, endure in hope or curse in vexation, exactly like all the rest of unregenerate humanity. Their likes and dislikes are as strong; their antipathies—and prejudices too I fear, are as pronounced as you will find anywhere; and the entrance to the inner sanctuary of their homes and hearts is as jealously guarded against profane intrusion.

What the dark man wants then is merely to live his own life, in his own world, with his own chosen companions, in whatever of comfort, luxury, or emoluments his talent or his money can in an impartial market secure. Has he wealth, he does not want to be forced into inconvenient or unsanitary sections of cities to buy a home and rear his family. Has he art, he does not want to be cabined and cribbed into emulation with the few who merely happen to have his complexion. His talent aspires to study without proscription the masters of all ages and to rub against the broadest and fullest movements of his own day.

Has he religion, he does not want to be made to feel that there is a white Christ and a black Christ, a white Heaven and a black

Heaven, a white Gospel and a black Gospel,—but the one ideal of perfect manhood and womanhood, the one universal longing for development and growth, the one desire for being, and being better, the one great yearning, aspiring, outreaching, in all the heart-throbs of humanity in whatever race or clime.

[...]

And this is why, as it appears to me, woman in her lately acquired vantage ground for speaking an earnest helpful word, can do this country no deeper and truer and more lasting good than by bending all her energies to thus broadening, humanizing, and civilizing her native land.

"Except ye become as little children" is not a pious precept, but an inexorable law of the universe. God's kingdoms are all sealed to the seedy, moss-grown mind of self-satisfied maturity. Only the little child in spirit, the simple, receptive, educable mind can enter. Preconceived notions, blinding prejudices, and shrivelling antipathies must be wiped out, and the cultivable soul made a tabula rasa for whatever lesson great Nature has to teach.

This, too, is why I conceive the subject to have been unfortunately worded which was chosen by Miss Shaw at the Woman's Council and which stands at the head of this chapter.

Miss Shaw is one of the most powerful of our leaders, and we feel her voice should give no uncertain note. Woman should not, even by inference, or for the sake of argument, seem to disparage what is weak. For woman's cause is the cause of the weak; and when all the weak shall have received their due consideration, then woman will have her "rights," and the Indian will have his rights, and the Negro will have his rights, and all the strong will have learned at last to deal justly, to love mercy, and to walk humbly; and our fair land will have been taught the secret of universal courtesy which is after all nothing but the art, the science, and the religion of regarding one's neighbor as one's self, and to do for him as we would, were conditions swapped, that he do for us.

It cannot seem less than a blunder, whenever the exponents of a great reform or the harbingers of a noble advance in thought and effort allow themselves to seem distorted by a narrow view of their own aims and principles. All prejudices, whether of race, sect or sex, class pride and caste distinctions are the belittling inheritance and badge of snobs and prigs.

The philosophic mind sees that its own "rights" are the rights of humanity. That in the universe of God nothing trivial is or mean; and the recognition it seeks is not through the robber and wild beast adjustment of the survival of the bullies but through the universal application ultimately of the Golden Rule.

Not unfrequently has it happened that the impetus of a mighty thought wave has done the execution meant by its Creator in spite of the weak and distorted perception of its human embodiment. It is not strange if reformers, who, after all, but think God's thoughts after him, have often "builded more wisely than they knew"; and while fighting consciously for only a narrow gateway for themselves have been driven forward by that irresistible "Power not ourselves which makes for righteousness" to open a high road for humanity. It was so with our sixteenth century reformers. The fathers of the Reformation had no idea that they were inciting an insurrection of the human mind against all domination. None would have been more shocked than they at our nineteenth century deductions from their sixteenth century premises. Emancipation of mind and freedom of thought would have been as appalling to them as it was distasteful to the pope. They were right, they argued, to rebel against Romish absolutism[1]—because Romish preaching and Romish practicing were wrong. They denounced popes for hacking heretics and forthwith began themselves to roast witches. The Spanish Inquisition in the hands of Philip and Alva was an institution of the devil; wielded by the faithful, it would become quite another thing. The only "rights" they were broad enough consciously to fight for was the right to substitute the absolutism of their conceptions, their party, their *"ism"* for an authority whose teaching they conceived to be corrupt and vicious. Persecution for a belief was wrong only when the persecutors were wrong and the persecuted right. The sacred prerogative of the individual to decide on matters of belief they did not dream of maintaining. Universal tolerance and its twin, universal charity, were not conceived yet. The broad foundation stone of all human rights, the great democratic principle "A man's a man, and *his own sovereign* for a' that"[2] they did not dare enunciate. They were incapable of drawing up a Declaration of Independence for humanity. The Reformation to the Reformers meant one bundle of authoritative opinions vs.

---

1 Romish is Roman Catholicism, dominant in Europe until the rise of the Protestant Reformation in the sixteenth century.

2 Here she plays on the words of Robert Burns's famous song, "A Man's a Man for a' That" (1795).

another bundle of authoritative opinions. Justification by faith, vs. justification by ritual. Submission to Calvin[1] vs. submission to the Pope. English and Germans vs. the Italians.

To our eye, viewed through a vista of three centuries, it was the death wrestle of the principle of thought enslavement in the throttling grasp for personal freedom; it was the great Emancipation Day of human belief, man's intellectual Independence Day, prefiguring and finally compelling the world-wide enfranchisement of his body and all its activities. Not Protestant vs. Catholic, then; not Luther vs. Leo, not Dominicans vs. Augustinians, nor Geneva vs. Rome;[2]—but humanity rationally free, vs. the clamps of tradition and superstition which had manacled and muzzled it.

The cause of freedom is not the cause of a race or a sect, a party or a class,—it is the cause of human kind, the very birthright of humanity. Now unless we are greatly mistaken the Reform of our day, known as the Woman's Movement, is essentially such an embodiment, if its pioneers could only realize it, of the universal good. And specially important is it that there be no confusion of ideas among its leaders as to its scope and universality. All mists must be cleared from the eyes of woman if she is to be a teacher of morals and manners: the former strikes its roots in the individual and its training and pruning may be accomplished by classes; but the latter is to lubricate the joints and minimize the friction of society, and it is important and fundamental that there be no chromatic or other aberration when the teacher is settling the point, "Who is my neighbor?"

It is not the intelligent woman vs. the ignorant woman; nor the white woman vs. the black, the brown, and the red,—it is not even the cause of woman vs. man. Nay, 'tis woman's strongest vindication for speaking that the world needs to hear her voice. It would be subversive of every human interest that the cry of one-half the human family be stifled. Woman in stepping from the pedestal of statue-like inactivity in the domestic shrine, and daring to think and move and speak,—to undertake to help shape, mold, and

---

1   John Calvin (1509–69) was an influential French pastor during the Protestant Reformation.

2   Martin Luther (1483–1546), an early Protestant reformer, was condemned in 1520 by Pope Leo X (r. 1513–21). Dominicans and Augustinians are two Roman Catholic religious orders. Many Protestant reformers, notably Calvin, moved to Geneva, where they were safe from arrest as heretics.

direct the thought of her age, is merely completing the circle of the world's vision. Hers is every interest that has lacked an interpreter and a defender. Her cause is linked with that of every agony that has been dumb—every wrong that needs a voice.

It is no fault of man's that he has not been able to see truth from her standpoint. It does credit both to his head and heart that no greater mistakes have been committed or even wrongs perpetrated while she sat making tatting and snipping paper flowers. Man's own innate chivalry and the mutual interdependence of their interests have insured his treating her cause, in the main at least, as his own. And he is pardonably surprised and even a little chagrined, perhaps, to find his legislation not considered "perfectly lovely" in every respect. But in any case his work is only impoverished by her remaining dumb. The world has had to limp along with the wobbling gait and one-sided hesitancy of man with one eye. Suddenly the bandage is removed from the other eye and the whole body is filled with light. It sees a circle where before it saw a segment. The darkened eye restored, every member rejoices with it.

What a travesty of its case for this eye to become plaintiff in a suit, Eye vs. Foot. "There is that dull clod, the foot, allowed to roam at will, free and untrammelled; while I, the source and medium of light, brilliant and beautiful, am fettered in darkness and doomed to desuetude." The great burly black man, ignorant and gross and depraved, is allowed to vote; while the franchise is withheld from the intelligent and refined, the pure-minded and lofty souled white woman. Even the untamed and untamable Indian of the prairie, who can answer nothing but "ugh" to great economic and civic questions is thought by some worthy to wield the ballot which is still denied the Puritan maid and the first lady of Virginia.

Is not this hitching our wagon to something much lower than a star? Is not woman's cause broader, and deeper, and grander, than a blue stocking debate or an aristocratic pink tea? Why should woman become plaintiff in a suit versus the Indian, or the Negro or any other race or class who have been crushed under the iron heel of Anglo-Saxon power and selfishness? If the Indian has been wronged and cheated by the puissance of this American government, it is woman's mission to plead with her country to cease to do evil and to pay its honest debts. If the Negro has been deceitfully cajoled or inhumanly cuffed according to selfish expediency or capricious antipathy, let it be woman's mission to plead that he be met as a man and honestly given half the road. If woman's own happiness has been ignored or misunderstood in our country's legislating for bread winners, for rum sellers, for property holders, for the family relations, for any or all the interests that touch her vitally, let her rest her plea, not on Indian inferiority, nor on Negro depravity, but on the obligation of legislators to do for her as they would have others do for them were relations reversed. Let her try to teach her country that every interest in this world is entitled at least to a respectful hearing, that every sentiency is worthy of its own gratification, that a helpless cause should not be trampled down, nor a bruised reed broken; and when the right of the individual is made sacred, when the image of God in human form, whether in marble or in clay, whether in alabaster or in ebony, is consecrated and inviolable, when men have been taught to look beneath the rags and grime, the pomp and pageantry of mere circumstance and have regard unto the celestial kernel uncontaminated at the core, when race, color, sex, condition, are realized to be the accidents, not the substance of life, and consequently as not obscuring or modifying the inalienable title to life, liberty, and pursuit of happiness,—then is mastered the science of politeness, the art of courteous contact, which is naught but the practical application of the principle of benevolence, the back bone and marrow of all religion; then woman's lesson is taught and woman's cause is won—not the white woman nor the black woman nor the red woman, but the cause of every man or woman who has writhed silently under a mighty wrong. The pleading of the American woman for the right and the opportunity to employ the American method of influencing the disposal to be made of herself, her property, her children in civil, economic, or domestic relations is thus seen to be based on a principle as broad as the human race and as old as human society. Her wrongs are thus indissolubly linked with all undefended woe, all helpless suffering, and the plenitude of her "rights" will mean the final triumph of all right over might, the supremacy of the moral forces of reason and justice and love in the government of the nation.

God hasten the day.

6. Sophia Alice Callahan, "Is This Right?," *Wynema: A Child of the Forest* (Philadelphia: Smith, 1891), 94–98

[Sophia Alice Callahan (1868–94) wrote poetry and fiction. Her father was a leader of the Creek Nation, although his ancestry is debated; her mother was the daughter of a Methodist missionary. She was educated at the Wesleyan Female Institute in Virginia and became a teacher, working at the Harrell Institute in Muskogee and then at the Wealaka School, a boarding school for Creek children established in 1881 and run by her father. She died of pleurisy aged 26.]

"Is This Right?"

"Wynema, this is a friend of ours whom we found in the Sioux country. Can you speak the language? If so, she will tell you all, and I should like for you to interpret for my benefit. Ask her to tell you about the 'starving time,' as the Indians call the time when they lived on one cent per day," said Robin one day, some weeks after his return home. He had been to Keithley College and had brought Chikena home with him that she might see the "squaw and papoose," as he laughingly called Wynema and Genevieve.

"Very well, dear," Wynema replied. "I learned to speak the Sioux language when quite a child. We had an old Sioux woman who lived with us until I was almost grown, when she died. And thus I became familiar with the language."

Then Wynema took the old woman's hand and kissed her softly, remembering the dear ones she had left behind in the burying-ground of the battle-field; and she spoke words of sympathy, leading her to talk of her troubles.

"My husband wishes to hear of your sufferings during the time you came near starving, before the Indian war. Can you tell me while I interpret."

This is the story she told Wynema and Robin as they sat by the window of the pleasant sitting-room of the Hope Seminary.

"There was a time when my people had plenty of land, plenty of cattle and plenty of everything; but after a while the palefaces came along, and partly buying, partly seizing our lands by force, drove us very far away from our fertile country, until the Government placed us on a reservation in the Northwest, where the cold wind sweeps away our tents and almost freezes us. Then the great and powerful Government promised us to supply us with bountiful rations, in return for our lands it had taken. But one day the agent told us the Government was poor, very poor, and could not afford to feed us so bountifully as in the past. So he gave us smaller rations than before, and every day the portion of each grew smaller, until we felt we were being starved; for our crops failed and we were entirely dependent on Government rations. Then came the days when one cent's worth daily was issued to each of us. How we all sickened and grew weak with hunger! I saw my boy, my Horda, growing paler and weaker every day, and I gave him my portion, keeping him in ignorance of it, for he would not have taken it if he had known. Our chiefs and warriors gathered around the medicine men and prayed him to ask the Great Father what we should do to avert this evil. So the medicine man prayed to the Great Father all night, in his strange, murmuring way; and the next morning he told us to gather together and dance the holy dance to the Great Father and to sing while we danced, 'Great Father, help us! By thy strong arm aid us! Of thy great bounty give us that we may not die.' We were to dance thus until dawn, when the Messiah would come and deliver us. Many of our men died dancing, for they had become so weak from fasting that they could not stand the exertion. Then the great Government heard of our dances, and fearing trouble, sent out troops to stop us.[1]

"Strange the great Government did not hear of your starving too, and send troops to stop *that*," remarked Robin, per parenthesis.

"Then our great chief, Sitting Bull,[2] told us the government would starve us if we remained on the reservation; but if we would follow him, he would lead us to a country teeming with game, and where we could hunt and fish at our pleasure. We followed him to the Bad Lands, where we struck tents, as we were tired, intending to resume our march after we had rested. But one day we saw a cloud of dust, and there rode up a crowd of Indian police with Buffalo Bill at their head. They called out our chief and ordered him to surrender, then

---

1   The dance known as the Ghost Dance originated with a Northern Paiute prophet called Wovoka (c. 1856–1932). It was adapted by many Indigenous groups; the Lakota version was a response to their forced settlement and starvation after crop failures in 1890.

2   Sitting Bull (c. 1831–90) was famous as one of the leaders who defeated Custer and the US 7th Cavalry at the Battle of Little Bighorn in June 1876. The following year, Sitting Bull and his followers moved across the border to Canada; most returned with him after four years.

arrested him. Sitting Bull[1] fired several shots, instructed his men how to proceed to recapture him, but all to no avail, for the police were backed up by the pale-faced soldiers; and they killed our chief, his son, and six of the bravest warriors. Thus began the war of which your husband has already told you. It ended in Indian submission—yes, a submission extorted by blood.

"Buffalo Bill is the assumed name of the man who went about everywhere, taking a crowd of Indians with him and showing them, is he not?" asked Wynema of her husband.

"Yes, he was at the exposition at New Orleans[2] with a band of Indians who he was then 'showing,' and thus gaining subsistence for himself."

"It is strange he would lead a police force against the people who have helped him to gain a livelihood. Do you suppose the Indians who travelled with him became wealthy thereby?

"Oh yes, very," he answered in the same tone. "Some of the Indians went from near us, and when they came back their friends and neighbors had to make up a 'pony purse' to give them a start. One trip with this 'brave' man was sufficient, though I never heard one of them express a desire to go again."

"There is an old man in the Territory, now, if he has not died recently, who traveled a great deal with Buffalo Bill, and I have never heard anything of the fortune he made. He is old and poor, and goes about doing what odd jobs he can get to do, and his friends almost entirely maintain him. It seems to me that gratitude, alone, to this benighted people who have served him would

---

1 The account of Sitting Bull's death here is not accurate; he was killed on Standing Rock Reserve by Indian agency police during an attempt to arrest him for fear he would support or join the Ghost Dancers. The Lakota were starving, but a media frenzy had erupted that depicted them as malcontents bent on war. Buffalo Bill Cody (1846–1917) was brought by the army to Standing Rock to help convince Sitting Bull—who had worked in his Wild West show—to surrender, but was forced to leave without seeing him. He played no further role in the event. Although the Ghost Dancers surrendered at Wounded Knee, the attempt to disarm the men led to a scuffle and then a massacre in which 25 US soldiers and 170 Lakota, mainly women and children, were killed, many by indiscriminate fire from four rapid-fire light artillery guns mounted on hills nearby.
2 The show wintered in New Orleans in 1884–85, during the World Industrial and Cotton Exposition, which ran from December 1884 to June 1885.

have rendered him at least neutral. If I could not have been for them, I most certainly would not have taken so prominent a part against them," Wynema said indignantly.

"Robin, there was such a scathing criticism of the part the United States government has taken against the Indians of the Northwest, in the *St. Louis Republic*. I put the paper away to show you, but it has gotten misplaced. The substance of the article was this: the writer commended the Government on its slaughter of the Indians, and recommended that the dead bodies of the savages be used for fertilizers instead of the costly guano Mr. Blaine has been importing. He said that the Indians alive were troublesome and expensive, for they would persist in getting hungry and cold; but the Indians slaughtered would be useful, for besides using their carcasses for fertilizers, the land they are now occupying could then be given as homes to the 'homeless whites.' I don't believe I ever read a more sarcastic, ironical article in any newspaper. I should like to shake hands with the writer, for I see he is a just, unprejudiced, thinking man, who believes in doing justice even to an Indian 'buck.' But here are more papers with dots from the battle-field; yet you know more and better about this than the writers of these articles, for you were all around and among the Indians, as well as the soldiers."

"Yes; but I should like to read their story and know their opinions. Good!" said he, reading. "Hear this from the *Cherokee Telephone* and interpret, for Chilkena can understand."

"The papers of the states are discussing the Indian war in the Northwest, its causes, etc. Here is what the matter is in a nutshell; Congress, the Secretary of the Interior, the Army and the Indian agents, have vied with each other in shameful dealings with these poor creatures of the plains. They buy their lands—for half price—make treaties and compacts with them in regard to pay, provisions, etc., then studiously turn and commence to lay plans to evade their promise and hold back their money to squander, and withhold the provisions agreed to be furnished. It must be remembered that these Indians buy, aye more than pay for all the United States Government lets them have—they have given the Government an acre of land for every pound of beef, sugar, coffee, and flour they have ever received. The Government has neglected to comply with treaties with these people—hence the war. They would rather die by the sword and bullet than to see their wives and children perish by degrees. Remember, too, that for every acre of land the United States Government holds to-day, which it acquired from the Indians of any tribe, from the landing of Columbus, it has not paid five cents on an average. The Government owes the Indians of North America justly to-day, ten times more than it will ever pay them. Search history and you will find that these are facts and figures and not mere sentimentalism. Newspaper editors in the states, who speak so vainly of the kindness of the Government to the Indians of this country, should post themselves a little, and each and every one could write a page of history on the United States Government's treatment of the Indians, as black and damnable as hell itself."

"Phew! That's pretty strong isn't it?" said Robin, finishing and looking up.

"What does Chikena say?"

"She says it is all so. I am glad the editors of newspapers are denouncing the right parties."

7. Zitkala-Ša / Gertrude Simmons Bonnin, "Why I Am a Pagan," *Atlantic Monthly* 90 (December 1902): 801–03

[Zitkala-Ša (1876–1938), "Red Bird," also known as Gertrude Simmons Bonnin, was a Sioux (Dakota) writer and activist. Raised by her Dakota mother after her Euro-American father left the family, she was taken to boarding school at the age of eight. A gifted musician, she played violin at the New England Conservatory of Music in Boston between 1897 and 1899. She then taught music at the Carlisle Indian Industrial School and began to publish in *Harper's Monthly* and *Atlantic Monthly*. However, her dislike of the school's rigid assimilation policies and her concern about her family led her to move back to the reservation, where she met and married Raymond Bonnin. After her children grew older, she became an activist and prominent member of the Society for American Indians (1916–19). She left the organization, eventually founding her own advocacy group, the National Council of American Indians in 1926.]

When the spirit swells my breast I love to roam leisurely among the green hills; or sometimes, sitting on the brink of the mur-muring Missouri, I marvel at the great blue overhead. With half closed eyes I watch the huge cloud shadows in their noiseless play upon the high bluffs opposite me, while into my ear ripple the sweet, soft cadences of the river's song. Folded hands lie in my lap, for the time forgot. My heart and I lie small upon the earth like a grain of throbbing sand. Drifting clouds and tinkling wa-ters, together with the warmth of a genial summer day, bespeak with eloquence the loving Mystery round about us. During the idle while I sat upon the sunny river brink, I grew somewhat, though my response be not so clearly manifest as in the green grass fringing the edge of the high bluff back of me.

At length retracing the uncertain footpath scaling the precipitous embankment, I seek the level lands where grow the wild prairie flowers. And they, the lovely little folk, soothe my soul with their perfumed breath.

Their quaint round faces of varied hue convince the heart which leaps with glad surprise that they, too, are living symbols of omnipotent thought. With a child's eager eye I drink in the myriad star shapes wrought in luxuriant color upon the green. Beautiful is the spiritual essence they embody.

I leave them nodding in the breeze, but take along with me their impress upon my heart. I pause to rest me upon a rock embedded on the side of a foothill facing the low river bottom. Here the Stone-Boy, of whom the American aborigine tells, frolics about, shooting his baby arrows and shouting aloud with glee at the tiny shafts of lightning that flash from the flying arrow-beaks. What an ideal warrior he became, baffling the siege of the pests of all the land till he triumphed over their united attack. And here he lay,—Inyan our great-great-grandfather, older than the hill he rested on, older than the race of men who love to tell of his wonderful career.

Interwoven with the thread of this Indian legend of the rock, I fain would trace a subtle knowledge of the native folk which enabled them to recognize a kinship to any and all parts of this vast universe. By the leading of an ancient trail I move toward the Indian village.

With the strong, happy sense that both great and small are so surely enfolded in His magnitude that, without a miss, each has his allotted individual ground of opportunities, I am buoyant with good nature.

Yellow Breast, swaying upon the slender stem of a wild sunflower, warbles a sweet assurance of this as I pass near by. Breaking off the clear crystal song, he turns his wee head from side to side eyeing me wisely as slowly I plod with moccasined feet. Then again he yields himself to his song of joy. Flit, flit hither and yon, he fills the summer sky with his swift, sweet melody. And truly does it seem his vigorous freedom lies more in his little spirit than in his wing.

With these thoughts I reach the log cabin whither I am strongly drawn by the tie of a child to an aged mother. Out bounds my four-footed friend to meet me, frisking about my path with unmistakable delight. Chän is a black shaggy dog, "a thorough bred little mongrel" of whom I am very fond. Chän seems to understand many words in Sioux, and will go to her mat even when I whisper the word, though generally I think she is guided by the tone of the voice. Often she tries to imitate the sliding inflection and long drawn out voice to the amusement of our guests, but her articulation is quite beyond my ear. In both my hands I hold her shaggy head and gaze into her large brown eyes. At once the dilated pupils contract into tiny black dots, as if the roguish spirit within would evade my questioning.

Finally resuming the chair at my desk I feel in keen sympathy with my fellow creatures, for I seem to see clearly again that all are akin.

The racial lines, which once were bitterly real, now serve nothing more than marking out a living mosaic of human beings. And even here men of the same color are like the ivory keys of one instrument where each resembles all the rest, yet varies from them in pitch and quality of voice. And those creatures who are for a time mere echoes of another's note are not unlike the fable of the thin sick man whose distorted shadow, dressed like a real creature, came to the old master to make him follow as a shadow. Thus with a compassion for all echoes in human guise, I greet the solemn-faced "native preacher" whom I find awaiting me. I listen with respect for God's creature, though he mouth most strangely the jangling phrases of a bigoted creed.

As our tribe is one large family, where every person is related to all the others, he addressed me:—

"Cousin, I came from the morning church service to talk with you."

"Yes?" I said interrogatively, as he paused for some word from me.

Shifting uneasily about in the straight-backed chair he sat upon, he began: "Every holy day (Sunday) I look about our little God's house, and not seeing you there, I am disappointed. This is why I come to-day. Cousin, as I watch you from afar, I see no unbecoming behavior and hear only good reports of you, which all the more burns me with the wish that you were a church member. Cousin, I was taught long years ago by kind missionaries to read the holy book. These godly men taught me also the folly of our old beliefs.

"There is one God who gives reward or punishment to the race of dead men. In the upper region the Christian dead are gathered in unceasing song and prayer. In the deep pit below, the sinful ones dance in torturing flames.

"Think upon these things, my cousin, and choose now to avoid the after-doom of hell fire!" Then followed a long silence in which he clasped tighter and unclasped again his interlocked fingers.

Like instantaneous lightning flashes came pictures of my own mother's making, for she, too, is now a follower of the new superstition.

"Knocking out the chinking of our log cabin, some evil hand thrust in a burning taper of braided dry grass, but failed of his intent, for the fire died out and the half burned brand fell inward to the floor. Directly above it, on a shelf, lay the holy book. This is what we found after our return from a several days' visit. Surely some great power is hid in the sacred book!"

Brushing away from my eyes many like pictures, I offered midday meal to the converted Indian sitting wordless and with downcast face. No sooner had he risen from the table with "Cousin, I have relished it," than the church bell rang.

Thither he hurried forth with his afternoon sermon. I watched him as he hastened along, his eyes bent fast upon the dusty road till he disappeared at the end of a quarter of a mile.

The little incident recalled to mind the copy of a missionary paper brought to my notice a few days ago, in which a "Christian" pugilist commented upon a recent article of mine, grossly perverting the spirit of my pen. Still I would not forget that the pale-faced missionary and the hoodooed aborigine are both God's creatures, though small indeed their own conceptions of Infinite Love. A wee child toddling in a wonder world, I prefer to their dogma my excursions into the natural gardens where the voice of the Great Spirit is heard in the twittering of birds, the rippling of mighty waters, and the sweet breathing of flowers. If this is Paganism, then at present, at least, I am a Pagan.

8. From Zitkala-Ša / Gertrude Simmons Bonnin, "An Indian Teacher among Indians," ch. 4: "Retrospection," *Atlantic Monthly* 85 (March 1900): 385–87

[This piece explains why Zitkala-Ša resigned from her teaching position at Carlisle Indian Industrial School. Founded in 1879 by Captain Richard Henry Pratt, it became the model for 26 schools run by the Bureau of Indian Affairs, and many more schools for Indigenous students run by religious denominations. It also influenced Canadian residential school policies (see Appendix D1).]

Leaving my mother, I returned to the school in the East. As months passed over me, I slowly comprehended that the large army of white teachers in Indian schools had a larger missionary creed than I had suspected.

It was one which included self-preservation quite as much as Indian education. When I saw an opium-eater holding a position as teacher of Indians, I did not understand what good was expected, until a Christian in power replied that this pumpkin-colored creature had a feeble mother to support. An inebriate paleface sat stupid in a doctor's chair, while Indian patients carried their ailments to untimely graves, because his fair wife was dependent upon him for her daily food.

I find it hard to count that white man a teacher who tortured an ambitious Indian youth by frequently reminding the brave changeling that he was nothing but a "government pauper."

Though I burned with indignation upon discovering on every side instances no less shameful than those I have mentioned, there was no present help. Even the few rare ones who have worked nobly for my race were powerless to choose workmen like themselves. To be sure, a man was sent from the Great Father to inspect Indian schools, but what he saw was usually the students' sample work made for the exhibition. I was nettled by this sly cunning of the workmen who hoodwinked the Indian's pale Father at Washington.

My illness, which prevented the conclusion of my college course, together with my mother's stories of the encroaching frontier settlers, left me in no mood to strain my eyes in searching for latent good in my white co-workers.

At this stage of my own evolution, I was ready to curse men of small capacity for being the dwarfs their God had made them. In the process of my education I had lost all consciousness of the nature world about me. Thus, when a hidden rage took me to the small white-walled prison which I then called my room, I unknowingly turned away from my one salvation.

Alone in my room, I sat like the petrified Indian woman of whom my mother used to tell me. I wished my heart's burdens would turn me to unfeeling stone. But alive, in my tomb, I was destitute!

For the white man's papers I had given up my faith in the Great Spirit. For these same papers I had forgotten the healing in trees and brooks. On account of my mother's simple view of life, and my lack of any, I gave her up, also. I made no friends among the race of people I loathed. Like a slender tree, I had been uprooted from my mother, nature, and God. I was shorn of my branches, which had waved in sympathy and love for home and friends. The natural coat of bark which had protected my oversensitive nature was scraped off to the very quick.

Now a cold bare pole I seemed to be, planted in a strange earth. Still, I seemed to hope a day would come when my mute aching head, reared upward to the sky, would flash a zigzag lightning across the heavens. With this dream of vent for a long-pent consciousness, I walked again amid the crowds.

At last, one weary day in the school-room, a new idea presented itself to me. It was a new way of solving the problem of my inner self. I liked it. Thus I resigned my position as teacher; and now I am in an Eastern city, following the long course of study I have set for myself. Now, as I look back upon the recent past, I see it from a distance, as a whole. I remember how, from morning till evening, many specimens of civilized peoples visited the Indian school. The city folks with canes and eyeglasses, the countrymen with sunburnt cheeks and clumsy feet, forgot their relative social ranks in an ignorant curiosity. Both sorts of these Christian palefaces were alike astounded at seeing the children of savage warriors so docile and industrious.

As answers to their shallow inquiries they received the students' sample work to look upon. Examining the neatly figured pages, and gazing upon the Indian girls and boys bending over their books, the white visitors walked out of the schoolhouse well satisfied: they were educating the children of the red man! They were paying a liberal fee to the government employees in whose able hands lay the small forest of Indian timber.

In this fashion many have passed idly through the Indian schools during the last decade, afterward to boast of their charity to the North American Indian. But few there are who have paused to question whether real life or long-lasting death lies beneath this semblance of civilization.

Appendix C: On the Six Nations

[The Six Nations are known for their system of governance, the Great Law of Peace. It was said to have influenced the Constitution of the United States, despite major differences between the two systems, for example in the role of women. The Law was composed and promulgated orally by Deganawidah and Hiawatha, his spokesman, before the arrival of Europeans on the continent. *The Iroquois Book of Rites*, transcribed from the memory of E. Pauline Johnson's grandfather by Horatio Hale with help from her father and published in 1883, provides information on how these traditions of governance were maintained. However, Henry Wadsworth Longfellow's *The Song of Hiawatha* (1855), which sold 50,000 copies in two years and inspired an array of art, music, and parodies, was much more influential: Johnson could recite most of it from memory by the time she was fourteen. Far from factual, as claimed, *Hiawatha* presents a noble savage whose world was safely in the past. It was written in the same tradition as many other Romantic synthetic epics based on fragments of early folklore in Europe, such as the *Poems of Ossian* (1760) and the Finnish *Kalevala* (1835; 1849).]

1. Duncan Campbell Scott, "The Onondaga Madonna," *Labour and the Angel* (Boston: Copeland and Day, 1898), 15

[Scott (1862–1947) was well known not only as a "Confederation Poet" and short-story writer, but also as the literary executor for his friend and fellow Confederation poet Archibald Lampman (1861–99). Scott joined the Department of Indian Affairs in 1879 as a clerk, rising to the highest position of deputy superintendent in 1913, which he held until his retirement in 1932. He firmly believed in assimilation enforced by education, a policy that led to a strict regime of residential schooling and cultural repression. First published in 1894 as "The Onondaga Woman and Her Child," and reprinted with this title in 1898, this poem was widely anthologized after World War II; see Fee.]

She stands full-throated and with careless pose,
This woman of a weird and waning race,
The tragic savage lurking in her face,
Where all her pagan passion burns and glows;
Her blood is mingled with her ancient foes,
And thrills with war and wildness in her veins;
Her rebel lips are dabbled with the stains
Of feuds and forays and her father's woes.

And closer in the shawl about her breast,
The latest promise of her nation's doom,
Paler than she her baby clings and lies,
The primal warrior gleaming from his eyes;
He sulks, and burdened with his infant gloom,
He draws his heavy brows and will not rest.

2. W.D. Lighthall, "The Caughnawaga Beadwork Seller," *Songs of the Great Dominion: Voices from the Forests and Waters, the Settlements and Cities of Canada*, ed. W.D. Lighthall (London: Walter Scott, 1889)

[The anthology compiled by W.D. Lighthall (1857–1954), which includes two poems by Johnson, was influential in establishing a national canon for Canadian poetry.]

KANAWÂKI,—"By the Rapid,"—[1]
 Low the sunset 'midst thee lies
And from the wild Reservation
 Evening's breeze begins to rise.
Faint the Kònoronkwa chorus
 Drifts across the currents strong;
Spirit-like the parish steeple
 Stands thine ancient walls among.

Kanawâki,—"By the Rapid,"—
 How the sun amidst thee burns!
Village of the Praying Nation,
 Thy dark child to thee returns.
All day through the palefaced city,
 Silent, selling beaded wares,

---

1 Caughnawaga, now Kahnawake, is a Mohawk village south of Montreal founded in 1718.

I have wandered with my basket,
Lone, excepting for their stares.

They are white men; we are Indians:
What a gulf their stares proclaim!
They are mounting; we are dying:
All our heritage they claim.
We are dying, dwindling, dying!
Strait and smaller grows our bound:
They are mounting up to heaven,
And are pressing all around.

Thou art ours,—little remnant,
Ours from countless thousand years,—
Part of the old Indian world:
Thy breath from far the Indian cheers.
Back to thee, O Kanawâki!
Let the rapids dash between
Indian homes and white man's manners,—
Kanawâki and Lachine!

O, my dear! O Knife-and-Arrows!
Thou art bronzed, thy limbs are lithe;
How I laugh when through the crosse-game[1]
Slipst thou like red elder-withe!
Thou art none of these pale-faces!
When with thee I'll happy feel;
For thou art the Indian warrior
From thy head unto thy heel!

Sweet the Kònoronkwa chorus
Floats across the currents strong;
Clear behold the parish steeple
Rise the ancient walls among!
Skim us deftly, noiseless paddle:
In my shawl my bosom burns!
Kanawâki,—"By the Rapids,"—
Thy own child to thee returns.

---

1 Lacrosse, an ancient Indigenous ceremonial game now played
   across North America and in Australia as a competitive sport.

3. Walt Whitman, "Red Jacket (From Aloft)," *Transactions of the Buffalo Historical Society. Red Jacket*, vol. 3 (Buffalo: The Society, 1885), 105

[Whitman (1819–92) subtitled this poem "Impromptu on Buffalo City's commemoration of and monument to the old Iroquois orator, October 9, 1884." He likely read about this ceremony, attended by Johnson and her sister Evelyn, in an article, "Honouring a Dead Indian," in *The Critic* (27 September 1884). He published the poem in *The Philadelphia Press* (10 October 1884) and it was reprinted in the "Sands at Seventy" annex to *Leaves of Grass* (1888). Johnson's "The Re-interment of Red Jacket" (see above, pp. 38–40) first appeared in the *Transactions*, just before Whitman's poem.]

Upon this scene, this show,
Yielded to-day by fashion, learning, wealth,
(Nor in caprice alone—some grains of deepest meaning,)
Haply, aloft, (who knows?) from distant sky-clouds' blended shapes,
As some old tree, or rock or cliff, thrill'd with its soul,
Product of Nature's sun, stars, earth direct—a towering human form,
In hunting-shirt of film, arm'd with the rifle, a half-ironical smile curving its phantom lips,
    Like one of Ossian's ghosts[1] looks down.

4. Ely S. Parker / Donehogawa, Speech at the Ceremony to Re-inter Red Jacket, *The Transactions of the Buffalo Historical Society. Red Jacket*, vol. 3 (Buffalo: The Society, 1885), 41–44

[Ely S. Parker / Donehogawa (1828–95), a Seneca descendent of Red Jacket, served as adjutant to General Ulysses S. Grant during the American Civil War, later rising to the rank of general. Grant later appointed him as Commissioner of Indian Affairs in

---

1 Ossian was an epic bard invented by Scottish poet James Macpherson (1736–96) in 1760. Widely believed to be ancient Gaelic tales, Macpherson's collections were translated into many languages and inspired writers such as Johann Wolfgang von Goethe (1749–1832) and Walter Scott (1771–1832), as well as many Romantic painters and composers. Disputes about authenticity erupted early, with Samuel Johnson (1709–84) denouncing the works as not only forgeries, but also bad poetry. The consensus now is that Macpherson interwove real ancient texts with his own poetry.

1869. E. Pauline Johnson was present at the re-interment of Red Jacket with her sister Evelyn and would have heard this speech.]

Mr. President, Officers and Members of the Buffalo Historical Society, and Ladies and Gentlemen of the City of Buffalo:

I regret the lateness of the hour at which I am called to speak to you, as the Indian question is an almost inexhaustible one, and I hardly know where to begin or where to end. It is a broad and complicated subject, and I can add but little to the very able, interesting and eloquent address delivered this evening on the Iroquois Indians and Red Jacket, the chief and orator. I also realize that you are exhausted from your long sitting, hence I promise you to be as brief as possible in what I say, a task, however, that I may find difficult to accomplish.

Much has been said and written of the Iroquois people. All agree that they once owned and occupied the whole country now constituting the State of New York. They reached from the Hudson on the east to the lakes on the west, and claimed much conquered territory.

I desire only to direct attention to one phase of their character, which, in my judgment, has never been brought out with sufficient forces and clearness, and that is, their fidelity to their obligations and the tenacity with which they held to their allegiance once it was placed. More that two hundred and fifty years ago, when the Iroquois were in the zenith of their power and glory, the French made the mistake of assisting the northern Indians with whom the Iroquois were at war. They never forgot or forgave the French for the aid they gave their Indian enemies, and the French were never afterward able to gain their friendship. About the same time the Holland Dutch came up the Hudson, and though perhaps they were no wiser than their French neighbors they certainly pursued a wiser policy by securing the friendship of the Iroquois. The Indians remained true to their allegiance until the Dutch were superseded by the English, when they also transferred their allegiance to the new comers. They remained steadfast to the faith they had given, and assisted the English people to put down the rebellion of the American colonies against the mother government. The colonies succeeded in gaining their independence and establishing a government to their liking, but in the treaty of peace which followed, the English entirely ignored and forgot their Indian allies, leaving them to shift for themselves. A portion of the Iroquois, under Captain

Brant, followed the fortunes of the English into Canada, where they have since been well cared for by the provincial and home governments. Those who remained in the United States continued to struggle for their homes and the integrity of what they considered their ancient and just rights. The aid, however, which they had given against the cause of the American Revolution had been so strong as to leave an intense burning hostility to them in the minds of the American people, and to allay this feeling and to settle for all time the question of rights as between the Indians and the whites, General Washington was compelled to order an expedition into the Indian country of New York to break the Indian power. The Indians left to themselves and bereft of British aid made Sullivan's success an easy one. He drove them from their villages, cut down their corn-fields and orchards, leaving the poor Indians homeless, houseless and destitute.[1] We have been told this evening that the "Long House" of the Iroquois had been broken. It was indeed broken by Sullivan's invasion. It was so completely broken that never again will the "Long House" be reconstructed.

The Indians sued for peace. They were now at the mercy of General Washington and the American people. A peace was granted them, and small homes allowed in the vast domain they once claimed as absolutely and wholly theirs by the highest title known among men, viz., by the gift of God. The mercy of the American people granted them the right to occupy and cultivate certain lands until someone stronger wanted them. They hold their homes to-day by no other title than that of occupancy, although some Indian bands have bought and paid for the lands they reside upon the same as you, my friends, have bought and paid for the farms you live upon. The Indian mind has never to this day been able to comprehend how it is that he has been compelled to buy and pay for that which has descended to him from time immemorial, and which his ancestors had taught him was the gift of the Great Spirit to him and his posterity forever. It was an anomaly in civilized law far beyond his reasoning powers.

---

1   In 1779, General John Sullivan (1740–95) was instructed by George Washington to destroy Iroquois villages and crops and to take as many prisoners as possible, in order to break the Confederacy's ability to support the British. His expedition destroyed more than 40 villages and killed some 1,000 Loyalist and Iroquois soldiers; many more non-combatants died of starvation in the hard winter that followed.

In the treaty of peace concluded after Sullivan's campaign the remnants of the Iroquois transferred their allegiance to the United States, and to that allegiance they have remained firm and true to this day. They stood side by side with you in the last war with Great Britain, in defence of this frontier, and fought battles under the leadership of the able and gallant General Scott. Again, the sons of Iroquois marched shoulder to shoulder with you, your fathers, your husbands and your sons in the last great Rebellion of the South, and used, with you, their best endeavors to maintain the inviolability and integrity of the American constitution, to preserve unsullied the purity of the American flag, and to wipe out forever from every foot of American soil the curse of human slavery. Such, in brief, has been their fidelity to their allegiance.

It was during the troublous times of the American Revolution that Red Jacket's name first appears. He is mentioned as a messenger, or bearer of dispatches, or runner, for the British. He subsequently appears at the treaty of peace, and at all treaties and councils of importance his name is always prominent. He was a devoted lover of his people, and he labored hard for the recognition and restoration to his people of their ancient rights, but in which he was unsuccessful. His political creed did not embrace that peculiar doctrine now so strongly believed in, that "to the victors belong the spoils." He did not know that the Sullivan campaign had taken from his people all the vested rights which God have given them, and when, subsequently, he was made to understand that a pre-emptive title hung over the homes of his people he was amazed at the audacity of the white man's law which permitted and sanctioned the sale and transfer by one person to another of rights never owned and of properties never seen. From the bottom of my heart I believe that Red Jacket was a true Indian and a most thorough pagan. He used all the powers of his eloquence in opposition to the introduction of civilization and Christianity among his people. In this, as in many other things, he signally failed. So persistent and tenacious was he in his hostility to the white man and his ways and methods that one of his last requests is said to have been that white men should not dig his grave and that white men should not bury him. But how forcibly now comes to us the verity and strength of the saying that "man proposes, but God disposes." Red Jacket had proposed that his remains should lie buried and undisturbed in the burial-place of his fathers. Very soon after his death his people removed from their old lands to other homes. Then God put it into the hearts of these good men of the Buffalo Historical Society to take charge of his remains, give him a decent burial in a white man's graveyard, and over his grave to erect a monument which should tell his story to all future generations. We have this day witnessed and participated in the culmination of their labors. Red Jacket has been honorably reburied with solemn and ancient rites, and may his remains rest there in peace until time shall be no more. While a silent spectator of the ceremonies to-day, the words of the blessed Saviour forcibly presented themselves to my mind, "the foxes have holes and the birds of the air have nests, but the Son of Man hath not where to lay his head." [Luke 9:58]. I applied this saying to the Indian race. They have been buffeted from pillar to post. They once owned much, but now have hardly anything they can call their own. While living they are not let alone—when dead they are not left unmolested.

I thank you for your kind attention, and I now bid you all, and each of you, a fair good-night; may you retire to sweet slumbers and pleasant dreams.

5. From Arthur C. Parker, "Certain Important Elements of the Indian Problem," *American Indian Magazine: The Quarterly Journal of the Society of American Indians* 3.1 (1915): 24–38

[Arthur C. Parker (1881–1955), of Scots-English and Seneca descent, became a well-known archaeologist. With other prominent Native Americans, he co-founded the Society of American Indians in 1911; he edited the society's *American Indian Magazine* from 1915 to 1920. In the article, he argues that the people of the United States, through the church and their government agencies, have taken basic rights from American Indians. In the excerpt below, Parker explains how the United States can return to American Indians the right of their native freedom. In his call for the recognition of the great American Indian leaders of the past, he uses the work of E. Pauline Johnson to exemplify their spirit, quoting from her "A Cry from an Indian Wife" (see above, pp. 131–33), which appeared in the best-selling anthology of her poetry, *Flint and Feather* (1912).]

[...]

The people of the United States through thir governmental agencies, and through the aggression of their citizens have ... [r]obbed the American Indian of his native freedom.... The Indian must be given back the things of which he has been robbed with the natural accumulation of interest, that the world's progress has earned. American civilization and Christianity must return the seven stolen rights without which no race or community of men can live.

[...]

4. *The Right of Freedom.* The first and greatest love of the American Indian was his freedom. Freedom had been his heritage from time immemorial. The red man by nature cannot endure enforced servitude or imprisonment. By nature he is independent, proud and sensitive. Freedom to the red man is no less sweet, no less the condition of life itself than to other men. With Dryden the red man may exclaim:

> "The love of liberty with life is given
> And life itself the inferior gift of heaven!"[1]

The fathers of the American Republic had suffered the hand of oppression. They could not endure the torment of being governed by a hand that wrote its laws across the sea. The will of the mother country was not the will of her children and there was a revolt. Patrick Henry arose and sounded the hearts of his compatriots when he shouted "Give me liberty or give me death."[2] Benjamin Franklin wrote, "Where liberty dwells, there is my country,"[3] and Thomas Jefferson in his Summary View of the Rights of British Americans laid down the principle, "The God who gave us life, gave us liberty at the same time."[4] In how many instances do all these thoughts paraphrase the expression and

---

1 John Dryden (1631–1700) was an English Restoration dramatist, poet, and literary critic who was made Poet Laureate in 1668. This line is from his poem "Palamon and Arcite," part of his *Fables, Ancient and Modern* (1700).

2 Patrick Henry (1736–99) was a founding father of America. "Give me liberty, or give me death!" is from a speech he gave for the Virginia Convention in 1775 in opposition to the Stamp Act.

3 These words are often attributed to Benjamin Franklin (1706–90), a founding father of the United States.

4 Thomas Jefferson (1743–1826) was a founding father of the United States, the main author of the Declaration of Independence (1776), and President of the United States (1801–09). *A Summary View of the Rights of British America* (Williamsburg: Clementina Rind, 1774).

the actions of the freedom-loving red men, who are governed not by their own kindred, or by their own volition, but by a hand that reaches out afar across the country.

The voice of great men rang out many times in the council halls of the nations of red men. The words of King Philip, Garangula, DeKanissora, Red Jacket, Tecumseh, Pontiac, Black Hawk, Osceola, Red Cloud and others, sound even yet, in eulogy of native freedom.[1] The time was when red men were not afraid to speak for back of them was power. How masterful was the speech of Garangula in reply to the Governor of Canada, who came to intimate the Five Nations and force them to trade with France alone, when he answered: "Hear, Yonondio, I do not sleep. I have my eyes open and the sun enlightens me. We are born free, we neither depend on Yonondio nor Corlear; we

---

1 Wampanoag chief King Philip (c. 1639–76) was an important leader in King Philip's War (1657–78). Garangula was the name given to the Iroquois Chief Otreouti (1659–88) by the French; he called the French Governor of New France, Joseph-Antoine de la Barre (1622–88), Yonondio. Corlear is the Iroquois name for Thomas Dongan, the British governor. In a speech entitled "Do Not Choke the Tree of Peace" (1684), he made it clear that the Iroquois viewed themselves as equal to the French. Dekanissora was a leader of the Five Nations who mediated between the British and the French during King William's War (1688–97). Red Jacket (1750–1830) was a Seneca orator perhaps best known for his 1805 address "Religion for the White Man and the Red," where he argues that Christianity is best suited to white men. Tecumseh (1768–1813), a Shawnee chief, led the Indigenous allies of the British in the War of 1812, including John "Smoke" Johnson, E. Pauline Johnson's grandfather. Pontiac (c. 1720–69), an Ottawa war chief, was prominent in Pontiac's War (1763–66). Black Hawk (1767–1838) was a war leader of the Sauk. He dictated his autobiography, entitled *Autobiography of Ma-ka-tai-me-she-kia-kiak, or Black Hawk*, in 1833. Osceola (1804–38), born Billy Powell, was a Seminole leader during the Second Seminole War (1835–42). He was captured in September 1837; tourists and portrait painters, notably George Catlin (1796–1872), visited him in jail. Red Cloud (1822–1909), or Makhpiya-Luta, was a Lakota chief best known for his military successes against the United States. In 1866 the United States signed the Fort Laramie Treaty with him, guaranteeing the Lakota possession of much of what is now South Dakota and Wyoming. Later US incursions on these lands led to the massacre at Wounded Knee in 1890, and the lands are the subjects of ongoing legal disputes in the US courts.

may go when we please and carry with us whom we please, buy and sell what we please. If your allies be your slaves, use them as such......"

Imagine a reservation chief talking that way today to so small an official as a politically appointed agent sent over his tribe! The chief would be sent to the lock up and the charge be labeled "insubordination."

How different the spirit of the Indian woman of the old day who saw her country wrested from her nation and bravely bade her sons go forth to war. She recited to them the woes of her people and urged them to be men. Pauline Johnson, (Tekaheonwake) of the Canadian Mohawks, speaks of the charge of the Indian wife to her warrior husband:

> "Then go and strike for liberty and life and bring back
>   honor to your Indian wife.
> Your wife? Ah what of that,—who cares for me,
> Who pities my poor love and agony?
> What white robed priest prays for your safety here
> As prayer is said for every volunteer
> That swells the ranks that Canada sends out?
> Who prays for victory for the Indian scout?
> Who prays for our poor nation lying low?
> None—therefore take your tomahawk and go!
> Go forth nor bend to greed of white man's hands,
> By right, by birth we Indians own these lands,
> Though starved, crushed and plundered lies our nation
>   low—
> Perhaps the white man's God has willed it so!"

A race of men and women to whom liberty was the condition of life itself must again have liberty restored, if it is again to live.

[...]

Appendix D: Canadian Residential Schools

[As the report by Nicholas Flood Davin produced in 1879 (Appendix D1) makes clear, industrial and residential schools for Indigenous children in Canada were modelled on those of the United States. A few such schools, including the Anglican-run Mohawk Institute in Brantford, antedated Confederation. By 1931, there were 80 residential schools across Canada; the last one closed in 1996. Only about a third of eligible children attended these schools; the rest attended day schools or avoided school altogether. As the pamphlet by P.H. Bryce (Appendix D2) makes clear, the health of the children in the schools was neglected; worse, they were often subjected to physical and sexual abuse and punished for using their native languages. The prime minister of Canada, Stephen Harper, apologized for the abuses of the residential schools in 2008; that year, the Indian Residential Schools Truth and Reconciliation Commission was founded to allow those who survived to testify to and educate the public about the schools' destructive effects on them, their languages, cultures, and communities; see *They Came for the Children*.]

1. From Nicholas Flood Davin, *Report on Industrial Schools for Indians and Half-Breeds* (Ottawa, 14 March 1879; CIHM microfilm, Early Canadiana Online)

[Nicholas Flood Davin (1840–1901), an Irishman, came to Canada in 1872 to report on the potential for the annexation of Canada by the United States. Once in Canada, he began a career as a journalist, speaker, author, poet, and playwright. He ran for the Conservative Party in 1878, losing by a narrow margin. He was then appointed by prime minister Sir John A. Macdonald to investigate American industrial schools for Native children; excerpts from his report, often called "The Davin Report," follow. In 1883, he founded a newspaper, the Regina *Leader*, with help from the Macdonald government; the paper subsequently supported both the CPR and the Conservative Party. He won Assiniboine West for the Conservatives in 1887.

Davin's assumption that even those Indigenous peoples regarded as "civilized" would require a great deal of effort to overcome what were viewed as hereditary and biological differences was a commonplace racist attitude of the time. Note that this report was written after the first Riel Resistance of 1869–70 and before the second Resistance of 1885.]

To the Right Honourable
The Minister of the Interior.[1]

Sir,—I have the honour to submit the following report on the working of Industrial Schools for the education of Indians and mixed-bloods in the United States, and the advisability of establishing similar institutions in the North-West Territories of the Dominion.

In accordance with your directions of the twenty-eighth of January, I went to Washington [and was given] every facility for becoming acquainted with the establishment, cost, and practical values of industrial schools among the Indian population of the United States.

The industrial school is the principal feature of the policy known as that of "aggressive civilization." This policy was inaugurated by President Grant in 1869. But, as will be seen the utility of industrial schools had long ere that time been amply tested. Acting on the suggestion of the President, Congress passed a law early in 1869, providing for the appointment of the Peace Commission. This Commission recommended that the Indians should, as far as practicable, be consolidated on few reservations, and provided with "permanent individual homes"; that the tribal relation should be abolished; that lands should be allotted in severalty and not in common; that the Indian should speedily become a citizen of the United States, enjoy the protection of the law, and be made amenable thereto; that, finally, it was the duty of the Government to afford the Indians all reasonable aid in their preparation for citizenship by educating them in industry and in the arts of civilization. After eight years' experience of the partial carrying out of these recommendations, the Board pressed for a still more thorough policy; they urged, among other things, that titles to land should be inalienable from the family of the holder for at least three generations. From 1869 vigorous efforts

---

1 John A. Macdonald (1815–91) retained this role from 1878 to 1887 during his second term as prime minister.

in an educational direction were put forward. But it was found that the day-school did not work, because the influence of the wigwam was stronger than the influence of the school. Industrial Boarding Schools were therefore established, and these are now numerous and soon will be universal. The cry from the Agencies where no boarding industrial schools have been established is persistent and earnest to have the want supplied.

The experience of the United States is the same as our own as far as the adult Indian is concerned. Little can be done with him. He can be taught to do a little at farming, and at stock-raising, and to dress in a more civilized manner, but that is all. The child, again, who goes to a day school learns little, and what little he learns is soon forgotten, while his tastes are fashioned at home, and his inherited aversion to toil is in no way combated.

[...]

The happy results of Industrial Schools are strikingly shown in the case of the five "civilized" nations,[1] the Cherokees, the Chickasaws, the Chocktaws, the Creeks [Muscogee] and Seminoles, who are all making undoubted progress in agriculture and in education. They number in all about sixty thousand, and occupy reservations on what it known as the "Indian Territory," where it is the policy of the United States to settle as many Indian tribes as possible. This territory lies, roughly speaking, between 34 and 37 latitude and 96 and 100 longitude. A large proportion of the income of these nations is devoted to educational purposes. They have their own schools; a code of their own; a judiciary; a national council which enacts laws; newspapers in the native dialect and in English; and they are, in effect, five little republics within the Republic, but of course without the high functions of Empire. The Honourable the Commissioner arranged that I should meet some of the principal men of these nations.

[...]

---

1   The application of the term "civilized" to those Indigenous groups seen as most assimilated is, of course, based on a European definition of what constitutes civilization and places those groups who continued traditional ways of life in an inferior position. These five tribes all farmed, which was seen as a step in the right direction as compared to those tribes who continued to hunt, fish, and gather their food.

Colonel Wm. P. Ross, (Cherokee), spoke as follows: "I was President of the Board of Education last year. We had in operation about seventy-eight primary schools (that is, neighbourhood or day schools) where the children are taught the ordinary elements of an English education. We have two high schools taught by white teachers—one male, the other female; in each there are two departments, one primary, the other academic. Last year we had an aggregate attendance at all our schools of 2,800 children, and an average of something less than 2,000. We have a Board of Education, consisting of three members, who have charge of all the schools in the county; they examine teachers and pay them, or rather they give certificates upon which they draw their pay from the treasury through the Chief. We support our schools out and out and the majority of our teachers are Indian teachers. About $75 000 a year is expended for educational purposes. The first public schools the Cherokees had, west of the Mississippi, were established in 1842. There were schools amongst them previously to that time, but they were partially or entirely supported by missionary institutions. But since 1842 we have had our own system of public schools, under the control and management of the Cherokee nation.

All the representatives of the five civilized tribes declared their belief that the chief thing to attend to in dealing with the less civilized or wholly barbarous tribes, was to separate the children from the parents. As I have said, the Indian Department, at Washington, have not much hope in regard to the adult Indian, but sanguine anticipations are cherished respecting the children. The five nations are themselves a proof that a certain degree of civilization is within reach of the red man while illustrating his deficiencies.

[...]

At Winnipeg, I met most of the leading men, clerical and lay, who could speak with authority on the subject of the inquiry, and to the experience, knowledge and courtesy of Mgr. Taché,[1]

---

1 Alexandre-Antonin Taché (1823–1894) was Oblate missionary to the Plains Indians and the first bishop (1851) and then archbishop (1871) of St. Boniface, Manitoba. The Canadian government asked him to help prevent the two Riel Resistances, as the Métis were mostly Roman Catholic, but his influence did not prevail.

Père Lacombe,[1] Hon. Jas. McKay and many others, this report is much indebted.

Among the Indians there is some discontent, but as a rule it amounts to no more than the chronic querulousness of the Indian character, and his uneasiness about food at this time of year will unfortunately leave no trace in his improvident mind when spring opens and fish are plentiful. The exceptions are furnished by one or two chiefs whose bands are starving, that is in the Indian sense of that word, without a certain prospect of food in the future. Distress will always exist among improvident people, and undoubtedly distress and misery exist in many Bands. The attitude of the chiefs referred to, and the language held by the chief on the occasion of a visit to St. Peter's Reservation—language which showed that he was in communication with the unsettled Bands open up, in the event of the disappearance of the buffalo (a disappearance no protective legislation can long retard), a prospect which demands the serious consideration of the Department. No race of men can be suddenly turned from one set of pursuits to another set of a wholly different nature without great attendant distress. But, suddenly, to make men long accustomed to a wild unsettled life, with its freedom from restraint, its excitement and charm, take to the colourless monotony of daily toil,[2] the reward of which is prospective, is impossible.

The half-breeds or mixed-bloods are thoughtful, if not anxious, regarding the Government's intentions respecting them. But the problem before the department cannot be settled by the issue of scrip.[3] The problem can be solved only by gradually educating Indians and mixed-bloods in self-reliance and industry.

Colonel Porter's testimony given above, that of Mr. Ross, the position of these gentlemen and the position of the five "civi-

---

1 Albert Lacombe (1827–1916) became an Oblate missionary, working with the Plains Cree.

2 Compare this passage to Johnson's "The Indian Corn Planter" above (p. 139).

3 A certificate redeemable for land or money, scrip was first issued to Metis applicants after the first Riel Resistance. The Canadian government's goal was to regularize land holding in what had been Hudson's Bay Company territory until its transfer to Canada in 1870 so that settlers could move in. Because of the new Manitoba government's inability or unwillingness to protect the Metis, many sold their scrip and left for what is now northern Saskatchewan, where further inroads on their settlements led to the second Riel Resistance in 1885.

lized" nations are instructive. Not merely is the only effective means of educating the Indians in self-reliance and self-support pointed out; the inference is not far-fetched that the mixed blood is the natural mediator between the Government and the red man, and also his natural instructor.

[...]

There is now barely time to inaugurate a system of education by means of which the native populations of the North-West shall be gradually prepared to meet the necessities of the not distant future; to welcome and facilitate, it may be hoped, the development of the country; and to render its government easy and not expensive.

[...]

The Indian character, about which some persons fling such a mystery, is not difficult to understand. The Indian is sometimes spoken of as a child, but he is very far from being a child. The race is in its childhood. As far as the childhood analogy is applicable, what it suggests is a policy that shall look patiently for fruit, not after five or ten years, but after a generation or two. The analogy is misleading when we come to deal with the adult, and is of course a mere truism and not a figure of speech when we take charge of the Indian in the period of infancy. There is, it is true, in the adult, the helplessness of the mind of the child, as well as the practical helplessness; there is, too, the child's want of perspective; but there is little of the child's receptivity; nor is the child's tractableness always found. One of the prime conditions of childhood is absent—the abeyance of the passions. Anybody who has tried to educate grown-up civilized men, with untrained minds, as are the minds of most civilized men, will understand the disturbing and dwarfing influence of the complex interests which crowd in on the adult. The Indian is a man with traditions of his own, which make civilization a puzzle of despair. He has the suspicion, distrust, fault-finding tendency, the insincerity and flattery, produced in all subject races. He is crafty, but conscious how weak his craft is when opposed to the superior cunning of the white man. Not to speak of him—even some of the half-breeds of high intelligence are incapable of embracing the idea of a nation—of a national type of man—in which it should be their ambition to be merged and lost. Yet he realises that he must disappear, and realizing this, and unable to associate himself with the larger and nobler idea, the motive power which inspired a Pontiac and a Tecumseh, is absent. The Indian's stolidity is in part assumed, in part the stupor produced by external novel and distasteful conditions, and in both respects has been manifested in white races at periods of helplessness and ignorance, of subjection to, and daily contact with, the power and superior skill and refinement of more advanced races, or even more advanced branches of the same race. We need not, therefore, recall the names of Indian heroes to make us respect the latent capacities of the red man. We have only to look to the rock whence we were hewn. The Indian, I repeat, is not a child, and he is the last person that should be dealt with in a childish way. He requires firm, bold, kindly handling and boundless patience. He exacts, and surely not unreasonably, scrupulous honesty. There ought to be a special exemplary punishment provided for those persons who, when employed by the government to supply the Indian with stores, cheat him.

It would be travelling beyond the record to comment on our Indian policy and our treaties with the Indians, though I have formed very decided opinions respecting both. But this remark is pertinent. Guaranteeing schools as one of the considerations for surrendering the title to land was, in my opinion, trifling with a great duty and placing the Government in no dignified attitude. It should have been assumed that the Government would attend to its proper and pressing business in this particular. Such a guarantee, moreover, betrays a want of knowledge of the Indian character. It might easily have been realized, (it is at least thinkable), that one of the results would be to make the Chiefs believe they had some right to a voice regarding the character and management of the schools, as well as regarding the initiatory step of their establishment.... The establishment and conduct of schools are matters which should have been left in a position to be considered apart from the disturbing and sometimes designing predilections of a Chief; the needs and aptitudes of the settlement are alone worthy of being weighed. The moment there exists a settlement which has any permanent character, then education in some form or other should be brought within reach of the children. This is not merely a matter of policy. It is that, of course, in the highest degree. It is a sacred duty.

[...]

The first and greatest stone in the foundation of the qua-si-civilization of the Indians, wherever seen, was laid by the missionaries, men who had a supreme object and who did not count their lives dear unto them. Schools are scattered over the whole continent, wherever Indians exist, monuments of religious zeal and heroic self-sacrifice. These schools should be utilized as much as possible, both on grounds of efficiency and economy. The missionaries' experience is only surpassed by their patient heroism, and their testimony, like that of the school teachers, like that of the authorities at Washington is, that if anything is to be done with the Indian, we must catch him very young. The children must be kept consistently within the circle of civilized conditions. Mgr. Taché in his work, "Sketch of the North-West of America"[1]—points out that the influence of civilized women has issued in superior characteristics in one portion of the native population. This influence in and out of the school must be con-stantly present in the early years. "Hitherto," says Mr. Meeker,[2] a man who could speak with authority of a large portion of the Indians of the United States, "young men have been boarded and clothed and instructed, but in time they were off to the hunting ground. The plan now is to take young children, give them the care of a mother, and have them constantly in hand." Such care must go *pari passu*[3] with religious training.

There are, as we have seen, some twelve hundred families of half-breeds—or mixed-bloods—in the North-West. Some of these are men of education and settled pursuits. But the great majority of them live under conditions which turn on the vanish-ing axle-tree of the buffalo's existence. It is no reproach to these men and their children to say that they will require training, whether supplied from within or without, before they can hap-pily and effectively settle down as farmers. Archbishop Taché's sketch of the virtues and views of the mixed bloods (*Sketch of the North-West of America*, pp. 98-110), a sketch drawn at once by a masterly and loving hand, can leave no doubt on the mind that training will be needed. Nor, as I have said, is this a reproach. The same thing had been true of men belonging to the best white

---

1 Alexandre-A. Taché, *Sketch of the North-West of America*, trans. D.R. Cameron (Montreal: John Lovell, 1870).

2 Davin quotes N.C. Meeker, Indian Agent, White River, Colorado, from the *Annual Report of the Commissioner of Indian Affairs to the Secretary of the Interior* (January 1878), p. 19.

3 "At one and the same time" (Latin).

races, and in modern times. The mixed-blood had already in high development many of those virtues which would make him a useful official where activity, intelligence, horsemanship and fidelity were required. But if the mixed-blood is to hold his own in the race for existence, which will soon be exigent, in lands where, even yet, for the greater part of the year, primeval silence reigns, it is not enough that he should know all the arts of the voyageur and trader; not enough even that he should be able to do a little farming; he must be educated and become susceptible to the bracing influence of complex wants and varied ambitions.

I should recommend at once, an extensive application of the principle of industrial boarding schools in the West, were it not that the population, both Indian and half-breed, is so largely migratory that any great outlay at present would be money thrown away.

[Davin makes detailed suggestions for the location of possible schools, based on nearby resources, such as timber and lakes for fishing, and suggests which religious denomination should run them.]

The importance of denominational schools at the outset for the Indians must be obvious. One of the earliest things an attempt to civilize them does, is to take away their simple Indian mythology, the central idea of which, to wit, a perfect spirit, can hardly be improved on. The Indians have their own ideas of right and wrong, of "good" Indians and "bad" Indians, and to disturb this faith, without supplying a better, would be a curious process to enlist the sanction of civilized races whose whole civilization, like all the civilizations with which we are acquainted, is based on religion. A civilized sceptic, breathing, though he does, an atmosphere charged with Christian ideas, and getting strength unconsciously therefrom, is nevertheless, unless in instances of rare intellectual vigour, apt to be a man without ethical backbone. But a savage sceptic would be open to civilized influences and moral control only through desires, which, in the midst of enlightenment, constantly break out into the worst features of barbarism. Where, however, the poor Indian has been brought face to face with polemics and settlements are divided, or think they are divided, on metaphysical niceties, the school should be, as at the White Earth Agency, Minnesota, nondenominational.

[Here Davin suggests how to reward parents whose children do attend school, as well as the children themselves. He suggests that education should be made compulsory in the future and makes recommendations about the qualities of the teacher, that he be paid well, and that he be supported by the religious denomination in charge of the school. He also recommends "competent inspection," and that boys or girls who show special aptitudes be trained to work for the Department as teachers or clerks, and be "fitted to launch out on commercial and professional careers." Apart from making residential school compulsory in 1920 and turning over the schools to religious denominations, the rest of these recommendations were ignored.]

2. From Peter Henderson Bryce, *The Story of a National Crime: Being an Appeal for Justice to the Indians of Canada; the Wards of the Nation, Our Allies in the Revolutionary War, Our Brothers-in-arms in the Great War* (Ottawa: James Hope, 1922)

[Peter Henderson Bryce (1853–1932) was Chief Medical Officer of the Department of the Interior between 1904 and 1921. This department included the Department of Immigration and the Department of Indian Affairs. In 1907 and 1909 he wrote reports condemning health conditions in the residential schools he visited, but those reports were buried and his career stalled. Retired in 1921 and released from his oath of confidentiality, he published a pamphlet, from which these extracts are taken, which was, unfortunately, also discounted because his conclusion (not included here) revealed that he was motivated not only by the desire to help Indigenous people, but also to get the retirement benefits he felt he deserved. However, his important role as an early and persistent public-health advocate for immigrants and Indigenous people has subsequently been widely recognized.]

[...]

I. For the first months after the writer's appointment he was much engaged in organizing the medical inspection of immigrants at the sea ports; but he early began the systematic collection of health statistics of the several hundred Indian Bands scattered over Canada. For each year up to 1914 he wrote an annual report on the health of the Indians, published in the Departmental report, and on instructions from the minister made in 1907 a special inspection of thirty-five Indian schools in the three prairie provinces.[1] This report was published separately; but the recommendations contained in the report were never published and the public knows nothing of them. It contained a brief history of the origin of the Indian Schools, of the sanitary condition of the schools and statistics of the health of the pupils, during the 15 years of their existence. Regarding the health of the pupils, the report states that 24 per cent. of all the pupils which had been in the schools were known to be dead, while of one school on the File Hills reserve, which gave a complete return to date, 75 per cent. were dead at the end of the 16 years since the school opened.

Recommendations of school report, 1907

Briefly the recommendations urged, (1) Greater school facilities, since only 30 per cent. of the children of school age were in attendance; (2) That boarding schools with school farms attached be established near the home reserves of the pupils; (3) That the government undertake the complete maintenance and control of the schools, since it had promised by treaty to insure such; and further it was recommended that as the Indians grow in wealth and intelligence they should pay at least part of the cost from their own funds; (4) That the school studies be those of the curricula of the several Provinces in which the schools are situated, since it was assumed that as the bands would soon become enfranchised and become citizens of the Province they would enter into the common life and duties of a Canadian community; (5) That in view of the historical and sentimental relations between the Indian schools and the Christian churches the report recommended that the Department provide for the management of the schools, through a Board of Trustees, one appointed from each church and approved by the minister of the Department. Such a board would have its secretary in the Department but would hold regular meetings, establish qualifications for teachers, and oversee the appointments as well as the control of the schools; (6) That Continuation schools be arranged for on the school farms and that instruction methods similar to those on the File Hills farm colony be developed; (7) That the health interests of the pupils be guarded by a proper medical inspection and that the local physicians be encouraged through the provision at each school of fresh air

---

1   See *Report on the Indian Schools of Manitoba and the Northwest Territories* (1907), Peel's Prairie Provinces, University of Alberta Library, Web.

methods in the care and treatment of cases of tuberculosis.

II. The annual medical reports from year to year made reference to the unsatisfactory health of the pupils, while different local medical officers urged greater action in view of the results of their experience from year to year. As the result of one such report the Minister instructed the writer in 1909 to investigate the health of the children in the schools of the Calgary district in a letter containing the following: "As it is necessary that these residential schools should be filled with a healthy class of pupils in order that the expenditure on Indian education may not be rendered entirely nugatory, it seems desirable that you should go over the same ground as Dr. Lafferty and check his inspection."

Recommendations based on the examination of 243 school children
These instructions were encouraging and the writer gladly undertook the work of examining with Dr. J.D. Lafferty the 243 children of 8 schools in Alberta, with the following results:—

(a) Tuberculosis was present equally in children at every age; (b) In no instance was a child awaiting admission to school found free from tuberculosis; hence it was plain that infection was got in the home primarily; (c) The disease showed an excessive mortality in the pupils between five and ten years of age; (d) The 10,000 children of school age demanded the same attention as the thousand children coming up each year and entering the schools annually.

Recommendations, made in this report, on much the same lines as those made in the report of 1907, followed the examination of the 243 children; but owing to the active opposition of Mr. D.C. Scott,[1] and his advice to the then Deputy Minister, no action was taken by the Department to give effect to the recommendations made. This too was in spite of the opinion of Prof. George Adami, Pathologist of McGill University, in reply to a letter of the Deputy Minister asking his opinion regarding the management and conduct of the Indian schools. Prof. Adami had with the writer examined the children in one of the largest

---

1 Duncan Campbell Scott (see Appendix C1) began as a clerk in the Department of Indian Affairs in 1879, moving through the ranks until he was promoted to Deputy Superintendent, a post he held from 1913 until he retired in 1932. The Deputy Superintendent was the highest non-elected official in this department.

schools and was fully informed as to the actual situation. He stated that it was only after the earnest solicitation of Mr. D.C. Scott that the whole matter of Dr. Bryce's report was prevented from becoming a matter of critical discussion at the annual meeting of the National Tuberculosis Association in 1910, of which he was then president, and this was only due to Mr. Scott's distinct promise that the Department would take adequate action along the lines of the report. Prof. Adami stated in his letter to the Deputy Minister:—

"It was a revelation to me to find tuberculosis prevailing to such an extent amongst these children, and as many of them were only suffering from the early incipient form of the disease, though practically everyone was affected, when under care it may be arrested, I was greatly impressed with the responsibility of the government in dealing with these children.... I can assure you my only motive is a great sympathy for these children, who are the wards of the government and cannot protect themselves from the ravages of this disease."

III. In reviewing his correspondence the writer finds a personal letter, written by him to the Minister dated March 16th, 1911, following an official letter regarding the inaction of the Department with regard to the recommendations of the report. This letter refers to the most positive promises of Mr. D.C. Scott that the Department would at once take steps to put the suggestions contained in the report into effect. The letter further says:—

"It is now over 9 months since these occurrences and I have not received a single communication with reference to carrying out the Suggestions of our report. Am I wrong in assuming that the vanity of Mr. D.C. Scott, growing out of his success at manipulating the mental activities of Mr. Pedley, has led him to the fatal deception of supposing that his cleverness will be equal to that of Prospero[1] in calming any storm that may blow up from a Tuberculosis Association or any where else, since he knows that should he fail he has through memoranda on file placed the responsibility on Mr. Pedley and yourself. In this particular matter, he is counting upon the ignorance and indifference of the public to the fate of the Indians; but with the awakening of the health conscience of the people, [that] we are now seeing on every hand, I feel certain that serious trouble will come out of

---

1 Prospero, the deposed Duke of Milan and a magician, is the main character in Shakespeare's *The Tempest*.

departmental inertia, and I am not personally disposed to have any blame fall upon me."

It will then be understood with what pleasure the writer hailed the appointment of Dr. W.A. Roche[1] as Superintendent General of Indian Affairs after the year's term of the Hon. R. Rogers, whose chief activity was the investigation of the Deputy Minister, which led up to his retirement. Now at last he said, "A medical minister exists who would understand the situation as relates to the health of the Indians." So an early opportunity was taken to set forth in a memorandum to Dr. Roche, dated Dec. 9th, 1912, data and statistics relating to the several hundred scattered bands on whose health the total expenditure was but little more than $2 per capita, while the death rate in many of the bands was as high as forty per thousand. The reply acknowledging receipt of this memorandum contained the following:—

Dr. Roche encouraged to act
"There is certainly something in your suggestions that should receive every consideration, and some time when I can find an opportunity and it is convenient for you, I shall be pleased to discuss this matter with you."

[...] As Dr. Roche became ill and was absent for some months nothing further was done; but on his return the writer in a personal interview urged that this serious medical Indian problem be taken up in earnest. It was stated that medical science now knows just what to do and what was necessary was to put our knowledge into practice. Dr. Roche stated that on his return from the West he would certainly take the matter up. Since that moment however, to the present, the matter has awaited the promised action.

The writer had done no regular inspection work since Mr. D.C. Scott was made Deputy minister in 1913, but had in each year up to 1914 prepared his medical report, printed in the annual report of the Department. About this time the following letter was received:

P.H. Bryce, M.D. Ottawa,
Medical Inspector, June 17, 1914.

---

1 William James Roche (1859–1937), Conservative MP from 1896–1917, a medical doctor who was Superintendent-General of Indian Affairs from 1912 to 1917.

Immigration Branch.

Dear Sir,

In reply to your letter of the first instant, asking that the files of the Department, containing our medical officers' reports be placed at your disposal, so that you may peruse them to enable you to furnish a report for publication, I desire to point out, that by the organization of this Department, under the Civil Service Act of 1908 you were not included therein and since that time your whole salary has been a charge against the Department of the Interior. It is true that since then we have availed ourselves of your services on a few occasions; but during the past year, so far as I am aware, you have not been called upon to do any duty for the Department. I may say also that Dr. [O.I.] Grain[1] of Winnipeg, has lately been appointed to oversee the Western schools and reserves and his time is fully occupied in the work. Under these circumstances, I do not think that you should be asked to furnish a report on the medical work in connection with Indians during the fiscal year. I must thank you cordially for the offer to again prepare a report for publication.

Yours sincerely,
DUNCAN C. SCOTT, D.S.G.I.A.

Dr. Scott's malign influence
The transparent hypocrisy contained in this remarkable communication sent, not by the Minister Dr. W.A. Roche, but by his deputy, will be seen in the fact that from 1908, five annual reports had been prepared by the writer, while the special report on the eight schools of the Calgary district with the recommendations already referred to had been made on the instructions of the Department in 1909. The other reason given, to the effect that a certain physician, since retired for good cause, quite inexperienced in dealing with Indian disease problems, had been appointed as Medical Inspector for the Western Provinces, showed how little the Minister cared for the solution of the tuberculosis problem.

---

1 Orton Irwin Grain (1863–1932) was a Winnipeg physician and a Conservative member of the Manitoba Legislative Assembly. Medical inspector for Indian Affairs from 1913 to 1918, his suggestions for improving health on reserves were rejected as too expensive.

[...]

IV. *Dr. Roche's culpable apathy*

As the war broke out in 1914 and immigration was largely suspended, an unexpected opportunity occurred through the greater time at his disposal for the writer's special knowledge and experience to be utilized in improving the health of the Indians; but in no single instance, thereafter, were the services of the writer utilised by this medical Minister, who in 1917 was transferred to preside over the Civil Service Commission, and who must be held responsible for the neglect of what proved to be a very serious situation. In 1917, the writer prepared, at the request of the Conservation Commission, a pamphlet on "The Conservation of the Man Power of Canada," which dealt with the broad problems of health which so vitally affect the man power of a nation.

Value of Man Power of Indians

The large demand for this pamphlet led to the preparation of a similar study on "The Conservation of the Man Power of the Indian Population of Canada," which had already supplied over 2000 volunteer soldiers for the Empire. For obvious reasons this memorandum was not published, but was placed in the hands of a minister of the Crown in 1918, in order that all the facts might be made known to the Government. This memorandum began by pointing out that in 1916 4,862,303 acres were included in the Indian reserves and that 73,716 acres were then under cultivation; that while the total per capita income for farm crops in that year in all Canada was $110 that from the Indian reserves was $69, while it was only $40 for Nova Scotia. It is thus obvious that from the lowest standard of wealth producers the Indian population of Canada was already a matter of much importance to the State. From the statistics given in the "Man Power" pamphlet it was made plain that instead of the normal increase in the Indian population being 1.5 per cent. per annum as given for the white population, there had been between 1904 and 1917 an actual decrease in the Indian population in the age period over twenty years of 1,639 persons whereas a normal increase would have added 20,000 population in the 13 years. The comparisons showed that the loss was almost wholly due to a high death rate since, though incomplete, the Indian birth rate was 27 per thousand or higher than the average for the whole white population.

[...]

As it was further desirable to obtain the latest returns of deaths by age periods and causes the writer communicated with the Secretary of the Indian Department asking for such returns. In reply he received the following letter.

Dear Dr. Bryce, Ottawa, May 7, 1918.

I have your letter of the third instant asking for certain vital statistics. I am unable to give you the figures you ask as we are not receiving any vital statistics now, and last year we obtained only the total number of births and deaths from each Agency. These were not printed and are not therefore available for distribution. The causes of deaths have never been noted in our reports and we have no information.

Your obedient servant,
(Signed) J.D. McLean,
Asst. Deputy and Secretary.

Entire absence of causes of death
Thus after more than a hundred years of an organized Department of Indian Affairs in Canada, though the writer had at once begun in 1904 on his appointment the regular collection of statistics of diseases and deaths from the several Indian bands, he was officially informed that in a Department with 287 paid medical officers, due to the direct reactionary influence of the former Accountant and present Deputy Minister [Scott] no means exists, such as is looked upon as elementary in any Health Department today, by which the public or the Indians themselves can learn anything definite as to the actual vital conditions amongst these wards of the nation.

A study of the 1916–17 statistics shows that in the wage earning period of life, from 21 to 65 years, the Indians of Alberta had 161 less population, of British Columbia 901 less, of Ontario 991 less and of Nova Scotia 399 less....

Extraordinary mortality from tuberculosis
Naturally it is asked; Why this decrease should have taken place? In 1906 the report of the Chief Medical Officer shows that statistics collected from 99 local medical officers having the care of a population of 70,000 gave a total of 3,169 cases of tuberculosis

or 1 case for every seven in a total of 23,109 diseases reported, and the death rates in several large bands were 81.8, 82.6, and in a third 86.4 per thousand; while the ordinary death rate for 115,000 in the city of Hamilton was 10.6 in 1921. What these figures disclose has been made more plain year by year, namely that tuberculosis, contracted in infancy, creates diseases of the brain, joints, bones, and to a less degree of the lungs and also that if not fatal till adolescence it then usually progresses rapidly to a fatal termination in consumption of the lungs.

The amazing reduction of tuberculosis in Hamilton

The memorandum prepared by the writer in 1918 on tuberculosis further showed that the city of Hamilton with a population greater than the total Indian population had reduced the death rate from tuberculosis in the same period, from 1904 to 1917, by nearly 75 per cent. having in 1916 actually only 68 deaths. The memorandum further states, "If a similar method had been introduced amongst the bands on the health-giving uplands of Alberta, much might have been done to prevent such a splendid race of warriors as the Blackfeet from decreasing from 842 in 1904 to 726 in 1916, or, allowing for natural increase, an actual loss of 40 per cent. since they should have numbered at least 1,011."

V. Such then is the situation made known to the Hon. N.W. Rowell, who applied to the writer in 1918 to supply him with such facts and arguments as would support the Bill he proposed to introduce into Parliament for the creation of a Federal Department of Health.

Occult influences again rob the Indians of a chance

It was with pleasure that the memorandum dealing with Indian health matters was given him, along with a proposed Bill for a Department of Health, which contained amongst its provisions one for including the Indian Medical Service along with the other Medical Federal services in the new Department. In the special medical committee called by Mr. Rowell to discuss the Bill, such inclusion was of course approved of and the clause appeared in the First Reading in Parliament. But something then happened: What special occult influences came into action may be imagined, when the Second Reading of the Bill took place with this clause regarding the Indian Medical Service omitted. It has been noted that from 1913 up to the time when Dr. W.A. Roche was eliminated from the government in 1917 to make room for a more hardy and subtle representative of Unionism the activities of the Chief Medical Inspector of the Indian Department, had in practice ceased; yet now he was to see as the outcome of all this health legislation for which he had been struggling for years, the failure of one of his special health dreams, which he has hoped to see realized.

One who failed them in their agony
If the writer had been much disturbed by the incapacity or inertia of a medical Minister in the matter of the Indian health, he now saw that it was hopeless to expect from them an improvement in it when the new Minister of Health,[1] who had posed as the Bayard of Social Uplift, the Protagonist of Prohibition, the Champion of Oppressed Labour, the Sir Galahad of Women's rights, and the *preux Chevalier* of Canadian Nationalism, could with all the accumulated facts and statistics before him condemn to further indefinite suffering and neglect these Wards of the Canadian people, whom one Government after another had made treaties with and whom deputies and officials had sworn to assist and protect.

A side light however, may serve to illumine the beclouded situation. With the formation of the Unionist Government the usual shuffle of portfolios was made and the then dominating Solicitor General, grown callous and hardened over a franchise Bill,[2] which disfranchised many thousands of his fellow native-born citizens, had now become Minister of the Interior. That the desire for power and for the control [of] appointments should override any higher consideration such as saving the lives of the Indians must be inferred from the following statement of the Hon. A. Meighen, Minister of the Interior and now Prime Minister. On June 8th, 1920, the estimates of the Indian Department were under consideration in Parliament. Page 3275 of Hansard has the following:—

---

1 Arthur Meighen (1874–1960), who was appointed as Minister of the Interior and Superintendent of Indian Affairs in 1917 as part of the Union (coalition) wartime government. He became prime minister in July 1920.

2 The War-Time Elections Act of 1917 gave the vote to women who were wives or close relatives of soldiers fighting overseas, but it disenfranchised "enemy-aliens" naturalized as Canadians after 31 March 1902, unless they had relatives serving in the armed forces.

Mr. D.D. McKenzie, "I understand that frightful ravages are being made amongst them (Indians) by tuberculosis and the conditions of life are certainly not such as to preserve them from the ravages of that dread disease. I should be pleased to know at the earliest possible moment if that branch of the Department was going to be transferred to the Department of Health."

Mr. Meighen, "The Health Department has no power to take over the matter of the health of the Indians. That is not included in the Act establishing the department. It was purposely left out of the Act. I did not then think and do not think yet that it would be practicable for the Health Department to do that work, because they would require to duplicate the organization away in the remote regions, where Indian reserves are, and there would be established a sort of divided control and authority over the Indians."

Mr. Beland, "Is tuberculosis increasing or decreasing amongst the Indians?"

Mr. Meighen, "I am afraid I cannot give a very encouraging answer to the question. We are not convinced that it is increasing, but it is not decreasing."

Red tape condemns the Indians because of a pitiable inertia
In this reply of the Minister we see fully illustrated the dominating influence, stimulated by the reactionary Deputy Minister, which prevents even the simplest effective efforts to deal with the health problem of the Indians along modern scientific lines. To say that confusion would arise is the equivalent of saying that co-operation between persons toward a desired social end is impracticable; whereas co-operation between Provincial and Federal Health Departments is the basis upon which real progress is being made, while further a world peace is being made possible in a league of once discordant nations. The Premier has frankly said he can give no encouraging answer to Dr. Beland's question, while at the same moment he condemns the Indians to their fate by a pitiable confession of utter official helplessness and lack of initiative, based upon a cynical "*non possumus*."[1]

Thus we find a sum of only $10,000 has been annually placed in the estimates to control tuberculosis amongst 105,000 Indians scattered over Canada in over 300 bands, while the City of

---

1 "We cannot do it" (Latin).

Ottawa, with about the same population and having three general hospitals, spent thereon $342,860.54 in 1919 of which $33,364.70 is devoted to tuberculous patients alone. The many difficulties of our problem amongst the Indians have been frequently pointed out, but the means to cope with these have also been made plain. It can only be said that any cruder or weaker arguments by a Prime Minister holding the position of responsibility to these treaty wards of Canada could hardly be conceived.

[...]

EPILOGUE. This story should have been written years ago and then given to the public; but in my oath of office as a Civil Servant swore that "without authority on that behalf, I shall not disclose or make known any matter or thing which comes to my knowledge by reason of my employment as Chief Medical Inspector of Indian Affairs." Today I am free to speak, having been retired from the Civil Service and so am in a position to write the sequel to the story.

[Here Bryce recounts the case for restoring his pension and superannuation payment.]

Works Cited and Select Bibliography

Books by Johnson

White Wampum. London: John Lane, 1895.

Canadian Born. Toronto: Morang, 1903.

"When George Was King" and Other Poems. Brockville, ON: Brockville *Times*, 1908.

Legends of Vancouver. Vancouver: Privately printed, 1911; Toronto: McClelland & Stewart, 1912.

Flint and Feather. Toronto: Musson, 1912.

The Moccasin Maker. Toronto: Briggs, 1913; new ed. with Introduction and notes by A. Lavonne Brown Ruoff. Norman: U of Oklahoma P, 1998.

The Shagganappi. Toronto: Briggs, 1913.

E. Pauline Johnson / Tekahionwake: Collected Poems and Selected Prose. Ed. Carole Gerson and Veronica Strong-Boag. Toronto: U of Toronto P, 2002.

North American Indian Silver Craft. Vancouver: Subway, 2004.

Works Cited and Further Reading

Acoose, Janice / Misko Kisikawikwe. *Iskwewak: Kah' Ki Yaw Ni Wahkomakanak: Neither Indian Princesses nor Easy Squaws*. Toronto: Women's, 1995.

Alfred, Taiaiake. *Peace, Power, Righteousness: An Indigenous Manifesto*. Don Mills, ON: Oxford UP, 1999.

Armstrong, Jeannette. *Whispering in Shadows*. Penticton, BC: Theytus, 2000.

Barman, Jean. "Taming Aboriginal Sexuality: Gender, Power, and Race in British Columbia, 1850–1900." *BC Studies* 115/116 (1997/98): 237–66.

Benn, Carl. *The Iroquois in the War of 1812*. Toronto: U of Toronto P, 1998.

Berger, Carl. *The Sense of Power: Studies in the Ideas of Canadian Imperialism, 1867–1914*. Toronto: U of Toronto P, 1970.

Brant, Beth. *Writing as Witness: Essay and Talk*. Toronto: Women's, 1994.

Bryant, William Clement. [Speech at the Ceremony to Re-inter Red Jacket.] *Transactions of the Buffalo Historical Society—Red Jacket.* Vol. 3. Buffalo: The Society, 1885. 15–23.

Cardinal, Harold, and Walter Hildebrandt. *Treaty Elders of Saskatchewan: Our Dream Is that Our Peoples Will One Day Be Recognized as Nations.* Calgary: U of Calgary P, 2000.

Carter, Sarah. *The Importance of Being Monogamous: Marriage and Nation Building in Western Canada to 1915.* Edmonton: U of Alberta P, 2008.

Chambers, Lori. *Married Women and Property Law in Victorian Canada.* Toronto: U of Toronto P for the Osgoode Society for Canadian Legal History, 1997.

Charlesworth, Hector. "The Indian Poetess: A Study." *Lake Magazine* (September 1892): 81–87.

Crate, Joan. *Pale as Real Ladies: Poems for Pauline Johnson.* Ilderton, ON: Brick, 1989.

Deerchild, Rosanna. "My Poem Is an Indian Woman." *Indigenous Poetics in Canada.* Ed. Neal McLeod. Waterloo: Wilfrid Laurier UP, 2014. 237–44.

Deloria, Philip J. "Four Thousand Invitations." *American Indian Quarterly* 37.3 (2013): 23–43.

Fee, Margery. "Publication, Performances, and Politics: The 'Indian Poems' of E. Pauline Johnson / Tekahionwake (1861–1913) and Duncan Campbell Scott (1862–1947)." *Anthologizing Canadian Literature: Theoretical and Cultural Perspectives.* Ed. Robert Lecker. Waterloo, ON: Wilfrid Laurier UP, 2015. 51–77.

Foster, Mrs. Garland W. *The Mohawk Princess Being Some Account of the Life of Tekahion-wake (E. Pauline Johnson).* Vancouver: Lion's Gate, 1931.

Gerson, Carole. "Postcolonialism Meets Book History: Pauline Johnson and Imperial London." *Home-work: Postcolonialism, Pedagogy and Canadian Literature.* Ed. Cynthia Sugars. Ottawa: U of Ottawa P, 2004. 432–33.

——. *A Purer Taste: The Writing and Reading in English in Nineteenth-Century Canada.* Toronto: U of Toronto P, 1989.

Gerson, Carole, and Veronica Strong-Boag. Introduction. *E. Pauline Johnson / Tekahionwake: Collected Poems and Selected Prose.* Ed. Gerson and Strong-Boag. Toronto: U of Toronto P, 2002. xiii–xliv.

Goeman, Mishuana. *Mark My Words: Native Women Mapping Our Nation.* Minneapolis: U of Minnesota P, 2013.

Gray, Charlotte. *Flint and Feather: The Life and Times of E. Pauline Johnson*. Toronto: HarperFlamingo, 2002.

Green, Rayna. "The Pocahontas Perplex: The Image of Indian Women in American Culture." *The Massachusetts Review* 16.4 (1975): 698–714.

Hoy, Helen. *How Should I Read These? Native Women Writers in Canada*. Toronto: U of Toronto P, 2001.

Johnson, Evelyn H.C. *Memoirs*. Ohsweken, ON: Chiefswood Board of Trustees, 2009.

Johnston, Sheila M.F. *Buckskin and Broadcloth: A Celebration of E. Pauline Johnson—Tekahionwake, 1861–1913*. Toronto: Natural Heritage, 1997.

Keller, Betty. *Pauline: A Biography of Pauline Johnson*. Vancouver: Douglas & McIntyre, 1981.

Knowles, Norman. *Inventing the Loyalists: The Ontario Loyalist Tradition and the Invention of Usable Pasts*. Toronto: U of Toronto P, 1997.

Matthias, Joe. Interview. *The Native Voice: Official Organ of the Native Brotherhood of British Columbia*. Special Commemorative Issue. 1961.

McRaye, Walter. *Pauline Johnson and Her Friends*. Toronto: Ryerson, 1946.

Monture, Patricia A. "Women's Words: Power, Identity, and Indigenous Sovereignty." *Canadian Women's Studies* 26.3/4 (2008): 154–59.

Monture, Rick. *We Share Our Matters: Two Centuries of Writing and Resistance at Six Nations of the Grand River*. Winnipeg: U of Manitoba P, 2014.

Moses, Daniel David. "Getting (Back) to Poetry: A Memoir." *Indigenous Poetics in Canada*. Ed. Neal McLeod. Waterloo, ON: Wilfrid Laurier UP, 2014. 121–35.

Niro, Shelley, and Anna Gronau, dirs. *It Starts with a Whisper*. Bay of Quinte Productions. 1992. Film.

Paul, Daniel N. *We Were Not the Savages*. 3rd ed. Halifax: Fernwood, 2006.

Piatote, Beth. "The Indian/Agent Aporia." *American Indian Quarterly* 37.3 (2013): 45–62.

——. *Domestic Subjects: Gender, Citizenship and Law in Native American Literature*. New Haven, CT: Yale UP, 2013.

Rak, Julie. "Double-wampum, Double-life, Double Click: E. Pauline Johnson by and for the World Wide Web." *Textual Studies in Canada* (2001). Web.

Rogers, Janet Marie. "Pauline Passed Here." *Indigenous Poetics in Canada.* Ed. Neal McLeod. Waterloo, ON: Wilfrid Laurier UP, 2014. 39–41.

———. *Pauline and Emily, Two Women.* Alexandria, VA: Alexander Street, 2006.

Ruffo, Armand Garnet. Interview with Neal McLeod. *Indigenous Poetics in Canada.* Ed. Neal McLeod. Waterloo, ON: Wilfrid Laurier UP, 2014. 23–29.

Stonechild, Blair, and Bill Waiser. *Loyal Until Death: Indians and the North-west Rebellion.* Calgary: Fifth House, 1997.

Strong-Boag, Veronica, and Carole Gerson. *Paddling Her Own Canoe: The Times and Texts of E. Pauline Johnson (Tekahion-wake).* Toronto: U of Toronto P, 2000.

They Came for the Children: Canada, Aboriginal Peoples, and Residential Schools. Truth and Reconciliation Commission. Report. 2012. Web.

Van Steen, Marcus. *Pauline Johnson: Her Life and Work.* Toronto: Hodder and Stoughton, 1965.

"Voting Rights." Human Rights in Canada: A Historical Perspective. Canadian Human Rights Commission. Web.

Warrior, Robert. "The SAI and the End(s) of Intellectual History." *American Indian Quarterly* 37.3 (2013): 218–35.

Wilmott, Glen. "Paddled by Pauline." *Canadian Poetry* 46 (2000). Web.

From the Publisher

A name never says it all, but the word "Broadview" expresses a good deal of the philosophy behind our company. We are open to a broad range of academic approaches and political viewpoints. We pay attention to the broad impact book publishing and book printing has in the wider world; we began using recycled stock more than a decade ago, and for some years now we have used 100% recycled paper for most titles. Our publishing program is internationally oriented and broad-ranging. Our individual titles often appeal to a broad readership too; many are of interest as much to general readers as to academics and students.

Founded in 1985, Broadview remains a fully independent company owned by its shareholders—not an imprint or subsidiary of a larger multinational.

For the most accurate information on our books (including information on pricing, editions, and formats) please visit our website at www.broadviewpress.com. Our print books and ebooks are also available for sale on our site.

On the Broadview website we also offer several goods that are not books—among them the Broadview coffee mug, the Broadview beer stein (inscribed with a line from Geoffrey Chaucer's *Canterbury Tales*), the Broadview fridge magnets (your choice of philosophical or literary), and a range of T-shirts (made from combinations of hemp, bamboo, and/or high-quality pima cotton, with no child labor, sweatshop labor, or environmental degradation involved in their manufacture).

All these goods are available through the "merchandise" section of the Broadview website. When you buy Broadview goods you can support other goods too.

broadview press
www.broadviewpress.com